*The Psychology
of Learning and Memory*

The Psychology
of Learning and Memory

Douglas L. Hintzman

University of Oregon

W. H. Freeman and Company
San Francisco

Library of Congress Cataloging in Publication Data

Hintzman, Douglas L
    The psychology of learning and memory.

    (A Series of books in psychology)
    Bibliography: p.
    Includes index.
    1. Learning, Psychology of. 2. Memory.
    I. Title.
BF318.H56   153.1   77-16295
ISBN 0-7167-0035-2

Printed in the United States of America

   2 3 4 5 6 7 8 9

To My Mother

Contents

Preface

This book encompasses the fields of both animal conditioning and human memory. Anyone writing such a book encounters a problem the author of a more specialized text does not face: How should material from these two largely independent areas be combined? I have attempted to turn this apparent difficulty to my advantage, since it provides a rationale for the discussion of important issues that might otherwise be ignored. These issues fall into three general categories: (1) Historical: How did the two fields develop historically? How have they influenced each other? How are their relationships changing? (2) Philosophical: How do the behaviorist and cognitivist approaches to learning differ and in what ways are they alike? What are the limitations of either approach? (3) Evolutionary: How is human learning related to conditioning in animals? More generally, in what ways did the ability to learn develop as more and more complex organisms evolved? Discussions of these broad issues are scattered throughout the book, although the historical material tends to be concentrated in the first three chapters and Chapter 13, while evolutionary issues are confronted most directly in Chapter 7.

From the very beginning, the psychology of learning and memory has undergone change. It has continually been shaped and reshaped by theoretical controversies. A major purpose of this book is to give the student, through many examples, some appreciation of this dynamic process—to show how theories determine the way experiments are performed and how the results of experiments influence theoretical ideas. I hope the naive seeker of truth will come to appreciate more fully how elusive the truth really is. Scientific progress—in any field—is a process whereby the "truth" is continually being redefined.

An earlier draft of the manuscript of this book was read, in whole or in part, by several persons. I am especially grateful to Alice Healy, Steven Keele, Roberta Klatzky, Robert Leeper, Alexander Polatsek, Howard Rachlin, Mary Rothbart, and Richard Solomon. Their criticisms have been most helpful. In revising the manuscript, I have attempted to take most of them into account.

Douglas L. Hintzman
March 1977

*The Psychology
of Learning and Memory*

1

Introduction

Of all the animal species that inhabit this planet, we humans are truly exceptional. Our uniqueness finds expression in many ways: We use fire, build machines, domesticate animals and cultivate crops, communicate through spoken and written language, legislate our own social controls, visit such inaccessible places as the surface of the moon and the floor of the sea, and alter the face of the earth itself. Central to all these accomplishments is our great flexibility—our unparalleled capacity to change our behavior to suit the circumstances we are in.

Underlying the flexibility of our behavior are the processes we call learning and memory. *Learning* is a change in an organism, due to experience, which can affect the organism's behavior. *Memory* is the persistence of that change over time. The flexibility of human behavior rests on our ability to profit from experience—that is, on our unsurpassed ability to learn.

Very simple animals behave only in rigid, stereotyped ways. They are limited to genetically pre-programmed responses which can be changed by experience little, if at all. Moderately complex animals can learn, but for many of them learning requires direct experience. Being rewarded or punished will change an individual animal's behavior, but seeing a companion rewarded or punished will not. Still more complex organisms, particularly the higher primates, can learn "vicariously" from the successes and failures of others. They are, however, restricted in this learning to direct observation—that is, to the here and now. Human beings are free from even this limitation.

1

Through the use of language, we can learn from the experiences of others. The experiences we learn about may concern events that were observed, inferred, or even imagined. Thus, we are freed in our learning not only from the here and now but also, to some extent, from reality.

The flexibility of human behavior has enabled us to adapt to an incredible variety of physical and social environments. Allowed free reign, human flexibility produces the great variability we see in the diversity of languages and social customs, and within cultures, among social roles, occupations, and individual interests. Given direction, human flexibility can produce remarkable accomplishments such as the exploration of the solar system and the conquest of disease. It seems clear that an understanding of learning and memory—the processes that give human behavior its great flexibility—would be a major step toward understanding the nature of intelligence itself. While learning and memory are topics that have provoked much speculation by philosophers and experiments by scientists, the mysteries of their nature and function are still largely unsolved.

THE IMPORTANCE OF LEARNING AND MEMORY

To psychologists in particular, the problem of learning is a central one. Hardly an area of psychological investigation can ignore it. The differences among individuals that we call personality are believed to be strongly influenced by experience. Girls and boys adopt the sex roles modeled for them by adults. Whether a person is violent or peaceful, anxious or confident, gregarious or solitary, thoughtful or impulsive, deceitful or candid—all depend to some extent on learning. Early childhood experiences, such as weaning, toilet training, and interactions with parents and siblings, may exert a strong influence on emotional and cognitive development. It may even be—if one controversial hypothesis is to be believed—that a person's ultimate level of intellectual ability is determined by what happens to him during the first few years of life.

The aspects of social behavior we place under the heading of "culture" are primarily learned: language, sex roles, occupations, religious beliefs, and attitudes toward the family, neighborhood, community, and nation. Prejudices regarding race, social caste, and sex are acquired by experience; and it is through experience that they can be changed. The nature of modern society reflects, in large part, the speed with which humans adapt. We are absurdly easy to indoctrinate, which accounts for the variety and instability of political and religious views. And technological developments—which affect the ways we relate to work, to leisure, and to each other—produce a never-ending spiral in which learning-produced changes necessitate further learning, which brings about further change.

Clinical psychologists and psychiatrists have a strong interest in an understanding of learning. Many mental and behavioral problems are assumed to result, at least in part, from experience. Phobias, social anxiety, depression, psychosomatic symptoms, and habits such as smoking are examples. And most methods of psychotherapy are designed to provide an experience that will bring about a change in the patient—either in his mental state or in his behavior. Many therapists have looked directly to the psychology of learning for hints as to how therapeutic techniques might be improved.

Even perception—the way things look and sound to us—depends partly on learning. One might suppose the perception of stimuli to be entirely unaffected by past experience, but this is not the case. A person who is reading will perceive an "important" extraneous stimulus such as the mention of his own name, even though other words spoken by the same voice are easily ignored. A conversation that sounds like jabbering to someone unfamiliar with the language sounds quite different to one to whom the language is known; what looks like a series of random squiggles to a nonreader is immediately recognized as a coherent message to one who can read; and chess pieces on a board, arranged as in a position from a game, look quite different to a novice than they do to a chess master. A once-blind person whose vision is repaired sees things very differently than you or I. There is even some evidence, from experiments with cats, that normal development of cells in the visual areas of the brain depends on visual stimulation during infancy.

Physiological psychologists also have an interest in learning. The biological basis of learning and memory remains one of the great unsolved problems of science. Psychological investigations should play a crucial role in solving this problem. The search for a solution cannot be conducted exclusively at the level of neurochemistry, neurophysiology, and neuroanatomy, since it is only by observing an organism's behavior that we can determine that it has learned. In addition, the physiological psychologist is likely to find clues to the nature of the learning mechanism he is seeking in the results of behavioral experiments.

Areas outside psychology also are deeply concerned with learning and memory. The philosopher reflecting upon the nature of knowledge can hardly ignore what is known about the process by which knowledge is acquired. The physical anthropologist concerned with human evolution must take into consideration the remarkable capacity of humans to learn, and must ask not only what ecological pressures brought this ability about, but also how the developing ability may have exerted its own influence on evolution.

Many computer scientists, in the field called "artificial intelligence," are concerned with building machines that can duplicate or even exceed human abilities. How does one construct a computer that can translate languages, play games such as chess, think creatively, generate and follow its own elaborate plans, read handwriting, control skilled acts, and retrieve complex information quickly from a vast and efficient memory? Computer scientists attempting to answer such questions cannot, rationally, ignore the fact that a device that does all these things already exists, in the human mind, and that a general ability underlying all such special ones is the ability to learn.

Educators, of course, have always had a practical interest in learning and memory, and the application of learning principles to educational practice has always been regarded by learning psychologists as an ultimate goal of their work. How can instruction and training be made more effective and efficient? Can forgetting be slowed or prevented? How should teaching methods be matched to subject matter and to the abilities of students? What special methods should be used in training the retarded, the blind, or the deaf? How is knowledge acquired through reading? And how is this remarkable skill itself learned? Educators have looked to psychology, perhaps too trustingly, for answers to such questions; and psychologists have attempted, sometimes too readily, to comply. Applications of learning principles to education have not always been successful—but this should not be surprising. There is much about learning and memory we still do not understand.

Practical interest in learning and memory, of course, is not restricted to clinical psychology and education. Professional animal trainers and ordinary pet owners want to teach their animals good habits and eliminate bad ones; ranchers and farmers want to cure wild animals of their destructive behavior; and wildlife managers want to keep animals from endangering themselves. Parents want to influence the behavior and beliefs of their children. Corrections officers want to rehabilitate their prisoners. Athletes and musicians want to improve their respective skills; coaches, military officers, and factory managers want to improve the skills of those under them. Public speakers and entertainers want to improve their own memories; politicians, advertisers, and propagandists have messages they want people to remember and facts they want them to forget. Each of us, in his own way, curses his faulty memory when important names and faces, shopping lists, routine appointments, urgent deadlines, bizarre dreams, creative ideas, and even trivial facts are forgotten. In one way or another, learning and memory touch on nearly all human activities.

THE PRESENT STATUS OF THE FIELD

Given the potential impact of an accurate understanding of learning and memory both inside and outside psychology, the uncertain accomplishments of the field may be viewed with disappointment. An outsider who asks a physicist about falling bodies, electricity, or nuclear reactions will receive a definitive reply. Further, if he asks another physicist the same question, he can be confident the answer will be essentially the same. One who asks a psychologist how repetitive drill contributes to learning or what causes forgetting should expect either a discussion of several competing theories or a single, coherent analysis with which other psychologists will not fully agree. If he asks enough different psychologists, he will discover that not all of them agree even on how one should go about seeking the answers to such questions. Some explain effects of past experience on behavior in terms of mental, or conscious, events; others prefer theories based on the "machinery of the brain"; still others argue that the investigator should simply describe observable behavior and not attempt to explain it at all. Such theoretical and methodological disputes often strike the layman as unscientific. They are not what the "hard sciences" have led him to expect. Several things should be said about this attitude.

In the first place, it is a mistake to think of science as a body of agreed-upon knowledge. Science is, instead, a method by which knowledge is acquired. What distinguishes science from other modes of thought such as religion is not general agreement but the way the agreement is eventually reached. In the scientific method, ideas are subjected to skeptical analysis, and solid evidence is demanded in their support. In this respect, experimental psychology is no different from physics and chemistry—the frontiers of knowledge in those disciplines are, like psychology, often the scenes of vigorous disputes.

In the second place, experimental psychology is not without agreed-upon facts. Thousands of phenomena uncovered in psychology experiments have proven to be replicable; that is, similar investigations done in different laboratories reliably produce equivalent results. Replicable experimental results are a prerequisite for the existence of a scientific discipline, and although failures to replicate do occur in psychology (as in other areas), replicability of results is a prerequisite the field easily meets.

What the psychology of learning and memory is lacking is not the methodology and attitude of science, or reliable phenomena to be explained. What is lacking is theoretical interpretations of the phenomena with which all psychologists agree. Learning and memory have been the subject of numerous theories; but no theory of learning has attained the status of the theories of Newton, Einstein, or Darwin, in their respective disciplines. No single theory has provided the kind of elegant, coherent, and complete explanation of the phenomena of learning and memory that would lead to its acceptance by all those working within the field.

It is interesting to speculate about why no such generally accepted theory of learning and memory exists. Psychology as a science is young. Experimental psychology is just a little over a century old. Physics is much older: Galileo's experiments were done nearly four hundred years ago, and Newton's *Principia* appeared in 1687. Perhaps the field is still waiting for some genius to come along and put things in order. Many psychologists fantasize themselves as psychology's Newton, but so far even the most brilliant and concerted efforts have fallen short.

A more valid reason for the lack of a universal theory of psychology may be the complexity of psychology's subject matter. Each animal species has evolved to fit a particular ecological niche. And within a species, individuals differ from one another in a multitude of ways—a diversity assured by both genetics and past experience. The human brain is an incredibly complex device, and it is always undergoing change. It may never be in exactly the same state at two different times. The very flexibility the psychologist wants to study makes his job difficult. The subject in an experiment adapts to the artificial nature of the experimental situation, often finding ways of coping with the task that are more complex than the experimenter intended. The subject may try to discover the purpose of the experiment, to aid or hinder the investigation; he may even cheat. The "subjects" of physics experiments may be subtle and difficult to comprehend, but they are uniform in their structure and behavior, and they do not have an intelligence and a contrary will of their own.

Disagreements and controversies, then, are to be expected in a science so young dealing with a subject matter so complex, and they are certainly characteristic of the psychology of learning and memory. Many of them are fascinating; they are what make the area an exciting one in which to work. Some textbooks in the field, in an attempt to protect the student from confusion, try to hide controversy. They either ignore important issues altogether or present only one side as though it were an established fact. This seems a mistake. Only a person who knows something of the nature of these controversies and the attempts that have been made to resolve them can truly be said to understand the field.

Thus, this book is not only about phenomena we are sure we understand. It is also about theoretical issues—some old and some recent, some resolved and some recurring, some famous and some obscure, some active and some that have been abandoned due to an apparent lack of progress. Through the analysis of these issues, the reader should learn more than the facts of learning and memory; he or she should learn in addition that interpretations of facts in this area are subject to challenge and change. A theory in great favor yesterday may be rejected today, only to be resurrected tomorrow in slightly different form. An appreciation of the complexities of the issues faced by investigators in this field may help prevent the contagious fads occasionally spread by psychologists (and pseudopsychologists) suffering from attacks of premature enthusiasm about the far-reaching implications of their work. The sophisticated onlooker should be skeptical about such excesses. But one should also appreciate the real progress that is being made in understanding learning and memory and realize that the confusion, disagreement, and controversy of the field stem primarily from the subject matter itself. The human mind is the most difficult challenge science has ever faced.

BACKGROUND AND OVERVIEW

The psychology of learning and memory has roots in two different disciplines. It inherited from philosophy an interest in knowledge, and from biology an interest in adaptation. Philosophers (particularly those in the field of epistemology) are concerned with the structure of knowledge, the way it is acquired, and the way it is used. Biologists are concerned with adaptation, not only through genetic selection, but also through experience. Thus, the traditions of both parent disciplines are concerned with learning, but in different ways. One might expect the relationship of the two traditions within psychology to be complementary, but for the most part the relationship has been an antagonistic one.

The philosophical tradition is represented within psychology by a collection of attitudes sometimes called *cognitivism*. A psychologist of this persuasion is interested in cognitions, or mental events—ideas, thoughts, purposes, conscious awareness, images, feelings, and acts of will. Cognitivism views learning primarily as the acquisition of knowledge.

The biological tradition is represented in psychology by *behaviorism*. From the point of view of behaviorism, learning refers to a change in behavior. If a behaviorist is interested in anything beyond observable behavior itself, it is the principles of operation of the device producing the behavior. These principles may be understood by making use of mechanical analogies, but not by referring to mental events. As we shall see in the following chapters, behaviorists are strongly against mentalistic explanations of behavior, which they view as inherently unscientific.

The psychology of learning and memory is today split, not only into the somewhat opposed camps of cognitivism and behaviorism, but also into two broad interest areas. In one of these areas investigators do research on animal learning; in the other they do work on human memory. It should be no surprise that interest areas and theoretical persuasions are related: animal learning researchers tend to adopt a behaviorist view of learning, while most human memory investigators have a strong cognitive bias. The differences in theoretical orientation mean that communication between animal learning and human memory researchers is not as frequent or as sympathetic as it might be. Communication does occur, however, and there are signs that the split between the two interest areas is diminishing.

A theme of this book, superimposed on discussions of more specific issues, concerns the forces that brought about the split between cognitivism and behaviorism and that have maintained it for many years. The present state of the field cannot be presented accurately in cross-section; it can be understood only in historical context. Likewise, projections of the future of the field can only be made with some knowledge of what past states have been. For these reasons, the organization of this book is partly historical.

To give the reader a kind of road map of the area to be covered, a brief overview of the history of the psychology of learning and memory should be useful. Figure 1.1 represents the history of the field in terms of changes in the relative influence of the cognitivist and behaviorist traditions over time. The vertical axis represents time. There are two curves, one for cognitivism and one for behaviorism, and the horizontal axis—the distance of each curve from the center line—indicates in a rough way the degree of interest in that tradition at a particular time. There have been many outside influences on the psychological study of learning and memory. The ones that have had the most impact are represented in the figure by heavy arrows. The names of the most influential individuals and schools of thought within the cognitivist and behaviorist traditions are located at points on the time scale that correspond, very roughly, to their most important works.

From the beginning of the scientific study of learning in 1885 until around 1920, the field was dominated by interest in the roles in learning and memory of mental events (ideas, images, awareness, and so on)—the position we have called cognitivism. Most of the problems that were studied had already been discussed at great length by philosophers; experimental psychologists simply attacked the same problems using scientific methods. Most of the research during this period used human subjects. In the 1920s and 1930s, however, there was a shift of influence toward behaviorism. Most learning research—although certainly not all of it—was done on animals, and most theoretical explanations of animal or human behavior avoided reference to mental events.

The period from around 1960 to the present has seen a dramatic resurgence of interest in cognitivism and an attendant increase in human learning research. This resurgence, as Figure 1.1 suggests, has been strongly influenced by computers. The existence of "thinking machines" has greatly affected how psychologists theorize about men-

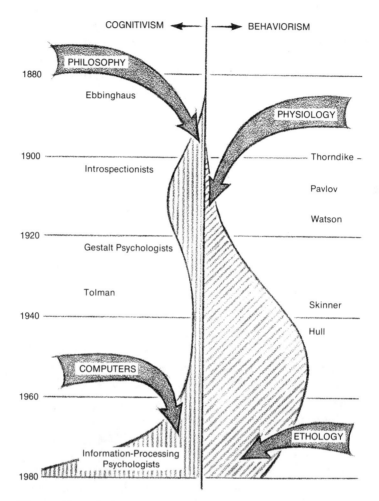

Figure 1.1 Time graph of the history of the psychology of learning and memory.

tal processes, including those involved in learning and memory. The behaviorist tradition today has many adherents, but it has lost the iron grip it once had on the field. It is being pressured by the new-found popularity of cognitivism, on one side, and the concepts and findings of ethology, on the other. Ethology, the study of the behavior of animals in their natural surroundings, is forcing behaviorists to radically alter their views of learning. This topic, like the others briefly mentioned here, is covered in detail in the following chapters.

Influential individuals and groups of psychologists, listed alongside the undulating curves of Figure 1.1, include the following: (a) Ebbinghaus, who did the first formal experiments on human learning and memory (see Chapter 2); (b) the introspectionists, who tried to study mental events directly by "looking inward" on the mind (again, see Chapter 2); (c) Thorndike and Pavlov, who both conducted pioneering research on animal learning around the beginning of this century (see the discussion of Thorndike's work in Chapter 4, and the discussion of Pavlov's in Chapter 3); (d) Watson, the founder of behaviorism (see Chapter 3); (e) the Gestalt psychologists, whose work on memory was not widely appreciated until the renaissance of cognitivism many years later (see Chapters 9 and 10); (f) Tolman, who championed a cognitivist theory of animal learning during a period when behaviorist sentiment prevailed (see Chapters 5 and 6); (g) Skinner and Hull, the most influential proponents of behaviorism (see Chapters 5 and 6); and (h) the information-processing psychologists, whose use of the computer analogy has revolutionized cognitive psychology in general and the area of human memory in particular (see Chapters 9, 10, 11, and 12).

This brief overview and cast of characters is too sketchy, of course, to answer the many questions it raises—questions about why the shift from cognitivism to behaviorism occurred, how information-processing theorists use the computer analogy, how behaviorism has come into conflict with ethology and so on. Filling in such details is the purpose of the remaining chapters of this book.

2

Cognitive Origins

In 1885, in the German city of Leipzig, a remarkable book was published—a book that was to have a profound effect on the infant science of psychology. It was an immediate success in academic circles, and for its author, a young philosopher named Hermann Ebbinghaus, the book earned nearly instant recognition. Ebbinghaus was a true creative genius. From an interest in the philosophy of the mind, a deep appreciation of the methods of natural science, and a personal dedication of truly heroic proportions, he fashioned the foundations of an experimental science of the higher mental processes. He did this in spite of the nearly universal view, in both philosophy and psychology, that the experimental study of learning, memory, and thinking was impossible. In his experimental investigations of memory, Ebbinghaus accomplished the "impossible" in such a convincing way that no one who read his book doubted that the prevailing view had been wrong. Furthermore, he did it in a way that can be recognized today as more sophisticated and more modern in tone than the work of many of those who were to build later upon the foundations he had laid.

Since Ebbinghaus's experiments are so important, some of them will be described later in this chapter in some detail. To better appreciate what Ebbinghaus accomplished, however, let us first examine briefly the philosophical and psychological backgrounds from which his work emerged.

BRITISH EMPIRICIST PHILOSOPHY

Long before psychology began to take shape as a separate discipline, philosophers had analyzed mental processes in great detail. The philosophical investigation of the mind can be traced back to ancient Greece; but Ebbinghaus took his cues most directly from the later writings of the school of British philosophy known as empiricism. British empiricism thrived in the period roughly between 1650 and 1850. Its contributors included such historic figures in philosophy as John Locke, George Berkeley, David Hume, and James Mill. The philosophies of these men differed somewhat from one another, but they all agreed on one point, which is the basic doctrine of empiricism: that all knowledge comes from experience. Put another way, the empiricists contended that the contents of the mind are learned.

In this view, they differed from the European rationalist philosophers, the most notable of whom were René Descartes and Immanuel Kant. The rationalists held that many of our ideas are innate—that is, given by heredity rather than by experience. The rationalists disagreed among themselves regarding the innateness of some ideas (for example, the idea of God) but agreed on others (for example, space, time, and causality). According to the rationalist view, we experience events in terms of space, time, and causality, not because that is the way the world is, but because that is the way the mind imposes structure on our experience of the world.

It is not hard to see why the writings of the empiricists, rather than those of the rationalists, provided the inspiration that ultimately led to the development of a psychology of learning. To the rationalists, intuition and reason were more trustworthy as sources of knowledge than the imperfect information given us by sensory experience. But to the empiricists, experience was the origin of all knowledge, and so the process by which raw experience is transformed into knowledge—the process of learning—was of paramount importance. Arguments concerning the relative importance of heredity and experience are still with us, of course, so it would be incorrect to conclude that either view, empiricism or rationalism, has been shown to be superior to the other. Nevertheless, it is undeniable that the empiricists had considerably more influence on the development of the psychology of learning. This influence arose not only from the importance they attached to the process of learning, but also from what they had to say about what that process was like.

In studying the contents of the mind, the British empiricist philosophers adopted a method that appeared quite appropriate for their
subject matter. They thought, and thought about their thoughts, and
wrote down their observations. One of their primary goals was to
analyze mental experience into its constituent elements. Under close
observation, they claimed, the contents of the mind could be seen to
consist of clearly defined units. These units of the mind they called
"ideas." They distinguished between two kinds of ideas. First, there
were *simple ideas,* which were the basic atoms of experience—ideas so
elementary that they could not be divided into component parts. Typically, simple ideas were thought to stand for elementary sensations
such as colors, tones, and taste qualities. Second, there were *complex
ideas,* which were combinations of simple ones. An example the empiricists commonly gave was the idea of "apple," which they said was
made up of the simple ideas of roundness, redness, and sweetness
(and perhaps others). All ideas, the empiricists claimed, were of these
two types: simple or complex.

Concerning the acquisition of knowledge, the empiricists sought
answers to two questions. The first had to do with the way simple ideas
become combined into complex ideas. How do roundness, redness,
and sweetness become unified into the concept "apple"? The second
had to do with the way in which ideas follow one another in awareness.
For most adult members of our society, the idea "salt" is regularly
followed by the idea "pepper," and likewise the idea "boy" is commonly followed by the idea "girl." Even when the mind wanders in a
seemingly undirected fashion, it is often noted in retrospect that the
ideas that follow one another are related. Why does the sequence of
ideas in the mind show these lawful regularities, rather than being
completely random?

To both these questions—the one concerning the formation of complex ideas out of simple ones, and the other concerning the sequence
of ideas in the mind—the empiricist philosophers proposed the same
answer. In both cases, they said, learning is involved. And in both
cases the basic mechanism of learning is the formation of *associations*
between ideas. The association was considered a kind of "mental glue"
that bonded ideas together. According to the view the empiricists
developed, two ideas experienced in *contiguity*—that is at the same
time or in immediate succession—become connected or associated.
Thus, because roundness, redness, and sweetness are experienced

simultaneously whenever we encounter (and taste) an apple, they become associated; and the resulting combination of these simple ideas represents the concept "apple." Likewise, since salt and pepper are frequently encountered together, their corresponding ideas become associated; and as a result, when the idea "salt" is present in the mind it tends to call up its associate "pepper." Ideas occur sequentially in awareness because they represent stimuli that have been encountered sequentially in the past.

This teaching of the British empiricist philosophers, that learning consists of the formation of associations between contiguously occurring ideas, has been called the *doctrine of associationism*. It played such an important role in the empiricists' thinking that they have also been given the label British associationists. The doctrine of associationism has had a dominant influence on the psychology of learning and memory right down to the present day. The concept of association and the notion that contiguity is necessary for learning to occur have been challenged but have never been abandoned by the majority of psychologists. Many theories incorporating these notions will be encountered in later chapters. The doctrine of associationism has been remarkably long-lived.

EARLY EXPERIMENTAL PSYCHOLOGY

In the late 1800s, when psychology was beginning to be considered a discipline separate from philosophy, psychologists made use of two different methods in investigating the nature of the mind. One, not much different from the method of philosophy, could be characterized as *naturalistic*. The other, borrowed from physical science, was *experimental*. The naturalistic method studies things as they naturally occur in the world, in the course of everyday life, while the experimental method deliberately creates artificial situations in which influential factors can be manipulated, eliminated, or carefully controlled. The use of the naturalistic method in psychology is perhaps best illustrated by the writings of William James. James's *Principles of Psychology*, a two-volume work published in 1890, is considered one of the great books of Western literature; it is still valued by psychologists for its brilliant insights into psychological processes and colorful descriptions of mental life. We shall have occasion to refer to some of James's observations in the chapters ahead.

The use of the experimental method, up to the time of Ebbinghaus's work, had been confined almost entirely to the study of the senses. One popular area of investigation, called psychophysics, had the goal of describing the relationship between the objective, physical world and the subjective, psychological one. A classic problem of psychophysics, to give just one example, was to determine a subject's *sensory threshold*—the weakest stimulus the subject could perceive. To determine the auditory threshold, an experimenter would present very faint tones of varying intensities and ask the subject to indicate whenever a tone could be heard.

A second type of investigation dealt with *reaction time*. In a simple reaction-time experiment, the subject is required to press a button, as quickly as he can, as soon as a stimulus appears. A typical finding of experiments of this sort is that the greater the intensity of the stimulus, the faster the subject responds.

In a third type of investigation, a subject was presented with a stimulus such as a color or an odor, under carefully controlled conditions, and was asked to report his subjective experience—that is, the elementary sensations and feelings produced by the stimulus. This technique, called *introspection,* made use of subjective observations, as did philosophical psychology. But in contrast to the naturalistic method of philosophy, the observations were made under artificially controlled conditions. Thus, the subjective method of "looking inward," used in philosophical psychology, had been adapted to the experimental setting.

None of these experimental techniques had been used to deal with problems of association, such as learning, memory, or thinking. Such processes were held to belong to philosophical psychology and to be by their very nature outside the realm of experimental science. Wilhelm Wundt, the founder of the first experimental psychology laboratory and the most powerful figure in German psychology, had himself declared that higher mental processes could not be studied experimentally. The ambitious project Ebbinghaus set for himself denied this generally accepted view. We do not know exactly how the notion of challenging this dogma occurred to Ebbinghaus, but we know that he was thoroughly familiar with British associationist philosophy, and this helps us understand both his choice of problem and his development of an appropriate method of investigation.

EBBINGHAUS'S WORK: EXPERIMENTS ON ASSOCIATIONS

Ebbinghaus's goal was to study the associative process described by the British empiricists by using the methods of natural science. He set out to study associations experimentally, by carefully controlling the conditions under which they were formed, the length of time they were retained, and the way in which they were recalled. Rather than adopting the naturalistic method of philosophy, in which the associations studied involved everyday ideas (such as "apple") that had been acquired at undetermined times under uncontrolled conditions, Ebbinghaus produced associations under artificial laboratory conditions. Rather than relying on purely subjective impressions, no matter how compelling, Ebbinghaus attempted to measure memory objectively. Is a frequently repeated event remembered better than a seldom experienced one? Is an event that occurred long ago more difficult to recall than one that occurred recently? Intuitively these statements seem to be true. But Ebbinghaus wanted precise statements of the laws involved—a goal his contemporaries thought unattainable.

Ebbinghaus's basic notion was that the sequence of associated ideas that makes up naturally occurring thought could be simulated in the laboratory by artificially impressing a chain of completely new associations on the mind. His reasoning was as follows: Suppose a human subject studies several stimuli in sequence (let us call them A, B, C, D, and E). Each stimulus, in turn, produces its corresponding idea in the mind. Thus idea a, produced by stimulus A, is followed by idea b, produced by B, and so on. According to the law of contiguity, ideas occurring in close succession should become associated. Thus, if stimuli A, B, C, D, and E are studied in order, the associative chain of ideas a–b–c–d–e should be formed. As a result, whenever stimulus A is encountered, the entire chain of ideas a through e should go through the subject's mind.

Since the goal here was to study the formation of *new* associations, without assistance or interference from associations already in the mind, Ebbinghaus invented what he hoped would be a relatively meaningless unit with no prior associations. He simply took two randomly selected consonants and put a vowel in between—for example, ZOT, BOK, KIF. As long as the combination did not form a German word, it qualified as a *nonsense syllable* and would serve as one of his stimuli. He generated a pool of some 2,300 such syllables. From this pool he selected items at random to make up his experimental lists.

The learning materials of his experiments consisted of *serial lists*—that is, series of nonsense syllables that had to be memorized in their proper order.

Ebbinghaus used himself as subject in all his experiments. In memorizing a list, he would read it aloud at a fast, regular rate paced by a metronome. He re-read the list repeatedly, without pausing between readings. When he felt he was close to mastery of the list, he tested himself, again without pausing, by looking only at the first syllable and trying to recite the list all the way through at the same fast rate. If he made an error or hesitated, he read through the rest of the list and then alternated reading and testing himself in this way until he was able to recite the list from memory without hesitation. At this point he immediately stopped a clock and recorded the number of seconds it had taken him to learn the list. Often he also kept track of the number of repetitions memorization of the list had required. Either measure served as an index of the difficulty of the list.

Great care was taken to control the conditions under which the experiments were performed. Distractions in the environment, time of day, and his mental attitude and health were all factors Ebbinghaus made note of and attempted to take into account in interpreting his results. In addition, from his study of mathematics he had acquired a

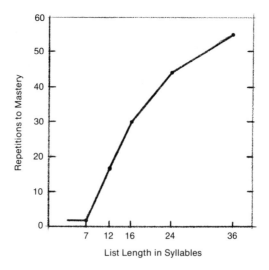

Figure 2.1 Effect of list length on learning difficulty. [Data from Ebbinghaus, 1885.]

sophisticated appreciation of statistical theory. He knew that the average of several observations is much more stable than the individual measurements on which it is based, and for this reason he always learned several lists conforming to each experimental condition. Considering the experiments reported in his book and the extensive preliminary experiments he conducted over a number of years, it is safe to say that in the course of his investigations Ebbinghaus must have memorized several thousand nonsense syllable lists. No one who has ever learned a serial list of nonsense syllables can deny the man's heroic dedication to the goal of making psychology an experimental science.

Ebbinghaus's investigations appeared in the year 1885, in a book entitled *Über das Gedächtnis (On Memory)*. In it, he described experiments concerning a number of aspects of the associative process. The results of only a few of his experiments will be presented here.

Effects of List Length

How is the difficulty of learning related to the amount of material to be learned? To answer this question, Ebbinghaus constructed and learned a number of lists varying in length or number of syllables. The lists were 7, 12, 16, 24, and 36 syllables long. As Figure 2.1 shows, the average number of repetitions necessary for one errorless reproduction increased from 1, for 7-syllable lists, up to 55, for 36-syllable lists. No one, of course, will be surprised to learn that long lists are harder to memorize than are short ones. But one might be surprised to learn that a 5-fold increase in length (from 7 to 36 syllables) results in a 55-fold increase in difficulty. Ebbinghaus's result with the shortest list corresponds to what is today called the *memory span*—the number of items that can be repeated without error after one exposure. The memory span is usually said to be around seven. It is slightly longer than seven for letter sequences, and somewhat shorter for unfamiliar items such as nonsense syllables. Ebbinghaus's memory span of seven nonsense syllables is unusually high. This may reflect his high intellectual ability—in fact, memory span tests are often included in intelligence tests. Alternatively, it may reflect the vast amount of practice Ebbinghaus had at committing strings of nonsense syllables to memory. It is now known that an individual's memory span increases somewhat with practice on the task.

Effects of Meaningfulness

Another problem studied by Ebbinghaus was the influence of meaningfulness on memory. Memorizing stanzas of the English poet
Byron's *Don Juan,* he found, was much easier than the rote learning of
serial lists of nonsense syllables. When nonsense syllable lists and
poetry were equated for length in syllables, the combined advantages
of meaning, rhyme, and rhythm amounted to about a 90 percent
reduction in effort. That is, nonsense syllables took about ten times as
long as the poetry to memorize.

Repetition and Savings

The primary concern of Ebbinghaus's work was the retention of associations over time. Subjectively, it seems clear that retention depends
on two factors: the initial depth of the impression on memory, and the
time the impression has had to fade away. But what precisely is the
nature of each of these relationships? Since "depth of impression" and
"fading away" are just figurative terms with no objective referents,
there is no way to tell. Ebbinghaus sought objective, quantitative measurements which would allow the functional relationships to be stated
in a manner similar to the statement of physical laws. "Depth of impression," he saw, could be replaced by a count of the number of times
the list was repeated in original learning. To determine the extent to
which the impression had been forgotten or had faded away, Ebbinghaus proposed that the list be relearned after a given retention interval. Forgetting could then be measured by comparing the number of
trials (or amount of time) needed to relearn the list to mastery with the
number of trials (or time) needed to learn it in the first place. The
comparison was expressed as a "savings" score, in terms of a
percentage:

$$\text{Percent savings} = 100 \times \frac{\text{Trials to learn} - \text{Trials to relearn}}{\text{Trials to learn}}$$

Suppose it took 30 trials to learn a list initially. Then according to
the formula if it takes 30 trials to relearn, savings equal 0 percent—no
effort is saved as a result of the previous practice on the list, and so
there is no evidence of retention at the time of relearning. Likewise, if
relearning requires no practice (the list can be recited perfectly on the
first attempt) savings equal 100 percent. If relearning takes 15 trials,

savings equal 50 percent, and so on. The savings score provides a very sensitive measure of retention. Even information that appears to have been completely forgotten often shows savings in relearning. Thus, the person who spoke French as a child but feels he has long since forgotten the language is underestimating his memory. A little training in French, for this person, will have a dramatic effect.

How is retention affected by the degree of learning? To answer this question, Ebbinghaus read 16-syllable lists either 8, 16, 24, 32, 42, 53, or 64 times, and relearned each list to mastery 24 hours after the initial learning. Altogether, he learned 60 different lists in each of these conditions. Retention, measured in terms of percent savings, is presented as a function of the number of original learning trials in Figure 2.2. Although the data are presented in a different way from that used by Ebbinghaus, they illustrate one of his conclusions: that there is a straight-line relationship between the number of original learning trials and the number of trials saved in relearning. The more trials of original practice, the less effort is necessary for relearning.

Note, however, that because of forgetting during the 24-hour retention interval one trial of original practice did not save one trial in relearning. These lists were 16-syllables long, and the study of learning as a function of list length (Figure 2.1) showed that 16-syllable lists

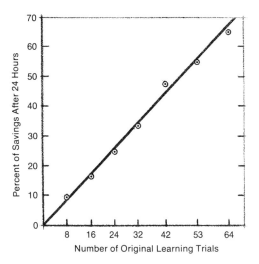

Figure 2.2 Savings after 24 hours as a function of trials of original learning. [Data from Ebbinghaus, 1885.]

required approximately 32 trials to learn. If Ebbinghaus's memory
for the lists in this study had been perfect, therefore, the savings
resulting from 32 trials of original learning would have been 100
percent. Instead, they were about 32 percent, which shows that the
degree of forgetting occurring in 24 hours was considerable. Notice
especially that repetition beyond the point of mastery (32 trials, in this
case) increases the degree of retention. This phenomenon has come to
be known as *overlearning*. The phenomenon of overlearning is something every student who studies for examinations could put to practical use.

Effects of Retention Interval

Savings of a barely mastered list on an immediate test would be about
100 percent. Savings on a test delayed 24 hours were 32 percent. This
raises a further question. What would savings be after 48 hours? In
general, what is the nature of the function relating forgetting to the
length of the retention interval? In still another experiment, Ebbinghaus set out to plot the course of retention as a function of time. He
learned lists to mastery, and later relearned different ones of these lists
after intervals of 19 minutes, 63 minutes, 1 day, 2 days, 6 days, and 31
days. Altogether, this experiment involved the learning and subsequent relearning of 1,228 lists of 13 syllables each! The results, in
terms of percent savings, are presented in Figure 2.3. Here it can be

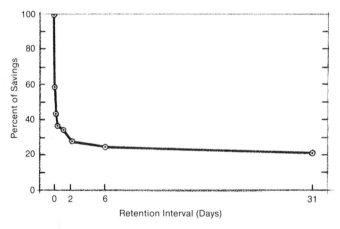

Figure 2.3 Savings as a function of retention interval. [Data
from Ebbinghaus, 1885.]

seen that retention dropped off rather precipitously at first. Forgetting amounted to over 41 percent after only 19 minutes, and over 55 percent after 1 hour. However, the rate of forgetting over longer intervals was much slower. While 72 percent had been forgotten after 2 days, only 79 percent was forgotten after 31 days. This change in the rate of forgetting over time, quite rapid at first and becoming slower at longer intervals, is sometimes called the *classic retention function*. It suggests that retention would reach 0 percent only after a very long interval, perhaps on the order of many years. Ebbinghaus, in fact, explored the possibility of fitting a mathematical function to his retention curve. The function he chose as providing the best fit is one in which retention approaches zero only as time approaches infinity.

The initial rapidity with which Ebbinghaus forgot his nonsense syllable lists is rather remarkable. He attributed forgetting primarily to the passage of time. But today we know that there are other more potent sources of forgetting, and that Ebbinghaus's technique of using himself as subject in all his experiments must have contributed substantially to the amount of forgetting he observed. One source of forgetting, called *proactive interference,* is produced by similar material learned in the past. Since Ebbinghaus had memorized a very large number of lists in prior investigations, proactive interference is a likely explanation for the rapid forgetting he observed. Another source of forgetting, called *retroactive inference,* is produced by similar material learned after the to-be-remembered material. Ebbinghaus's routine was to learn several lists in a session and then relearn them all in a later session. Inevitably, therefore, the learning (or relearning) of several other nonsense syllable lists occurred between the time a given list was learned and the time at which it was relearned—a likely source of retroactive interference.

Evaluation of Ebbinghaus's Work

Ebbinghaus's work has been criticized on several grounds. One criticism has been that nonsense syllables are not completely homogeneous and without meaning, as Ebbinghaus had hoped they would be. In fairness, however, it must be said that Ebbinghaus recognized that the syllables did not perfectly meet his goal of having no prior associations. He wanted to study the formation and breakdown of new associations, uncontaminated by old ones, but he knew that, like the physicist seeking a perfect vacuum, he could only approximate the ideal conditions. Other criticisms have centered on the fact that Ebbinghaus used himself as subject in all his experiments. For example, it has been asserted (a) that this situation produced massive amounts of proactive and retroactive interference, (b) that Ebbinghaus knew the purpose of each experiment, and this may have had a subtle influence on the outcome, and, (c) that the laws of association for a single subject might be atypical, so that generalization to other individuals would be unwarranted.

Whatever the merits of the various criticisms, they appear trivial when contrasted with the tremendous positive contribution Ebbinghaus made. At a time when higher mental processes were the sole province of philosophical psychology, when observations of the processes were all subjective and the conditions of observation were uncontrolled, Ebbinghaus introduced a method of measuring memory objectively in a situation where the time and degree of original learning could be carefully specified. Observations were not only objective, but quantitative as well. Precise measurement and the control of such factors as mental attitude and the time of day of learning were almost an obsession for Ebbinghaus. In the experiments just described and a number of others, Hermann Ebbinghaus showed convincingly that the associative processes could be studied using the methods of natural science. The publication of his book in 1885 opened an entirely new area to scientific investigation.

INTROSPECTIONISM AND HIGHER MENTAL PROCESSES

With the publication of Ebbinghaus's book it became clear that the higher mental processes could be brought under experimental investigation. It is important to note, however, that while psychologists influenced by Ebbinghaus set out to study these processes experimentally, not all of them did it objectively. Those who studied learning followed Ebbinghaus's lead in using objective measures of relearning, recall, or recognition. But others were reluctant to give up the method of introspection, which had served philosophical psychology so well and which appeared to be indispensable in the experimental analysis of perception. These investigators, called *introspectionists,* studied higher mental processes subjectively, as the British empiricists had done; but unlike the philosophers, they adapted the method for use in a controlled experimental setting.

Subjective Versus Objective Observations

Today, with the benefit of hindsight, we can see that the introspectionists' failure to break with philosophy as completely as Ebbinghaus had done was a mistake. Their insistence on subjective observation would eventually bring about their downfall and discredit the entire cognitivist tradition. At the time, however, adopting a subjective experimental approach to the study of higher mental processes must have seemed like the obvious and appropriate thing to do.

There is nothing inherently unscientific about subjective observation. Like objective data, subjective reports can be analyzed and classified in systematic ways, and theories explaining the observations can be proposed. But all such activities require data that are reliable—that is, observations on which all investigators agree. Scientists can, and normally do, disagree about explanations of their observations; but it is upon the observations themselves that decisions about the validity of a theory ultimately rest. Without agreement on observations, disagreements concerning theories can never be resolved.

The advantage of objective observations is that they are more likely than subjective observations to produce consensus. This is not because subjective observations never agree (nearly everyone presented with an extremely loud sound will report a feeling of pain) or because objective observations always do (view the celebrated controversy in astronomy concerning whether canals could be seen on Mars). But objective observations can be aided by precise instruments. Given a reading on a clock, a mark on a ruler, or a score on an intelligence test, all observers will agree closely on what the observation is. If subjective observations had a comparable degree of reliability, they would be an invaluable source of psychological data.

As we have said, it is essential in any science that investigators agree on what the data are. The quandary in which introspectionism eventually found itself involved disagreements about the data. Thus, the possibility that the mind could be studied scientifically was seriously brought into question.

The Imageless-Thought Controversy

Around the turn of the century, a flurry of experiments were done using introspection to study higher mental processes. Typically, the subject, or "observer," as he was usually called, was asked to make a more or less complex judgment as quickly as he could. The primary interest was in the observer's introspective account, taken immediately afterward, of what had passed through his awareness as the judgment was being made. Tasks varied widely. The observer might lift two weights and decide which was heavier, or give the opposite of a word, or indicate esthetic preference for one painting over another, or express agreement or disagreement with a statement, or complete a sentence, or draw a conclusion from a syllogism. Always, immediately after his response he was to describe what had gone through his mind. Sometimes he was asked leading questions about visual imagery, words, and feelings he experienced as the judgment was being made.

Traditional introspective analysis had identified three kinds of elements in the mind: *feelings,* which gave experience its emotional tone; *sensations,* which arose from stimulation of the sense organs; and *images,* which were like copies of sensations, but which could occur without external stimulation. The image was considered to be the vehicle of thought. It therefore played much the same role in introspective psychology as the idea had played in the philosophy of the British empiricists. The fact that introspectionism assigned the image this key role led to the "imageless-thought" controversy, which helped bring about introspection's downfall.

The imageless-thought controversy developed from the types of experiments just described. A simple stimulus or problem was presented, requiring a response of some kind, and after responding the observer described the mental events that led him to make that response. Many observers, it turned out, reported that answers came to them without the experience of intermediary images. In some cases, the answers came so quickly that hardly any conscious content at all could be observed. For example, consider a simple mathematical problem: "I will say a number, and you are to add six to it. Ready? . . . Nine." Attempts by observers to scrutinize the mental events of the fraction of a second between "nine" and the production of the answer met with little success. This was a minor embarrassment to introspectionism since it was obvious that there were important events occurring during the interval that were not available to introspective analysis. There was some argument about the existence of images during the brief instant. But the experience of imageless thought in this case could be explained away as an instance of direct association, a process in which images would not be expected to intervene.

Far more serious were problems requiring a complex judgment by the observer. "Bravery is to courage as humor is to . . . ?" Given such problems, some highly trained observers consistently reported thinking without images, either visual or verbal in nature. There was, to be sure, an awareness of a train of thought, of getting close to the answer, a feeling of wanting to do well—but no images. Others, upholding the traditional view that the image is the vehicle of thought, objected. *They* experienced imagery—a laughing face perhaps, or the sound of the word "synonym." But the upstarts argued that their thoughts were abstract, and not at all like copies of sensory events.

The defenders of the traditional view, most notably E. B. Titchener, of Cornell University, replied in various ways. Perhaps those reporting imageless thought had fallen into the trap of reporting the *object* of the thought (which may very well be abstract), rather than describing the nature of the thought itself. This would be somewhat like reporting that the *idea* of "dog" was furry or the *idea* of "chocolate" was brown. But this objection raises a further problem. How can one examine and describe a thought independent of its content? If a thought is to be examined and described, doesn't the thought itself have to be the object of thought? And how can a thought be about itself? Such an argument calls the entire method of introspection into question. The problem is apparently solved by noting that a thought is subjected to introspective analysis only *after* it has occurred. The thought doing the analysis is a different one; it has as its object remembered thoughts of the immediate past.

The observers reporting imageless thought considered Titchener's criticism that they may have been describing the objects of thought, rather than the thoughts themselves; but they were sure they were indeed describing the thoughts. Perhaps, Titchener countered, the images had become so habitual that they were largely subconscious and hardly recognizable as images as they appear in awareness. By appealing to subconscious images, however, Titchener and other traditionalists were shaking the foundations of their science. If the crucial mental events cannot be observed introspectively, then what is the value of the method? Perhaps introspection should be abandoned.

And increasingly, observers were emphasizing the abstract nature of thought. They claimed that when images did occur they were an irrelevant by-product of the actual thought process. How could the image of a laughing face lead one to correctly respond with "wit,"

rather than with "laugh," or "face," or "joke"? Thus, even when images were observed, they did not constitute a complete explanation of
the process of thought.

The important point about the imageless-thought controversy is
that different observers disagreed about the data. Titchener and other
traditionalists reported that thought always consisted of images. The
opposing camp reported the frequent occurrence of abstract thought.
Perhaps they were both right. Perhaps the two groups of observers
had different types of minds. Or perhaps the traditionalists so firmly
believed thought consisted of images that this belief affected what they
observed. Whatever the cause, the scandalous disagreement among
observers set the stage for the abandonment of subjective observation
in experimental psychology.

Other Applications of Introspection

Imageless thought was the most celebrated problem confronting introspectionism, but not the only one. If a method is to be of general
value to psychology, it should be useful in investigating personality
differences, insanity, the mind of the child, and even animal psychology. Introspectionists enthusiastically attempted to apply their
method to these areas of investigation.

It might seem brash to suppose that through introspection one
could study any mind other than one's own. However, appeal to something called "ejective consciousness" made this seem less absurd than
it at first appeared. Margaret Washburn (1917) stated the critical assumption as follows:

> I am perfectly willing to admit that the psychological basis of
> ejective consciousness may be a kind of inner imitation of the
> behavior of others, but the inevitable accompaniment of such
> inner imitation is the consciousness of other people's states of
> mind, and this consciousness may be directly observed by intro-
> spection . . . (p. 16).

Thus the objective observation of others can lead to a state of em-
pathy, in which the others' mental processes are mimicked by our
own. This allows us to study other minds by introspection.

Nor was the use of the method restricted to the study of other
normal adult human minds—it was extended even to animal psychology. If the most careful and conservative application of introspection

by similarly trained psychologists produced bitter disagreement over the existence of imageless thought, one can imagine the perils of attempting to analyze the contents of the mind of a dog, rat, snake, or ant through introspection. Yet the method was applied in such cases, with the inevitable result. A good example is found in the following quotation from Wundt (1896):

> I had made myself, as a boy, a fly-trap, like a pigeon-cote. The flies were attracted by scattered sugar, and caught as soon as they had entered the cage. Behind the trap was a second box, separated from it by a sliding door, which could be opened or shut at pleasure. In this I had put a large garden spider. Cage and box were provided with glass windows on the top, so that I could quite well observe anything that was going on inside. At first nothing particular happened. When some flies had been caught, and the slide was drawn out, the spider, of course, rushed upon her prey and devoured them, leaving only the legs, head, and wings. That went on for some time. The spider was sometimes let into the cage, sometimes confined to her own box. But one day I made a notable discovery. During an absence the slide had been accidentally left open for some little while. When I came to shut it, I found that there was an unusual resistance. As I looked more closely, I saw that the spider had drawn a large number of thick threads directly under the lifted door, and that these were preventing my closing it, as though they had been so many cords tied across it.
>
> What was going on in the spider's mind before she took this step towards self-preservation—a step, mark you, which but for the *vis major* of the boy-master would have been perfectly adequate to effect the desired result? The animal psychologist will possibly say: "the spider must first of all have come to understand the mechanism of the sliding door, and must have said to herself that a force operating in a definite direction could be compensated by another in the opposite direction. Then she set to work, relying upon the perfectly correct inference that if she could only make movement of the door impossible, she would always have access to the victims of her murderous desires. There you have a consideration of general issues, an accurate prevision, and a cautious balancing of cause and effect, end and means." Well, I am rather inclined to explain the matter otherwise. I imagine that as the days went by there had been formed in the mind of the spider a determinate association on the one hand between free entry into the cage and the pleasurable feel-

ing attending satisfaction of the nutritive instinct, and on the other between the closed slide and the unpleasant feeling of hunger and inhibited impulse. Now in her free life the spider had always employed her web in the service of the nutritive , impulse. Associations had therefore grown up between the definite positions of her web and definite peculiarities of the objects to which it was attached, as well as changes which it produced in the positions of certain of these objects—leaves, small twigs, etc. The impression of the falling slide, that is, called up by association the idea of other objects similarly moved which had been held in their places by threads properly spun; and finally there were connected with this association the other two of pleasure and raising, unpleasantness and closing, of the door. Any other intellectual or inventive activity is entirely unnecessary. If she had not had these associations at her disposal, she would certainly never have hit upon the plan she did (pp. 351–352).

The principle of *parsimony* says that one should never invoke a complex explanation when a simple one would do as well. In this passage, Wundt criticizes animal psychologists for the overly complex explanation they would give for the behavior of the spider and proposes instead a parsimonious one. To a modern psychologist, Wundt's explanation seems hardly less outrageous than that of his imagined adversaries.

In animal psychology, as in the imageless-thought controversy, the method of introspection produced disagreement among observers. A result of this disagreement, as we shall see in the next chapter, was the rise of behaviorism. Behaviorism entailed a fundamental change in the assumptions psychologists made about their science, the kinds of experiments they did, the method of observation they used, and the way they constructed their theories.

3

The Behaviorist Revolution

In his book *The Structure of Scientific Revolutions,* Thomas Kuhn describes the pattern of events surrounding revolutionary changes in scientific thought. The conceptual framework that scientists in a given field impose on the subject matter they study, Kuhn calls a "paradigm." A scientific revolution, in Kuhn's view, can best be understood as a process whereby the prevailing paradigm of an area of investigation is replaced by another paradigm that is fundamentally different. Several points about this process are worth noting. First, investigators working within the original framework are bothered by certain anomalies—problems that will not yield to solution by the commonly accepted methods the paradigm provides. Second, an alternative approach is proposed. At first, this alternative may be relatively crude, but it deals with the anomalies in a convincing way and holds out the promise of eventually developing into a more complete and adequate way of organizing the subject matter of the field. Third, the new approach demonstrates its value, either by identifying and solving new problems or by redefining old ones in a way that leads to more elegant solutions, and thus gains adherents. Finally, the majority of investigators in the field—with the possible exception of a few of the older ones—become converted. Once again the area is held together by a single, commonly accepted paradigm which appears to promise continuous progress. The cycle is complete.

The last chapter sketched the beginnings of the experimental study of higher mental processes and noted in particular certain anomalies that were encountered by the introspectionists. The imageless-thought issue, in particular, could not be ignored or dismissed as unimportant, since it led the introspectionists to question some of the assumptions underlying their whole approach to psychology.

In this chapter, we shall see how a new school of psychology, called behaviorism, gained support by providing a radical solution to the problem encountered by introspectionism, and eventually rose to become the established point of view. Behaviorism proposed that the unreliable subjective methods of observation be replaced by objective methods and that terms which alluded to mental states be banned not only from observation but from explanation as well. In essence, behaviorism was proposing that the field of psychology be redefined as "the study of behavior," rather than "the study of mental life."

The founder of behaviorism in America was John B. Watson. He was the chief advocate of the new view, and the most prominent leader of the revolution. By attacking introspectionism in particular, and the cognitivist approach in general, Watson prepared psychology for the sweeping changes that were to come. But if Watson's polemics against the past were virulent, his program for the future was vague. How could a psychology that studied only behavior and ignored the mind deal with psychological processes of central importance such as learning and thinking? Watson maintained that such an approach could succeed, but provided no concrete evidence which showed convincingly that he was right. The ultimate victory of behaviorism, therefore, may have been due less to Watson's testimonial than to the positive example provided by Pavlov's work. We shall, therefore, delay a more thorough discussion of Watson's views. It is to the research of the Russian physiologist Ivan P. Pavlov that we now turn.

PAVLOV'S WORK

Pavlov was the first-born son of a poor Russian clergyman. His education was at first oriented toward a career in the ministry, like his father's. But as a seminary student, Pavlov took several classes at the University of St. Petersburg and soon became fascinated with physiology. What particularly intrigued him was the digestive system. He wondered how such a complex mechanism worked. Pavlov left the seminary and entered the university, where, under the direction of one of the professors, he was able to gain first-hand experience in physiological research. After graduating, Pavlov entered the Military-Medical Academy to pursue an M.D. degree and prepare himself for a research career. In 1883, at the age of thirty-three, Pavlov received his M.D. degree. His dissertation concerned neural control of the heart. From this research, he developed an appreciation for the control of the internal organs by the nervous system—an influence to be seen in all his later work.

After Pavlov received his M.D. degree, his interests turned again to digestion. Working with others, he perfected a surgical technique that allowed secretion of digestive juices to be studied in an animal that was alive and well. The technique involved creating an isolated pouch of stomach tissue, with its nerve supply intact, sealed off from the rest of the stomach (and therefore from food) but opening directly to the outside of the body. This allowed easy measurement of gastric secretion. Experiments done on dogs prepared in this way enabled Pavlov to specify the relationships between gastric secretion and such variables as amount of food eaten, kind of food eaten, and time since eating.

To study the secretion of saliva, Pavlov developed a similar surgical technique. The duct from a dog's salivary gland was diverted through an incision, to the outside of the cheek. Thus, the amount, quality, and rate of secretion of the saliva could be measured directly. The relation between salivary and gastric secretion was found to be complex. For example, both food and an acid solution placed in the dog's mouth would lead to salivation, but the food would also produce gastric secretion, while the acid solution would not. Pavlov also noted that the nature of the saliva in the two cases was different. This finding led him to distinguish two different kinds of salivary reflex—one which was involved in the digestion of food and one which was defensive and apparently served the purpose of washing foreign substances from the mouth. In 1897 Pavlov's research was published in a book entitled *Lectures on the Work of the Principal Digestive Glands*. In 1904, for his immense contributions to the understanding of the physiology of digestion, he was awarded the Nobel Prize.

In 1902 Pavlov made a decision that was to make him as famous in psychology as he was in physiology. For the most part, the secretions of the digestive glands appeared to be innate reflexes—that is, inborn, genetically determined responses to stimuli such as food in the mouth, esophagus, and stomach. But Pavlov had noticed while studying the reflexes of the salivary glands that if the same dog was used repeatedly in an experiment salivation soon began to occur even before the food was placed in the mouth. The sight of the food or the experimenter or even the sound of the experimenter's footsteps was often enough to elicit the salivary response. Pavlov viewed this as a *learned* reflex, which was produced somehow by the pairing of a neutral stimulus with food in the mouth. His name for it was "psychic secretion." At first, he treated the phenomenon as an annoyance, since it made experiments on innate salivary reflexes difficult to perform. He did recognize it as important, however, for the psychic secretion appeared to represent a simple form of learning, and learning was something that was a complete mystery to science. Pavlov's momentous decision was to turn all his efforts to the investigation of this phenomenon. It was a project that occupied him for the rest of his life.

How should one go about studying learning? The first approach Pavlov tried was introspection. He and his assistant tried to imagine what subjective experiences the dog was having. What ideas, feelings, and expectations were going through the dog's mind? These efforts proved fruitless. Pavlov's observations and those of his assistant did not always agree. And it was clear that the method itself was flawed since disagreements would be possible whenever subjective observations were used. Furthermore, the method of introspection was contrary to Pavlov's training and experience as a physiologist. What was the "mind" other than the working of the brain? And wasn't the brain an organ of the body, to be studied like any other? The functioning of the nervous system, Pavlov decided, could never be unraveled using the subjective methods of psychology. The brain would eventually be understood only if treated as a biological mechanism, to be studied (like the stomach) by objective observations in carefully controlled experimental settings.

The Basic Experiment

The research program Pavlov and his co-workers developed over the next three decades involved many elaborations of a simple basic experiment. A dog was held in a harness which secured its neck and all four legs, making gross body movements impossible. The salivary duct was diverted to the outside of the cheek in the way previously described, and a device for measuring the amount of saliva secreted was attached to the duct. Food or acid solution could be introduced into the animal's mouth at a precise moment, and various neutral stimuli could be presented through the senses of vision, hearing, and touch. To eliminate distracting noises from outside, the experimental subject and apparatus were enclosed in a sound-deadened room.

Under these conditions a neutral stimulus such as a tone, if presented just before food or acid solution was placed in the mouth, was found to acquire power to elicit salivation. It took many presentations of the tone and food, sometimes extending over several days, before salivation would occur when the tone was presented alone; and once acquired, this "learned reflex" was easily disrupted. Nevertheless, the result was striking. The dog now salivated when presented with a stimulus that previously had elicited no salivation at all. It appeared that any neutral stimulus paired repeatedly with food would eventually elicit salivation.

The learned connection between the tone and salivation was referred to formally by Pavlov as a "conditional reflex." This is to be contrasted with the "unconditional reflex" to food in the mouth (unconditional because it does not depend on past training). The first translation of Pavlov's work into English used the term *conditioned reflex,* and since this has become the customary expression, we shall use it here.

The food, in our example, is called the *unconditioned stimulus* (the innate or natural stimulus of the reflex), and the tone is called the *conditioned stimulus* (the stimulus of the conditioned reflex). These two terms are frequently abbreviated UCS and CS, respectively. Salivation produced by the food is called the *unconditioned response* (UCR), and that elicited by the tone, after training, is called the *conditioned response* (CR).

Pavlov thought the conditioning procedure established a conducting pathway in the brain, linking the neural centers for the CS and CR. A necessary condition for establishing such a pathway was that the CS occur at about the same time as the UCS; that is, the two had to occur in temporal contiguity. A diagram of the formation of a conditioned reflex, as interpreted by Pavlov, is presented in Figure 3.1. An energy field surrounding the pathway of the unconditioned reflex (solid arrow) was assumed to divert energy from the neural center for the CS, and pull it toward the center for the UCR. With repeated pairing of the CS and UCS, a new pathway was thought to be formed (dashed arrow), mediating the conditioned reflex.

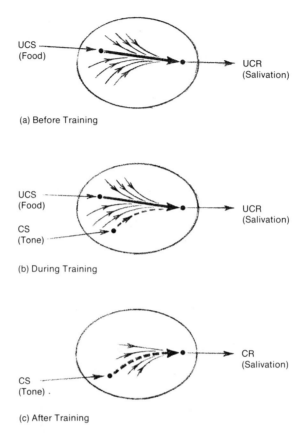

Figure 3.1 Pavlov's model of the brain activity underlying conditioning. [Adapted from H. Rachlin, *Behavior and Learning.* Copyright © 1976 by W. H. Freeman and Co.]

Extinction and Recovery

Interestingly, Pavlov did not spend much time studying the acquisition of conditioned reflexes, but concentrated instead on how they could be manipulated, once established. One phenomenon Pavlov demonstrated was what he called *extinction*. A conditioned reflex, no matter how well practiced, can be eliminated if the CS is presented several times in succession alone (without the food). An example of extinction, taken from one of Pavlov's experiments, is presented in Figure 3.2.

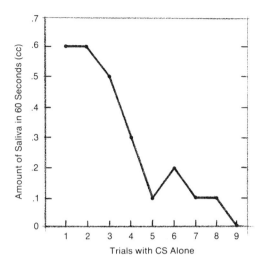

Figure 3.2 Extinction of a conditioned salivary reflex. CS presentations were 16 minutes apart; saliva was measured in cubic centimeters (cc). [Data from Pavlov, 1927.]

What is extinction? Has the conditioned reflex, so difficult to acquire, been so easily lost? Is extinction the destruction of the reflex? Pavlov had a different theory. There was evidence, from physiological research, that the operation of the nervous system was based on two opponent processes—*excitation* and *inhibition*. Pavlov thought the conditioned reflex was based on excitation of the CS–CR pathway in the brain. Extinction, he thought, was due to the build-up of inhibition, directly opposing the tendency of the reflex to occur. Thus, extinction was assumed to be due not to destruction or erosion of the CS–CR pathway, but rather to temporary blocking of its activity by the inhibitory process.

There were several pieces of experimental evidence favoring the inhibition account of extinction. One was that when extinction was complete or nearly so (that is, when repetition of the CS alone had brought the amount of salivation elicited by the CS back to zero), a loud sound or other distracting stimulus could produce reappearance of the conditioned reflex. If the CS was presented soon after such a distracting event, it elicited salivation. This phenomenon Pavlov called *disinhibition* since it suggested that the inhibitory process was disrupted by the distractor, releasing the conditioned reflex so it could again occur. Another bit of evidence that extinction was not permanent destruction of the conditioned reflex was obtained simply by waiting a while after extinction was complete and then presenting the CS again. If several minutes or hours were allowed to pass before the CS was presented, it would again elicit the response. This result has been called *spontaneous recovery*. While the degree of recovery is usually not complete—that is, the magnitude of the response does not return to the level reached before the beginning of extinction—the existence of any recovery at all indicates that during extinction the conditioned reflex was not destroyed.

Stimulus Generalization and Differentiation

Pavlov attached great importance to the phenomenon called *stimulus generalization*. Once a conditioned reflex has been established to a certain CS, it will also occur when stimuli similar to the CS are presented. The magnitude of the response becomes less as the test stimulus becomes less similar to the CS. An example of stimulus generalization is found in an experiment done in Pavlov's laboratory by G. V. Anrep. The CS for the salivary reflex was activation of a vibrator attached to the dog's thigh, and the UCS was food. After the salivary reflex had been conditioned, tests were made applying vibratory stimuli to other locations along the dog's side—the hind paw, the pelvis, the middle of the trunk, the shoulder, the foreleg, and the front paw—in addition to the thigh (the original point of stimulation). Figure 3.3 presents the number of drops of saliva secreted during 30-second periods of vibratory stimulation at each point. The magnitude of the reflex was greatest when the test stimulus was the CS itself, and it dropped off in a regular way with distance from the CS along the animal's skin. The gradual drop in response strength with decreasing similarity to the CS is called the *generalization gradient*.

The form of a generalization gradient such as that represented in Figure 3.3 can be altered considerably through a procedure of Pavlov's called *differential conditioning*. In the experiment just described, the animal was trained with the vibratory stimulus applied to the thigh, always followed by the UCS. In the test for generalization, a stimulus applied to the pelvis elicited nearly as much salivation as did the CS. Suppose, however, that *both* the stimulation of the thigh and stimulation of the pelvis were presented during training, with stimula-

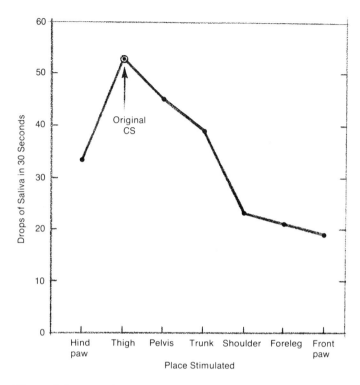

Figure 3.3 Generalization of a conditioned salivary reflex. [Data from Pavlov, 1927.]

tion of the thigh always followed by food and stimulation of the pelvis never followed by food. Let us call the stimulus followed by the UCS the *CS +*, and the stimulus never followed by the UCS the *CS−*. What happens is that early in the course of training the dog with salivate to the CS− (generalization), as well as to the CS+; but as training progresses, the response to the CS− gradually declines and is eventually extinguished altogether. Thus the CS+ produces salivation, while the CS−, although highly similar to the CS+, does not. This is called differential conditioning because the animal has learned to respond differently to the two stimuli.

Pavlov thought that generalization and differential conditioning revealed a great deal about the physiological processes of the brain. He theorized that the neural centers representing the stimuli were arranged spatially on the surface of the cerebral cortex of the brain according to the similarity of the stimuli they represented. Generalization was assumed to be due to the spreading or "irradiation" of excitation from the point corresponding to the CS+ to the neighboring areas of the cortex. The spread of excitation could be counteracted by building up inhibition at one or more of the neighboring points (that is, by presenting a CS–). Many of the experiments done by Pavlov and his colleagues were designed to measure the amount of time it took for excitation and inhibition to spread over the cortex after their respective stimuli had been applied, and to determine the nature of the interaction between the two opposing processes. Excitation and inhibition were never observed directly, of course—they were inferred from the results of the laboratory experiments on conditioned reflexes. Pavlov's writings leave a clear impression that he firmly believed this theory about the working of the brain. It seemed to him to follow necessarily from the experimental results. Actually, he had constructed an ingenious but highly speculative theory which, although stated in physiological terms, was supported only by the data it was invented to explain. The theory, as we shall see, influenced a number of later investigators, but it is not generally accepted today (for one thing, it is known that conditioning can occur in an animal whose cerebral cortex has been removed). Pavlov's basic experimental results, on the other hand, have been repeated many times. Most of what is known about conditioned reflexes (often called *classical conditioning*) was first discovered in Pavlov's laboratory.

Psychopathology

Before we leave Pavlov's work, one other famous experiment should be described. Pavlov and his co-workers had discovered that through a modification of the differential conditioning procedure a dog could be induced to make extremely fine discriminations. This was done by beginning with a CS– that was very different from the CS+ and then making it more and more similar. For example, in one experiment a piece of paper that was white and one that was a very light shade of grey were used as the CS+ and the CS– in the standard differential conditioning procedure, in which the CS+ and CS– are both presented during training, one followed by the UCS and the other not. The dog was unable to learn the discrimination between white and light grey. Then the procedure was changed. At first, a dark grey, which looked very different from the CS+, was used as the CS–. As this easy discrimination developed, successively lighter shades of grey were substituted as the CS– until the discrimination impossible to learn under the original procedure had been established. Pavlov reported that dogs could learn to discriminate shades of grey on successive trials that humans could not tell apart side by side, suggesting that the capacity for brightness discrimination in dogs is much greater than that in humans.

This procedure, called *gradual differentiation*, was used by one of Pavlov's students, Shenger-Krestovnikova, to study the limits of discriminability of shapes. The CS+ in her experiment was a circle, and the initial CS– was an ellipse. The ratio of the horizontal and vertical axes of the ellipse was 2 : 1—that it, it was twice as wide as it was tall. Once this circle versus ellipse discrimination developed the 2 : 1 ellipse was replaced as the CS– by an ellipse having a ratio of 3 : 2. This procedure was repeated until a ratio of 9 : 8—not very different in shape from the circle—was reached (see Figure 3.4). On this final problem, some differentiation developed at first, but it did not improve with training. In fact, it became worse and finally disappeared. After about three weeks of training on this difficult discrimination, Pavlov relates,

> The whole behavior of the animal underwent an abrupt change. The hitherto quiet dog began to squeal in its stand, kept wriggling about, tore off with its teeth the apparatus for mechanical stimulation of the skin, and bit through the tubes connecting the animal's room with the observer, a behavior which never happened before. On being taken into the experimental room the dog now barked violently, which was also contrary to its usual custom; in short it presented all the symptoms of a condition of acute neurosis. On testing the cruder differentiations they were also found to be destroyed, even the one with the ratio of the semi-axes 2 : 1 (1927, p. 291).

Why did this unusual behavior occur? No punishment was involved; all the dog did was stand in the harness, to be fed after presentation of a circle and not fed after an ellipse. Many dogs learned the difficult discrimination without exhibiting such behavior. Pavlov interpreted the "neurotic" behavior of the dog as due to the clash of inhibition and excitation in an animal whose nervous system was of a type especially prone to such a pathological state.

Pavlov lived to be eighty-six. In the later years of his life, his interests turned to the application of all he had learned about the nervous

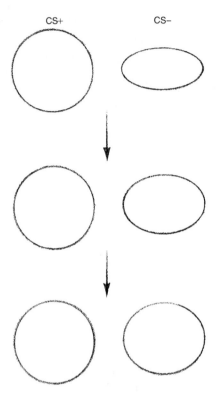

Figure 3.4 Stimuli like those used in the Shenger-Krestovnikova experiment.

system to the field of psychiatry. Different personality types, he thought, reflected different relative strengths of excitation and inhibition in the nervous system. Pathological cases resulted from an extreme imbalance between the two opposing forces or from a violent clash between them caused by a particularly stressful experience. Sleep, Pavlov thought, was a state in which inhibition dominates the entire cortex, allowing the nervous system to recuperate from the excitatory activity of waking life. He recommended sleep as a treatment for many mental problems.

Higher Mental Processes

While Pavlov believed that his experiments on dogs provided important insights into the causes of human behavior, he came to realize also that humans were different in a fundamental way. In this respect, his view differed from the views of many American psychologists who were to attach so much importance to the experiments he had done. The fundamental difference between humans and other animals, Pavlov felt, lay in our capacity for symbolic communication—that is, language. Symbolic representation not only enables one person to control the behavior of another without resorting to the inefficient and unreliable procedures of conditioning, but in addition enables a person to attain control over his own behavior. To emphasize the difference between conditioned reflexes, on the one hand, and behavior that is under symbolic control, on the other, Pavlov used the term *second signal system* to refer to language. This system he viewed as having evolved out of the *first signal system*, which was concerned with conditioned reflexes. The behavior of animals, according to Pavlov, was determined solely by the first signal system, while in humans the first and second signal systems were thought to coexist. The complexities of human behavior were considered a product of their interaction. Pavlov did little to elaborate further on the nature of the second signal system. But much recent research in the Soviet Union has had as its primary goal achieving an understanding of the system of symbolic control that Pavlov saw as making human behavior unique.

BEHAVIORISM

The experiments by Pavlov on conditioned reflexes were known to very few Americans prior to 1927, when a series of Pavlov's lectures were translated into English and published under the title *Conditioned Reflexes: An Investigation of the Physiological Activity of the Cerebral Cortex*. The research reported there, which had spanned a period of about twenty years, struck a responsive chord in American psychology. Some of the reasons for this responsiveness have already been discussed.

First, recall that among psychologists the dominant view regarding learning, memory, and thinking was one that had been inherited from British empiricism—that these processes could best be understood in terms of the concept of the association. The concept of the conditioned reflex was obviously very similar. The philosophers and psychologists had spoken of associations between ideas; Pavlov's conditioned reflex was an association between a stimulus and an overt (that is, objectively observable) response. Otherwise the two concepts seemed to be essentially the same. Further, Pavlov had found that formation of a conditioned reflex required the pairing of the CS and UCS, and thus it appeared to obey the British empiricists' principle of contiguity. His experiments appeared to reveal in raw form the processes by which associations are built up and broken down. This suggested the possibility that the basic nature of learning could be uncovered by studying conditioning in lower organisms.

Second, the methods used by many psychologists at that time were subjective. While some had followed Ebbinghaus's example in making observations objectively, others had found the method of introspection more appealing. But introspectionism, as was pointed out in the last chapter, had fallen into disrepute because of scandalous failures of observers, in many experimental situations, to agree. Pavlov's method was in sharp contrast to that of introspectionism. Like Ebbinghaus, Pavlov relied only on objective observations. But he distrusted even theories that were stated in mentalistic terms. Thus while Ebbinghaus's aim had been to study associations between ideas—the British empiricists' atoms of the mind—Pavlov's theory made no reference to ideas or other mental events. Instead, a physiological mechanism was described, in which the interaction of excitation and inhibition on the cortex determined the animal's behavior. The dogs in Pavlov's experiments behaved "as if" their brains were mechanisms of the sort his theory described—and indeed, Pavlov assumed that they were. Most important, however, was the emphasis Pavlov placed on objectively observing and measuring both the stimulating conditions and the behavior the conditions produced. His work strongly suggested that the essential facts about associative processes could be uncovered without any reference to the mind.

A third important fact about the psychology of the day was that it was interested not only in the normal adult human mind (the study of which, in principle, might be conducted by introspection), but also in the minds of animals, children, and the mentally disturbed. It could easily be seen that Pavlov's method, pioneered on the dog, could be used to study the psychology of any organism, regardless of whether the subject was capable of introspection. Studies from Pavlov's laboratory using the method of gradual differentiation had shown that even problems of psychophysics, such as questions about the limits of perceptual discrimination, could be explored in a completely objective way.

Watson's Position

Pavlov's work gave added force to arguments already being made by the American psychologist John B. Watson. In several articles and books, beginning in 1913, Watson had advocated a revolutionary change in psychology toward a position he called *behaviorism* (Watson, 1913, 1919, 1930). Simply stated, his position was that psychology should cease trying to be a science of mental life and become a science of behavior. While introspectionists had blamed each other for the disagreements that plagued their investigations, Watson saw the problem, instead, in their method. He argued that subjective observations were inherently unreliable because they were private, not public. A true science could be based only on observations of overt behavior—defined as activities of the glands and muscles—and the conditions under which the behavior occurs. Only objective observations, according to his view, could be accepted in science. The goal of psychology was to establish stimulus–response (S–R) laws, in order "to be able, given the stimulus, to predict the response—or, seeing the reaction take place, to state what the stimulus is that has called out the reaction" (Watson, 1930, p. 18).

In advocating an objective psychology, Watson's position was in agreement with some of the work psychologists were already doing. But Watson went even further. He proposed that *all* metalistic language be banned from psychology—not only as descriptions of introspective observations, but as explanations of behavior, as well. Nearly all psychologists of the time made reference to consciousness, ideas, feelings, sensations, thought, and the will. The prevailing view was that rigorous definitions were not necessary because everyone knew what the terms meant. But Watson's claim, to the contrary, was that *nobody* knew what they meant. No one, he maintained, knows what the term consciousness refers to because "consciousness has never been seen, touched, smelled, tasted, or moved" (Watson and McDougal, 1929, p. 14). Psychology had earlier abandoned the term soul, being unable to find anything—even through introspection—to which the term referred. Watson's position was that mind, awareness, memory, purpose, and all the other mentalistic terms that constituted the language of psychology deserved the same fate. They were relics of a savage and ignorant past—mythological entities woven into our folk wisdom, corresponding to nothing in the real world. They sounded like satisfactory explanations of behavior, but close analysis showed the "explanations" to be illusory. Psychology would become a science only when psychologists abandoned the use of such terms altogether.

How, then, should psychologists proceed? A beginning could be seen in Pavlov's concept of the conditioned reflex. Some of the basic laws of learning had apparently been uncovered in Pavlov's conditioning experiments, and Watson felt that eventually nearly all behavior would be explained in terms of conditioned reflexes. He developed a theory in which conditioned stimulus–response connections had the primary explanatory role. Even thinking was seen by Watson as nothing but "word behavior." When we talk, word behavior can be observed. When we think, it cannot, at least not in the usual way. But sensitive recording devices indicated that thinking is accompanied by subtle movements of the vocal apparatus—the tongue, lips, larynx, and diaphragm. Thus, even the presumably complex processes of human thought, in Watson's view, could be analyzed in terms of an objective psychology consisting of S–R laws.

The Conditioning of Fear

Watson is most famous for his philosophy regarding how psychology should be done. His theory of learning was crude even by the standards of his day, and his experimental contribution was not a major one. In one well-known series of studies, however, Watson extended the conditioning procedure to the learning and extinction of emotional reactions in humans. These experiments deserve mention not only because they illustrate how the conditioning procedure can be applied to behavior other than salivation, but also because Watson's application was the forerunner of behavior therapy—an important recent development in clinical psychology.

The experiments concerned the acquisition and extinction of the emotional reaction commonly called fear. Watson and Rayner (1920) chose for their subject an eleven-month-old infant named Albert. Their goal was to determine whether Albert would learn to show fear in response to a stimulus when it was paired with another stimulus that already produced the fear reaction. For their neutral stimulus, Watson and Rayner chose a white rat—something to which little Albert showed no fear initially. For their fear-producing stimulus, they chose a loud sound, produced by striking an iron bar with a hammer, just behind the child's head. Described in Pavlov's terms, the white rat was the CS, to which the fear reaction was to be conditioned, and the clanging sound was the UCS, which produced the fear reaction before the experiment began. According to Pavlov, the pairing of the CS and the UCS (or more accurately, the pairing of the CS and fear reaction or UCR) should form a conditioned reflex in which the fear reaction is produced by the CS alone—a possible model of how phobias and other emotional responses are learned. The laboratory notes of Watson and Rayner (1920) describe little Albert's acquisition of the fear reaction to the white rat:

11 Months 3 Days [of age]
1. White rat suddenly taken from the basket and presented to Albert. He began to reach for rat with left hand. Just as his hand touched the animal, the bar was struck immediately behind his head. The infant jumped violently and fell forward, burying his face in the mattress. He did not cry, however.
2. Just as the right hand touched the rat, the bar was again struck. Again the infant jumped violently, fell forward, and began to whimper.
In order not to disturb the child too seriously no further tests were given for one week.

11 Months 10 Days
1. Rat presented suddenly without sound. There was steady fixation but no tendency at first to reach for it. The rat was then placed nearer, whereupon the infant began tentative reaching movements with the right hand. When the rat nosed the infant's left hand, the hand was immediately withdrawn. He started to reach for the head of the animal with the forefinger of the left hand, but withdrew it suddenly before contact. It is thus seen that the two joint stimulations given the previous week were not without effect. He was tested with his blocks immediately afterwards to see if they shared in the process of conditioning. He began immediately to pick them up, dropping them, pounding them, etc. In the remainder of the tests the blocks were given frequently to quiet him and to test his general emotional state. They were always removed from sight when the process of conditioning was under way.
2. Joint stimulation with rat and sound. Started to touch rat, then fell over immediately to right side. No crying.
3. Joint stimulation. Fell to right side and rested upon hands, with head turned away from rat. No crying.
4. Joint stimulation. Same reaction.

5. Rat suddenly presented alone. Puckered face, whimpered and withdrew body sharply to the left.

6. Joint stimulation. Fell over immediately to right side and began to whimper.

7. Joint stimulation. Started violently and cried, but did not fall over.

8. Rat alone. *The instant the rat was shown, the baby began to cry. Almost instantly he turned sharply to the left, fell over on left side, raised himself on all fours and began to crawl away so rapidly that he was caught with difficulty before reaching the edge of the table*. (Watson and Rayner, 1920, pp. 4–5.)

Next, Watson and Rayner tested for generalization to other stimuli. When the wooden blocks were presented, there was not the slightest evidence of the fear response. However, a rabbit, suddenly placed on the mattress in front of the child, produced crying and an attempt to crawl away. A dog elicited a similar, but less pronounced, reaction. A seal-fur coat likewise produced a fear reaction. Albert showed some reluctance to touch cotton wool, and even Watson's hair. In short, the fear reaction of withdrawal, crying, and crawling away appeared to have been transferred by conditioning from the loud sound to the white rat, and once this had occurred other objects similar to the white rat produced a fear reaction, as well.

Watson and Rayner were well aware of the ethical problems posed by their research. Subjecting a child to emotional trauma purely out of scientific curiosity seems callous, and Watson and Rayner were criticized by many for conducting the experiment. Still, in deciding whether to undertake such research, the investigator must consider the likely benefits, as well as the possible risks. A great many people suffer from phobias, and in some cases the fear prevents the person from leading a normal, productive life. An accurate understanding of how phobias develop might lead to their effective treatment and prevention. The experiment on little Albert was a crucial test of the hypothesis that phobias are acquired through conditioning. Given the importance of the problem, Watson and Rayner felt that the potential benefits greatly outweighed the risks.

The Elimination of Fear

The importance of the demonstration that phobias can originate in conditioning lies primarily in its suggestion of a way in which they might be eliminated. If a phobia is a learned reaction, then a learning technique may be the best way to treat it. Mary Cover Jones, a student of Watson, explored various techniques for removing children's fears. Among them were disuse (waiting for the child to "outgrow" the fear), verbal organization (talking with the child about the feared object), social imitation (placing the child in a situation in which other children play with the feared object), extinction (presenting the feared object repeatedly), and counterconditioning. According to Jones (1924), the method of counterconditioning showed the most promise. The method will now be described.

Peter, aged three, showed extreme fear of a variety of objects, including rabbits, white rats, fur coats, feathers, cotton wool, frogs, fish, and mechanical toys. His phobia was, in fact, much like little Albert's, except that Peter's was "home grown" and more pronounced. The only procedure attempted that led to a marked improvement in Peter's situation was *counterconditioning*. The basic idea of counterconditioning is to replace the unwanted response with another response with which it is incompatible. In the case of Peter, it was thought that the activity of eating would be incompatible with the crying, escape attempts, and visceral reactions we call fear.

Peter was served his regular mid-afternoon meal of crackers and milk in a high chair, at one end of a 40-foot-long room. At the other end of the room, just as he began eating, the experimenters introduced a rabbit in a cage, far enough away so that it did not disturb the child's eating. The place was marked, and the next day the rabbit was moved closer and closer until Peter began to show slight signs of fear. This place was also marked, and on succeeding days the same routine was followed. Eventually, Peter allowed the rabbit to be placed in his lap, and he stroked it with one hand as he fed himself with the other. Subsequent tests with other stimuli, such as the fur coat and feathers, showed that the fear reaction to furry objects had been completely eliminated. Apparently, the original negative emotional reaction had been gradually replaced by the positive emotional reaction that normally accompanies eating. The conditioned fear reaction had been "countered" or replaced by a conditioned reaction incompatible with fear. The procedure of gradually introducing the feared object into a positive situation is the basis of the therapy procedure called *systematic desensitization*, which will be discussed in a later chapter.

Effects of the Behaviorist Movement on Psychology

Scientific revolutions, like political ones, are often followed by periods of extremism in which more of the old system is discarded than can be justified by its failings. The failings of introspective psychology and the successes of Pavlov's research produced a situation in which Watson's philosophy of how psychology should be done received enthusiastic support. One could debate whether Watson's writings helped to cause the behaviorist revolution or whether they were merely products of it; but whichever is the case, there was a remarkable correspondence between the positions he advocated on a number of issues and the trends that dominated the psychology of learning for many years thereafter. The effects of the behaviorist revolution reverberated throughout psychology, and affected related disciplines as well. In the field of learning, behaviorism produced four effects especially worth noting.

First, subjective methods of observation (introspection) were disallowed. All observations were to be of public facts. Behaviorists described the observable responses made by the subject and the conditions under which those responses occurred. While it was, in principle, possible to treat subjective *reports* as behavior—since they are, after all, spoken or written responses—this apparent loophole was little used. Verbal reports themselves could be used as data, but the subjective contents of the reports could not be accepted as fact, since they referred to mental states.

Second, in agreement with Watson's view, mentalistic explanations of behavior were frowned upon. Events hypothesized as intervening between the experimental manipulations and the behavior (that is, between the S and R), were usually of a mechanistic sort. In other words, rather than explaining behavior as the result of purposes, feelings, images, and so on, passing through the subject's mind, theorists tried to specify the principles of operation of a machine that would behave in the same way as the organism under investigation. The mechanistic model could be stated in physiological terms (like Pavlov's theory) or in terms of some other kind of physical analogy. As we shall see, the preference for mechanistic over mentalistic explanations was not universal. However, most psychologists interested in learning, whether in humans or animals, considered mechanistic theories to be more "scientific" than mentalistic ones.

Third, learning was emphasized as a cause of behavior, to the virtual exclusion of heredity. As we have seen, this emphasis on learning had its roots in British empiricism. In the hands of behaviorists, the emphasis was taken to such an extreme that Watson once boasted:

I should like to go one step further tonight and say, "Give me a dozen healthy infants, well-formed, and my own specified world to bring them up in, and I'll guarantee to take any one at random and train him to become any type of specialist I might select—a doctor, lawyer, artist, merchant-chief, and, yes, even into a beggar-man and thief, regardless of his talents, penchants, tendencies, abilities, vocations and race of his ancestors" (Watson, 1926, p. 10).

This extreme emphasis on environment was primarily a reaction to the notion of instincts. Among some psychologists, instinct was the preferred explanation for almost any complex behavior. The lists of instincts produced by such writers were nearly endless, and included the instincts of pugnacity, hunting, acquisitiveness, constructiveness, play, secretiveness, cleanliness, shame, and maternal love. Certainly, calling these behaviors instincts can lead one to overlook the importance of learning in their development. But behaviorists took such an extreme position on the dogma of instincts that they sometimes seemed to deny the existence of *any* genetic influences on behavior.

A fourth effect of behaviorism was a general preference for animal subjects in learning experiments. Watson's view, which was shared by many psychologists, was that the nature of learning in animals and in humans was basically the same. If one accepts this notion (Pavlov, as we have seen, did not), then the advantages of working with animals cannot be denied. Since animals are simpler, one should be able to study the learning process in animals in its most basic form. Animals can also be laboratory raised. This gives the experimenter a degree of control over past experience that, for both ethical and practical reasons, cannot be achieved with human subjects. (An attempt to eliminate the influence of past learning, as we have seen, was behind Ebbinghaus's invention of the nonsense syllable. A more elegant and successful solution is to raise the organism in an environment in which learning experiences are carefully controlled.) Now if there is no such thing as instinct, and if the process of learning is the same regardless of the animal studied, then a further simplification is possible: research can be done on whatever animal is docile, readily available, and easy to raise. The albino rat and the pigeon have provided most of our information about learning in animals. As we shall see in Chapter 7, the assumptions underlying decisions to base learning research primarily on these two species have returned to haunt psychology in recent years.

Uses of the Term "Behaviorism"

From around 1930 to approximately 1960, the psychology of learning was dominated by the four characteristics of behaviorism listed above. Actually, behaviorism is a cluster of attitudes that tend to go together but do not always do so, and for this reason the term behaviorism is difficult to define in simple terms. Different authors use the term in different ways, the result being frequent failures to communicate exactly what is meant. Considering the present discussion to this point, at least three different meanings of behaviorism can be usefully contrasted. Their difference is one of breadth.

What we shall call *behaviorism-1* (often called methodological behaviorism) is the broadest. It refers only to the first effect of behaviorism noted above—namely, the rejection of introspection as a means of making observations. In the sense of behaviorism-1, the behaviorist revolution was virtually complete. While there has been a very slight loosening of the rules in recent years, it is the general practice of experimental psychologists—and of the journals in which they publish—to accept as observations only data that are, in principle, public. In this sense, nearly all of modern experimental psychology could be called behavioristic; and the work of Ebbinghaus would also fall into this category.

Somewhat narrower is *behaviorism-2*. This point of view follows Watson's strictures. It excludes not only subjective observations but mentalistic explanations, as well. Thus, it would be quite acceptable to say that the dog, when presented with the CS, produced 12 drops of saliva in a 10-second period (an objective observation), but not to say that this occurred because the dog had developed a strong expectation that the CS would be followed by food. Expectations—like ideas, purposes, and will—are mentalistic concepts, and would not be considered acceptable explanations of behavior. To say the dog salivated because an excitatory pathway had developed in the brain, linking the point representing the CS with that for salivation, however, would be acceptable. The explanation is mechanistic, since it attempts to describe a physical device which could produce behavior that would mirror that of the dog. Pavlov, under this definition, would be called a behaviorist, while Ebbinghaus would not.

Narrowest of all is *behaviorism-3*. This position is sometimes called descriptive behaviorism. Its most prominent defender is B. F. Skinner. To the descriptive behaviorist, neither mentalistic nor mechanistic processes are acceptable explanations of behavior. The proper interest of the psychologist is limited to what can be observed—responses of the organism and the conditions under which they occur. Inferences of any kind regarding hypothetical events inside the organism's skull—whether they are mentalistic events such as purposes and expectations, or physical events such as opponent processes of excitation and inhibition—are not permitted. Neither Ebbinghaus nor Pavlov would qualify as a behaviorist under this extreme restriction of the meaning of the term.

As we use the term behaviorism here, neither the broadest nor the most restricted meaning is intended. In Chapter 1, behaviorism was contrasted with cognitivism, the approach that recognizes mental events and accepts mentalistic language in its explanations of behavior. Thus, the meaning intended there was behaviorism-2, and that is what will be meant throughout this book whenever the unmodified term behaviorism is used. Our selection of the behaviorism-2 meaning does not mean that the other distinctions are not worth making, however. Behaviorism can be thought of as consisting of two subcategories: neobehaviorism, in which mechanistic theories of behavior are constructed, and descriptive behaviorism, in which they are not. The distinctions being made here should become more clear in Chapter 5, where the theoretical positions of three psychologists will be compared: a cognitivist, E. C. Tolman; a neobehaviorist, C. L. Hull; and a descriptive behaviorist, B. F. Skinner.

To set the stage for that comparison and much of the discussion to follow, the next chapter describes the basic procedures used in studying animal learning, and defines some terms every student of learning should know.

4

Experimental Procedures
in Animal Learning

This chapter examines some of the basic types of animal learning experiments. Experiments, of course, differ from each other in many ways; but animal learning experiments are usually categorized into a few basic types. These types are referred to as experimental *paradigms*. The word paradigm, in general, means "pattern." Here it refers to the pattern around which an experiment is designed. This use of the term should be distinguished from Thomas Kuhn's concept of the scientific paradigm, referred to in the last chapter. Kuhn uses the word paradigm to refer to the conceptual framework through which a scientist views the research in his field. The two meanings of the term paradigm are quite different, although the "pattern" concept can be seen in both.

Four basic experimental paradigms will be described. They are (1) habituation and sensitization, (2) classical conditioning, (3) instrumental conditioning, and (4) operant conditioning. Most of the information in this chapter is relatively noncontroversial. The types of experimental manipulations defining each paradigm are described, along with typical results of those manipulations. Additional experimental results will be presented in later chapters, where they are relevant to theoretical issues under discussion. The material in the present chapter is intended to provide the background necessary for understanding those issues and the experiments bearing upon them.

HABITUATION AND SENSITIZATION

Habituation

In 1887, in an article entitled "Some Observations on the Mental Powers of Spiders," Peckham and Peckham described an experimental demonstration of a very simple type of learning. They repeatedly sounded a tuning fork near a spider in its web, recording each time the spider's response of dropping on its thread. With the first sounding of the stimulus, the response was pronounced. The response declined with repetitions of the tone on a given day, recovering somewhat from one day to the next, and eventually ceased altogether. The decrease of an innate reaction to a stimulus due to repetition, as demonstrated by this experiment, is called *habituation*. To borrow terms from Pavlov, habituation can be considered a decrease in an unconditioned (or innate) reflex due to repetition of the UCS.

Habituation is considered by many investigators to be the simplest form of learning. While habituation undoubtedly has some limited adaptive value, the organism does not learn to do anything new, or to do something better, but only *not* to do something already in its unlearned behavioral repertoire. Habituation is also the most widespread form of adaptive change, common to all animals from the single-cell protozoa through humans (Razran, 1971). In vertebrates, habituation can apparently take place in the spinal cord, without involvement of the brain, for if the nerve fibers linking the brain and spinal cord are cut (producing what is called a "spinal" animal), reflexes mediated by the spinal cord, such as flexion of the hind limb in response to shock to the foot, will still habituate.

The number of stimulus exposures necessary to produce habituation varies widely, depending upon the organism being tested, the response being measured, and the strength of the stimulus used to elicit the response. Certain general characteristics of habituation, however, are remarkably independent of such factors. Thompson and Spencer (1966) have listed the common characteristics of habituation. The following discussion borrows from their account.

Typically, the magnitude of the UCR decreases with the number of stimulus presentations in the way illustrated in the first panel of Figure 4.1. A curve of that shape is described as a "negative exponential function." The magnitude of the response may or may not eventually

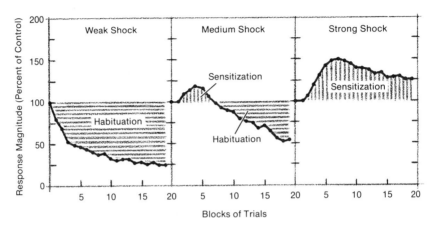

Figure 4.1 Habituation and sensitization as a function of stimulus intensity and trials. [Adapted from Groves and Thompson, 1970.]

reach zero. Whether it does or not depends partly on the strength of the stimulus (habituation is more effective with repetition of a weak stimulus than a strong one).

Habituation shows stimulus generalization; that is, if a response is habituated by presenting a particular UCS repeatedly, tests with similar stimuli will tend to show habituation as well. The magnitude of the response increases as the test stimulus becomes less similar to the original UCS.

Habituated responses show *spontaneous recovery*. If the UCS is not presented for a time following habituation training, the tendency for the UCS to elicit the UCR will increase, eventually approaching its original level. If the response is then habituated again, allowed to recover again, rehabituated, and so on, habituation becomes more and more rapid each time it occurs.

How do we know that habituation is not simply a matter of fatigue? One bit of evidence is seen in stimulus generalization. If the response could not occur because of muscle fatigue, stimuli dissimilar to the original UCS would not be able to elicit it. The experimental evidence, however, is that they do. A second finding that is contrary to the fatigue explanation is a phenomenon called *dishabituation*. Suppose a UCS is repeatedly presented, resulting in habituation of the UCR. Then another, especially strong stimulus (such as a loud noise) occurs. If the UCS is presented immediately after the strong stimulus, it elicits the UCR at nearly its original strength. This is called dishabituation because it appears to eliminate the habituation that was produced by repetition of the UCS. An interesting finding regarding dishabituation is that it spontaneously disappears. In a matter of several seconds after presentation of the dishabituating stimulus, the habituation returns even without new repetitions of the UCS (Groves and Thompson, 1970). Dishabituation therefore appears to be a temporary increase in the strength of the response which leaves the underlying habituation intact.

By now it should be apparent that there are many parallels between the habituation of innate reflexes and the extinction of conditioned reflexes, as studied by Pavlov. Many of the manipulations are the same. In extinction, a *learned* response to a CS grows weaker because the CS is presented without the UCS. In habituation, an *innate* reflex to a UCS simply decreases with repeated presentation of the stimulus. Despite this difference, both phenomena show stimulus generalization and spontaneous recovery. And the phenomenon of dishabituation is remarkably similar to what Pavlov called disinhibition—a recovery of the response, due to presentation of a strong stimulus such as a loud noise. The similarities of habituation of the unconditioned reflex and extinction of the conditioned reflex have suggested to many investigators that the underlying mechanisms are essentially the same.

Sensitization

It is important to note that not all innate reflexes habituate. In fact, many reflexes that will habituate when the UCS is weak will not habituate when its is strong. Repetition of a strong stimulus can result in an effect opposite to that of habituation—namely, an increase in the magnitude of the response. Such an increase is called *sensitization*. An example of the effect of stimulus intensity on habituation and sensitization is shown in Figure 4.1. The data, taken from Groves and Thompson (1970), show how flexion of the hind limb in response to shock, in a spinal cat, changes with repetition of the shock stimulus. With a weak shock, the flexion response habituates; with a strong shock, sensitization occurs. An everyday example of the phenomenon shown in Figure 4.1 can be found in the effects of unwanted noise. If a neighbor's radio is playing softly, we may hear it at first but soon stop attending to it (habituation). However, if it is playing very loudly, it may become more and more distracting. With repeated exposure our annoyance increases (sensitization).

There is a rather interesting finding regarding the way habituation and sensitization are related to stimulus intensity, as illustrated in Figure 4.1. Ordinarily, the response to an intense stimulus will simply become sensitized with repetition. But the response can be habituated if the stimulus is first presented at a very weak intensity and then is gradually made more and more intense as training proceeds. Habituation training is much more effective following this gradual procedure than it is if the intense (final) stimulus is the only one presented. This outcome has been obtained with the startle response in rats (Davis and Wagner, 1969) and also with the hind limb flexion reflex in spinal cats (Groves and Thompson, 1970). This is one illustration of the effectiveness of gradual training procedures—a point to which we shall return later in this chapter.

The experimental operations for producing habituation and sensitization are the same. In both cases a UCS is presented repeatedly. If the strength of the UCR decreases, habituation has been obtained. If it increases, sensitization has been observed. As was just indicated, one factor determining which will occur in the intensity of the stimulus. Sensitization may be considered a higher form of learning than habituation. The simplest organisms in which it is found are planaria, or flatworms, and earthworms (Razran, 1971). Sensitization gives certain reflexes of these organisms a primitive ability to increase in strength with practice—an important characteristic of higher forms of learning.

Pseudoconditioning

Sensitization has not been studied thoroughly, so we can say little more about it. We do know, however, that sensitization generalizes to stimuli quite different from the original UCS. This fact has important consequences for the design of adequate conditioning experiments.

Suppose an investigator repeatedly elicits the hind limb reflex in a spinal cat, using shock to the leg as the UCS. He then pinches the animal's tail. Pinching the tail would not ordinarily elicit the hind limb flexion response. It may do so now, however, if the reflex has become highly sensitized and has generalized to stimuli quite different from the UCS. In other words, the tail pinch may be enough like leg shock to produce the flexion reflex, providing the reflex is highly sensitized. Ordinarily, it would not do so.

Now imagine the situation of an investigator who is attempting to condition the hind limb reflex by repeatedly pinching the tail (as a CS) and then shocking the leg (as the UCS). If after several trials the tail pinch alone elicits the reflex, he might very well conclude that he has obtained conditioning. In reality, however, the response to the pinch might have nothing to do with the *pairing* of the CS and UCS. It could result from sensitization, in the way just described; and sensitization does not involve the learning of new associations.

Since such a result could easily be mistaken for conditioning, it has been called *pseudoconditioning*. To make sure that the response to a CS reflects true conditioning, rather than pseudoconditioning, a careful investigator will compare the performance of a group of animals for which the CS and UCS are paired (the conditioning group) with that of another group of animals to which the CS and UCS are presented, but *not* paired (the pseudoconditioning control). Any sensitization resulting from repeated presentation of the UCS should be the same for both groups. Only if the CR is more pronounced in the conditioning group than in the control group is the investigator justified in concluding that conditioning has been obtained. (When this precaution is taken, many experiments on spinal animals fail to show evidence of conditioning. Others have produced positive evidence, however. Thus the possibility of true conditioning occurring in the spinal cord is still an open question.)

CLASSICAL CONDITIONING

In 1902, at about the time Pavlov's work on salivary conditioning was getting well under way, a graduate student named E. B. Twitmeyer submitted a PH.D. dissertation to the University of Pennsylvania, entitled "A Study of the Knee-Jerk." In it, he described a phenomenon he had discovered by accident. He had been conducting an experiment on the knee-jerk reflex. On each trial of the experiment a bell was sounded to warn the subject that a hammer was about to strike his knee. While testing one subject, Twitmeyer accidentally sounded the bell without tripping the hammer. The knee jerk occurred even though the natural stimulus for the reflex (the hammer blow) had not. Recognizing the importance of this discovery, Twitmeyer immediately redesigned his experiment in order to study it. Unfortunately, other psychologists showed little interest in the result, and Twitmeyer abandoned the project without even publishing his dissertation in a scientific journal. (Twitmeyer's experiments were finally published, in recognition of their historical importance, in the December, 1974, issue of the *Journal of Experimental Psychology*.)

The phenomenon Twitmeyer independently discovered is usually called *classical conditioning*. Other terms that are often applied are *respondent conditioning* and *Pavlovian conditioning*. If Twitmeyer had been a Nobel Prize winner instead of an unknown graduate student, or if he had possessed the determination and forceful personality of Pavlov, perhaps the procedure would be called Twitmeyerian conditioning today. If he had done nothing more than publish his dissertation, American psychology would have become familiar with the classical conditioning paradigm twenty years before Pavlov's work became widely known.

Recall that the classicial conditioning procedure involves the pairing of two stimuli: the CS, a neutral stimulus that does not elicit the response prior to conditioning, and the UCS, which elicits the response (UCR) before conditioning begins. Through pairing of the two stimuli, the CS alone comes to elicit the response (now called the CR). Thousands of experiments have been done using this procedure. Evidence of classical conditioning has been found in animals as simple as earthworms and as complex as humans. Baby chickens have been conditioned in the egg, and baby humans in the uterus. Responses that have been classically conditioned include salivation, changes in electrical rhythms of the brain (EEG), constriction of blood vessels, the knee jerk, vomiting, the eye-blink reflex, and changes in respiration (Kimble, 1961).

Several features of classical conditioning have already been mentioned in connection with Pavlov's work: Elimination of the UCS and presentation of the CS alone results in *extinction;* if time is allowed to pass following extinction and the CS is again presented alone, the CR shows partial *spontaneous recovery;* a strong unexpected stimulus results in *disinhibition,* the reappearance of the extinguished response. A CR that has been established using a particular CS will generalize to other stimuli according to their similarity to the CS; but generalization can be restricted by presenting during training both a CS+, which is followed by the UCS, and a CS–, which is not—a procedure called *differential conditioning*.

Temporal Arrangements of CS and UCS

An important variable in classical conditioning experiments has to do with the arrangement of the CS and UCS in time. In Figure 4.2 are presented several different types of conditioning arrangements. In the *simultaneous* procedures the CS and UCS are presented at exactly the same time. In the *delay* procedure, the CS goes on and remains on until the UCS is presented. The duration of the CS—that is, the delay from onset of the CS to onset of the UCS—can be varied. It is generally found that a delay of .5 to 1.0 second is most effective for conditioning, although there are striking exceptions to this rule, which will be discussed in Chapter 7. In the *trace* procedure, the CS comes on and then goes off some time before the UCS occurs. Conditioning presumably involves an internal trace of the CS, since the physical stimulus is no longer present when the UCS occurs. Conditioning is difficult to establish with traces longer than a few seconds, although it can be done. Long-trace conditioning is most easily established by first

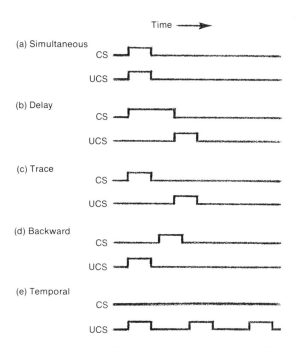

Figure 4.2 CS–UCS arrangements defining different classical conditioning paradigms.

training with a delay or short-trace procedure, and then gradually lengthening the time from CS offset to UCS onset.

In the *backward* conditioning procedure, the UCS precedes the CS. Backward conditioning is difficult to achieve, and there is some controversy concerning whether it exists at all. One reason backward conditioning may be difficult to show has been discussed by Razran (1971). He points out that in the backward conditioning paradigm both the onset and the offset of the UCS precede the CS. Because of this, the CS may become conditioned both to UCS-onset reactions and to UCS-offset reactions, and these reactions may be incompatible with each other. Consider the situation where the UCS is shock. The onset of shock produces a negative reaction which we might call "pain," while the offset produces a positive reaction which we might call "relief." Since the shock goes on and then off before the CS occurs, both reactions are available to become conditioned to the CS. The offset of the shock, however, is more nearly contiguous with the CS than is onset of the shock. Thus, according to the principle of contiguity, the "relief" reaction should be more strongly conditioned to the CS than the "pain" reaction. Since relief and pain are in a sense opposite responses, little if any evidence will be found that the negative "pain" response has been conditioned to the CS.

Finally, in the *temporal* conditioning procedure, there is no observable CS at all. The UCS is simply presented repeatedly, with the interval between presentations always the same. After prolonged training, the animal will come to make the response in anticipation of the UCS—that is, just before it occurs. The temporal conditioning procedure may be thought of as similar to the trace conditioning procedure; but in temporal conditioning it cannot be the "trace" of a CS that becomes conditioned to the response, since there is no CS as such. Instead, it may be the "trace" of the previous UCS (or possibly of the UCR). In one of Pavlov's experiments, temporal conditioning of the salivary reflex was achieved with an interval as long as 30 minutes (Pavlov, 1927).

CS Interactions

A number of important phenomena of classical conditioning, first discovered in Pavlov's laboratory, involve the pairing or combining of more than one CS. One such phenomenon is *higher-order conditioning*. A higher-order conditioned response is established in two stages. First, a CS such as a light is paired with a UCS such as food until it comes to elicit the response (salivation). Let us call the light CS_1. Next, another stimulus which we shall call CS_2 (say a buzzer) is paired repeatedly with CS_1, in the absence of the UCS. The CS_1, in this pairing, plays the role of the UCS in the simple conditioning paradigm. It does not elicit the response as an innate reflex, however, but as a previously conditioned one. Higher-order conditioning is established if the CS_2 comes to elicit the response through its pairing with the CS_1. Such conditioning can be obtained, but it is sometimes difficult. The UCS (food, in this case) is not presented during the second phase of the experiment, while the CS_1 and CS_2 are being paired. Thus, the response to the CS_1 tends to extinguish at the same time that we are trying to condition it to the CS_2. If extinction of the CS_1–CR connection is too rapid or acquisition of the CS_2–CR connection is too slow, higher-order conditioning will not occur.

A second phenomenon involving more than one CS is *compound stimulus conditioning*. Here, a compound stimulus, composed of CS_1 and CS_2, is paired with the UCS. The two CS's may be either from the same modality (for example, two lights) or from different modalities (for example, a light and a tone). They are presented together, followed by the UCS. Typically, once the CR has been conditioned to the compound stimulus, it can also be elicited by either CS_1 or CS_2 presented alone. After extensive training, however, it may be elicited only by the compound, and not by either component alone—showing that the animal is responding to the two-stimulus combination as a unit. This phenomenon, called "configuring," will be discussed further in Chapter 7.

A third result produced by CS interactions has attracted considerable recent interest. It is called *blocking*. Suppose that in a compound stimulus conditioning experiment, as just described, one of the component CS's we use has already been conditioned to the response. That is, our experiment has two stages: First, CS_1 is paired with the UCS, until it reliably elicits the response. Next, the compound stimulus CS_1 plus CS_2 is paired repeatedly with the UCS. Under these circumstances, CS_1, which was used in stage one of the experiment, maintains its power to elicit the CR, while CS_2, which is new, acquires little or no power to do so. Prior conditioning of one component of the compound stimulus apparently prevents, or blocks, the conditioning of the other component—hence the term "blocking." Just why this happens is not clear, but there is some indication that the animal fails, in the second stage, to pay attention to the CS_2 (Dickinson, Hall, and Mackintosh, 1976).

INSTRUMENTAL CONDITIONING

In 1898 a young American psychologist named Edward L. Thorndike published a monograph describing a number of experiments on the general topic of animal intelligence. The experiments, using cats, dogs, and baby chicks as subjects, were designed to provide objective experimental evidence regarding the reasoning abilities of animals. At the time, animals were thought by many authorities to be almost human in their ability to reason and solve problems. However, the evidence was unsystematic and fragmentary, and primarily based on anecdotes—a method that Thorndike considered untrustworthy. Not only were the situations in which the behavior occurred uncontrolled, but the anecdotal method itself was selective. It reported *only* remarkable occurrences and thereby made the unusual appear typical. As Thorndike put it:

> Dogs get lost hundreds of times and no one ever notices it or sends an account of it to a scientific magazine. But let one find his way from Brooklyn to Yonkers and the fact immediately becomes a circulating anecdote. Thousands of cats on thousands of occasions sit helplessly yowling, and no one takes thought of it or writes to his friend, the professor; but let one cat claw at the knob of a door supposedly as a signal to be let out, and straightaway this cat becomes representative of the cat-mind in all the books (Thorndike, 1898, p. 4).

Cats unlatching doors were supposed, by some, to understand the inner workings of the door latch. Thorndike's experiments suggested, however, that such behavior was learned in a blind trial-and-error fashion, and showed no reasoning ability whatever.

In the experiments for which Thorndike became best known, an "utterly hungry" cat was placed in a device called a *puzzle box*. Outside the box was placed some food. The puzzle box was constructed in such a way that the cat could escape by performing a response that released a latch holding the door. The response bringing freedom (and food) varied. Some boxes required pressing a lever; in others, pulling a string or sliding a bolt would open the door. Upon being confined in the box for the first time, the cat would thrash and jump about in a seemingly aimless fashion. Eventually, a response would be made that opened the door. Thorndike measured the animal's escape *latency*—that is, the amount of time it took for the correct response to occur. The cat was then returned to the box, and again it thrashed

about until the response unlatching the door was made. This procedure was repeated over and over again; for each trial Thorndike
recorded the latency of the correct response.

Escape latency varied considerably from trial to trial, but over a
number of trials the latency tended to become shorter and shorter.
The amount of thrashing gradually decreased until eventually the
animal calmly performed the required response almost immediately
after being placed in the box. The escape latency data of two of
Thorndike's cats (one in Box A, which required pulling a wire loop
hanging from the ceiling in front of the door, and one in Box C, which
required rotating a wooden crosspiece) are presented in Figure 4.3
(Thorndike, 1898).

Thorndike's puzzle box experiments illustrate what is usually called
instrumental conditioning or *instrumental learning*. This name derives
from the fact that the behavior learned is instrumental in obtaining
some desired outcome or reward. The neutral term *reinforcement* is

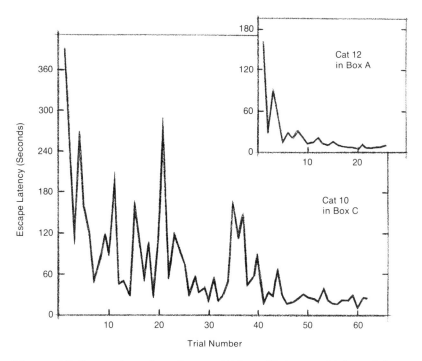

Figure 4.3 Escape latencies of two of Thorndike's cats. [Adapted from
Thorndike, 1898.]

often used in the psychological literature in place of the more common term *reward*. In the experiment by Thorndike just described, the reinforcer was food. (A second reinforcer was escape from the confines of the box, which the animals apparently found aversive.) The characteristic that differentiates instrumental from classical conditioning is that, in instrumental conditioning, the critical stimulus called the reinforcer is presented only if the animal first makes an appropriate response. In classical conditioning, presentation of the reinforcer (the UCS) does not depend on whether or not the animal first responds.

Experimental Apparatus

The puzzle box has received little use since Thorndike's first experiments. Psychologists have devised a variety of types of apparatus for investigating instrumental conditioning. The apparatus used in a particular experiment depends upon a number of factors—primarily the organism being studied, the manipulations the experimenter wants to perform, and the type of response he wants to measure. A description of several kinds of apparatus will illustrate the variety of experimental situations used in the instrumental conditioning paradigm.

A device once popular in animal psychology but little used today is the *complex maze* (Figure 4.4a). Typically, a complex maze consists of a *start box*, where the animal is placed initially, a *goal box*, which contains the reward, and a pathway linking the start and goal boxes. The pathway may double back or branch off into many blind alleys. The experimenter places the animal in the start box, trial after trial, and on each trial measures either the *speed* with which the animal traverses the maze or the *number of errors* (that is, entrances into blind alleys). One finding regarding behavior in the complex maze is that the animal first learns to avoid entering blind alleys nearest the goal box. It appears that the ease of learning a choice between two paths depends in part on how quickly the choice is followed by reward.

Mastery of a complex maze obviously requires the learning of a complex sequence of behavior. To aid in the analysis of learning, psychologists have simplified the maze through a process of gradual evolution. A common apparatus used to study choice behavior is the *T-maze*, which as the name suggests is shaped like a T, having a start box at its base and a single choice point branching off toward two goal boxes (Figure 4.4b). The T-maze can be used to study preferences, by placing one reward (say sugar water) in one goal box and another

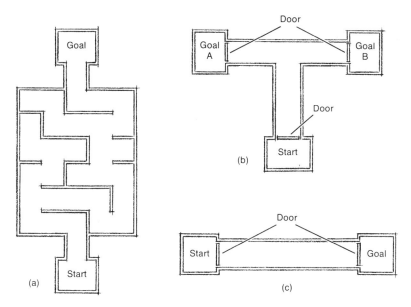

Figure 4.4 Floor plans of some typical animal learning mazes: (a) complex maze; (b) T-maze; (c) straight-alley maze, or runway.

(plain water) in the other goal box. It is also used to study *discrimination learning*. One arm of the T, for example, might be painted black and the other white. The black and white paths are switched back and forth randomly between the left and right sides from one trial to the next, and the animal must learn that the black path leads to reward, regardless of which side it is on.

More simple yet (and hardly deserving to be called a maze) is the *straight-alley maze* or straight runway, which consists of a start box and goal box with a runway in between (Figure 4.4c). Two measures of behavior are frequently used in the straight-alley maze: one is response *latency*—the amount of time from the opening of a door connecting the start box and the alley until the animal enters the alley; the other is response *speed*—the rate at which the animal traverses the alley once it has entered it. The straight-alley maze has found its greatest use in the investigation of effects on performance of reinforcement variables such as the amount of reward, kind of reward, and delay of reward. It is also possible, however, to study discrimination learning in a straight-alley. A tone might be sounded when the animal is in the start box, a high tone indicating that there is food in the goal box, and a low tone indicating that the goal box is empty. This type of task is called a *go–no go discrimination,* since the choice is between making the response and not making it. The situation is much like that of differential classical conditioning, in which the CS+ and CS− determine whether the animal responds or not. The two situations differ in one crucial respect, however. In the go–no go situation, the response is an instrumental one that the animal must make in order to obtain the reinforcer, while in the classical conditioning situation the arrival of the reinforcer (the UCS) does not depend on whether the animal responds.

Another piece of apparatus, called the *shuttle box,* is often used to study the effects of aversive stimuli such as electric shock. The shuttle box consists of two compartments separated by a barrier over which the animal must jump. The floors of both compartments are electrified grids, which can be turned on independently. If the animal is in one compartment and shock is administered through the floor, it can escape the shock by jumping into the other compartment. The acquisition of a response that will terminate the aversive stimulus (for example, jumping the barrier) is called *escape learning* (see Figure 4.5a). A further complication can be introduced by preceding the onset of shock with a signal such as a tone or blinking light. By jumping the barrier shortly after the signal occurs, the animal can avoid the shock altogether. Learning to respond to a warning signal in a way that prevents any exposure to the aversive stimulus is called *avoidance learning* (Figure 4.5b). These two situations are easily confused, but the names given them point out the crucial difference. In escape learning, the animal receives no warning, but by responding quickly when the aversive stimulus first occurs, it can escape the pain. In avoidance learning, onset of the aversive stimulus is predictable—usually because it is heralded by a warning signal. By responding when the signal occurs, the animal can avoid any contact with the aversive stimulus.

Positive Versus Negative Reinforcement

In instrumental conditioning, the animal comes to make the response that leads to reinforcement, and not to make responses that do not. Because reinforcement plays a central role in this process, investigators have been interested in just what reinforcement is and how it works. Some of the theoretical disputes surrounding reinforcement

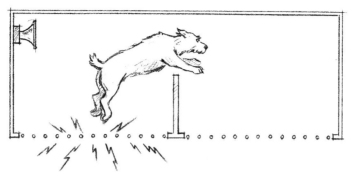

(a) Escape Conditioning

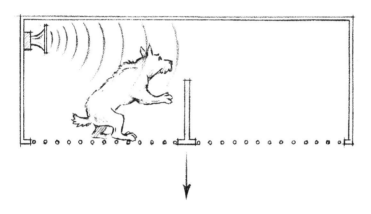

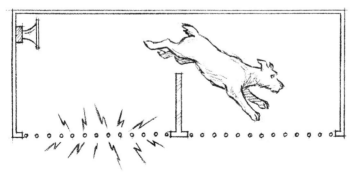

(b) Avoidance Conditioning

Figure 4.5 Two uses of the shuttle box: (a) escape conditioning and (b) avoidance conditioning.

will be discussed in Chapter 6. Here we shall attempt to stay clear of controversy, while examining reinforcement phenomena more closely.

Reinforcement is a manipulation that, if it follows a particular response, increases the tendency of that response to occur again. If the manipulation having this effect is the *presentation* of a stimulus, the stimulus is called a *positive reinforcer*. If the manipulation increasing the response tendency is the removal or *termination* of a stimulus, the stimulus is called a *negative reinforcer*. Thus negative reinforcement and escape learning (which was just described) are two ways of referring to the same manipulation.

Stimuli that are reinforcing because of the animal's genetic makeup, rather than because of the animal's experience, are called *primary reinforcers*. Primary positive reinforcers are usually stimuli that an appropriately deprived animal will approach, such as food, for a hungry animal, or water, for a thirsty one. Such stimuli are called *appetitive* stimuli (note the relation to the word appetite). Primary negative reinforcers are typically stimuli that an animal will learn to avoid (such as shock). Such stimuli are called *aversive* stimuli.

Negative reinforcement, then, is the termination of an aversive stimulus upon the performance of a response. Since the term suggests a negative consequence of the act, it has been used also to refer to *presentation* of an aversive stimulus following a response. The latter use of the term negative reinforcement, however, is no longer accepted, since reinforcement refers only to events that make the response more likely. Following a response with the presentation of an aversive stimulus is correctly referred to as *punishment*. Thus negative reinforcement and punishment are not synonyms. The two operations are quite different—and so are their effects on behavior.

Reinforcement Parameters

Fortunately, most of the laws governing the effects of reinforcement on behavior appear to be essentially the same for positive and negative reinforcers. Therefore, the following statements can be considered to apply to both types of reinforcement.

One frequently studied variable in instrumental conditioning is the *amount of reward*. "Amount" is a somewhat ambiguous term. It may refer to the size of a chunk of food, the number of food pellets, the concentration of a sugar solution, the amount of time a male is allowed to copulate with a female, or the degree of reduction of shock current. If animals are trained in a straight-alley runway, with different groups of animals receiving different amounts of reward in the goal box, the typical finding is that running speed increases with the magnitude of the reward. On the first trial, of course, running speeds are uniformly slow and do not depend on the amount of reward. As training progresses, speed increases for all the groups, but it levels off (reaches an *asymptote*) at a speed determined by the amount of reward. The larger the reward, the greater the speed. The same general relationship holds for the latency of the response of leaving the start box and entering the runway. (The larger the reward, the shorter the latency.)

Delay of reward is another variable that has strong effects on instrumental conditioning. By delay of reward we simply mean the time between performance of the response and administration of reinforcement. The effect of delay of reward depends to some extent on the species of animal being tested and on the nature of the task. With rats, even very short delays can have devastating effects on learning. This is well illustrated by an experiment done by Grice (1948). Grice required rats to make a black–white discrimination, taking a right-hand turn on some trials and a left-hand turn on others. Both the right and left pathways included a delay box, in which the animal's progress could be held up for a short time between the choice point and the goal box. One group of animals (the control group) was allowed to run straight through the delay box to the goal box. Other groups were delayed for different amounts of time before being allowed to continue to the goal box. The delays were 0.5, 1.2, 2.0, 5.0, and 10.0 seconds. Figure 4.6 shows how performance of the different groups of rats changed over trials. The shorter the delay, the more quickly the animals learned. Since there were two choices, the "chance" rate of success would be 50 percent. The animals with a 10-second delay of reward showed no evidence of improvement over the 50 percent rate even after several hundred trials.

If an animal has been trained to perform an instrumental response for reinforcement and the reinforcement is now withheld, the strength of the response gradually drops back to its original low level. As in the case of classical conditioning, the decrease in response tendency that results from withholding reinforcement is called *extinction*. Also similar to what is found in classical conditioning is the *spontaneous*

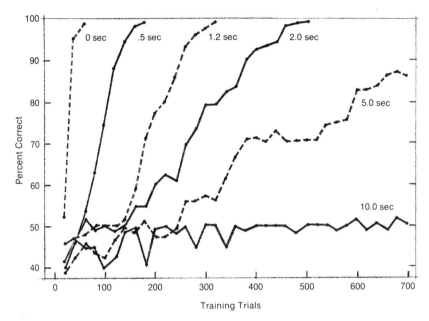

Figure 4.6 Effects of delay of reward (0 to 10 seconds) on learning in a T-maze. [After Grice, 1948. Copyright 1948 by the American Psychological Association. Reprinted by permission.]

recovery of an extinguished instrumental response with the passage of time. Extinction and spontaneous recovery are two of many properties that classical and instrumental conditioning have in common.

A manipulation with interesting effects on instrumental behavior is that of presenting reward on only some fraction of the training trials. Rewarding an animal on every trial is called 100 percent or *continuous reinforcement*. Rewarding the animal on some fraction of the trials is called *partial reinforcement*. If reinforcement is given randomly, with a certain probability of occurring on each trial, the manipulation is simply identified in terms of the percentage of trials that are reinforced—say 25 percent or 50 percent. One of the most dramatic effects of partial reinforcement is seen in extinction. The responses of a group receiving partial reinforcement during training extinguish *more slowly* than those of a group receiving reinforcement on every trial. This counter-intuitive result is called the *partial-reinforcement effect* (sometimes abbreviated PRE). It has been the focus of a number of theoretical disputes.

A good example of the partial-reinforcement effect is found in an experiment by Bower (1960). Unlike most studies of the partial-reinforcement effect, this one used negative, rather than positive reinforcement. The experimental apparatus was a straight-alley runway with an electrified grid as the floor. The grid in the start box and runway and the grid in the goal box could be turned on independently. At the start of a trial, a rat was placed in the start box and the shock turned on. On reinforced trials, the animal experienced termination of shock immediately upon entering the goal box. On nonreinforced trials, shock was present in the goal box, as well as in the alley (the animal was removed from the goal box after spending 20 seconds there). There were four groups of animals tested, receiving reinforcement on different proportions of trials: 100 percent, 75 percent, 50 percent, and 25 percent. Following training, extinction trials were administered to the 100 percent and 50 percent groups. During these

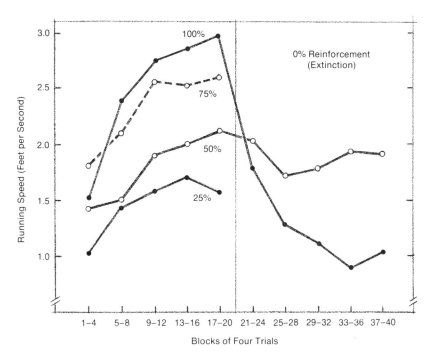

Figure 4.7 Effects of partial reinforcement on acquisition and extinction of an escape response. [After Bower, 1960. Copyright 1960 by the American Psychological Association. Reprinted by permission.]

trials, entering the goal box never produced termination of shock (0 percent reinforcement). The acquisition and extinction data are presented in Figure 4.7. As the graph shows, the greater the probability of shock termination, the faster the animals ran during acquisition. However, the opposite was true during extinction. The running of group that had been rewarded with shock termination 100 percent of the time during acquisition extinguished much more rapidly than that of the group that had received 50 percent reinforcement. This is the partial-reinforcement effect.

OPERANT CONDITIONING

The apparatus most frequently used to study animal behavior is the *Skinner box*. Much of the popularity of this apparatus derives from the fact that experimental manipulations are easily automated, leaving the experimenter free from laboratory drudgery to construct theories, devise new experiments, and write. B. F. Skinner (1956) has given us a charming account of the evolution of the device that bears his name. The desire to avoid laboratory drudgery played an important role in development of the Skinner box. As a graduate student at Harvard University in the late 1920s, Skinner was studying the behavior of rats traversing an eight-food long runway for food. To save himself the trouble of having to move the rat from the goal box of the runway to the start box after every trial, he constructed a return path for the rat to take on his own. The result was a maze with a floor plan in the form of a rectangle, with a direct path from the start box to the goal (the original runway), and a roundabout path leading from the goal back to the start box. Next, Skinner invented a way to save himself the trouble of reinforcing the animal for each trip to the goal box. He constructed the ingenious apparatus shown in Figure 4.8. The entire rectangular-shaped runway was balanced in the center so that it tipped back and forth as the rat moved from one end to the other. Whenever the runway tipped back, the attached arm hooked a wheel and moved it one notch. This allowed a piece of food in one of the notches around the perimeter of the wheel to drop through a funnel into the food dish. Thus, the animal produced its own reward each time it shuttled back and forth in the maze. Finally, Skinner discovered that by winding a string around the central spindle of the wheel (which turned one notch each time the rat ran around the runway)

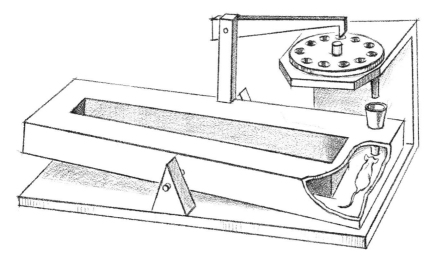

Figure 4.8 A precursor of the Skinner box. [After Skinner, 1956. Copyright 1956 by the American Psychological Association. Reprinted by permission.]

and attaching the string to a pen held against a continuously moving drum, he could preserve a complete record of the behavior of the animal while the experimenter was out of the room. Each time the wheel turned, the string unwound slightly, displacing the string downward. The resulting curve was a stair-step tracing that was steep when the rat was active, and less steep when the animal made few trips around the maze.

The "Skinner Box"

The apparatus in Figure 4.8, of course, is nothing but a huge lever. From this realization, it was only a small step to the experimental chamber known as the "Skinner box." A diagram of a modern Skinner box is shown in Figure 4.9. The apparatus consists of a chamber, which may be sound-deadened to eliminate distracting noise, a floor which may or may not be an electrified grid designed for studying effects of shock, a food magazine for dispensing positive reinforcers, and a "manipulandum"—typically a lever for rats, or a pressure-sensitive key for pigeons. The manipulandum is connected to the food magazine (or shock apparatus) through an electronic circuit, allowing complex relations between responses and reinforcement to be pro-

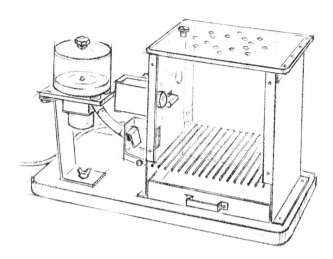

Figure 4.9 A Skinner box. [Courtesy of Ralph Gerbrands Co., Arlington, Mass.]

grammed. In addition, secondary stimuli, called discriminative stimuli, may be presented in various ways to control the animal's behavior. The discriminative stimuli may be tones or lights. When a pigeon is tested, it is common practice to illuminate the response key from behind. In this way, various colors and patterns can be projected on the key as discriminative stimuli. The experimenter is assured that the bird will look at the stimulus, since it must peck the key in order to obtain a reward.

Behavior in a Skinner box is recorded by means of a *cumulative recorder*. In principle, the idea is the same as that behind Skinner's unwinding string. A sheet of paper is moved through the recorder at a slow, steady rate. A pen leaves a continuous line on the paper. If the animal makes no response, the pen does not move, and a straight horizontal line results. When the animal responds, the pen is displaced slightly upward, to a new position. The result is a *cumulative curve* that reflects the animal's *response rate*. If the animal responds at a fast rate, the curve is steep. If the response rate is slow, the slope of the curve is more gradual. Cumulative records showing acquisition, extinction, and spontaneous recovery of the lever-pressing response by a rat are shown in Figure 4.10. The data are taken from Skinner's *Behavior of Organisms* (1938).

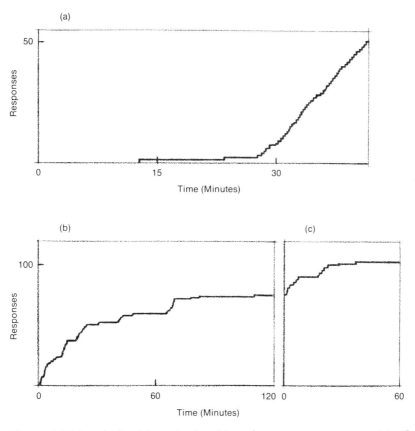

Figure 4.10 Acquisition (a), extinction (b), and spontaneous recovery (c), of an operant response. [After B. F. Skinner, *The Behavior of Organisms: An Experimental Analysis*, © 1938 renewed 1966. Reprinted by permission of Prentice-Hall, Inc., Englewood Cliffs, N.J.]

A response (for example, pressing a lever) which the subject can repeat as often as desired is called a *free operant*. The term "operant" has essentially the same meaning as instrumental response. The response is called a free operant in this situation because there is no restriction on when the manipulandum is made available to the subject; the response can be made at any time. The learning of a free operant is often called *operant conditioning*. No important theoretical distinction is made between operant and instrumental conditioning; in fact, the terms are often used interchangeably. However, the term operant conditioning is used mostly in connection with a response that can be made at any time, while the term instrumental conditioning usually refers to the kinds of trial-by-trial learning situations described in the last section. While the instrumental situation gives the experimenter control over intervals between responses, which is an advantage for some purposes, the operant conditioning procedure allows one to measure response rate—a measure that is not possible in instrumental conditioning.

There are two areas of investigation in which the operant conditioning procedure has proved most useful. One is in the study of schedules of reinforcement, and the other is in the investigation of control of behavior by discriminative stimuli. We shall turn first to a discussion of schedules of reinforcement.

Schedules of Reinforcement

A *reinforcement schedule* is a rule relating the presentation of reward to the behavior of the animal. In *continuous reinforcement,* the animal receives a reward every time the correct response is made. Other schedules are called *intermittent,* because not all responses are reinforced. (The term intermittent, rather than partial, is customary in the operant conditioning literature.)

A simple intermittent schedule is the *fixed-ratio* schedule, in which every nth response is reinforced. Thus, if n is 5, the animal must make five responses for every reward. On a *variable-ratio* schedule, likewise, the animal must make a certain number of responses, $n,$ to obtain the reward—but n varies from one reward to the next. Variable-ratio schedules are usually specified by the *average* number of responses necessary to produce the reward. Many games of chance can be viewed as variable-ratio schedules. Thus, in throwing a die for let us say a three, one wins on the average once every six throws. The schedule is a "variable ratio—6." Ratio schedules are so named because there is a predetermined ratio of responses to reinforcements. The animal must make so many responses to obtain the reward; when he makes them does not matter.

In contrast to ratio schedules are *interval schedules.* In an interval schedule, regardless of the animal's behavior, a certain period of time must follow a reward before another reward can be obtained. On a *fixed-interval* schedule, responses can be rewarded no more often than once every t seconds. Thus on a fixed-interval 60-second schedule, the animal can receive at the most one reinforcer every 60 seconds. The first response occurring after 60 seconds have elapsed since the last reward will be reinforced; a response occurring sooner than 60 seconds after the last reward will not be reinforced. On a *variable-interval* schedule, likewise, a certain time interval must elapse after each reward before another reward can be obtained, but the length of the interval varies. A variable-interval schedule is usually identified by the *average* length of the interval during which reinforcement cannot occur.

Notice that with an interval schedule the number of reinforcements that can be obtained in a fixed period of time is strictly limited. This is not the case with a ratio schedule, in which the number of reinforcements is directly proportional to the rate of responding—the more responses per unit time, the more reinforcements are received.

Typical cumulative records for the simplest types of reinforcement schedules are shown in Figure 4.11. All four curves depict responding by hungry pigeons for food. A fixed-ratio schedule, once the animal is well trained, produces a faster rate of responding than does continuous reinforcement. However, there is usually a pause in responding just after each reward is consumed. At the end of the pause, responses

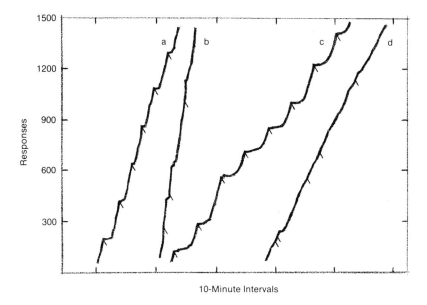

10-Minute Intervals

Figure 4.11 Cumulative records produced by four schedules of reinforcement: (a) fixed ratio, 200 responses per reinforcement; (b) variable ratio, 360 responses per reinforcement; (c) fixed interval, 4 minutes; (d) variable interval, 3 minutes. [Adapted from Ferster and Skinner, 1957.]

are made at a steady, rapid rate until the next reinforcement occurs (curve *a* in Figure 4.11). A variable-ratio schedule produces a fairly steady, fast rate of responding, with shorter pauses following reward than those that characterize the fixed-ratio schedule. Generally, the higher the average ratio of a variable-ratio schedule (that is, the more responses per reward), the higher is the response rate (curve *b* in Figure 4.11). A fixed-interval schedule produces, with a well-practiced subject, what is called a *scallop*. Following each reward there is a pause and then a gradual increase in response rate, reaching a peak at just about the time reinforcement is due (curve *c* in Figure 4.11). It is the gradual, rather than abrupt, increase that differentiates the effect of a fixed-interval schedule from that of a fixed-ratio schedule. A variable-interval schedule produces a slow, steady rate of responding. The longer the average interval, the slower is the overall response rate (curve *d* in Figure 4.11).

In operant conditioning, as in instrumental conditioning, extinction is fastest following continuous reinforcement. It is slowest following variable-ratio and variable-interval schedules, and fixed-ratio and fixed-interval schedules fall in between.

There are many other types of schedules in addition to the ratio and interval varieties. For example, reinforcement can occur only when the animal responds at a slow rate (this is called the DRL schedule—for differential reinforcement of a low rate of responding). One can also train the animal to respond only with a certain degree of force. Deliberate manipulation of characteristics of the response, such as its force, is called *response differentiation*. An almost unlimited number of complex schedules can be created by combining simple schedules in various ways. Two schedules can alternate; they can be chained, so that the requirements of both must be satisfied in order to produce a reward; they can operate simultaneously, so that meeting the requirements of either will produce reinforcement; two operants (for example, two response keys), each with its own schedule, can be made available at the same time; and the nature of the schedule can be made to change, depending on the subject's performance. A whole area of research has grown up around complex reinforcement schedules.

Stimulus Control

If a special stimulus such as a tone or colored illumination of a key is present whenever responding leads to reinforcement and is absent when it does not, the animal learns to respond only when the stimulus is present. The behavior is then said to be under *stimulus control,* and the stimulus that signals availability of reward is called a *discriminative stimulus* (S^D). Following such training, the animal may be tested in the presence of other stimuli with varying degrees of similarity to the S^D. Response rates are higher the more the test stimulus resembles the S^D—thus, operant behavior displays *stimulus generalization.*

Suppose that nonavailability of reinforcement was signalled, not by the absence of the S^D as just described, but by presentation of another stimulus, similar to S^D. A stimulus associated with absence of reinforcement is denoted S$^\Delta$. Both the S^D ("S-D") and the S$^\Delta$ ("S-Delta") are called discriminative stimuli; but the S^D indicates availability and the S$^\Delta$ nonavailability of reward. The effect upon generalization of training with short periods of S^D interspersed with periods of S$^\Delta$ is compared, in Figure 4.12, with that of training without S$^\Delta$. The data are

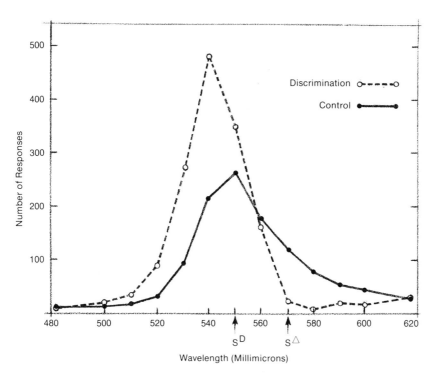

Figure 4.12 Effects of operant discrimination training on stimulus generalization. [After Hanson, 1959. Copyright 1959 by the American Psychological Association. Reprinted by permission.]

taken from an experiment by Hanson (1959). The subjects in Hanson's experiments were pigeons, and the S^D was illumination of the key with light of 550-millimicron wavelength. In the control condition, where training did not include an S^Δ, the generalization test revealed a typical generalization gradient peaking at the wavelength of the S^D. However, when periods of S^D illumination were interspersed, during training, with periods of S^Δ illumination (570 millimicrons), signalling no reward, the form of the generalization gradient was different. Not only was the tendency to respond in the range of the S^Δ depressed (which simply indicates that a discrimination between the two stimuli developed), but there was a shift of the point of maximum responding, in the direction *away* from the S^Δ. Thus, the group of animals trained with both an S^D and S^Δ did not respond maximally to the S^D of 550; instead, a test stimulus of 540 produced the greatest response rate. This phenomenon, produced by the standard discrimination training procedure, is called the *peak shift*, because there is a shift in the peak of the generalization gradient.

Fading

A different procedure for training a discrimination between an S^D and S^Δ is called *fading*. This procedure has a number of interesting properties—among them the fact that it does not produce the peak shift. Consider one of a series of experiments on fading described by Terrace (1966). In the first stage of the experiment, pigeons were taught to peck a red response key (S^D). In the second stage, the key was first made to go dark very briefly every 30 seconds. The duration of the dark period was gradually increased to 30 seconds. During this phase of training, the pigeons pecked at the key when it was lighted, but never did so when it was dark. In the third stage, an S^Δ was introduced by illuminating the key with very dim green light during the darkened periods and gradually increasing the intensity of the green illumination. Thus, dark periods were gradually introduced in stage two, and then in stage three the darkened key was gradually changed into a green one. The pigeons learned to discriminate red from darkness, and then red from green, with virtually *no errors*. In a fourth stage of training, the birds were taught to discriminate between a horizontal and a vertical white bar—an even more difficult discrimination to establish using the standard procedure. First, the vertical line was superimposed on the red key (S^D), and the horizontal line was superimposed on the green key (S^Δ). Then the colors were gradually faded out. The result was that the difficult horizontal–vertical discrimination, like the simpler red–green one, was learned with no errors; the pigeons pecked the key only when it was illuminated with the vertical bar, and never when it was illuminated with the horizontal bar.

Terrace (1966) has noted a number of differences between the behavior of animals given errorless discrimination training, through the fading technique, and those learning a discrimination in the standard way, through alternated periods of S^D and S^Δ. First, fading produces errorless discrimination learning, while the standard procedure produces many errors. Second, when fading is used a test for generalization reveals no peak shift—the animal responds maximally to the S^D itself, not to a stimulus value displaced away from the S^Δ. Third, pigeons trained without errors calmly wait, in the presence of the S^Δ, for the S^D to appear, while those trained with errors demonstrate emotional behavior (wing flapping, jumping, and the like) similar to that produced in the presence of an aversive or punishing stimulus such as shock. Fourth, pigeons trained in the standard way often produce bursts of responses to the S^Δ, even after the discrimination has been completely mastered, while those trained without errors never do. It has been suggested that errorless discrimination learning and the standard error-producing procedure differ, not only in effectiveness, but in the underlying mechanism, as well. An S^Δ to which the subject has responded (without receiving reward) apparently acquires aversive properties, while one that has been faded in gradually and has never been responded to is simply part of the background from which the S^D—the signal to respond—is contrasted.

Animal Psychophysics

One of many uses to which operant conditioning techniques have been put is the study of "animal psychophysics"—the investigation of the sensory capabilities of animals. A pioneering study in this area was done by Blough (1958). The purpose was to investigate the pigeon's visual threshold—the lowest intensity of illumination the pigeon can see. Through a painstaking procedure, Blough taught a pigeon to peck two keys according to the appearance of a single visual stimulus above them. A peck on key A increased the intensity of the light very slightly. A peck on key B decreased it slightly. Pecks on key B also occasionally turned the stimulus off—an event heralding reinforcement. But of course the light could not go off unless it was on. Thus, when the illumination was too weak to be seen, the pigeon pecked key A, which eventually made it bright enough to be visible. But as soon as the stimulus could be seen, the bird pecked key B in an attempt to obtain reward. Since pecking key B produced reward only infrequently, and otherwise reduced the intensity of the stimulus, the stimulus-intensity value increased and decreased repeatedly, according to the animal's responses on the two keys. When light could be seen, the pigeon made it dimmer; and when it could not be seen, the bird made it brighter. The value around which the intensity fluctuated was taken to be the bird's visual threshold. The threshold was found to decrease with time in the dark (dark adaptation) and to vary with the wavelength or color of the stimulus in a regular way. Both types of data parallel similar findings from studies with humans. (Normal human adults, of course, do not have to be conditioned, since they can be instructed verbally how and when to respond.)

A COMPARISON OF PARADIGMS

Four basic experimental paradigms for studying animal learning have been described. In the first, a UCS—a stimulus reflexively eliciting an innate response—is presented repeatedly. Either of two opposite response tendencies may be produced by this manipulation: *habituation,* a decrease in the strength of the UCR; and *sensitization,* an increase in its strength. In the second paradigm, a neutral stimulus, the CS, is paired repeatedly with a UCS, and as a result comes to elicit the response when presented alone. This procedure is called Pavlovian, or *classical conditioning.* In the third paradigm, the animal makes a response and is rewarded, either through presentation of a positive reinforcer or through removal of an aversive stimulus or negative reinforcer. As a result, on the next trial, the reinforced response is more likely to occur. This procedure is called *instrumental conditioning.* In the fourth paradigm, as in the third, the animal makes a response which is then reinforced. Since the response is freely available (there are no discrete events called trials), the result is an increase in the rate or frequency with which the response is made. This is the *operant conditioning* paradigm.

Habituation and Sensitization Compared with Conditioning

It is interesting to note how much habituation and sensitization, both very primitive kinds of learning, have in common with the true conditioning procedures. Both, for example, display stimulus generalization, which is a prominent characteristic of classical, instrumental, and operant conditioning. Habituation is much like extinction of a conditioned response—not only in showing a decrease in response strength with repetition, but also in showing spontaneous recovery over time. Dishabituation, produced by an intense extraneous stimulus, is much like disinhibition of an extinguished conditioned reflex, as studied by Pavlov. It was once thought that disinhibition could not be obtained with instrumental or operant responses, but recent evidence shows that it can be (Brimer, 1970).

Another way in which habituation resembles conditioning is illustrated by the observation that a reaction to an intense stimulus can be habituated by first presenting the stimulus in weak form and then gradually increasing its intensity. A similar principle was used by Mary Cover Jones (1924) to counter-condition fear in children (see Chapter 3). The feared stimulus was introduced at a distance in a pleasant situation, and gradually brought closer. Likewise, Pavlov taught a difficult discrimination between white and light grey by first establishing an easy discrimination and then making the CS− more and more similar to the CS+. And in the operant conditioning situation, Terrace (1966) showed how a difficult discrimination between an S^D and S^Δ could be taught without errors through the use of fading. Perhaps the term *fading* could be used to refer to all these procedures. A simple principle seems common to all of them: A behavior that is difficult or even impossible to teach an organism by means of one technique may be produced readily if an easy version is trained first and then gradually made more and more like the difficult one.

The general principle of fading has proved useful in educational practice—particularly in training people who are physically and mentally handicapped. Indeed, the principle was applied in those fields more than a century before it was discovered in the learning laboratory. Lane (1976) recounts how Abbé Sicard, the eighteenth-century French educator of deaf-mutes, first taught his charges to read by inscribing a word inside a drawing of the corresponding object and then gradually fading out the outline and shape of the drawing, leaving the pupil to rely on the letters alone (see Figure 4.13). Related

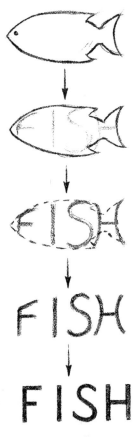

Figure 4.13 Fading as a way of teaching reading.

procedures were employed in the last century to teach skills to the deaf and the retarded, and in one celebrated case, to civilize the "wild boy of Aveyron" (Lane, 1976).

Classical Compared with Instrumental and Operant Conditioning

As we have seen, both instrumental and operant conditioning require the subject to make a particular response in order to obtain reward. But in instrumental conditioning the experimenter gives the animal individual opportunities (that is, discrete trials) to make the response, and measures the response's latency, amplitude, and probability; while in operant conditioning the response is always available, and the preferred measure is response rate. The two experimental procedures are so different that they have given rise to different ways of describing and thinking about learning research. Nevertheless, all theorists consider the mechanisms underlying learning in the two situations to be the same, and most writers, as a result, apply just one label (either instrumental or operant) to both. Since it is generally agreed that the underlying learning process is the same, we shall cease making the distinction for the remainder of this chapter. Whenever something is said about instrumental conditioning, it is meant to apply to operant conditioning as well.

A fundamental question theorists have debated is whether the mechanism underlying classical conditioning differs from that underlying instrumental conditioning. This is a subject that will be considered further in Chapter 6. For the present, we shall ignore this theoretical question; but it is important to understand the difference between the two forms of learning simply in terms of experimental procedure.

It is sometimes said that instrumental conditioning involves reinforcement, while classical conditioning does not. But this is misleading. The UCS plays a role in classical conditioning similar to that of the reward in instrumental conditioning—it is necessary in order for learning to occur, and when it is removed the behavior extinguishes. Indeed, many stimuli that can be used as the UCS in classical conditioning (for example, food and electric shock) also serve as reinforcers in instrumental conditioning.

The basic difference between the two conditioning procedures was pointed out by Skinner (1937). In both classical and instrumental conditioning there is a reinforcer or UCS; but in classical conditioning the reinforcer is presented just after the CS, while in instrumental conditioning it is presented just after the response. The difference, therefore, can be described in terms of *contingencies*. In classical conditioning, reinforcement is contingent on a stimulus (the CS), whereas in instrumental conditioning reinforcement is contingent on a response. Another way to describe the difference is to say that in classical conditioning reinforcement occurs regardless of whether the animal responds, while in instrumental conditioning the animal must respond in order to receive reinforcement.

An intriguing puzzle concerning the relationship between classical and instrumental conditioning has been pointed out by Razran

(1971). Up to this point, we have treated the CS in the classical conditioning situation as a neutral stimulus that elicits no innate reaction. This is an oversimplification, however. A tone ordinarily causes a dog to prick up its ears and move its head; and a light will cause the animal to move its eyes and its head. This kind of reaction is called an *orienting response* (OR). In the classical conditioning situation, then, one really begins with two reflexes: the CS–OR orienting reflex, and the UCS–UCR reflex. Conditioning takes place when the CS–OR reflex is replaced by the CS–CR reflex (in which the CR is similar to the UCR).

Note, however, that the conditions for instrumental conditioning are seemingly satisfied by this arrangement. Suppose we present a tone (CS) and the animal pricks up its ears (OR). Then we present food (UCS) and the animal salivates (UCR). The response of pricking up the ears is followed by a positive reinforcer. Why doesn't instrumental conditioning occur? That is, why doesn't the probability of the OR increase? Instead, it decreases and is replaced by the CR of salivation. Razran (1971) has proposed that what determines whether classical or instrumental conditioning will occur is the *habituability* of the response that is followed by the reinforcer. Most OR's (such as pricking up the ears) habituate easily with repeated presentation of the CS; most responses that can be instrumentally learned are not easy to habituate. Razran's suggestion, then, is that instrumental conditioning will occur only if the response that is to be conditioned does not easily habituate. This hypothesis is beginning to receive some attention from other investigators (for example, Kimmel, 1973).

The above analysis shows that the classical conditioning situation includes the basic components of the instrumental conditioning paradigm—a response is followed by reward. It is also true that the basic elements of the classical conditioning paradigm are present during instrumental conditioning. In fact, classically conditioned behavior is often observed during instrumental learning. A dog performing an instrumental response for food will salivate; and a rat running in a straight alley for food may be seen to gnash its teeth and smack its lips—responses that would be elicited as UCR's by the food. Likewise, in avoidance learning, in which a signal warns that shock is about to occur, animals often respond to the signal by squealing, defecating, or crouching in a corner—behavior that would be reflexively elicited by the shock.

Theorists have had difficulty determining whether classical and instrumental conditioning involve different underlying mechanisms.

One reason for this difficulty is that a "pure" case of instrumental conditioning—in which no classically conditioned behavior occurs—may be impossible to produce. In fact, the pecking of an illuminated key by a pigeon (the most commonly studied operant response) can be trained through a purely classical conditioning procedure. All one needs to do, apparently, is to repeatedly follow the lighting of the key (CS) by the delivery of food (UCS). The pecking response (the UCR to food) is transferred from the food to the key. Soon the pigeon is pecking the key, even though it need not do so in order to obtain the food (Brown and Jenkins, 1968). This phenomenon, which has come to be known as *autoshaping,* is discussed further in Chapter 7.

Secondary Reinforcement: A Mixed Paradigm

In the previous discussion of instrumental conditioning, the concept of primary reinforcement was introduced. Primary reinforcers, whose reinforcing power is genetically determined, are to be contrasted with secondary reinforcers, whose reinforcing power is acquired through learning. The paradigm demonstrating *secondary reinforcement* involves two stages: one of classical conditioning, and one of operant or instrumental conditioning. Consider a hungry rat fed in the presence of a previously neutral stimulus. We know that this situation fits the classical conditioning paradigm. The neutral stimulus is the CS; through its pairing with the UCS it can come to elicit the CR, part of the response the animal naturally makes to food. But the pairing of the CS and UCS has another effect on the animal's reaction to the CS, as well. It gives the CS the power to reinforce an instrumental response.

A good example of secondary reinforcement is provided by an experiment by Saltzman (1949). In the first stage of the experiment, hungry rats were fed in a distinctive goal box. For half the rats the goal box was white, and for the other half it was black. In the second stage the rats were given 15 trials of training in a maze which required a choice between two paths, one branching to the right and the other to the left. One of these paths led to the white goal box, and the other led to the black one; thus, for an individual rat, one goal box was the one in which food had been found during the first stage and the other was not. The animals were never fed in this maze; yet they learned to choose the path leading to the "correct" goal box—the one that had previously been associated with food—more often than the path leading to the "incorrect" one. Saltzman noted, however, that choices of the path leading to the previously rewarding goal box first increased, but then *declined* over the 15 trials. He suggested that in stage two the secondary reinforcing power of the goal box might have gradually extinguished because it was no longer paired with food. To test this hypothesis, he performed a second experiment. In this experiment the stage-one trials, in which food was paired with the goal box, were interspersed with the stage-two trials, which required a choice between the right and left paths of the maze. Under these conditions, the preference for the path leading to the "correct" goal box was maintained. The rats chose that path on 77 percent of the trials, as opposed to only 56 percent of the trials in the first experiment.

The experiments by Saltzman illustrate the crucial test of whether a CS has become a secondary reinforcer—it must have the power to reinforce *new learning.* In this case the animals learned to go left or right, even though this response was never directly reinforced with food. Stimuli of the goal box provided the only "reinforcement" for this behavior. The experiment also illustrates the fact that secondary reinforcers tend to lose their reinforcing power if they are not occasionally paired with the primary reinforcer (the UCS). Saltzman was able to forestall this loss in his second experiment by interspersing the choice tests with pairings of the goal box and food.

Secondary reinforcers, like primary reinforcers, can be either positive or negative. A *secondary positive reinforcer* is produced by pairing a neutral stimulus with a primary positive reinforcer, as in the Saltzman study. A *secondary negative reinforcer* is produced by pairing a neutral stimulus with a primary negative reinforcer, such as shock.

The test for secondary negative reinforcement, like that for secondary positive reinforcement, is whether or not the previously neutral stimulus will reinforce new learning. For example, suppose that in stage one a rat is placed in a white box (the CS), where it is repeatedly shocked (the UCS). In stage two the rat is again placed in a white box, but is never shocked. A lever is made available which, whenever it is pressed, opens a door permitting the rat to escape from the white box into another compartment. If the animal learns to make this response (and does so more quickly than a control rat that was never shocked in the white box), the white box has been shown to be a secondary negative reinforcer. Intuitively, an observer might assume that the rat had become "afraid" of the white box because it was shocked there. Thus, the paradigm for demonstrating secondary negative reinforcement is often referred to as a *fear conditioning* paradigm. Little Albert, in the experiment by Watson and Rayner (1920), performed an instrumental response (crawling away) to escape the white rat, which had become a secondary negative reinforcer by being paired with the loud noise.

A great deal of theoretical significance has been attached to secondary reinforcement as a link between animal learning studies and human behavior. While most complex human behavior appears to be instrumental or operant in the sense that it accomplishes a particular desired outcome, it is infrequent that the immediate outcome is a primary reinforcer. Students work for A's, laborers for wages, politicians for votes, celebrities for publicity, and amateur artists and hobbyists for whatever they produce plus occasional praise. Can the reinforcing power of such events be understood as examples of secondary reinforcement? That is, did these outcomes become reinforcing by being paired with primary (innate) reinforcers? There have been experimental attempts to make this connection. For example, a study by Wolfe (1936) found that chimpanzees that had learned to put a poker chip in a vending machine for a grape would work for poker chips even when the vending machine was not immediately available—a finding with an obvious parallel to the role of money in human behavior. The explanation of complex human behavior in terms of secondary reinforcement is not without its problems, however. It is not always evident that the "reinforcing" outcome has been paired with an appropriate primary reinforcer (with that UCS has the letter grade A been paired?), and there remains the fact that without such occasional pairings, most secondary reinforcers lose their reinforcing power. If A's, wages, votes, publicity, and praise are secondary reinforcers, they are remarkably resistant to extinction.

5

Theories of Animal Learning

Research on animal learning has been shaped to a considerable degree by the theoretical efforts of a few psychologists. The most influential theoretical positions have been those of Clark L. Hull, Edward C. Tolman, and B. F. Skinner. It is worthwhile becoming acquainted with the theories of these men, not only because their theories have had wide-reaching influence, but also because they illustrate three fundamentally different approaches to psychological explanation. Hull, as was indicated earlier, can be categorized as a neobehaviorist; Tolman as a cognitivist; and Skinner as a descriptive behaviorist. We shall examine the three approaches in turn.

NEOBEHAVIORISM: HULL'S THEORY

Neobehaviorism differs from descriptive behaviorism principally in its willingness to explain behavior in terms of hypothetical events occurring between the stimulus and the response—that is, within the animal's nervous system. It differs from cognitivism in the kinds of explanatory events it accepts. Mechanistic theories are accepted, but mentalistic ones are not. It is not necessary that a neobehaviorist theory refer directly to physiological events; it may be stated in terms of mechanical analogies. If the animal behaves *as though* a particular hypothetical mechanism were guiding its behavior, then the mechanism constitutes an acceptable theoretical explanation of the behavior. The actual nervous system of the animal, of course, may bear no physical resemblance to the proposed machine. The assumption is simply that both mechanisms—the neural one in the animal's head and the hypothetical one in the theory—are governed by the same principles. The proposed mechanism functions as a *model,* giving the theorist a concrete representation to aid in thinking through the implications of the theory. In some cases (for example, Deutsch, 1960; Walter, 1953) the theorist may actually fashion a working robot from relays, motors, and wheels, to show that his theory is indeed a complete and adequate explanation of the particular behavior it attempts to account for. More often, however, the theorist is content to carefully spell out the principles of operation of the machine in a formal or logical way.

Clark Hull's system is an excellent sample of a formal theory of behavior. His method of theorizing was deliberately and self-consciously patterned after that of classical physics. Hull—like many others then and now—considered physics, with its elegant mathematics and impressive precision, the science that psychology should try most to emulate.

Hull's goal was to construct a theory that could be stated in terms of a few basic postulates, from which numerous predictions regarding the animal's behavior could be derived in a logical, unambiguous way. The strategy was to construct such a theory, derive predictions, and compare the predictions with experimental data. If the predictions held, the theory would not be changed; if they failed, key postulates of the theory would be changed to bring the theory into agreement with the experimental outcomes. This strategy is called the *hypothetico-deductive method.* The method is one of evolution; ultimately, the theorist hopes, it will produce a theory that is true. By "true," in this case, we mean that the theory that evolves is perfectly adapted to its experimental environment, so that it correctly predicts the outcomes of all relevant experiments, past and present.

Because the hypothetico-deductive method requires the theory to evolve or change in response to predictive failures, Hull was quite willing to alter his theoretical assumptions, and he did so many times. The last revision of Hull's theory was completed shortly before his death in 1952. But the most complete version of his theory—and the most influential—was given in a book entitled *Principles of Behavior,* published in 1943. It is his 1943 theory that will be described here.

The theory is considerably more complex than the following discussion suggests. We shall focus on only its most basic assumptions. These should convey the general outline of the mechanistic theory Hull proposed.

Habit Strength

Hull's efforts were influenced not only by classical physics, but also by the writings of Pavlov. Hull assumed that the basic element of behavior was the stimulus–response connection (the S–R bond), a concept similar to Pavlov's conditioned reflex. The central construct of Hull's theory was the concept of *habit strength,* which was the strength of the association linking a stimulus situation (S) with a response (R). Habit strength was represented symbolically as $_sH_R$. An increase in $_sH_R$ occurred, according to Hull, only when three events occurred in contiguity: (a) the stimulus, S; (b) the response, R; and (c) reinforcement. Hull identified reinforcement primarily with the reduction of a physiological need, such as hunger, thirst, or pain. The assumption that reinforcement is necessary for learning places Hull's theory in a category of learning theories called *reinforcement theories.*

Hull's equation relating habit strength to the number of reinforced pairings of S and R was:

$$_sH_R = M (1 - 10^{-iN}).\qquad(1)$$

Here, i is an arbitrary constant which determines the individual subject's learning rate, N is the number of reinforced trials, and M is the maximum value $_sH_R$ can reach. The value of M was assumed to be greater the larger the reward was and the sooner it followed after the response. Thus, the variables of size of reward and delay of reward acted directly on the degree of learning, represented by $_sH_R$. This assumption is quite plausible for a reinforcement theory and, at the time the theory was published in 1943, appeared to be in accord with experimental results. Hull proposed that $_sH_R$ be measured on a 100-unit scale. (The unit of measurement of $_sH_R$ he called the *hab,* for habit.) Figure 5.1 plots Hull's equation for $_sH_R$ as a function of N, the number of reinforced trials, for two situations—one in which M is 100 (large, immediate reward) and one in which it is 50 (small or delayed reward). To account for stimulus generalization, Hull assumed that $_sH_R$ spreads to other stimuli in proportion to their similarity to S.

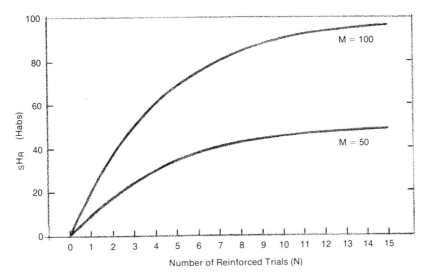

Figure 5.1 Growth of $_sH_R$ as a function of reinforced trials for large, immediate reward ($M = 100$) and small or delayed reward ($M = 50$), according to Hull (1943).

Drive

An animal is not likely to run down a runway for food or press a bar for water unless it is hungry or thirsty, no matter how well it has learned the response. Thus habit strength alone will not predict behavior; motivation must be taken into account. Hull represented motivation with the symbol D (for *drive*). He assumed that D increased as the animal's physiological needs increased, and thus could be manipulated by depriving the animal of such things as food, water, or sex. (The unit of measurement of D was called the *mote*.)

The role of drive in behavior was to activate habit strength:

$$_sE_R = {_sH_R} \times D. \tag{2}$$

Here, $_sE_R$ is the *reaction potential*—the potential for response R to occur in the presence of stimulus S. ($_sE_R$ was to be measured in *Wats*, named for Watson.) Equation (2) indicates that $_sE_R$ is a multiplicative function of $_sH_R$ and D. Thus, the tendency for R to occur in the presence of S will increase if either $_sH_R$ increases as a result of reinforced practice, or D increases as a result of increased deprivation. If either $_sH_R$ or D is zero, the behavior will not occur.

Inhibition

So far we have seen how reinforced practice and motivation affect behavior. But what about nonreinforced practice? We know that behavior that is not reinforced extinguishes. How is extinction to be explained? There is no provision in the theory for $_sH_R$ to decrease; it can only increase or stay the same. Behavior will disappear if the stimulus is removed or motivation is reduced to zero. But extinction also takes place when the stimulating conditions are unchanged and motivation is high. All that is necessary is elimination of reinforcement.

Hull dealt with extinction and spontaneous recovery by modifying Pavlov's concept of inhibition (he honored Pavlov by naming the unit of inhibition the *Pav*.) He assumed two kinds of inhibitory forces acting against the occurrence of the response. One was called *reactive inhibition* (symbolized by I_R). Reactive inhibition was assumed to be temporary, and to dissipate with rest. The dissipation of I_R during rest intervals allowed the theory to explain spontaneous recovery. The other kind of inhibition, called *conditioned inhibition,* was symbolized as $_sI_R$. Conditioned inhibition was assumed to be permanent. It was a kind of negative habit, opposing $_sH_R$—that is, a habit of *not* making R in the presence of S. The permanence of $_sI_R$ enabled the theory to account for the fact that spontaneous recovery is seldom—if ever—complete. The roles of I_R and $_sI_R$ in producing behavior were subtractive, expressed as follows:

$$_s\overline{E}_R = {}_sE_R - {}_sI_R - I_R. \qquad (3)$$

Hull called $_s\overline{E}_R$ the *effective reaction potential*. During extinction training, $_s\overline{E}_R$ will decrease, owing to the increasing values of both I_R and $_sI_R$. I_R is short-lived, while $_sI_R$ is permanent. Thus, if a rest interval occurs following extinction, I_R will gradually decline to zero. As a result, $_s\overline{E}_R$ will spontaneously recover, reaching the value $_sE_R - {}_sI_R$. Repeated extinctions will eventually increase $_sI_R$ to the point where no spontaneous recovery can occur.

Prediction of Behavior

So far we have considered Hull's most basic assumptions regarding learning and motivation and have seen how they combine to explain behavior. But there are two more problems that must be dealt with before the theory can be applied to the behavior of real animals in real experiments. The first has to do with variability, and the second with failures to respond.

Consider first the problem of variability. A rat running down an alleyway trial after trial does not smoothly increase its speed as learning progresses. On the average, the speed of running becomes faster with training, but the speed on any particular trial is not necessarily faster than that on the previous trial. The animal may get a poor start, stop to examine part of the apparatus, or simply run slowly. Thus, the behavior of a real rat does not reflect the smooth increase in $_sH_R$ shown in Figure 5.1. How should this variability in behavior be explained? Hull accounted for it with an additional concept called *oscillation*, represented by $_sO_R$. Oscillation was thought to be a kind of inhibition that varied randomly in amount from moment to moment. If the animal was tested at a time when $_sO_R$ was low, it would run fast; if it was tested when $_sO_R$ was high, it would run slowly. Since $_sO_R$ varied randomly from one trial to the next, the exact speed of the animal on any given trial could not be predicted. But on the average, speed would increase with practice, reflecting the increase in $_sH_R$.

What about failures to respond? This problem was handled by assuming that there was a threshold, or "limen," value that had to be exceeded in order for the response to occur. Specifically, a response occurs when the *momentary* effective reaction potential ($_s\bar{E}_R - _sO_R$) exceeds the threshold value $_sL_R$. If the threshold is not exceeded, the response does not occur. The speed of a response when it does occur is determined by the difference between the momentary effective reaction potential and $_sL_R$. The further the value is above the threshold $_sL_R$, the faster is the response.

The roles of $_s\bar{E}_R$, $_sO_R$, and $_sL_R$ in determining the final response are shown schematically in Figure 5.2. The increasing curve represents $_s\bar{E}_R$, which increases with practice because of the growth of $_sH_R$. The horizontal line represents $_sL_R$, the threshold that must be exceeded for a response to occur. The dotted lines extending below the $_s\bar{E}_R$ curve represent the inhibitory effects of $_sO_R$, varying randomly from one trial to the next. The combined influences of these three variables determine the behavior. Thus, on trials 1 and 2 of Figure 5.2, $_s\bar{E}_R$ is too low for a response to occur. On trial 3, $_s\bar{E}_R$ is high enough; but the inhibitory effect of $_sO_R$ is too great, so there is no response. On trial 4, $_s\bar{E}_R - _sO_R$ is high enough to produce a response; but on trial 5, $_sO_R$ is so

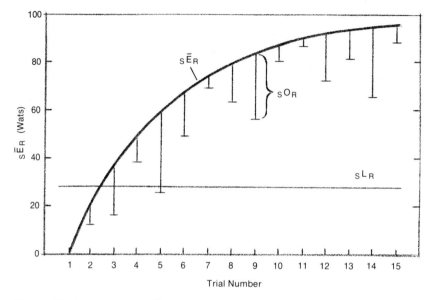

Figure 5.2 Interaction of $_s\bar{E}_R$, oscillation ($_sO_R$), and threshold ($_sL_R$) in determining performance, according to Hull (1943).

great that the response again fails to occur. On all remaining trials the animal responds, but the response speed varies according to the distance of $_s\bar{E}_R - {_sO_R}$ above $_sL_R$. Thus, on trial 7 the response is more rapid than on either trial 8 or 9. Overall, in spite of this variability, the probability that a response will occur increases with practice; and the responses that do occur, on the average, increase in speed.

A Summary of Basic Concepts

Figure 5.3 summarizes the relationship between Hull's theory and the manipulations and measurable outcomes of an experiment. Listed at the top are various *independent variables.* These are events over which the experimenter can exert control (for example, how long the animal has been deprived of water). At the bottom of the figure are four *dependent variables*—measurable characteristics of behavior which can vary, and which *depend* upon the values of independent variables. Hull considered the four dependent variables listed—probability, latency, amplitude (strength or speed), and resistance of the response to extinction—all to be reflections of the same underlying process. Between the independent and dependent variables lie *intervening vari-*

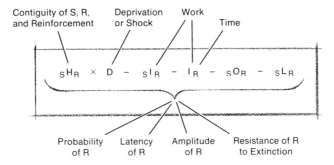

Figure 5.3 The intervening variables of Hull's (1943) theory, and their relationships to independent variables (top) and dependent variables (bottom).

ables, which cannot be directly manipulated or measured, but which the theory assumes to be present. They constitute a link in the causal chain—affected by the independent variables manipulated by the experimenter, and interacting with one another, in turn, to produce the animal's behavior.

The advantage of formulating a theory in explicit terms is that such a theory makes unambiguous predictions. When a prediction fails, one knows the theory must be changed. Notice, for example, that Hull's theory correctly predicts the effect on performance of delay of reward. This effect is mediated through $_sH_R$, which increases less when reward is delayed than when it is immediate. Notice also that the theory fails to predict correctly the effects of partial reinforcement on resistance to extinction. Continuous reinforcement, according to the theory, should lead to greater resistance to extinction than does partial reinforcement. As we saw in Chapter 4, just the opposite effect is usually found. Predictive successes and failures such as these, ideally, should help the theorist understand which parts of his theory are right and which are wrong. The faith underlying the hypothetico-deductive method is that repeated alterations and tests of the theory will eventually lead to an adequate explanation of behavior.

Derived Concepts

Two more of Hull's theoretical concepts are worth mentioning here. Recall from Chapter 4 that, with repeated trials in a complex maze, a rat first eliminates the errors that occur closest to the goal box. Hull explained this finding, in his 1943 theory, using the principle of the *goal gradient*. This principle stated that the power of reward to reinforce a particular S–R connection decreased the farther that particular choice point was from the goal. Hull was unable to account for the goal gradient solely in terms of the effect of delay of reward on $_sH_R$ because Grice's 1948 experiment (Figure 4.6) had shown that a reward delayed as long as 10 seconds produced virtually no learning—and learning in a complex maze involves delays that are much longer. Thus Hull based the goal gradient principle, not only on the effect of delay of reward, but also on secondary reinforcement. A stimulus followed by reward was assumed to become a secondary reinforcer, which then helped strengthen any S–R habit that reliably produced it. Thus, the goal gradient was assumed to be due primarily to the chaining of reinforcing power from stimulus to preceding stimulus, backward from the primary reinforcer in the goal box.

A particularly useful concept that Hull derived from the goal gradient assumption was that of the *habit-family hierarchy*. Suppose a hungry rat is placed in the start box of a maze that has not just one, but three possible paths to the goal box, all three branching from a single choice point. Imagine further that the three paths are of different lengths. Let us identify the shortest path as A, the medium-length path as B, and the longest path as C. Now as the rat explores the maze, trial after trial, it sometimes takes A, sometimes B, and sometimes C, and each path choice is followed eventually by reinforcement in the goal box. Thus three conflicting habits will be learned: S–R$_A$, S–R$_B$, and S–R$_C$, where S represents the single choice point, R$_A$ is the response of taking path A, and so on. Because of the goal gradient, the three habits will not be of equal strength. R$_A$ leads to reward most quickly, and so the S–R$_A$ connection will be strongest. The three habits, ranked in order of strength, will be:

$$_sH_{R_A} > {}_sH_{R_B} > {}_sH_{R_C}.$$

These three habits are all connected to S, the stimuli at the choice point, and all lead to the same goal. For this reason, Hull called them a habit family; and because the habits can be ranked in terms of strength, they constitute a hierarchy. Thus the name: habit-family hierarchy.

What does the habit-family hierarchy help us understand? First, there is the fact that rats trained in a maze such as the one just described eventually come to choose the shortest path on most of the trials. When they take another, it is likely to be the second shortest path. The longest path is seldom taken. This, of course, is exactly as predicted by the hypothesis of the habit-family hierarchy. But in addition, the hypothesis explains what happens when a pathway is blocked. Suppose a block is put in path A, so that only paths B and C will lead to the goal. According to the theory, encountering the block will produce inhibition of R_A. When this inhibition ($_sI_{R_A}$ and I_{R_A}) is great enough, its effect will outweigh the difference in habit strengths favoring A, and $_s\bar{E}_{R_A}$ will become less than $_s\bar{E}_{R_B}$. Thus, the predicted effect of a block in path A is that the animal will now prefer path B. This, too, is in accord with the experimental findings.

Hull's theory was testable—and this inevitably led to a number of predictive failures. The failures led Hull to change his theory in several fundamental ways. In the next chapter we shall examine some of the experiments that have been done to test key assumptions of Hull's theory. Many of these experiments have been conducted by psychologists favoring cognitive learning theories. We turn to cognitive theories next.

COGNITIVISM: TOLMAN'S THEORY

Cognitivism, which explains behavior in terms of mental events such as purposes, beliefs, decisions, and so on, was not particularly popular among those who studied learning during the 1930s, 1940s, and 1950s. This was one result of the behaviorist revolution. Because behaviorists had turned away from studying the mind, their work began to seem far removed from everyday experience and from the interests of psychology's parent discipline, philosophy. As one philosopher lamented, "First psychology lost its soul; then it lost its mind; and now it has lost consciousness."

Through this period, however, the basic approach of Ebbinghaus, which involved objective observations and mentalistic explanations, maintained a small following. Most of those choosing the approach of cognitivism were interested in human learning and memory, but there were a few who studied animals. Cognitivists interested in animal behavior typically preferred to study complex tasks over simple ones. Thus, Köhler (1925) studied the behavior of apes in situations in which some problem had to be solved in order to obtain a reward—

usually, a banana. Reaching the banana might require stacking several boxes to climb up on, for example, or putting two sticks together to reach through the bars of the cage. When such problems were solved, the solutions appeared to come suddenly. This suggested a process akin to the "aha" experience, which Köhler called *insight.* Likewise, Krechevsky (1932) studied the behavior of rats learning a discrimination in a T-maze. He, too, found that the problems seemed to be solved suddenly. Further, he noted that the patterns of choices the rats made before solution were not random, but systematic. Such behavior was taken as evidence of *hypothesis testing* in the lowly rat.

The most influential cognitivist studying animal learning was E. C. Tolman, who taught at the University of California at Berkeley. Tolman did more than anyone else to help psychology "regain consciousness." As the leader of the small group of cognitivists, Tolman was Hull's chief rival. Much of his experimental work had the aim of showing that animals—particularly the rat—were more intelligent than S–R theories such as Hull's implied. Despite the success of many of his experiments in this regard (to be discussed in Chapter 6), Tolman's theory was not widely accepted. Tolman's theory was very informal compared with Hull's. It was often stated in terms that had not been clearly defined, and it was, in addition, unashamedly mentalistic. Tolman's method was not hypothetico-deductive. As Tolman (1938) described it, he constructed theories by "imagining how, *if I were a rat,* I would behave" in a particular situation, deriving rules from such imaginings, and eventually translating the rules into "some kind of objective and respectable sounding terms" constituting the theory. Despite this mentalistic, even introspective, approach to theory building, Tolman agreed with the behaviorists that the *testing* of theories must be done by completely objective means. Let us examine the theory that this method produced.

Purposive Behavior

Tolman considered himself a behaviorist. But this was true only in the sense of the broadest definition of the term (behaviorism-1, or "methodological behaviorism," as discussed in Chapter 3). He insisted that theories be tested by means of objective observation; but the nature of his theory definitely excludes it from the more strict definitions of behaviorism (behaviorism-2 and -3). He was a cognitivist in the tradition of Ebbinghaus.

The major statement of Tolman's position was the book *Purposive Behavior in Animals and Man,* published in 1932. Other theoretical papers appeared in the 1930s and 1940s, and in a paper written shortly before his death, Tolman (1959) attempted to formulate his theory in a more formal way, to make it more comparable to Hull's. In his various writings, Tolman invented theoretical terms freely, often substituting one forbidding hyphenated term (for example, sign-Gestalt-expectation) for a different term he had used previously, without any real change in meaning. But while the terminology changed considerably, the basic assumptions of the theory changed very little. The following discussion attempts to present the fundamental ideas of Tolman's theory without the frequently confusing language.

In contrast to Watson, Hull, and others, who proposed that what is learned is an S–R bond, Tolman assumed that what is learned is a belief, or *expectancy.* In traversing the maze, the rat learns that food is in the goal box, that a right turn follows the first left turn, and so on. Upon being shocked in a shuttle box, the animal comes to expect shock in that situation. If the sound of a bell is reliably followed by food, the animal expects food whenever the bell sounds. In general, the animal learns *what will lead to what.* Behavior is *purposive,* because it is produced by the desire or demand for a particular outcome. This view is in sharp contrast to that of Hull, who assumed in his 1943 theory that the animal is pushed around its environment by stimuli it encounters, making whatever responses have happened to become conditioned to those stimuli in the past. The Tolmanian rat anticipates the consequences of its action; the Hullian rat does not.

Tolman further distinguished between his view and that of S–R theorists regarding the units of behavior that could be studied most profitably. Following Pavlov, many S–R theorists felt that behavior should be described in terms of its *molecular* structure—that is, glandular secretions and muscular contractions. They assumed that what the animal learned was to respond to a given stimulus by contracting particular muscles in a particular pattern. Tolman did not question that behavior ultimately consists of secretions and contractions, but argued that behavior was purposive, and that it was therefore more fruitful to describe it in *molar* terms—that is, in terms of acts and accomplishments. What the rat in the Skinner box learns, according to Tolman, is to push the bar down. The particular muscles used may vary from trial to trial, but the act is the same. Likewise, the animal in a maze may learn to approach the choice point, turn toward the light from the window, pass two paths branching to the right, and enter the third. The sequence of steps with left and right feet is irrelevant; it varies from trial to trial (as do speed and number of stops to scratch), but the path taken is the same. It is the molar, goal-directed *act* that is learned. The molecular (muscle-twitch) responses produced on a given trial simply constitute one way the learned act can be performed.

Because Tolman considered particular responses relatively unimportant in describing behavior, he had little to say about them. He concentrated instead on describing the knowledge an animal must have in order to behave in a particular way. This disinclination to consider the question of how knowledge leads to action led one S–R theorist to charge that Tolman left the rat at a choice point, "buried in thought" (Guthrie, 1952, p. 143). In the final statement of his theory, Tolman (1959) attempted to take the response into account—but it was still the molar, goal-directed act he had in mind, rather than the molecular, muscle-twitch response.

With this preliminary overview out of the way, let us turn to a more detailed treatment of Tolman's theory.

Beliefs and Expectancies

When an animal experiences two stimuli in succession (S_1 followed by S_2), a *belief*, $S_1 \rightarrow S_2$, is established. The belief can be paraphrased as saying "when S_1 occurs, S_2 tends to follow." Likewise, when the animal makes R_1 in the presence of S_1, and this is followed by S_2, a belief $S_1R_1 \rightarrow S_2$ is learned. This belief is paraphrased as "when I perform R_1 in the presence of S_1, S_2 occurs." Thus, there are two kinds of beliefs—$S_1 \rightarrow S_2$ and $S_1R_1 \rightarrow S_2$. Stimulus events play two roles in beliefs—the role of S_1 (called a *sign*) and that of S_2 (the *consequence*). A sign indicates either that S_2 is likely to occur, or that R_1 is likely to lead to S_2.

Beliefs can vary both in terms of strength, or "confidence," and in terms of the perceived probability of the consequence (S_2). These are different kinds of magnitudes, and they are not necessarily correlated. For example, the animal could be very confident that S_1 will *not* be followed by S_2.

When the animal encounters the sign appropriate for a particular belief (or a stimulus similar to that sign) the belief becomes aroused. An aroused belief is called an *expectancy*. Whether or not an expectancy will influence the animal's behavior depends upon motivation or *demand*—a concept to which we shall return shortly.

Belief Structures: Chains and Maps

It may appear that the concept of belief, or expectancy, does not differ appreciably from that of the S–R bond. However, an S–R bond simply links an S and an R, while an expectancy (either $S_1 \rightarrow S_2$ or $S_1R_1 \rightarrow S_2$) has the property of linking a sign (S_1) and a consequence (S_2). Since S_1 and S_2 are both stimuli, it is possible for expectancies to be *chained*. Thus, following experience in a Skinner box a rat may possess the following beliefs: $S_1R_1 \rightarrow S_2$; $S_2R_2 \rightarrow S_f$; $S_fR_f \rightarrow S_{hr}$. They may be paraphrased as follows: "In this situation (S_1), a bar press (R_1) makes the feeder mechanism produce a click (S_2); moving to the feeder (R_2) following the click produces the sight and smell of food (S_f); eating the food (R_f) produces hunger reduction (S_{hr})." Since the consequences of some beliefs are the signs of others, the beliefs constitute a chain with interlocking elements. A chain of beliefs or expectancies can be "telescoped." For example the rat in the Skinner box expects: $S_1R_1 \rightarrow S_{hr}$; "pressing the bar in situation S_1 will (eventually) lead to hunger reduction." Likewise, the rat has experienced what happens when it fails to press the bar ($\bar{R}_1$). This sequence does not lead to reduced hunger, so the expectancy is: $S_1\bar{R}_1 \rightarrow S_{\overline{hr}}$; "No bar press in situation S_1 does not lead to hunger reduction."

It is a simple matter to construct a set of beliefs for a rat in a complex maze. Such a set of beliefs will include not only the chain of events that leads from the start box to the goal box, but also the chains that lead into various blind alleys, and thus to no food. In the case of the maze, which was Tolman's favorite apparatus for studying learning, the entire set of beliefs constitutes what Tolman called a *cognitive map*—an integrated representation of the local environment which includes not only simple sequences of events, but also information about directions, distances, and even time relations.

> [The nervous system] is far more like a map control room than it is like an old-fashioned telephone exchange. The stimuli, which are allowed in, are not connected by just simple one-to-one switches to the outgoing responses. Rather, the incoming impulses are usually worked over and elaborated in the central control room into a tentative, cognitive-like map of the environment. And it is this tentative map, indicating routes and paths

and environmental relationships, which finally determines what responses, if any, the animal will finally release (Tolman, 1948, p. 192).

Tolman did not really explain how a cognitive map can develop out of a set of expectancies; but many of his predictions about the behavior of rats in mazes obviously derived from the rather vague notion that the animal's behavior is governed by a kind of "map" in the head.

Demand

What about the role of motivation? Like Hull, Tolman realized that both motivation and learning are necessary to produce behavior. In Hull's theory motivation (D) simply helps the stimulus push the response out. In Tolman's theory, however, motivation produces goals; and anticipated goals, in a sense, pull the animal toward them.

Whether or not an expectancy $S_1R_1 \rightarrow S_2$ will influence behavior, according to Tolman, depends on the *demand* for the consequence, S_2. Demand can be either positive or negative, and can vary in degree. An example of a consequence or S_2 with negative demand would be shock. If S_2 has negative demand, the animal will probably not produce R_1. If S_2 has positive demand, on the other hand, R_1 will be likely to occur. The probability of R_1 occurring will depend on the strength of the demand for S_2, as well as the demands of competing expectancies. For example, if the animal has two expectancies, $S_1R_1 \rightarrow S_2$ and $S_1R_1' \rightarrow S_2'$, and the demand for S_2' is greater than that for S_2, then R_1' will be more likely to occur than R_1. In general, the expectancy with the consequence having the most positive (or least negative) demand is the one that will control behavior.

How do demands come about? Ultimately, they arise from physiological needs. These needs lead automatically to demands for certain innately determined goals, such as the reduction of hunger or thirst. In the example of the rat in the Skinner box, hunger reduction ($S_{\overline{hr}}$) has zero demand as long as the animal is not hungry; but if it is deprived of food, the demand for S_{hr} becomes positive and that of $S_{\overline{hr}}$ becomes negative. An important principle is that demand can be passed along an expectancy chain, from the consequence of one expectancy to the consequences of the preceding links in the chain. Thus, in the hungry rat's set of expectancies, $S_1R_1 \rightarrow S_2$, $S_2R_2 \rightarrow S_f$,

$S_fR_f \rightarrow S_{hr}$, the positive demand for the goal S_{hr} induces positive demand in S_f, which in turn induces positive demand in S_2. If S_1 is present and S_2 has positive demand, R_1 will occur. In this way the first act of the sequence is elicited.

Thinking: Inference and VTE

Tolman's theory attributed to animals a rudimentary capacity for thought. One example is the process of *inference*, which derives from the fact that two beliefs with a sign and consequence that match can be chained. Chaining can occur even when the animal has not experienced the corresponding events in close succession. Suppose that on one occasion an animal learns $S_1R_1 \rightarrow S_2$, and on another occasion it learns $S_2R_2 \rightarrow S_3$. Because the expectancies resulting from these two experiences have S_2 in common, they constitute a chain: it can be telescoped as $S_1R_1 \rightarrow S_3$. Through "inference" the animal now knows how to get from S_1 to S_3, even though it has never done so before.

A second thought process, related to decision making, is represented by Tolman's concept of *vicarious trial and error* (VTE). Typically, a rat at a choice point in a maze does not simply turn one way or the other without hesitation. Instead it may pause, turn part way down one branch and return to the choice point, peer down the other branch and turn back to the choice point again, and so on—perhaps repeating this several times before making a final choice. Tolman referred to these "lookings back and forth" or "runnings back and forth" as VTE (Tolman, 1938). His notion was that the rat was sampling cues in the two branches in order to enhance the corresponding expectancies. This caution allowed the animal to experience the different outcomes in a "vicarious," or purely cognitive, way resulting in fewer overt errors. In higher animals, Tolman thought, VTE became a "mere feint at running back and forth"—the beginning of *ideation* in problem solving.

These are the essentials of Tolman's theory of learning. As we have seen, Tolman assumed that the basic unit of learning is an expectancy. The expectancy links two stimuli—the sign and the consequence—and this makes it quite different from the S–R bond. Tolman was not just a theorist. He and his students did a number of ingenious experiments contrasting his theory with S–R conceptions of the learning process. Some of their experiments will be examined in Chapter 6.

DESCRIPTIVE BEHAVIORISM: SKINNER'S SYSTEM

The chief proponent of descriptive behaviorism has been the Harvard psychologist B. F. Skinner. Descriptive behaviorists advocate that psychology study only overt behavior and the conditions under which it occurs—renouncing explanatory theories, such as those of Pavlov, Hull, and Tolman, which hypothesize psychological mechanisms (for example, irradiation, habit strength, and expectancy) that cannot be directly observed. A descriptive behaviorist does not propose fanciful causes of behavior inside the animal's nervous system or mind; he attempts to restrict himself to reporting what is observed.

The position of descriptive behaviorism has been characterized as "anti-theory." Indeed, Skinner (1950) entitled one of his most provocative articles "Are theories of learning necessary?" His answer was that they are not; and he further suggested that they may be harmful, in that they entice experimenters into relatively unproductive research directed toward the testing of hypotheses, rather than the gathering of important new facts. In truth, Skinner does not oppose all psychological theories, but only *explanatory* ones. He and his followers have themselves developed a theory of a different sort—a purely *descriptive* theory, which makes no claims to explanation.

The "theory" produced by descriptive behaviorism is a set of laws relating input (experimental manipulations) to output (behavior). There is no speculation about the inner workings of the device that transforms input into output; there are only descriptions of the device's effects. Some have characterized this approach as one that treats the organism as a "black box." From the standpoint of the theory itself, the organism is "empty." No reference is made to events, either mechanistic or mentalistic, inside the animal's head. (This does not mean that Skinner denies that the immediate causes of behavior are inside the animal's head. Knowing their nature, he says, would be very helpful. However, their nature is for the physiologist to discover, not for the psychologist to infer from behavioral experiments.)

What is the advantage of a purely descriptive study of behavior? Skinner feels that hypothesizing an inner determinant of behavior such as a purpose or an instinct suggests that the search for the cause of the behavior is at an end. In fact, he claims, our understanding is complete only when we have discovered the ultimate causes of the behavior in the present and past environments of the organism. Since explanatory theories locate the causes of behavior in the animal's nervous system or mind, where they cannot be observed, their solution to the mystery is only an illusory one. A true science or behavior can exist, in Skinner's view, only when the practice of explanatory theorizing is abandoned.

> We can follow the path taken by physics and biology by turning directly to the relation between behavior and environment and neglecting supposed mediating states of mind. Physics did not advance by looking more closely at the jubilance of a falling body, or biology by looking at the nature of vital spirits, and we do not need to try to discover what personalities, states of mind, feelings, traits of character, plans, purposes, intentions, or other perquisites of autonomous man really are in order to get on with a scientific analysis of behavior (Skinner, 1971, p. 15).

Thus, according to this point of view, only a theory that traces the origins of behavior to observable environmental conditions constitutes a truly scientific understanding of that behavior. Such a theory will tell us how the behavior can be controlled, and control, Skinner feels, is the only meaningful test of whether the causes of behavior are understood.

The causes of behavior are to be sought at two levels: (1) in the past history of the individual organism—especially its history of reinforcement, and (2) in the past history of the species—particularly its history of selective adaptation to the environment. The first is responsible for the repertoire of behavior acquired during the individual's lifetime, and the second for the genetically determined predispositions inherited by the individual from its ancestors. Skinner has aimed his own program of research at the first of these levels, for the obvious reason that at the second level very few of the determinants of behavior can actually be observed. Any guesses about what the past history of the species must have been are no less speculative or fanciful than guesses regarding unseen causes of behavior inside the animal's head.

If the researcher is not to develop and test hypotheses, just what course is he to follow? Skinner plainly feels that the ideal strategy is one of empirical discovery. Through sharp observation, the researcher notices apparent relationships between environmental events and behavior. These relationships are then subjected to careful experimental analysis. If they prove to be regular and lawful, they become part of the established knowledge of the field. The type of "theory" advocated by descriptive behaviorism, then, is a system of empirically

determined laws. Ideally, such a system will contain only true statements, since all the laws must be confirmed by experiment before
being admitted to the system.

That is the ideal. However, one can be certain only of the truth of
the particular experimental observations that have been made—for
example, that a particular white rat in a particular apparatus on a
certain day at a certain time, subjected to a particular set of manipulations, behaved in a certain way. Even if the experiment is repeated
many times, one can only say with certainty that the particular animals
tested exhibited that particular behavior. But experimental observations are of scientific value only if they are taken as examples of more
general phenomena—that is, as illustrations of scientific laws. When
one treats particular observations as illustrations of general laws, however, one runs the risk of including untrue statements in his system.
The problem of reasoning from particular observations to general
laws is called the *problem of induction*. It is a problem because a law may
not hold in all the situations where it is assumed to apply. Thus, the
difficulty is in deciding how general the lawful relationship really is.
Does the finding hold for all white rats, or just those raised in a
particular way? Does it hold for all rodents? All mammals? Does it
hold for motivating conditions other than hunger? For measures of
behavior other than those used in the particular experiments that
have already been done? Does it hold for times of the day or seasons of
the year other than those during which the testing was done?

Someone obsessively concerned with the difficulties inherent in the
problem of induction, of course, could never become a scientist; for
induction—the process of arguing from specific findings to general
principles—is the essence of scientific knowledge. Skinner has been
criticized, however, for generalizing too widely. His experimental
work has primarily concerned bar-pressing by hungry white rats and
key-pecking by hungry pigeons, isolated in small experimental cham-
bers and rewarded with food for their efforts. Yet he describes his
findings as *general* laws of behavior. And he has not hesitated to draw
from them numerous implications regarding human behavior, including even the use of language, and behavior in complex social and
cultural situations seemingly far removed from the Skinner box.
Thus, while Skinner has been vehemently opposed to inferences of
one kind—to events occurring inside the animal's nervous system—he
has had few qualms about inferences of another kind—to behaviors,
organisms, and situations very different from those providing the ex-

perimental support on which the behavioral laws rest. Of course such a strategy can be justly criticized only if it often leads to generalizations that are incorrect. The problems of reasoning from animal experiments to human behavior is an important one; and it will be considered in more detail in Chapter 7.

Construction of the System

Skinner's original goal, described in his 1938 book *The Behavior of Organisms*, was to develop a *functional analysis of behavior*. This was to be a set of empirically derived rules, discovered through experimentation, relating experimental manipulations to their effects on behavior. The system was envisioned as a means not only of describing behavior, but also of controlling it. If one wanted to make an animal behave in a certain way, he could do so by applying the rules of the system in an appropriate fashion. The rules were to be stated formally—that is, in a logical and unambiguous form. Eventually, it was hoped, mathematical expression of the rules would be possible.

A beginning was made in the direction of a formal system in the 1938 book, in which were stated twenty-four "laws of behavior." Skinner's system has changed since then, with some of the original laws abandoned and important new principles added. However, Skinner has not presented a formal restatement of his system. The main concern of his recent writings—including a book with the promising title *Contingencies of Reinforcement: A Theoretical Analysis* (Skinner, 1969)—has been a rather questionable extrapolation of principles of operant conditioning to the complex social behavior of humans. Whatever the reason for Skinner's failure to provide us with a formal restatement of his system, we have only the 1938 book to rely on for examples of the type of empirically derived rules he once envisioned as the end product of a science of behavior. Let us examine some of those rules.

Classes of Events

Skinner's analysis (1938) begins with two basic classes of events: *stimuli* and *responses*. A stimulus is defined as a part or a change in a part of the environment, having an effect on behavior. A response is defined as behavior that is correlated with a stimulus. Thus by definition, stimuli and responses are interrelated events. A crucial role is played by a subclass of stimuli called reinforcing stimuli, or simply *reinforcers*.

If the experimenter knows that a given stimulus is a reinforcer, he can control an animal's behavior by manipulating the conditions under which the stimulus is presented. A very important manipulation is to simply withhold a reinforcer, or to sharply limit the animal's access to it, for a period of time. Such a manipulation defines a level of *deprivation*. By directly describing conditions of deprivation, the experimenter can avoid using terms such as hunger or thirst (which are unobservable states of the organism). He refers only to directly measurable environmental events, such as the passage of time since feeding.

There are two general types of responses in Skinner's system, defined according to the effects of certain experimental manipulations. A response that is elicited by onset or offset of a stimulus is called a *respondent*. A response that is emitted by the organism in the absence of an identifiable eliciting stimulus (that is, a response that is not elicited reflexively by onset or offset of a stimulus) is called an *operant*. The distinction between respondents and operants is important in Skinner's system, because the laws of conditioning differ for the two types of response.

Lawful Relationships Among Events

The *law of respondent conditioning* was stated by Skinner (1938) as follows:

> 1. The approximately simultaneous presentation of two stimuli, one of which (the "reinforcing" stimulus) belongs to a reflex existing at the moment at some strength, may produce an increase in the strength of a third reflex composed of the response of the reinforcing reflex and the other stimulus.

Notice that this law simply describes the experimental operations for producing classical or Pavlovian conditioning. The two stimuli are the CS and UCS or reinforcing stimulus, and the "third reflex" is that linking the CS and CR. Skinner calls this type of conditioning respondent conditioning. The *law of respondent extinction* is:

> 2. If the reflex strengthened through [respondent conditioning] is elicited without presentation of the reinforcing stimulus, its strength decreases.

In addition to these two laws concerning respondents, Skinner (1938) presented a number of others based primarily on Pavlov's work. They need not be presented here.

The *law of operant conditioning* is:

> 3. If the occurrence of an operant is followed by presentation of a reinforcing stimulus, the strength is increased.

And the *law of operant extinction* is:

> 4. If the occurrence of an operant already strengthened through conditioning is not followed by the reinforcing stimulus, the strength is decreased.

The term "strength," where operant behavior is concerned, is usually translated as response rate. The two preceding laws (3 and 4) simply describe results such as those shown in parts a and b of Figure 4.10.

It is an interesting historical fact that something Skinner called the *reflex reserve* played an important role in his 1938 system. Reinforcement of an operant was said to produce a certain number of "potential responses," which were then exhausted during extinction. The concept of the reflex reserve was used to explain a number of findings. It was obviously not just a descriptive concept, however, since the "reserve" could not be observed directly. Skinner later explicitly discarded this notion, declaring that it was not very fruitful. A more important reason for abandoning the concept of the reflex reserve was the fact that it violated his philosophy of how psychology should proceed: the focus of interest should be on describing input–output relationships, not on developing hypotheses about intermediary events.

The four laws of behavior presented above give us some idea of what a purely descriptive theory of behavior would be like. The primary advantage of such formal rules, according to Skinner, is that they tell us how behavior can be controlled. Knowledge of such laws should enable one to change behavior without understanding the internal workings—either real or hypothetical—of the nervous system. To increase the tendency of a response to occur in a given situation, one must (a) decide whether the behavior is a respondent or an operant (by determining which definition fits) and (b) find a convenient reinforcing stimulus. (Whether or not a stimulus is a reinforcer is determined by observing its effects on behavior.) Armed with this knowledge and the laws of conditioning, one then can bring about the desired behavior change by following the appropriate rules.

Other Skinnerian Concepts

In addition to clarifying the distinction between classical (respondent) and instrumental (operant) conditioning, Skinner's system has contributed to the psychology of learning in a number of ways. Among the topics discussed in Chapter 4 which are part of Skinner's system are the distinction between *positive and negative reinforcers*, the analysis of the roles of *discriminative stimuli* (S^D and S^Δ) in controlling behavior, and the investigation of various *reinforcement schedules*. Three other important concepts attributed to Skinner, which were not discussed in Chapter 4, are *shaping*, *chaining*, and *superstitious behavior*. Let us consider them next.

In the instrumental and operant conditioning paradigms, the response must occur before it can be reinforced. This fact somewhat limits the variety of responses that can be trained using these paradigms. However, the limitation is not nearly as confining as it may at first appear. If the animal emits a response even remotely resembling the desired behavior, then a technique Skinner calls *shaping* can be used to bring the desired behavior about. Shaping is an art that must be acquired through practice, but the basic idea is simple enough. Beginning with the original response, one can gradually change its form by successively reinforcing closer and closer approximations to the response one wants the animal to make. In teaching a dog to roll over, for example, one should first reward the dog for sitting, then for lying down, then for lying on its side, and so on. If the changes in the required behavior are small enough, then at each stage of training the response one wishes to reward will be likely to occur simply as a variation of the response rewarded in the previous stage. In this way the original behavior is shaped into the new, desired form.

Response chaining could be considered a special case of shaping. Here the desired behavior is more complex, but it can be analyzed into a series of fairly well-defined responses. In response chaining, one first trains the animal to perform the final act in the desired sequence. This response should be followed immediately by reinforcement. Once the final response has been established, the opportunity to perform it (and receive reward) is made contingent on the next-to-last response in the chain. This principle is applied repeatedly, and the response chain is gradually built up. To establish the response chain R_a–R_b–R_c–R_d, for example, the successive stages are:

R_d–reinforcement
R_c–R_d–reinforcement

R_b–R_c–R_d–reinforcement

R_a–R_b–R_c–R_d–reinforcement

Response chains established in this way can be quite complex; Skinner has described an experiment in which a rat was taught to pull a string releasing a marble from a rack, pick the marble up and carry it in its forepaws to a tube, and drop the marble into the tube. Such chains are frequently developed in training animals to perform at circuses and fairs.

Suppose the feeder mechanism of a Skinner box is wired directly to a clock, so that reinforcers occur repeatedly at a certain interval—say once every minute. Reinforcement, in this situation, does not depend in any way on what the animal does. (For this reason, this does *not* qualify as a fixed-interval schedule, in which the animal must make a particular response in order to receive reinforcement.) One might expect the animal to learn nothing in such a situation, since no behavior is required to produce the reward. According to Skinner's (1948) description, however, what happens is quite different. Just by chance, some behavior must precede the first reward, and the effect of the reward is to increase the strength of that behavior. This makes it more likely that the behavior will occur again, and if it occurs just before the next reward, its strength will be increased still further. Eventually, purely by "accident," the animal may come to spend a great deal of time engaging in a particular, stereotyped behavior. Skinner calls this phenomenon *superstitious behavior,* suggesting that human superstitions may be learned in much the same way. The importance of this demonstration, however, is that it appears to show that reinforcement has a "blind", or automatic, effect on behavior. The response preceding the reward is strengthened even though there is no real causal connection between the two (a quite different analysis of the superstition experiment is given in Chapter 7).

Applications

Of psychologists studying learning and memory, Skinner has been the leading advocate of the application of laboratory discoveries to the solution of problems in the "real world." In part, this emphasis stems from his opposition to explanatory theories. If asked about the solution of some complex problem in psychotherapy or education, the typical learning theorist is likely to reply that an answer cannot be given until some basic problems concerning the nature of learning have been solved; that premature guesses are unlikely to be helpful;

and that only when we have a reasonably accurate theoretical understanding of the causes of behavior will we be ready to apply our
knowledge to the complex setting outside the laboratory. Contrast this
view with Skinner's assertion that the functional analysis of behavior
has already discovered many fundamental laws of behavior which can
and should be applied. In Skinner's view, psychologists should not
waste time inventing and testing theoretical notions and quarreling
about which theory is right; instead, they should be expanding our
knowledge of behavior and applying it to important practical
problems.

Skinner's leadership in applied research has been impressive. Skinner has written books and articles on the technology of teaching
(1968), the treatment of psychoses (1961), and the training of animals
(1951). Certainly one of the most unusual examples of applied psychological research is a classified Defense Department project Skinner
began during World War II. The goal of the project, called Project
Pigeon or ORCON (an acronym for "organic control"), was to develop
a guided missile. The problem was that electronic guidance systems
available at that time were unreliable, and too bulky to fit into existing
missiles. Skinner's ingenious scheme was to use pigeons, which were
neither bulky nor unreliable, as pilots. A system of lenses in the nose
of the missile was to project an image of the scene ahead on a
translucent screen in front of the pigeon. The bird was to be trained to
peck at certain targets (for example, the image of an enemy ship).
Whenever the bird pecked the screen a sensing device was to send a
report of the location of the peck to the guidance system of the missile,
which would alter the course as much as necessary to direct the craft
toward the target. Project Pigeon, now declassified, never became op-
erational, partly because of the increasing sophistication of electronic
guidance devices, which eliminated the need for the feathered pilots.
Skinner's (1960) account of the project, however, hints that Defense
Department officials' prejudice against pigeons may have also contributed to the project's demise.

Most applications of behavior technology that Skinner has advocated have been less bizarre. His practical orientation has been particularly popular in education and psychotherapy. There is even a
journal (the *Journal of Applied Behavior Analysis*) almost exclusively devoted to reports of applied "Skinnerian" research. Some of the applications growing out of the Skinnerian tradition will be considered,
with an eye toward what they tell us about the nature of learning, in
Chapter 7.

A COMPARISON OF THEORIES

The theories of Hull, Tolman, and Skinner differ in a number of important ways. First, they differ regarding the conditions that are assumed to be necessary for learning. All three agree that temporal contiguity is necessary (whether between stimuli or between stimulus and response); but Hull and Skinner go further and specify that reinforcement is necessary as well. Hull identifies reinforcement with reduction of a primary drive, while Skinner defines reinforcement only in terms of its effects on behavior. In Tolman's theory, expectancies can be built up even in the absence of reinforcement; thus only contiguity is necessary for learning to occur. For this reason, Tolman's theory is classified as a *contiguity* theory, while the systems of Hull and Skinner are called *reinforcement* theories.

Second, the theories differ in their answers to the question, what is learned? For Hull, an S–R bond is learned. In the presence of a drive state, the bond becomes ready to conduct energy from the stimulus to the response. The degree to which it does so depends on the strength of the habit or S–R bond. Skinner's position is much the same, except that the terms bond, association, and habit, referring to hypothetical events in the nervous system, are not used. For Skinner, what is learned is a tendency to behave in a particular way in a particular situation. Again, Tolman's position differs most. For Tolman, $S_1 \rightarrow S_2$ and $S_1 R_1 \rightarrow S_2$ expectancies are learned. Learning of S–S relationships can take place in the absence of any overt response; and behavior is "purposive," in that it is determined not only by the current stimulus situation, but also by its anticipated effects.

Third, the theories differ with regard to the distinction between classical and instrumental, or operant, conditioning. Hull's theory makes no distinction. Both kinds of conditioning are assumed to involve an increase in strength of an S–R bond whenever it is exercised in close proximity to reinforcement. Whether reinforcement occurs before the response (as in classical conditioning) or after it (as in instrumental conditioning) makes little difference.

Skinner's theory, concentrating as it does on experimental manipulations, draws a sharp distinction. Classical conditioning (which he calls respondent conditioning) is based on stimulus–reinforcement contingencies, while instrumental, or operant, conditioning is based on response–reinforcement contingencies. Skinner even suggested at one time that the two types of conditioning might involve different parts of the nervous system. Respondents, it was hypothesized, were responses of the viscera, controlled by the autonomic nervous system, while operants involved movements of the trunk, head, and limbs, under control of the skeletal nervous system.

In Tolman's theory, classical and instrumental conditioning can be related to the two types of expectancy. The Pavlovian situation reflects an $S_1 \to S_2$ expectancy; the dog salivates to the bell because it expects food. The CR occurs in "anticipation" of or in preparation for the UCS. Instrumental conditioning reflects an $S_1R_1 \to S_2$ expectancy; the animal produces R_1 in order to achieve S_2, the anticipated consequence of the act.

Fourth, the theories differ in their treatment of secondary reinforcement. For Skinner, secondary reinforcement is just a fact of behavior like any other, and can be fit into the system through addition of an appropriate law. Skinner prefers the term "conditioned reinforcement," which is descriptive of how secondary reinforcers are produced.

Hull attempted to relate reinforcement to drive reduction, and so to his theory secondary reinforcement, which involves no obvious drive reduction, was something of an embarrassment. Secondary *negative* reinforcement can be explained by assuming that what is rewarding is the reduction of a fear drive; some evidence for this position was provided by Miller (1948). But what about secondary *positive* reinforcement? Is it plausible to assume that a stimulus previously associated with drive reduction has itself acquired the power to reduce the drive? (Are we less hungry in the dining room than in the living room, where we seldom eat?) Several experimenters attempted to show that a stimulus previously paired with food reduced an animal's hunger, but the hypothesis was not supported. Thus Hull (1943) dealt with secondary reinforcement not by explaining it in terms of other postulates of his theory, but by adding a separate postulate describing the elementary facts of secondary reinforcement.

Tolman's theory appears to explain secondary reinforcement in a natural way. A rat will run to a goal box where food was previously found because it expects to find food there; it will learn to press a lever to turn off a tone previously associated with shock because it expects the tone to be followed by shock. Thus, secondary reinforcement, like classical conditioning, is accounted for by $S_1 \to S_2$ expectancies; no special treatment of the phenomenon is needed.

Finally, of course, there is the difference in basic philosophy underlying the three theories. Hull's preference was for an explanatory theory, modeled after Newtonian physics, specifying the principles of operation of the machine in the head. Tolman's approach was to develop an explanatory theory that made use of his intuitive understanding of the causes of behavior: purposes, expectancies, and general knowledge of what leads to what. Skinner feels that explanatory theories referring to hypothetical processes in the head are a waste of time and effort. In his view, psychologists should approach behavior from a purely descriptive point of view, with the aim of developing a system of empirical laws relating behavior to past and present manipulations of the environment.

6

Theoretical Issues in Conditioning

In psychology, as in other disciplines, research tends to focus on particular theoretical issues. Some of these issues, of course, are of more fundamental importance than others—and it is primarily these questions that are able to hold the interest of the research community over long periods of time. This chapter discusses three questions of traditional concern to learning theorists. First: Do classical and instrumental conditioning represent two basically different types of learning, or are they fundamentally the same? Second: Is contiguity a sufficient condition for learning to occur, or is reinforcement also necessary? Third: What is learned—expectancies or S–R bonds?

CLASSICAL AND INSTRUMENTAL CONDITIONING

In Chapter 4 we saw that the procedures for producing classical conditioning, on the one hand, and instrumental or operant conditioning, on the other, differ in one important respect. In classical conditioning, the reinforcer (the UCS) occurs regardless of whether the experimental subject makes a response. Presentation of the UCS is contingent only on occurrence of the CS. In instrumental or operant conditioning, reinforcement occurs only if the organism has made the required response. This is a difference in procedure. The question that has interested learning theorists is this: Are classical and instrumental conditioning just two slightly different ways of training an organ-

120

ism to make a particular response in a particular situation, or is there some more fundamental difference between them?

This problem is usually approached by noting that the responses used in classical conditioning experiments typically are different from those trained by instrumental conditioning. Is there some characteristic of a response that would allow an investigator to tell beforehand which training procedure would bring it under experimental control? Alternatively, given a demonstration of learned behavior, is there some way an investigator could determine which conditioning procedure was used to establish it?

Elicited Versus Emitted Responses

One distinction was proposed by Skinner (1938). As we saw in Chapter 5, he defined two kinds of responses: respondents, which are elicited reflexively by stimuli, and operants, which are not. The classical (or respondent) conditioning procedure, he maintained, could be applied only to the first type of response, and the instrumental (or operant) procedure only to the second. In drawing this distinction, Skinner was appealing to direct observation. The occurrence of a respondent appeared always to follow closely an identifiable eliciting stimulus. In the case of an operant, no eliciting stimulus could be observed.

Let us compare discrimination learning in the classical and operant conditioning situations. In classical discrimination conditioning, the CS+ (the signal that the UCS is about to occur) triggers a response, while the CS− (which signals no UCS) does not. In operant discriminative conditioning, the S^D (which signals that reward is available) results in responding, while the S^Δ (which signals no reward) does not. These two situations seem quite similar. Nevertheless, Skinner pointed out, in the classical procedure there is a direct temporal relationship between onset of the CS+ and occurrence of the response. The CS+ appears to *elicit* the response. In the operant situation, in contrast, there is no direct relationship in time between onset of the S^D and occurrence of the response. The S^D is simply the occasion for the organism to *emit* the response. Thus, the two types of behavior can be thought of as elicited and emitted, respectively. Other theorists have used the less precise (and suspiciously mentalistic) terms *involuntary* and *voluntary* to make the same point. In classical conditioning, the response is directly correlated with occurrence of the CS, and appears to be an involuntary reflex. In operant conditioning, the behavior appears to be more spontaneous, and hence appears voluntary.

Is the elicited versus emitted distinction a valid means of differentiating classical and instrumental conditioning? In general, it seems to work quite well. Responses that are typically trained by classical conditioning (for example, salivation, the eye blink, sweating of the palms) tend to be triggered reflexively by particular stimuli. Those that are trained by instrumental methods (for example, running, bar-pressing, pecking) appear to be emitted spontaneously by the animal. However, one can find cases in which the distinction breaks down.

Consider the case of temporal conditioning. Recall that Pavlov fed a dog at regular intervals (say once every 5 minutes), and the dog soon came to salivate regularly, on schedule, just before being fed. Responses other than salivation can also be trained in this way. Soviet psychologists have explored a number of variations of the temporal conditioning technique. In one of the few papers on this subject that has been translated into English, Dmitriev and Kochigina (1959) described the acquisition of the paw flexion response in dogs, in a situation in which shocks to the forepaw occurred regularly at 5-minute intervals. Early in training, flexion responses occur frequently, all during the 5-minute interval between one shock and the next. Later in training, the responses tend to occur only near the end of the interval, just prior to the next shock. Data from a typical 5-minute interstimulus interval, at an intermediate stage of training, are shown in Figure 6.1. These data have been redrawn from the original report, in the form of a cumulative record. Following the shock terminating one 5-minute interval, there were no leg flexions for about 2.5 minutes. Then responses began to occur. Their rate increased as the end of the interval approached.

The reader should compare the "scallop" of this curve with the scallops produced by an operant fixed-interval schedule (Figure 4.11). In both cases, the response rate is very low immediately following reinforcement (or UCS) and then increases as the next reinforcement becomes imminent. In fact, given just the cumulative curve of Figure 6.1, an investigator would have no way of knowing that the training procedure was classical temporal conditioning rather than an operant fixed-interval schedule.

The important point is this: In temporal conditioning, no eliciting stimulus can be identified. The responses, which (in Figure 6.1) begin

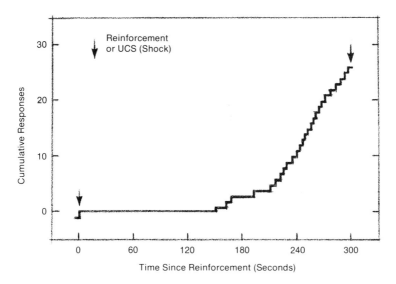

Figure 6.1 Cumulative record of the paw flexion response in classical conditioning. The dog's paw is shocked every 300 seconds. [Adapted from Dmitriev and Kochigina, 1959.]

to occur in the middle of the interval, are emitted by the organism in a seemingly spontaneous fashion. If one wants to call operant responses emitted or voluntary because of the absence of an identifiable eliciting stimulus, then in order to be consistent one must call responses trained by temporal classical conditioning emitted or voluntary, as well. Thus, while Skinner's proposal that respondents are elicited and operants are emitted works fairly well as a rule of thumb, it cannot be applied rigidly to distinguish respondents from operants. There are exceptions to the rule.

The similarity between the temporal conditioning data of Figure 6.1 and the typical fixed-interval scallop suggests that the animal may be learning something similar in the two situations—perhaps something to do with the time interval itself. Evidence from a study by Trapold, Carlson, and Myers (1965) suggests that this is the case. These researchers trained three groups of rats in a two-stage experiment. In the first stage, the three groups received different training. One group of rats was fed regularly in a Skinner box, once every 2 minutes, in 12 daily sessions; feeding was *not* contingent on any response. This, of course, is the classical temporal conditioning procedure. A second group was fed the same number of times, but on a random, rather than a regular, schedule. The third group—the control group—was not given any special training. Then, in stage two, all three groups of animals were trained on an operant fixed-interval 2-minute schedule, with feeding contingent on the bar-press response. All the rats acquired the fixed-interval scallop, but those initially given 2-minute temporal conditioning training learned it more rapidly than the others. This demonstration of *transfer* of learning from the classical to the operant situation indicates a common component. Apparently, if the mechanisms underlying the two types of conditioning differ at all, they are not completely separate. If they were, such transfer would not occur.

Autonomic Versus Somatic Control

A second distinction between responses that can be classically and instrumentally conditioned was first proposed by Stefan Miller and Jerzy Konorski (1928) and was later adopted by Skinner (1938, 1953). It is to Skinner that the distinction is usually attributed. The notion is that different parts of the nervous system might be involved in the two types of conditioning.

The nervous system is known to consist of two parts which are to some extent independent of one another, both anatomically and functionally. One part, the *somatic nervous system,* controls motions of our skeletal muscles. Our interactions with the external environment require the use of these muscles. They are largely under voluntary control, and when we are asleep they exhibit little activity. The other part of the nervous system controls the activity of our glands and the muscles of our internal organs—responses such as increases and decreases in heart rate, constriction and dilation of blood vessels, secretions of the digestive glands, and so on. It does not require conscious control, and functions perfectly well even when we are asleep. For this reason it is thought of as "autonomous," and has been named the *autonomic nervous system.*

A quick glance at lists of responses that have been classically and instrumentally conditioned in the laboratory suggests the distinction that occurred to Miller and Konorski (1928). Running, lever-pressing, rope-pulling, and key-pecking are all typical instrumental responses, and they all are under the somatic nervous system's control. Salivating, sweating, and fear responses (such as an increase in heart rate) are typical classically conditioned responses, and are controlled by the autonomic nervous system. Does this mean that the somatic nervous system learns according to the laws of instrumental conditioning and the autonomic nervous system according to the laws of classical conditioning? Unfortunately such a rule will not work. We know that skeletal responses such as leg flexion, the knee jerk, and the eye blink can be classically conditioned; therefore the relationship cannot be quite so simple.

The notion popularized by Skinner was that the somatic nervous system is capable of both classical and instrumental conditioning, while the autonomic nervous system is subject only to classical conditioning. When one considers the functions of the two systems, this seems reasonable enough. Our internal organs do not act directly on the environment to produce rewards. Therefore, there is no apparent need for them to be instrumentally conditioned. In fact, it is easy to imagine that such conditioning could be harmful. The autonomic nervous system controls our internal environment, and must maintain the proper balance and coordination of various internal functions. If the many responses of the autonomic nervous system could be increased or decreased by accidental reinforcement contingencies, the coordination of our internal organs would be difficult to maintain. It is reasonable, on the other hand, for our internal organs to be subject to classical conditioning. A stimulus that signals food can begin the internal processes necessary for digestion. One that signals an aversive stimulus can trigger preparation of the body for flight.

The hypothesis that instrumental conditioning of autonomic responses is impossible was supported by failures in a few early experiments. Apparently these failures, together with the plausible argument that autonomic responses are not ordinarily instrumental in obtaining reward, convinced nearly everyone. Instrumental control of autonomic responses became a dead issue, and it was not revived until the early 1960s.

The studies that revived interest in the issue used human subjects, training them to increase or decrease sweating of the palms (the galvanic skin response, or GSR) for "rewards." Fowler and Kimmel (1962), for example, found that subjects whose GSR increases were reinforced by onset of a flashing light raised the magnitude of their GSR's. Other investigators reported successful attempts to instrumentally condition human heart rate; and still others reported that instrumental conditioning could be used to raise or lower blood pressure.

But there is an important question about such demonstrations, which is difficult to answer adequately when human subjects are used. The question is, are the autonomic responses being conditioned directly, or are the subjects "cheating"—that is, using skeletal responses or cognitive activity to exert indirect control? A subject might learn to indirectly control his blood pressure, for example, by rapidly tensing and untensing his muscles (a skeletal response). In an adequate experiment on human subjects, therefore, a variety of skeletal responses must be monitored to insure that observed autonomic changes are not the result of voluntary activity of the somatic nervous system. The problem of cognitive control is even more difficult to deal with. A subject might learn to increase his GSR by imagining himself being chased by a horrible monster, or to increase his heart rate by thinking about sex. It is virtually impossible to do experiments on instrumental conditioning of autonomic responses in human subjects that cannot be explained in terms of cognitive control.

Experimentation has been aided, however, by the recent use of drugs of the curare family, which have the interesting property of interfering with the chemical transmitters that communicate nerve impulses to the skeletal muscles. Various uses have been found for these drugs in different cultures. South American Indian tribes used to dip their arrows in curare, enabling them to paralyze a victim with even an indirect hit. What makes curare useful for modern psychological researchers, however, is the additional fact that it does not interfere with autonomic responses. A curarized animal cannot make skeletal responses, but its autonomic functions are unimpaired. Humans who have been curarized report having been fully conscious the whole time; they are able to solve problems and remember the answers later, after the drug wears off (Leuba, Birch, and Appleton, 1968). The selective interference of curare with skeletal responses makes it possible to investigate instrumental conditioning of autonomic responses in an animal that cannot "cheat" by increasing or decreasing the rate of a skeletal response that, in turn, affects autonomic activity.

A number of experimental reports from the laboratory of N. E. Miller, at Rockefeller University, have claimed to demonstrate the instrumental conditioning of autonomic responses in curarized rats.

In a remarkable series of experiments, rats were apparently trained to increase or decrease their heart rates, to increase or decrease rate of urine formation in the kidney, to dilate or constrict the blood vessels of the tail, and to dilate the blood vessels of one ear while constricting those of the other ear—all for reinforcement by electrical stimulation of the brain. In another experiment, curarized rats learned to increase or decrease their blood pressure, independent of heart rate, in order to avoid an electrical shock. These experiments have been reviewed in two papers by Miller (1969) and DiCara (1970). Both papers speculate on possible applications of autonomic conditioning to medicine. A bold new era is envisioned, in which heart patients voluntarily control irregular heart beats, epileptics detect and inhibit abnormal brain rhythms to prevent convulsions, and everyone can reduce his blood pressure at will. Unfortunately, recent attempts to replicate the findings of the curarized rat experiments have failed (Miller and Dworkin, 1974). The most dramatic evidence in favor of instrumental conditioning of autonomic responses should not be accepted unquestionably until the reasons for this failure are known.

Where does this leave the question of instrumental conditioning of autonomic responses? The evidence just reviewed is not convincing, because of problems in eliminating skeletal or cognitive control in the studies on human subjects, and because of failures to replicate in the studies on curarized rats. There is still other evidence, however, that argues for such conditioning. Shapiro and Herendeen (1975) have reported that dogs can be trained to inhibit salivation in order to be fed. In stage one of the experiments, the dogs were classically conditioned to salivate at the sound of a tone. Then, in stage two, in order to receive food they had to keep their mouths dry for a specified period of time following the tone. If the previously conditioned salivary response occurred during that period, the food was withheld. Under this contingency, the number of trials on which salivation occurred dropped to about 20 percent. Such a decrease in salivation might simply be due to extinction, of course, since during stage two the tone often was not followed by food. However, an "extinction" control group eliminated this interpretation. Food was withheld from the control animals, in stage two, on just as many trials as it was from the experimental animals. The only difference between the experimental and control groups was that the former received reinforcement about 80 percent of the time, contingent on the nonoccurrence of salivation, while the control group received it on 80 percent of the trials regardless of whether salivation occurred. Performance of the control group showed very little extinction of the classically conditioned response. Apparently, then, it was the contingency between not salivating and being fed that decreased the rate of salivation in the experimental dogs. The inhibition of salivation was under instrumental control.

In addition to this experimental evidence, we may cite an observation of everyday life. Urination is controlled by the urethral sphincters, which are innervated by the autonomic nervous system. The fact that children can be toilet trained and pets can be housebroken suggests that this autonomic response can be brought under instrumental control. And Lapides, Sweet, and Lewis (1957) have reported that human subjects paralyzed with curare are able to initiate and stop urination on command, nearly as well as before paralysis. Thus urination, like salivation, appears to be a response of the autonomic nervous system that can be instrumentally controlled.

Biofeedback and "Alpha Control"

The general technique of electronically monitoring some bodily activity of which a person is normally unaware, and reproducing the recorded activity as sounds or other signals the person can easily perceive, has been given the name *biofeedback*. The rationale of biofeedback research is to enable the subject to monitor unconscious processes and bring them under voluntary control. The use of biofeedback to permit a human subject to bring the electrical activity of his brain under conscious control has been an offshoot of the research on autonomic conditioning.

In a paper presented at the annual meeting of the Western Psychological Association in 1962, Kamiya (1962) described an experiment in which a tone was sounded as feedback to a subject whenever "alpha waves"—changes in electrical potential of about 8 to 12 cycles per second—were detected in his EEG record. With a little practice, Kamiya's subjects were able to produce alpha, to sound the tone—or nonalpha, to turn it off—according to instructions. Alpha waves have been related to a calm, contemplative, relaxed state of mind, and they are reportedly characteristic of meditative states in practicioners of Zen and Yoga.

Kamiya's report and others that followed gave rise to a fad, fueled by interest in meditation and promoted by electronics firms offering "biofeedback" gadgets for sale to the general public. The wave of enthusiasm caught up a few trained scientists, as well as many laymen. The following passages, taken from a book on popular psychology, are representative of the extreme claims that have been made:

> It is difficult to capture on paper the sense of exhilaration felt by the person who, through biofeedback training, is able to master his body through his own power. All his life he has been taught he cannot control his "involuntary" nervous system. All his life he has been encouraged to "let the pill do the job" or "go ask Mr. Jones for the answer." All his life his capacity to control his own body, his own mind, his own fate has been challenged, deprecated, even ridiculed. And then, suddenly, there he is controlling his own nervous system, a man on his own magical mastery tour. "My God, I really did it by myself, didn't I?" one patient proudly announced after she had learned to control her own nervous system. "Yes," answered the doctor, "and that's the beauty of it." . . . If self-determination is to survive and prosper, people must come to believe—not merely hope or wish—that man is more than a biological automaton, that he is capable of controlling himself, by himself and for himself. People must believe that man has the intuitive wisdom to move in ways that are beneficial both for himself and for others. Biofeedback research is an important scientific enterprise because it is validating these optimistic beliefs with empirical evidence. Even if biofeedback training does not develop as rapidly as anticipated, its value to our democracy—indeed, to the perpetuation of the free spirit everywhere—will still be incalculable (Andrews and Karlins, 1975, pp. 66–67).

More sober analyses have been slow to develop—but the questions they ask are central ones. How is control of alpha brought about? Does one really achieve direct control over activity of the brain? Just what is the "alpha state"? How does it differ from other "states of consciousness"?

To begin with, we must realize that the control of alpha waves is quite commonplace. Closing one's eyes and relaxing typically increases alpha activity; opening one's eyes and scanning the environment produces "alpha blocking"—that is, the replacement of the alpha waves by high-frequency beta waves. Several questions immediately arise. Can subjects, given feedback training with eyes open, increase alpha activity beyond that produced when they are relaxed, with eyes closed? Results of an experiment by Paskewitz and Orne

(1973) suggest that they cannot. Even with extended training, in that study, the production of alpha waves never went above the eyes-closed baseline. Apparently the ability to increase alpha output through feedback is rather strictly limited. The fact that alpha only approaches, but does not exceed, the optimal level under training suggests that subjects may be learning not to increase alpha, but rather to decrease the blocking of alpha.

What activities block the alpha rhythm? Mulholland and Peper (1971) have found that decreases in alpha activity are related to changes in visual control systems—that is, the tracking of stimuli in the visual field, convergence and divergence of the eyes according to distance of the object from the viewer, and accommodation or focusing of the lens. In an alpha training session, they measured these visual activities and found that they were correlated with the production and blocking of alpha waves. Mulholland and Peper (1971) concluded:

> Autoregulation of the aipha rhythm by alpha feedback is likely to be mediated by learned control of oculomotor and lens adjustment processes. However, the learner may not be aware of the mediating process (p. 574).

In other words, subjects given alpha feedback, instead of directly controlling their brain states, may be making subtle responses such as focusing and defocusing the eyes, which in turn produce changes in alpha.

So there may be nothing special about what subjects learn to do when given alpha feedback. Further, the feedback training may be completely unnecessary. In a study conducted by Beatty (1972), one group of subjects was given alpha feedback training and a second group was given "false feedback," uncorrelated with alpha production. Subjects in this second group were told the feedback would help them learn to produce an alpha state consisting of feelings of calmness, pleasant relaxation, and increased inner awareness. Subjects given false feedback, together with these instructions, produced as much alpha activity as did the subjects given standard alpha feedback training. Thus, the electronic gadgets may be completely unnecessary—in this study, a simple verbal instruction worked just as well as feedback did. Plotkin (1976) has concluded that subjects who succeed in producing alpha through a cognitive strategy do so only because their strategy involves the visual control system. Thus, attempting to relax or "look inward" may result in defocusing of the eyes, and this may increase alpha.

The relationship between alpha waves and the subjectively described alpha state has been also called into question. Walsh (1974) gave subjects alpha feedback training during which he had them describe their mental states. Some subjects were told to expect a state of calm, dreamlike contemplation. Others were told that the mental state they would experience could not be predicted exactly, but might be any of three possibilities: (a) calm, dreamlike contemplation; (b) alert hyperattention; or (c) drowsiness or dullness. Walsh found that while the two groups of subjects learned to produce alpha waves equally well, only the subjects who had been told to expect the calm, contemplative "alpha state" reliably reported that state. Thus, subjective reports of mental events during alpha activity are apparently at least partly determined by suggestion. The considerable agreement among subjects in most alpha conditioning experiments may be due to common expectations, formed prior to or during the experiments, about the mental state alpha conditioning will produce.

The enthusiasm triggered by the first experiments on alpha conditioning is giving way to a more cautious, objective point of view. This change of attitude would seem to be necessary if anything of lasting value is to result. As Neal Miller has stated:

> I deplore the exaggerated publicity in the popular press about this and other kinds of work commonly called biofeedback. I fear that such exaggerated articles are raising impossible hopes which will inevitably result in a premature disillusionment that will interfere with the hard work that is necessary and desirable to explore this new area of research (Miller and Dworkin, 1974, p. 325).

Conclusion

No doubt claims regarding the variety of responses that can be brought under instrumental control have been exaggerated in recent years. Nevertheless, urination and salivation provide two fairly clear counterexamples to the rule that autonomic responses cannot be instrumentally conditioned. The statement that instrumental conditioning is restricted to responses controlled by the somatic nervous system may be considered a useful rule of thumb, but like the rule relating classical conditioning to elicited responses and instrumental condition-ing to emitted responses, it does not hold all the time. The failure to discover any hard and fast distinction between behaviors subject to the two types of conditioning has led many investigators to suggest that the mechanisms underlying classical and instrumental conditioning may, indeed, be the same.

IS REINFORCEMENT NECESSARY FOR LEARNING?

In the last chapter we saw that one of the fundamental issues separat-ing theories of learning concerns the function of reinforcement. Learning theories fall into two categories, depending upon their stand on this issue: *Contiguity theories* hold that all that is necessary for learn-ing to occur is that two events be experienced in contiguity. *Reinforce-ment theories* maintain that while contiguity is necessary for learning, it is not sufficient. If learning is to occur, the two contiguous events must be followed or accompanied by reinforcement. Thus reinforcers—according to this view—are special events that produce learning, and when reinforcement is not present, learning will not occur. Let us examine here theoretical and experimental developments surround-ing this question: Can learning occur without reinforcement?

The first investigations of conditioning, both classical and instru-mental, demonstrated that reinforcement plays a crucial role in be-havior. Pavlov (1927) noted the importance of the UCS in the classical conditioning paradigm. It must be present if a conditioned reflex is to be established; if it is removed (the CS is presented alone) the con-ditioned reflex will extinguish. The extinguished reflex can be reestab-lished rather quickly, however, with just a few pairings of the CS and UCS. The UCS, Pavlov said, is necessary to strengthen and maintain the conditioned reflex. Pavlov referred to this process as "reinforcement."

The first instrumental conditioning experiments were those of Thorndike (1898), described in Chapter 4. Recall that Thorndike placed a hungry cat in a puzzle box, with food visible on the outside, and the cats gradually learned to perform the response necessary to escape from the box and reach the food. Thorndike assumed that the correct response gradually replaced ineffective responses because it was strengthened—an automatic effect of the reward:

The cat does not look over the situation, much less *think* it over, and then decide what to do. It bursts out at once into the activities which instinct and experience have settled on as suitable reactions to the situation *"confinement when hungry with food outside."* It does not ever in the course of its successes realize that such an act brings food and therefore decide to do it and thenceforth do it immediately from *decision* instead of impulse. The one impulse, out of many accidental ones, which leads to pleasure, becomes strengthened and stamped in thereby, and more and more firmly associated with the sense-impression of that box's interior. Accordingly it is sooner and sooner fulfilled. Futile impulses are gradually stamped out (Thorndike, 1898, p. 45. Italics original).

Later, Thorndike turned his attention to educational psychology, conducting many experiments on human learning. These experiments, Thorndike believed, further demonstrated that reward was necessary for learning, and that its effect was automatic. For both animals and humans, the most important principle of learning was what he called the *Law of Effect*, which he stated formally as follows:

> When a modifiable connection between a situation and a response is made and is accompanied or followed by a satisfying state of affairs, that connection's strength is increased: When made and followed by an annoying state of affairs, its strength is decreased (Thorndike, 1913, p. 4).

Experiments on the effects of punishment later led Thorndike to abandon the second part of this law. He concluded that punishment or annoying consequences did not weaken an S–R connection directly, but only indirectly, by strengthening competing connections (Thorndike, 1932). The first part of the Law of Effect, however—attributing the strengthening of an S–R bond to a "satisfying state of affairs"—remained intact.

When John Watson, the founder of behaviorism, presented his theory of learning, the principle of reinforcement was conspicuously absent. Why? Apparently, Watson was offended by the seemingly subjective nature of the Law of Effect as it had been stated by Thorndike. As Watson said, "[Most psychologists] believe habit formation is implanted by kind fairies. For example, Thorndike speaks of pleasure stamping in the successful movement and displeasure stamping out the unsuccessful movement" (1925, p. 206). Watson hoped to account for the different strengths of S–R bonds objectively, simply on the basis of the frequency and recency with which they had been exercised, and to do away with the notion of reinforcement altogether. Unfortunately, this approach did not even allow him to account for the elementary fact of extinction in classical conditioning. During an extinction session an S–R connection is being exercised—but repetition without the UCS decreases rather than increases its strength. Clearly, as Pavlov had realized, the crucial event here is the deletion of the reinforcer. Any adequate theory of learning must—somehow—take reinforcement into account. But no behaviorist could accept as a scientific law a statement employing mentalistic terms. Thorndike's "satisfying state of affairs" had to be replaced by some more objective, mechanistic principle. Only when this was done could the Law of Effect be incorporated into behaviorist psychology.

The Nature of Reinforcement

Clark Hull took a major step in this direction when he identified reinforcement with reduction of a physiological need. His version of the Law of Effect, often referred to as the *drive-reduction theory of reinforcement,* attracted considerable attention because it appeared to be an objective, and therefore testable, hypothesis. In addition, it fitted in well with one of the major goals of Hull's behavior theory: to describe the principles of operation of an adaptive organism. An organism that learns to do those things which lead to reduction of its physiological needs is clearly better able to adapt to new situations than one that does not.

   The basic advantage of testable assumptions is one that may seem more like a drawback—it leaves them open to possible disproof. And there are now many apparent disconfirmations of the drive-reduction theory of reinforcement. Many species of animal, for example, will perform responses to drink a saccharin-flavored solution. Saccharin is sweet-tasting, but has no nutritive value. Rats will learn to press a bar to turn a light on or to turn it off. A change of illumination fulfills no known physiological need. Monkeys will press a lever to get a brief glimpse, through a window, of another monkey or a human being. Should this be attributed to "social" or "curiosity" drives, and if so, can they realistically be considered physiological needs? Male animals will repeatedly perform responses such as maze-running for the opportunity to copulate with a female, even if never allowed to reach the point of ejaculation; and humans pay money to see erotic movies, even though such stimulation increases the sex drive rather than reducing it.

There have been other attempts to identify reinforcers by characterizing objectively what they all have in common, but these attempts have not been much more successful than drive-reduction theory. B. F. Skinner, in fact, has refused to attempt to explain why reinforcers are reinforcing. This, of course, is in keeping with his anti-theoretical bias. A reinforcer, Skinner says, is *anything that functions as such in a conditioning situation*. That is, a reinforcer is defined by what it does. A positive reinforcer is a stimulus which, if presented just after an operant response, increases the operant's strength; a negative reinforcer is a stimulus that has the same effect if removed.

To some investigators, this treatment of reinforcement is a refreshing relief from theoretical squabbling, but to others it appears to solve no problems at all. They have severely criticized Skinner's treatment of reinforcement as empty, or "circular." Here is why: if we substitute Skinner's definition of a positive reinforcer into his law of operant conditioning (his version of the Law of Effect) we obtain:

> If the occurrence of an operant is followed by presentation of [a stimulus which, if presented just after an operant response, increases its strength], the strength is increased.

This presumably all-important rule for changing behavior, restated in this way, appears trivial. It seems to tell us nothing useful at all.

The key to the problem of circularity was pointed out by Meehl (1950). Meehl noted that in order to avoid circularity one need only demonstrate that reinforcers are *trans-situational*. Thus, if you can train an appropriately deprived rat to press a bar for stimulus X, you should also be able to get it to run through a maze for it, jump over a barrier for it, roll over and play dead for it, and so on. Once you have observed that X is a reinforcer in one situation, you know of many situations in which it can be applied with predictable results. The law of operant conditioning is still a useful rule because it tells us how stimuli that have been identified as reinforcers can be used in new situations.

The trans-situationality of reinforcers has been seriously questioned in recent years. One reason is that certain relationships between behaviors and reinforcers appear to be genetically determined. Thus reinforcement may be, to some extent, situation-specific. This possibil-

ity will be discussed in Chapter 7, under the heading "biological determinants of learning."

Another difficulty with the notion of trans-situational reinforcers
has been given theoretical treatment by David Premack (1965). Reinforcement, in Premack's theory, is *a behavior that is more preferred* than
the one being reinforced. Thus, if a rat has been deprived of water, it
will run to obtain water. But if a nonthirsty rat has been deprived of
exercise, and the opportunity to run is made contingent on drinking
water, the rate of drinking will increase. Thus, the relationship between drinking and running can be reversed simply by reversing degrees of deprivation. Premack proposes that, in order to determine
whether behavior X will reinforce behavior Y, one must determine
whether X is preferred to Y. A more preferred behavior will reinforce
a less preferred one, but not vice versa. If X is preferred to Y and Y is
preferred to Z, then the opportunity to engage in Y will reinforce
behavior Z, but not behavior X. According to this view, then, there is
no such thing as a class of trans-situational reinforcers. Reinforcement
is relative. The *Premack principle,* as this rule is sometimes called, has
proven especially useful in techniques of behavior modification.

While Premack's insight that reinforcement is relative is an important advance over Skinner's simple classifications system, it has the
disadvantage of being stated in terms of reinforcing "behaviors." This
somewhat limits its generality because some reinforcers seem to be
much more readily described as stimuli than as behaviors. Increases
and decreases in illumination can be reinforcing, for example, and so
can electrical stimulation of the brain.

The accidental discovery by Olds and Milner (1954) of reinforcing
effects of electrical stimulation of the brain generated considerable
excitement, for it seemed to promise that the physiological nature of
reinforcement would soon be understood. These investigators implanted electrodes deep in the brains of rats, and then passed electrical current to specific locations in the brain. Some of these locations
were found to be "reinforcing"—that is, the rats would repeat behavior that preceded the electrical stimulation. Interest focused on just
where these locations were and how the stimulation had its effect.
Perhaps a single "reinforcement pathway" could be found which fired
whenever any reinforcing event occurred, "stamping in" the immediately preceding act (as Thorndike had put it) and making it more
likely to occur again. Twenty years after the initial discovery and

excitement, however, it does not appear that a single reinforcement pathway will be found. There are many sites in the mammalian brain which, when stimulated, produce reinforcing effects. Some appear to be related to the thirst, hunger, and sex drives, although others are not obviously related to any drives at all.

The reinforcing effects of electrical stimulation of the brain are popularly attributed to stimulation of "pleasure centers." This view gains partial support from studies of human patients who have had electrode implantations as treatment for severe neurological problems such as epilepsy. When allowed to press buttons for electrical stimulation, patients will respond at high rates for stimulation of some sites, and not at all for others. Their subjective reports often stress the pleasurable result of the stimulation, frequently relating it to the build-up to sexual orgasm. Various electrode sites, however, produce various kinds of reports—for example, a "cool taste" or a "drunk feeling." One patient (reported in Heath, 1963), given an array of buttons each associated with a different electrode site, pressed one button more frequently than any other, including one that gave him what he described as sexual pleasure. His subjective report, however, was one of frustration. He said he felt on the verge of being able to recall something. The self-stimulations were an effort to retrieve an elusive memory.

This report illustrates the danger of classifying all "reinforcing" effects of brain stimulation as pleasurable. It is also worth emphasizing, once again, that "pleasure," like a "satisfying state of affairs," cannot be considered an adequate explanation of reinforcement. Even if it were known that all reinforcers were subjectively experienced as pleasurable, the question would still remain of just *how* pleasure increases the likelihood of the preceding response. To say, "If I found the outcome of a response pleasant I would repeat it," is simply to describe the effect of pleasure on one's own behavior—it does not explain why pleasure has that effect. This is just the kind of pseudo-explanation that John Watson found so easy to ridicule (and that mentalistic theories of behavior find so hard to avoid).

Fortunately, we do not have to have a good general theory of reinforcement in order to determine whether reinforcement is necessary for learning. We can simply identify it by its effects on behavior. In both classical and instrumental conditioning, reinforcement increases the likelihood of the response, and withdrawal of reinforcement leads to extinction. Many experimental reports have sidestepped the problem of explaining reinforcement, and dealt directly with the question of whether it is necessary for learning.

Sensory Preconditioning

In classical conditioning, the experimental paradigm used to study learning without reinforcement is called *sensory preconditioning*. Recall that the higher-order conditioning paradigm includes three stages: (1) the pairing of CS_1 with the UCS, (2) the pairing of CS_2 with CS_1, and (3) the test to determine whether CS_2 elicits the response. In sensory preconditioning, the design is the same, except that stages one and two are reversed. Thus in stage one, CS_2 is paired with CS_1; in stage two, CS_1 is paired with the UCS; and in stage three, CS_2 is tested for the tendency to elicit the response.

The logic relating the sensory preconditioning paradigm to the reinforcement issue, of course, rests upon the fact that the reinforcer (the UCS) is not introduced until the second stage of the experiment. If the pairing of CS_2 and CS_1 produces learning, the learning must have occurred without reinforcement. Learning occurring in stage one, supposedly, will show up in stage three, when CS_2—which has *never* been paired with the UCS—is tested for its tendency to elicit the response that was conditioned to CS_1 during stage two.

According to Tolman's theory, the animal in a sensory preconditioning experiment acquires two expectancies: $CS_2 \rightarrow CS_1$, in stage one, and $CS_1 \rightarrow UCS$, in stage two. These expectancies form a chain so that on the test CS_2 indirectly leads the animal to expect the UCS, and this expectancy produces the response. An expectancy can develop in stage one, according to Tolman's theory, because only contiguity is necessary for learning; reinforcement is not.

The first experiment on sensory preconditioning was done by Brogden (1939). The subjects in his study were eight dogs. In stage one, the sound of a bell preceded a flash of light, 20 times a day for 10 days. In stage two, one stimulus (the bell for four dogs, and the light for the other four) was paired repeatedly with shock to the left foreleg. The conditioned response was leg flexion. In stage three the stimulus that had not been presented in stage two was tested for its ability to elicit the leg flexion response. On the first day of this testing procedure, the response was elicited on 21 percent of the test trials— by the stimulus that had never been directly paired with shock.

Certain experimental controls should be included in experiments on sensory preconditioning, of course, to eliminate pseudoconditioning as an explanation of the tendency for CS_2 to elicit the response. Pseudoconditioning, as was pointed out in Chapter 4, is a kind of generalized sensitization of a response that can easily be mistaken for evidence of conditioning. Seidel (1959) carefully reviewed a number of published experiments that refined the sensory preconditioning procedure by including pseudoconditioning controls. He concluded that sensory preconditioning is indeed a real phenomenon. When two stimuli are paired they become associated, even though reinforcement may not be present at the time. Thus, while reinforcement may be necessary for classical conditioning to be observed, it apparently is not necessary for the conditioning to occur.

Reward-Shift Experiments

The role of reinforcement in instrumental conditioning has been the subject of considerable controversy. The amount and delay of reinforcement have well-known effects on key behavioral measures, such as running speed. In Hull's 1943 theory, as we have seen, it was assumed that these variables acted directly to affect the degree of learning, or habit strength. Rats trained with large rewards were assumed to run faster because the running response was more strongly associated with the stimuli of the runway. In fact the maximum value $_sH_R$ could reach was determined by size, quality, and delay of reward (see Figure 5.1). The assumption that the amount of learning is directly related to the amount of reward was one that Thorndike also had made. It is sometimes called the "strong law of effect."

Experiments indicating that the effects of magnitude of reward on performance are not simply mediated by habit strength were reported by Crespi (1942) and Zeaman (1949). In these studies, sometimes called *reward-shift* or reinforcement-shift studies, rats learned to run down a runway for food. After a rat had been trained for several trials with a certain amount of reward, the amount was changed or "shifted."

Let us consider what Hull's 1943 theory predicts about the effects of shifts in amount of reward. Suppose an animal has been trained to run for a small reward, and therefore runs down the runway to the goal box at a slow but fairly steady rate, trial after trial. Suddenly on one trial, and on all the trials following, the animal finds in the goal box a much larger reward. Hull's theory, incorporating the strong law of effect, predicts a slow increase in running speed after the amount of reward has been increased—the rationale being that $_sH_R$ leveled off at a fairly low value under small reward, and that now the large rewards can gradually push it up to a higher value. Suppose an animal trained with large reward is shifted to small rewards. The strong law of effect predicts no change in the animal's running speed; large rewards produced a strong habit, and smaller rewards should prevent extinction. Thus, the animal should continue to run fast even though the magnitude of reward has decreased.

In Zeaman's (1949) experiment, rats were first trained for 19 trials to run either for large (2.4 grams) or small (.05 grams) amounts of food. On trial 20, the amount was shifted, large to small and small to large. It remained at this new value for the next seven trials. Figure 6.2 presents average latency times for leaving the start box, for the animals in Zeaman's study. For 7 trials preceding the shift, the difference between groups in response latency was quite large, and both groups of animals were gradually becoming quicker. On the trial following the shift, however, the response latencies of the two groups

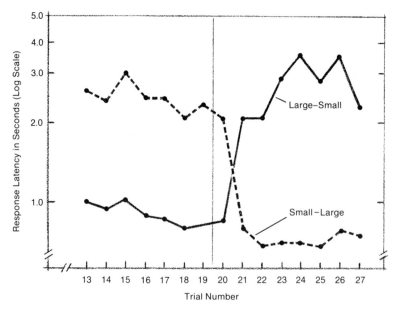

Figure 6.2 Effect of a shift in reward magnitude on start-box latency, in rats. [Adapted from Zeaman, 1949.]

dramatically reversed. The Large–Small group responded as slowly as the Small–Large group had before the shift, and the Small–Large group responded as quickly as had the animals in the Large–Small condition. Indeed, for the next several trials the Small–Large animals seem to have responded even more quickly, and the Large–Small animals more slowly, than the animals initially trained on the new amounts. These findings, known as positive and negative *contrast effects*, are beyond the scope of the present discussion. For our purposes, it is sufficient to note that the predictions of Hull's 1943 theory are not borne out. According to the strong law of effect, performance of the Large–Small animals should remain the same; and that of the Small–Large animals should change gradually following the reward shift. Instead, behavior of both groups was affected by the change, and the effect occurred in a single trial.

Latent Learning

An even stronger case could be made against reinforcement theories if it could be shown that instrumental conditioning can occur without reinforcement. The logic of experiments designed to demonstrate such learning is similar to that of the sensory preconditioning paradigm. In instrumental conditioning, the phenomenon is called *latent learning*.

In Chapter 4, the secondary reinforcement paradigm was introduced. It involves two stages: one in which there is a primary reinforcer, and a second in which it is shown that learning occurs in the absence of the primary reinforcer. Stimuli paired with the primary reinforcer in stage one apparently acquire reinforcing power, which is demonstrated in stage two. In Chapter 5, we saw that reinforcement theories such as Hull's find secondary reinforcement awkward to deal with. The latent learning paradigm is essentially the reverse of the secondary reinforcement paradigm. In stage one a learning experience is provided in which no primary reinforcer is used. In stage two reinforcement is introduced to show, by eliciting the appropriate behavior, that learning took place in stage one. During stage one, it is assumed, the learning was "latent" or unobservable, because the animal had no reason to show what it knew. Stage two provides the incentive, so that the latent learning can manifest itself in overt behavior.

A classic study of latent learning was done by Tolman and Honzik

(1930b). Three groups of hungry rats were given one run a day in a complex maze with 14 choice points. One group (Reward) was run for 17 days, and always found food in the goal box. A second group (No Reward), was also run for 17 days, but never found food in the goal box. The third group of animals (No Reward–Reward) was trained in two stages. In stage one, which lasted for 10 days, they were treated like the No Reward group. In stage two, lasting from day 11 to day 22, they were treated like the Reward group. The average numbers of errors, or entries into blind alleys, are shown for all three groups of animals in Figure 6.3. During the first stage, of course, rats in the No Reward–Reward group made as many errors as those in the No Reward group. After day 11, when these animals started finding food in the goal box, their performance dramatically improved. On the next

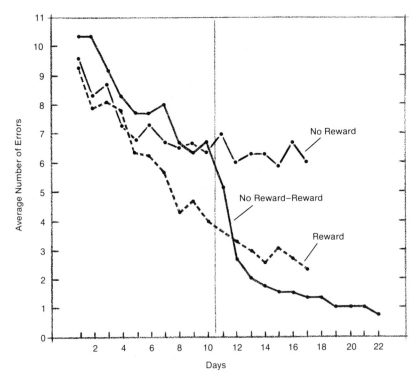

Figure 6.3 Effect of introduction of reward on errors (blind-alley entrances). [After Tolman and Honzik, 1930b. Published in 1930 by The Regents of the University of California; reprinted by permission of the University of California Press.]

trial, in fact, their error rate dropped by half, and was even slightly better than that of the Reward animals, which had been rewarded with food in the goal box for 11 previous trials.

The sudden improvement in performance is essential for establishing that latent learning occurred. The No Reward–Reward group improved so much more rapidly than the Reward group had originally that Tolman and Honzik concluded that these animals must have learned their way around the maze during stage one. Knowledge had been acquired even though reinforcement was not present. When food was found, on day 11, it provided the incentive to run directly to the goal box on the next trial.

Few topics in experimental psychology have elicited as much theoretical debate and experimental research as has latent learning. While the subject has largely disappeared from the journals as a research problem of current interest, a review by Thistlethwaite, published in 1951, cited over ninety articles dealing with latent learning. The interest shown in the topic attests to the theoretical importance once attached to the reinforcement-versus-contiguity issue.

The Current Status of Reinforcement Theory

Probably the most important reason that the latent learning controversy has died away is that the most influential reinforcement theorist, Clark Hull, changed his theory. Let us examine the role of reinforcement in Hull's revised theory, published in 1952.

In the 1943 theory, as we have seen, reinforcement affected behavior by increasing habit strength. In the 1952 version, reinforcement affected behavior in two ways: It increased $_sH_R$ and in addition provided incentive. The role of incentive, symbolized as K, was to provide motivation; and the effect of incentive on behavior was multiplicative:

$$_sE_R = {_sH_R} \times D \times K. \tag{1}$$

Notice what equation (1) implies. Previously, only habit and drive had to be present to produce behavior. But in the 1952 system, incentive has to be present as well. If K is near zero, the tendency for the response to occur will be minimal. If K jumps from a low to a high value from one trial to the next, the tendency to respond will increase accordingly. K is directly affected by the size of reward on immediately preceding trials. The ability of K to explain effects of reinforcement shift and latent learning experiments rests on the assumption that K can increase or decrease very rapidly from trial to trial. $_sH_R$, by contrast, can only increase, and this it does only gradually.

With this change in the theory, it becomes a simple matter to account for effects of changes in amount of reward. With a shift from small to large reward, the value of K suddenly increases; with a shift from large to small reward, it suddenly decreases. These shifts in incentive are more sudden than any effects of amount of reward on $_sH_R$, so the effects on $_sH_R$ are not apparent in the animal's behavior (Hull, 1952).

Latent learning is dealt with in a similar manner. The reader no doubt noticed in the Tolman and Honzik data (Figure 6.3) that even the rats given no reward learned to some extent to avoid entering blind alleys as they became familiar with the maze. This suggested to Hull that reinforcement of some kind—perhaps secondary reinforcement—was present during stage one of the experiment. Any reinforcement of the habit of running from the start box to the goal box, of course, would produce some $_sH_R$, and make possible the sudden elimination of errors in stage two due to the increase of K from near zero to a high value. Thus for Hull, the latent learning shown in the Tolman and Honzik study was just a special case of shift of reinforcement magnitude, which could be understood as the result of a change in the magnitude of K.

This change in Hull's theory, while preserving the law of effect, was a large step in the direction of Tolman's formulation, because it emphasized effects of reinforcement on incentive rather than on the strengthening of habits. It was also a step in the direction of complexity, since Hull assigned two functions to reinforcement—one, the incentive function, more powerful than the other.

Other research on latent learning, however, posed serious problems even for the weakened law of effect incorporated into Hull's 1952 theory. Hull supposed that during the "No Reward" stage of the Tolman and Honzik study the S–R bonds needed to get from start box to goal box were being strengthened by secondary reinforcement of some kind. In an experiment by Herb (1940), however, food reward was introduced into blind alleys at the beginning of stage two, instead of into the goal box. Her rats, in contrast to those of Tolman and Honzik, showed a sudden tendency in stage two to make more blind-alley entries. These habits are opposed to those that Hull assumed to be strengthened during stage one. Thus, the learning acquired during stage one in latent learning studies apparently is not confined to the habit that appears to be strengthening—that of running the maze with few blind alley entrances—but encompasses general knowledge of the spatial layout of the maze.

Thistlethwaite's (1951) extensive review of the latent learning literature concluded that instrumental conditioning can take place without reinforcement. Most animal learning researchers have now accepted this conclusion. Even Kenneth Spence, who carried on the tradition of Hullian learning theory after Hull's death, eventually adopted a contiguity theory of instrumental conditioning (Spence, 1956). Thus did the most influential learning theory of the 1940s and 1950s change in response to a growing body of experimental evidence: The strong law of effect, which assigned to reward the sole function of strengthening learning (Hull, 1943), gave way to a weak law of effect, which conceded to reward an additional incentive function (Hull, 1952), and then even the weak version of the law of effect was abandoned (Spence, 1956). Reinforcement was now assumed to affect motivation, and not learning. This was what Tolman's original position on the question had been (Tolman, 1932).

If the reinforcement-versus-contiguity issue was won by the contiguity theorists, as appears to be the case, how can we understand the position of Skinner, who has continued to emphasize reinforcement for nearly forty years? Skinner, it must be remembered, insists on accounting for behavior with empirical laws that relate experimental manipulations directly to behavior. There is no place in such a system for a distinction between learning and performance, because only performance can be observed. To assume the existence of learning that cannot be observed—that is, "latent" learning—is simply inadmissible. For good or ill, this is a restriction of purely descriptive theories such as Skinner's. The reasoning behind "latent learning" experiments is seen by Skinner and his followers as misguided; and the experimental outcomes are seen as irrelevant within the context of a descriptive theory of behavior.

WHAT IS LEARNED?

The most central question for theories of learning is, "What is learned?" Historically, it has been answered in two ways. One answer goes back to the British empiricist philosophers, who held that when events occur in contiguity, an association is formed between the corresponding ideas. This was the view that provided the rationale behind Ebbinghaus's experiments. It was also the view of Tolman. The *S–S association* (or expectancy) is basically a cognitivist notion. The other answer is that what is learned is an association or bond between a stimulus and a response. Thorndike, Watson, and Hull, among others, adopted this interpretation—and Skinner's position differs only in that he objects to terms such as association or bond. The *S–R association* is the traditional behaviorist answer to the question of what is learned.

The question regarding what is learned has been even more controversial than the issue concerning the role of reinforcement. Many experiments have been done to determine what is learned. Let us consider some of the basic ways of attacking this problem.

Response Generalization

A number of experiments have had the aim of showing that animals are more flexible in dealing with changes in the experimental situation than the S–R position predicts. If the animal learns to make particular movements in the presence of particular stimuli, as the S–R formulation suggests, then it should be incapable of dealing with a change in the situation which makes the old movements ineffective. The tendency of an experimental subject to respond in a slightly changed situation with movements different from those used in initial training, but having an equivalent effect, is called *response generalization*. An experiment performed by a student of Tolman will illustrate the phenomenon.

Macfarlane (1930) performed a maze learning experiment in which rats had to negotiate the same maze by two different means. In stage one, hungry rats learned to swim through a complex maze filled with water, to reach food in the goal box. Once the task had been mastered, stage two was begun. A submerged bottom was placed in the maze, just an inch below the surface of the water. The water was too shallow for swimming, so the rats had to wade—an act requiring quite different movements from swimming. Other rats learned to wade in stage one and had to swim in stage two. On the first trial of stage two, there was some slight hesitation and a few errors were made; but by the second trial the rats negotiated the maze virtually without error. Apparently the rats "knew" how to get through the maze independently of the specific movements required.

There have been several other experiments showing response generalization. Lashley and Ball (1929), for example, trained rats in a darkened maze and then cut their spinal cords in various places, producing difficulties in running. The normal movement patterns of some of the animals were greatly impaired; nearly all exhibited some lack of coordination. Despite these difficulties, when placed in the darkened maze most of the rats displayed perfect retention of the maze habit. In this experiment neither visual information nor proprioceptive feedback from the muscles could be used for guidance in stage two.

As was pointed out in the last chapter, Tolman emphasized the molar nature of behavior, declaring that the molecular nature of the response (the specific muscle contractions) was not important in learning. Experiments on response generalization demonstrate this fact rather clearly. In dealing with the phenomenon of response generalization, S–R theorists were forced to make a concession to Tolman's point of view. The general S–R formulation was salvaged by accepting the molar definition of the response. A stimulus situation was assumed to be associated with a molar response, such as turning right, or approaching a stimulus, or depressing a bar, regardless of the actual muscular contractions making up the act. Thus, a rat that had learned to make a left turn at a choice point while swimming could correctly make a left turn while wading. Hull was vague about whether molar or molecular responses were learned, and so in accounting for response generalization he was easily able to adopt the molar definition of the response.

Learning Without Responding

Even this altered version of S–R theory, however, requires that a response be made, while Tolman's notion of expectancy does not. Other experiments, accordingly, have been conducted to demonstrate *learning without responding*. One such study investigated classical conditioning in animals that were unable to respond. Beck and Doty (1957) immobilized cats by injecting the drug bulbocapnine into their muscles. This drug induces a "cataleptic stupor," in which the animal adopts a grotesque rigid posture similar to that of a human cataleptic patient and fails to respond to normally effective stimuli. While in this drugged state, the cats were given several hundred pairings of a tone (the CS) and a shock to the foreleg (the UCS), which, of course, they could not escape. After the effects of the drug had worn off, the cats were given repeated tests in which the tone was sounded alone, and was never followed by shock. On 70 percent of these trials, the tone elicited flexion of the foreleg—a response that had not occurred during the training trials. This, of course, is what one would expect if classical conditioning involved the formation of S–S expectancies, rather than S–R associations.

Sensory preconditioning, presented in the previous section as evidence that classical conditioning does not require reinforcement, has also been cited as evidence that learning does not require responding. In stage one of the sensory preconditioning experiment, two stimuli such as a tone and a light are paired. Reinforcement (the UCS) does not occur during this stage, and neither does the response, because the UCS is needed to elicit it. Sensory preconditioning, therefore, does not just favor the contiguity theory over reinforcement theory; it also provides evidence for the S–S interpretation of classical conditioning.

One of the more intriguing experiments on learning without responding was performed by McNamara, Long, and Wike (1956), in response to an earlier suggestion by Thorndike. In a critical review of Tolman's theory, Thorndike (1946) had suggested that evidence favoring the expectancy over the S–R point of view might be obtained by pulling a rat through a maze in a little wire cart, and then showing that the rat knows the way to the goal box just as well as an animal trained in the usual way. McNamara et al. used two groups of rats: an experimental group and a control group. Each rat in the experimental group was matched with one in the control group, for reasons that will become apparent shortly. The maze that was used was a T-maze. For half the rats in each group food was found at the end of the left branch, and for the other half it was always on the right. During stage one of the experiment each control animal was given several trials in which it was allowed to turn either to the left or to the right, and find food or no food, accordingly. Each experimental animal was given the same experience as the control animal with which it was matched, except that the experimental animal was not allowed to run—instead it was pushed along in a little basket and released in the goal box. If the control rat had turned left, the experimental animal was pushed left; if the control rat had turned right, its "yoked" mate was pushed right. Thus the sequence of right and left turns and of rewards and nonrewards was the same for experimental and control animals of a matched pair. In stage two of the experiment, all the animals were allowed to run through the T-maze. They were given 16 trials during which there was no reward. The result was that experimental animals took the previously rewarded path on 66 percent of the trials, compared to the control animals' 64 percent—almost exactly the same figure. The McNamara et al. study appears to demonstrate that instrumental learning can occur in the absence of an emitted response. Not even a molar response was required of the animal being pushed along in the basket—yet it apparently learned as well as the animal that responded by turning right or left.

Latent Extinction

Recall that Hull's 1943 theory explained extinction by using the concept of inhibition. I_R is the temporary tendency not to repeat a response, and sI_R is a permanent "negative habit," due to nonreinforced responding in the presence of stimulus S. Both concepts figured in Hull's explanation of extinction, and both required that the subject make the response R. Without R, neither I_R nor sI_R could occur. In Tolman's theory, by contrast, extinction occurs when the subject stops expecting reward. If Tolman's theory is correct, a clever experimenter should be able to extinguish a learned behavior even though the behavior does not occur. All he must do is manipulate the expectancy of reward, without requiring the animal to make the response. The phenomenon of extinction without responding is called *latent extinction*.

The first experiment showing latent extinction was published by Seward and Levy (1949). In stage one of their experiment, hungry rats learned to traverse a runway for food. In stage two, rats in the experimental group were repeatedly placed in the goal box, which they found empty. Rats in the control group received similar treatment, except that the location in which they were placed in stage two was not connected to the runway. Finally, in stage three of the experiment, all animals in both groups were given extinction training—they were allowed to run repeatedly to the empty goal box. The average number of trials to extinguish the running response was 3.12 for the experimental animals, which had been shown the empty goal box during stage two, and 8.25 for the control animals, which had not. On the very first trial of extinction training, before the running response had ever been followed by nonreward, the average latency, or time to leave the start box, was 7.70 seconds for the experimental group, and 2.55 seconds for the control group—a difference of three to one. Apparently the experience of seeing the empty goal box had been quite effective in extinguishing the running response. A number of other experiments have been done on latent extinction. A review by Moltz (1957) concluded that the phenomenon had been demonstrated conclusively.

Expectancies

Experiments on response generalization, learning without responding, and latent extinction were all designed to demonstrate phenomena contrary to S–R theory. Most experiments done by cognitive theorists were aimed at disproving S–R theories, rather than providing positive evidence for expectancies. One exception, though, was a *substitution experiment,* done by O. L. Tinklepaugh (1928), a student in Tolman's laboratory.

In Tinklepaugh's study, three monkeys were trained in what is called a *delayed reaction* task. The monkey sat in a chair and observed the experimenter, about eight feet away, as he placed a reward under one of two tin cups. Then a board was raised, blocking the monkey's view of the cups. Finally, after a predetermined period of time, the experimenter told the monkey it could come around the board and get the food. The question motivating such experiments, on monkeys and other animals, was how long the animal could remember which cup contained the reward. Monkeys are quite good at delayed reactions—in a modification of the basic experiment Tinklepaugh found they could delay as long as twenty hours.

The substitution experiment was performed after the monkeys had been given considerable experience in the delayed reaction task. In preparation for the critical test, Tinklepaugh trained the animals with two different rewards—banana on some trials, and lettuce on others. While the monkeys much preferred banana to lettuce, they would perform quite well in the delay task when lettuce was used, going to the correct cup when instructed to, taking the lettuce and eating it. Tinklepaugh wanted to demonstrate that the behavior of the monkey was guided by an internal representation of a particular reward—an expectancy for banana when banana had been placed under the cup, and for lettuce when the perceived reward had been lettuce. On the critical trial, unseen by the subject, he substituted the less preferred reward for the preferred one. Typical behavior on a substitution trial was described by Tinklepaugh as follows:

> The experimenter displays a piece of banana, lowers the board and places the banana under one of the cups. The board is then raised, and working behind it, with his hands hidden from the view of the monkey, *the experimenter takes the banana out and deposits a piece of lettuce in its place.* After the delay, the monkey is told to "come get the food." She jumps down from the chair, rushes to the proper container and picks it up. She extends her hand to seize the food. But her hand drops to the floor without touching it. She looks at the lettuce, but (unless very hungry) does not touch it. She looks around the cup and behind the board. She stands up and looks around her. She picks the cup up and examines it thoroughly inside and out. She has on occasion turned toward observers present in the room and shrieked at them in apparent anger. After several seconds spent searching, she gives a glance toward the other cup, which she has been taught not to look into, and then walks off to a nearby window. The lettuce is left untouched on the floor (Tinklepaugh, 1928, pp. 224–225). [Italics in the original.]

The behavior of monkeys in this situation left little doubt in the minds of Tinklepaugh or other observers that the animal's behavior was guided by an expectancy, or internal representation of the reward.

A Detour Experiment

A final experiment worthy of mention here is a *detour experiment* done by Tolman and Honzik (1930a). This experiment was intended to provide positive evidence for the existence of cognitive maps, by showing that rats could "reason out" which detour to take when the preferred path in a multiple-pathway maze was blocked. The maze used by Tolman and Honzik is illustrated in Figure 6.4. It had no blind alleys, but three alternate paths of unequal length leading from the start box to the goal box. During stage one of the experiment, the rats were given several trials in the maze, with food in the goal box. As we saw in Chapter 5, in this type of situation animals initially take the three paths about equally often, but soon come to prefer the shortest one. This is the finding on which Hull's concept of the habit-family hierarchy was based. During stage two of the experiment, a block was

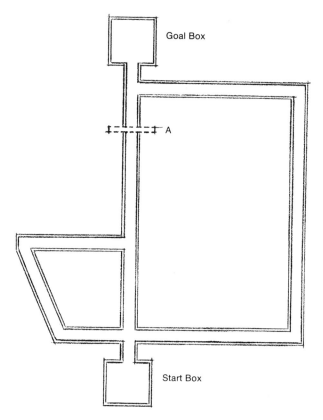

Figure 6.4 A three-pathway detour maze. A block is placed at point *A*. [Adapted from Tolman and Honzik, 1930a.]

placed across the path at the spot marked "A" in Figure 6.4. The rats, placed in the start box, ran down the short path and encountered the barrier. Then they were removed and placed in the start box again.

After encountering the block at point A, what will the rat do? Hull's theory makes a straightforward prediction, the basis of which was discussed in Chapter 5. Since the rat has exercised the S–R bond for running straight ahead, and the response has gone unrewarded, that habit should tend to extinguish (increase in I_R and sI_R). Now the second-ranked habit in the habit-family hierarchy should take over— and the rat should take the medium-length path, turning to the left. This would obviously be an inappropriate response for an animal that has just encountered a barrier blocking both the short and medium-length paths, but it is just what Hull's theory predicts. Tolman's theory, however, assumes that the rat possesses a cognitive map of the maze. The rat "knows" that the barrier at A blocks both the short and medium-length paths. Instead of turning left, it should take the long path, turning to the right. This is exactly what most of the rats in the Tolman and Honzik study did.

Modifications of S–R Theory

What is learned—S–R bonds or expectancies? The evidence just reviewed seems overwhelming. A rat that learns a task performing one set of movements has little difficulty switching to another set of movements that accomplishes the same result. Rats, cats, and dogs apparently can learn without making any overt responses, and sometimes they may learn as well as control animals that take an active part in mastering the task. Maze-running in the rat can be extinguished in the absence of responding. In addition, animals performing an instrumental task seem to anticipate a fairly specific reward, as is shown by the disruption of a monkey's behavior when a less preferred goal object is substituted for the expected one. And rats display the ability to choose detours in a maze in a way that strongly suggests familiarity with the general layout of the apparatus—that is, a cognitive map.

One might imagine that investigators faced with such evidence would have abandoned S–R theory and embraced Tolman's cognitive theory instead. But that did not happen, at least not immediately. Instead, during the 1940s and 1950s Hull's theory became more and more popular and Tolman's theory gradually faded from the scene. One reason for this was that Tolman's theory was too mentalistic to fit into the strongly behaviorist bias of the time. Another reason—some thought this was a consequence of its being mentalistic—was that it was relatively vague and imprecise. While Hull and Spence and other S–R theorists attempted to formalize their theories and sharpen the definitions of their concepts, Tolman based his theory largely on intuition, and never did satisfactorily explain many of his concepts. For example, just what is a "cognitive map" and how is it formed? How is it transformed into behavior? The lack of precise rules for generating predictions from the theory compared unfavorably with S–R theory, particularly as the latter was refined and advanced by Hull.

The most important reason for continued preference for S–R theory, however, was that it overcame many of the experimental disconfirmations by changing. It became more and more like Tolman's theory, but avoided the mentalistic language and conceptual fuzziness of Tolman's approach. As we saw earlier, response generalization studies were encompassed by S–R theory by dropping the molecular definition of the response as a glandular secretion or muscle contraction and adopting instead Tolman's molar definition, which viewed the response as an act that accomplished something (for example, depressing a lever or turning to the right). Learning without responding was handled by S–R theorists by assuming that responses did not have to be overt—they could be covert or "hidden." In fact, they could be completely internal "symbolic responses" that behaved just like overt responses in every way except that they could not be observed.

Moving responses inside the nervous system gave S–R theorists the freedom to invent a whole new system of explanations of the phenomenon that "pure" S–R theories, such as the one Hull had presented in 1943, could not handle. The central mechanism of this covert response system was the *fractional anticipatory goal response*, symbolized by r_g. This response was related to the subject's reaction to the goal object (for example, eating), and so it could represent or "stand for" the reward. It was fractional, meaning it was not overt and could not easily be observed; and it was anticipatory, meaning that once it had been acquired it tended to occur when the animal was placed in the experimental apparatus, before the animal reached the goal box. The r_g mechanism was given several theoretically useful properties: it had stimulus consequences (r_g produced s_g), so that observable habits could be connected to it (through s_g–R associations); it had an energizing property, which allowed Hull to relate it to the concept of incentive, K; and it could be conditioned and extinguished independently of the overt habit it guided and energized. As the dominant version of S–R theory developed (Hull, 1952; Spence, 1956; Amsel, 1958; Moltz, 1957), unobservable "fractional" responses came to do more and more of the work of explaining behavior.

A "fractional anticipatory goal response," being unobservable and anticipatory, is essentially an expectancy of the goal object, dressed up in different-sounding terms. With this addition, S–R theories became very similar to Tolman's theory. The main remaining difference was that Tolman assumed that expectancies were formed for all kinds of objects and events, while the r_g mechanism could anticipate only goal objects, or reinforcers. This meant that even the transfigured S–R theory could not handle the detour experiment, for even that theory possessed no concept equivalent to Tolman's cognitive map.

The Current Status of Expectancy Theory

In the last several years new evidence has emerged which seems extremely difficult to integrate into an S–R framework—even one that includes fractional anticipatory responses. Recall that Tolman speculated that expectancies carried two magnitudes—a strength (or confidence) and a probability. (This is in contrast to r_g, which only varies in strength.) Thus, an organism can learn that S_1 is usually followed by S_2, or that in the presence of S_1, R_1 and R_1' are equally likely to lead to S_2. While the notion that animals could learn probabilities was not made very precise in his theory, it enabled Tolman to explain the partial-reinforcement effect or PRE (the fact that resistance to extinction is greater following partial than following continuous reinforcement). The PRE was assumed to reflect the animal's ability to recognize that the probability of reinforcement had changed. Thus, a change from 100 percent to 0 percent reinforcement is more obvious than one from 50 percent to 0 percent, which in turn is easier to detect than a 25 percent to 0 percent shift. An experimental topic of current interest concerns numerous other situations in which animals seem to *learn correlations,* or the relative probabilities with which events co-occur.

An influential experiment conducted by Rescorla (1968) demonstrated the importance of correlations in classical conditioning. In stage one of Rescorla's study, rats spent 10 hours in a situation in which 2-minute periods during which a tone was sounded as a CS were alternated with longer periods of silence. The UCS was electric shock. During the CS-on periods, the probability of the rat being shocked varied, with different groups of animals having shock probabilities of .0, .1, .2, and .4. Traditional learning theories predict that the effectiveness of classical conditioning will vary directly with this probability—the more frequent the pairing of the tone and shock, the stronger should be the tone–fear connection. In addition, however, Rescorla allowed shock to occur during the periods of silence. These CS-off periods were divided up into 2-minute intervals, and the probability of shock in each 2-minute interval also varied from .0 to .4. Altogether, Rescorla had ten groups of rats, defined by ten different combinations of probability of shock during the tone and probability of shock during silence. The conditions are represented in panel (a) of Figure 6.5. Notice that for four of the conditions (the diagonal in the diagram) the two probabilities are equal. Thus, tone and shock were uncorrelated; the tone provided no reliable clue to whether the shock might occur. For the other six conditions (above the diagonal) shock was more likely during the tone than it was during silence. In these conditions, the CS and UCS were correlated; the tone could be used to predict the occurrence of shock.

During stage two of the experiment, Rescorla measured the tendency for the animals to respond to the CS with fear. The actual response measured was "freezing"—a kind of "shrinking back" from the behavior that otherwise would have occurred—technically referred to as the *conditioned emotional response.* To measure freezing, one first trains an animal to perform an operant response, such as bar-pressing for food. Then, while the operant response is being performed, the CS is presented. The suppression of the operant response, due to freezing, is measured from the cumulative record (see Figure 6.6). The response suppression percentages from stage two of Rescorla's experiment are shown in panel (b) of Figure 6.5. Notice that the tendency to freeze was directly related, not to the probability

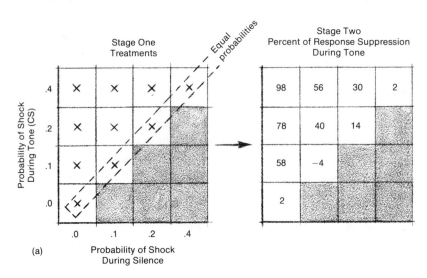

Figure 6.5 The conditions (a) and results (b) of Rescorla's experiment. [Data from Rescorla, 1968.]

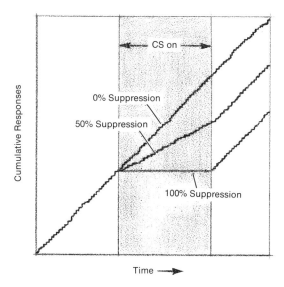

Figure 6.6 The suppression of operant responding as a measure of the conditioned emotional response.

of shock during the CS in stage one, but to the difference between the
CS-on and CS-off shock probabilities. In fact, for the zero-correlation
conditions (those on the diagonal), response suppression was virtually
zero.

This demonstration is important because it suggests that it is not the
number of CS–UCS pairings that determines classical conditioning
but rather the degree to which the CS predicts the occurrence of the
UCS. In stage one of Rescorla's study, animals in the .1–.0 condition
experienced only a quarter as many CS–UCS pairings as animals in
the .4–.4 condition experienced. Yet in the .1–.0 condition, the CS
acquired the power to elicit freezing, while in the .4–.4 condition it did
not.

From results such as these, one might argue that when there is a
zero correlation between two events—that is, when one event does not
predict the other—no learning occurs. A quite different interpretation
is possible, however. Perhaps when two events are uncorrelated the
animal learns just that: event A has no relationship to event B. That is,
rather than learning nothing about A and B, it learns that A cannot be
used to predict B. Such learning might be expected to interfere with

later learning when A is correlated with B. Evidence suggesting that this is the case has been uncovered in a series of recent studies on what is called *learned helplessness.*

One of the early studies of learned helplessness was done by Overmeier and Seligman (1967). In the first stage of this experiment, dogs were suspended in a "hammock" that severely restricted their movement, and were subjected to 64 shocks of 5-seconds duration. There was no way they could escape the shocks. A group of control animals was not subjected to inescapable shock. In the second stage of the experiment, 24 hours later, all the dogs were given avoidance training in a shuttle box of the type described in Chapter 4. On each trial, the lights blinked off as a warning signal. Ten seconds later, shock was administered through the grid in the floor of the apparatus. If the animal jumped the barrier, it could escape the shock. If it learned to jump within 10 seconds of the warning signal, it could avoid shock altogether.

Overmeier and Seligman noted markedly different behavior in the two groups of animals. Both groups of dogs initially yelped, ran, and jumped about in response to the shock, but the dogs that had received inescapable shock in stage one soon quieted down and experienced the shock in silence. The control animals, in contrast, kept moving about until they accidentally jumped the hurdle to safety. They soon learned to escape the shock, and in some cases to avoid it. Few of the dogs in the experimental group ever learned. In fact, 62.5 percent of the experimental animals failed to jump the hurdle even once, as compared with only 12.5 percent of the dogs in the control group.

Further research on learned helplessness has extended the findings to cats, rats, fish, and humans, and has eliminated most of the obvious interpretations of the phenomenon (for example, habituation to shock by the experimental animals). This literature has been reviewed in the book *Helplessness,* by Seligman (1975), and in a more technical article by Meier and Seligman (1976). The interpretation Seligman and his co-workers offer for the failure of the experimental animals to learn to escape is that an animal subjected to inescapable shock learns that the shock is not correlated with its behavior, and therefore there is nothing it can do to prevent the shock or escape from it. The animal has, in effect, learned to be helpless, even in a new situation in which it is possible to escape from the shock. Seligman (1975) interprets what is learned in cognitive terms—the animals have learned an expectancy "that responding and an outcome are independent" (p. 48). He offers some fascinating insights into the implications of this hypothesis, particularly if it is extended to human social behavior, personality, and psychotherapy. Such extensions, of course, should not be accepted without question, but learned helplessness promises to be a lively topic of discussion outside the field of animal conditioning as well as within it in the years to come.

Today, cognitive theories of conditioning are becoming more acceptable than they were in the days of Hull and Tolman. This is the result of several factors: (a) recognition of the fact that the changes that were made in S–R theory made it more and more similar to expectancy theory, (b) evidence that animals learn correlations, a fact difficult to reconcile with S–R theory, and (c) the fact that behaviorism has lost its grip on related areas of study, such as human learning and memory. Several recent conditioning theories have been remarkably similar to Tolman's. For example, Seligman and Johnston (1973) have proposed a theory of avoidance learning that employs an expectancy concept very similar to that of Tolman. And Boneau (1974) has presented a theory of operant behavior that assumes that animals learn $S_1R_1 \rightarrow S_2$ expectancies with probabilities assigned to them. All the information is organized into what Boneau calls an "internal model of the environment"—a concept much like the cognitive map. Menzel (1973) has investigated spatial memory in chimpanzees. The animals were carried around in a field and shown the locations of hidden foods, and later were released. They went from one hiding place to another in a route that nearly minimized the distance traveled— behavior suggesting to Menzel that the chimpanzees possessed a kind of cognitive map of the field.

Thus, the revival of cognitive learning theory has led to a resurgence of interest in Tolman's long-neglected concepts. This is not to say that current cognitive theories are "nothing but" Tolman's theory in new clothing. Expectancy theories are not all the same—and the vagueness and lack of precision for which Tolman was often criticized must be avoided in any present-day theory if it is to gain wide acceptance.

Robots

It is also of interest to compare certain of Tolman's ideas with recent work in a quite different field—that of *robotry*. To build a mechanical man is a dream nearly as old as machines themselves, but it has only been with the advent of electronic computers that the dream has appeared capable of coming true. In order to be useful, a robot should be able to perform many tasks ordinarily assigned to humans. This requires the ability to carry out instructions, and to adapt flexibly to a number of different environments. For their first efforts, workers in this field have begun with simple environments and' simple tasks, hoping to be able to gradually increase their complexity as the more and more complex technical problems associated with such an undertaking are recognized and solved.

Perhaps the most ambitious robot project was one carried out at the Stanford Research Institute (SRI) during the period 1968–1973. The SRI robot, named "Shakey" because of its apparent unsteadiness, is shown in Figure 6.7. It moved about in an environment consisting of

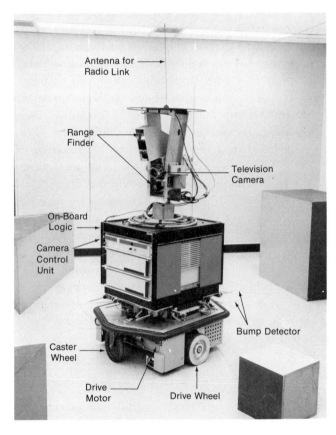

Figure 6.7 "Shakey," the SRI robot.

five rooms which contained various stationary and movable objects. Even in this simple environment, carrying out instructions can require solving some fairly complex problems. For example, if the robot is now in room 2, the instruction to turn off the light in room 4 might require a sequence of acts including moving through the door into room 3, pushing aside an interfering box and moving through the door leading to room 4, going into room 5 to retrieve a tall box, pushing the box into room 4 and up against the wall beneath the light switch, climbing up on the box, and turning off the light (see Raphael, 1976).

Apparently, engineers have not seriously considered the possibility of building S–R machines to carry out such tasks. The only approach that seems feasible is to give the robot knowledge of its environment and rules for manipulating the environment to achieve certain ends. Shakey used a "world model"—a kind of cognitive map of its five-room environment—which was useful for route planning and included information about the present positions of the robot and other objects.

In preparing to carry out an instruction, the robot (actually, a nearby computer that communicated to Shakey by radio) would form a "plan." The units of the plan consisted of two "states of the world" connected by an "operator," which would transform one state into the other:

$$(\text{State 1}) \ (\text{Operator 1}) \rightarrow (\text{State 2})$$

As an example, the operator PUSH can be applied to an object, moving it from location X to location Y, if State 1 consists of the following conditions: the object is pushable; the object is at location X; and the robot is at location X. Applying the operator PUSH to such a state leads to State 2, in which both the robot and the object are at location Y. This type of unit, of course, is very similar to Tolman's $S_1R_1 \rightarrow S_2$ expectancy.

In planning to carry out an instruction, the robot searched for a chain of such units leading from the present world state to the state specified by the instruction (for example, light off in room 4). This method is much like the "inference" process described by Tolman. But it does not suffer from the vagueness that characterized many of Tolman's concepts. As anyone who has ever programmed a computer knows, communicating an instruction to a machine requires that one specify every logical step to be carried out and the conditions under which it is to be applied. The similarities between Tolman's ideas and techniques applied in the SRI robot project suggest that although Tolman's theory was often stated in a vague and imprecise way, his approach to a theory of behavior was logically sound.

The TOTE Unit

Before we leave the question of what is learned, we must return to the problem of the nature of the response. Guthrie's charge that Tolman had failed to deal adequately with this problem, leaving the rat at a choice point "lost in thought" applies to any theory that deals with behavior strictly on the molar level. Thus, the shift of S–R theorists from molecular to molar concepts of the response in order to deal with demonstrations of response generalization was made at some cost. The problem is that, ultimately, behavior does consist of glandular secretions and muscular contractions. Any complete and adequate theory of behavior, if it assumes that molar responses are learned, must specify how molar responses or acts are transformed into responses at the molecular level.

An elegant attempt to solve this problem was made in the book *Plans and the Structure of Behavior,* by Miller, Galanter, and Pribram (1960). As the basic unit of behavior, these authors proposed the *negative feedback loop*—a control system that initiates action when a particular goal state fails to occur, continually monitors the results of this action (the feedback), and terminates action when the goal state has been achieved. A simple example of a negative feedback loop is a thermostat, set to turn on a heater whenever the temperature goes below 70° (the goal state). Another example is the "do loop" of a computer program, which executes a series of instructions repeatedly until a particular condition is satisfied and then transfers control to some other part of the program, in accordance with instructions. The analogy between the behavior of a living organism and that of a computer executing a program exerted a strong influence on the way Miller, Galanter, and Pribram developed their theory.

Miller, Galanter, and Pribram give the negative feedback loop a special name: the *TOTE unit.* TOTE is an acronym standing for Test-Operate-Test-Exit, the sequence of events that occurs when one of these units is activated. A diagram of a basic TOTE unit is shown in Figure 6.8. The arrows in the diagram represent the transfer of

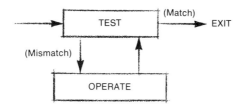

Figure 6.8 A TOTE unit. [After *Plans and the Structure of Behavior* by George A. Miller, Eugene Galanter, and Karl Pribram. Copyright © 1960 by Holt, Rinehart and Winston, Inc. Reprinted by permission of Holt, Rinehart and Winston.]

"control"—which is to say that by following the arrows, one can tell at each point which step is to be executed next. The arrow entering the box labeled "test" represents the transfer of control from other parts of the behavioral program to the particular TOTE unit shown. The function of the test phase is to make a decision. It compares a particular stimulus with a representation of a goal state, and if the stimulus matches the goal state, control is transferred out of the TOTE unit (it "exits"), passing to another part of the behavioral program. If the stimulus does not match the goal state, action is taken to bring the stimulus and goal state into agreement. This action is represented by the "operate" box in the diagram. The arrow returning from "operate" to "test" represents feedback; that is, once the operation has been executed, control is returned to the test phase to determine whether the goal state is now satisfied. If not, the operate phase is executed again until the stimulus and goal state match.

A particularly useful example of a TOTE unit at work is the act of hammering a nail (Miller et al., 1960, pp. 32–37). A hypothetical unit controlling this behavior is shown in Figure 6.9. The goal is to have the head of the nail flush with the surface of the board. The stimulus that is compared with this goal state is the nail. If it is flush with the board, no further action is taken; if it sticks up, it is hammered, checked to see whether it is flush, hammered again, and so on. The operation of hammering the nail is executed repeatedly, until the goal state is satisfied.

Consider some of the advantages of the TOTE unit as the basic unit of a behavior theory. The TOTE unit differs from the S–R bond in

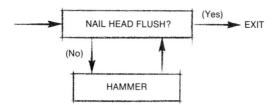

Figure 6.9 A TOTE unit for hammering a nail. [Adapted from Miller, Galanter, and Pribram, 1960.]

emphasizing that behavior is not simply triggered by external stimuli, but is guided by the relationship between external stimuli and internal representations of goals. In this respect it is essentially equivalent to Tolman's $S_1R_1 \rightarrow S_2$ expectancy. (Take S_1 to be the actual stimulus, S_2 to be the goal state, and R_1 to be the operation that the animal believes will transform S_1 into S_2.) Unlike the expectancy, however, the TOTE unit emphasizes the repetitive nature of much goal-directed behavior. The TOTE unit also differs from the expectancy in being able to deal with the relationship between molecular and molar behavior.

Miller et al. (1960) solve the problem of molar versus molecular behavior by borrowing another principle from computer programming. TOTE units, like "do loops" in a computer program, can be "nested" inside each other in a hierarchical fashion. Low-level TOTE units can be parts of the operate phase of a higher-level unit. An example of such *hierarchical nesting* of TOTE units is given in Figure 6.10. There, the operate phase of the unit for hammering a nail has been expanded into two lower-level units—one for lifting the hammer and one for striking the nail. One can imagine this kind of hierarchical nesting including any number of levels. For example, the "hammer" unit may be part of a unit for putting a board in place, which is in turn part of a unit for building a wall. The ultimate goal of the "super" TOTE unit guiding all of this behavior may be to complete construction of a house (or simply to earn a living).

Thus behavior can be described in terms of the goal states of the TOTE units guiding it at any level. To say that the person is lifting his arm, driving a nail, putting a board in place, building a wall, or constructing a house are all correct descriptions of the behavior. They differ in that they refer to goals of different levels, but all the goals are guiding behavior simultaneously. Each low-level goal is part of the

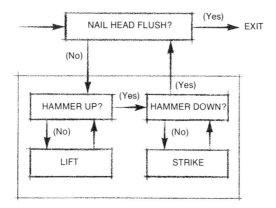

Figure 6.10 A hierarchically nested TOTE unit. [After *Plans and the Structure of Behavior* by George A. Miller, Eugene Galanter, and Karl Pribram. Copyright © 1960 by Holt, Rinehart and Winston, Inc. Reprinted by permission of Holt, Rinehart and Winston.]

operate phase of a higher-level TOTE unit that has as its function the achievement of some higher-level goal. If learning consists of establishing higher-level goals (or expectancies), the actual muscle contractions that are used in accomplishing those goals can vary, depending upon the circumstances. Thus, the molecular responses of an animal that has learned the way through a maze can change (from swimming to wading, for example) without disrupting the overall organization of the animal's behavior.

Many psychologists find TOTE units intuitively satisfying as basic units of behavior—they are guided both by goals and by stimuli, they capture the repetitive nature of much behavior, and they can be hierarchically nested, integrating molecular responses with molar acts. But is there any objective evidence that such negative feedback loops control behavior? There is. Two examples of TOTE-like systems, identified at the physiological level, are the regulation of eating, and muscle contraction.

An essential function of the nervous system is to regulate conditions of the internal environment such as body temperature, oxygen supply, and the availability of various substances necessary for life. Consider hunger. Although the details are in some dispute, a prominent hypothesis holds that the regulation of food intake begins with signals from particular brain centers that are sensitive to blood sugar level. When blood sugar level drops below a certain level, these centers begin to fire, arousing the animal to seek food. One might imagine feeding to be regulated by a simple TOTE device—the animal will seek food, and then eat until blood sugar level again exceeds the goal state. However, the facts are more complicated than this, since it takes some time for digestion to occur, and animals stop eating long before blood sugar level has had a chance to rise significantly. Apparently, other information enters into the decision to stop seeking food. One other source of information is the stretch receptors of the stomach. When the stomach is full, food seeking will not occur. An appropriate TOTE unit is shown in Figure 6.11. The test phase of the unit makes two tests—comparing blood sugar with the criterion level c, and testing to determine whether the stomach muscles are stretched. Only if both tests fail to produce a match is the operate phase of the unit activated. Food-seeking, of course, could involve many different kinds of activities, depending upon the environment and the animal's experience in it. Thus the TOTE unit for food-seeking would occupy the top level of a TOTE hierarchy. Food, necessary for life, is a high-level goal. The regulation of feeding behavior is apparently more complex than Figure 6.11 suggests—but there is no reason to doubt that the control mechanism involves the principles of the negative feedback loop.

For our other example of a TOTE unit, let us consider the lowest level of the hierarchy—the muscle contraction. One might suppose that our voluntary skeletal muscles respond directly to signals from the brain, which tell them when and how much to contract. Recent physiological evidence, however, suggests that this is not the case. Signals from the brain apparently travel, not to the muscle fiber itself,

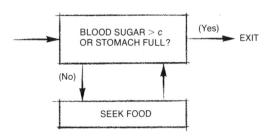

Figure 6.11 A TOTE unit for feeding behavior.

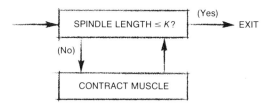

Figure 6.12 A TOTE unit for control of a muscle fiber.

but to tiny organs called *muscle spindles* embedded in the muscle fiber. The muscle spindles can contract without the muscle itself contracting, and it has been hypothesized that it is tension on the muscle spindle rather than contraction of the muscle that is set directly by the brain. Merton (1972) has proposed that the muscle fiber is controlled by the muscle spindle, in the following way. The spindle contains sense organs that are sensitive to stretch or tension. A muscle spindle will be stretched whenever the length of the muscle in which it is embedded does not correspond to the length specified by the signal to the spindle from the brain. The stretch receptor in the spindle sends a signal to the spinal cord, which relays the impulse to the muscle fiber, causing it to contract. The muscle will continue to contract until the spindle stops sending signals, indicating that it is no longer stretched. This hypothesis explains the well known knee-jerk reflex. When the knee is struck just below the kneecap, pressure is exerted on a tendon. This stretches the muscle spindles in the tendon, and they relay a signal through the spinal cord telling the muscle to contract. The sudden movement in the leg is in the direction appropriate to relieve tension on the muscle spindles that were stretched.

A TOTE unit embodying Merton's hypothesis is shown in Figure 6.12. Here it is assumed that the goal state, set by the brain, is for the muscle spindle to be of length k. If it is longer than k, impulses are relayed through the spinal cord to the muscle, causing its contraction. As soon as the spindle reaches length k (or less) the muscle ceases to contract.

Now we see how the relationship between molar and molecular responses can be handled by a TOTE-unit hierarchy. The evidence suggests that the highest-level molar acts, such as food-seeking, and the lowest-level molecular responses, such as contracting a muscle, are guided by negative feedback loops. All one need do is imagine the intermediate levels of the hierarchy, consisting of TOTE units for achieving intermediate-level goals such as turning right or pressing a lever. Convincing evidence that these intermediate levels can best be characterized as TOTE units is presently lacking, but it seems like a potentially fruitful hypothesis to pursue.

7

How Much Have We Learned About Learning?

R esearch in the field of learning is sometimes criticized for being concerned with seemingly trivial problems. For example, how can one get a dog to salivate to a flashing light? A rat to press a lever? A pigeon to peck a red key but not a blue one? How can the behavior be broken down, once it is acquired? Such questions, as the nonpsychologist readily observes, are not intrinsically interesting. That is, there is nothing particularly important about salivation in dogs or lever-pressing in rats—salivation is certainly one of the least fascinating things that dogs do, and in nature not one rat in a billion ever presses a lever for food.

As the preceding chapters have suggested, the great interest shown in such experiments is attributable, not to the significance of the particular behavior under investigation, but to what that particular behavior is assumed to tell us about behavior in general. It has been assumed that learning follows general laws, and that these laws can be discovered just as easily by studying lever-pressing in the white rat as by studying any other combination of behavior and organism. Such details of the experiment are often decided by custom and convenience. They have been assumed to be unimportant, since all behavior should demonstrate the same general laws.

The assumption that the laws of learning are the same regardless of stimulus, response, reinforcer, or organism has been called the *general process view of learning*. Historically, this view has been deeply ingrained in learning theory, as the following quotes illustrate. Here is Pavlov on stimuli:

> Any agent in nature which acts on an adequate receptor apparatus of an organism can be made into a conditioned stimulus for that organism (Pavlov, 1972, p. 38).

Skinner on responses:

> I suggest that the dynamic properties of operant behavior may be studied with a single reflex (Skinner, 1938, p. 46).

Skinner on organisms:

> Pigeon, rat, monkey, which is which? It doesn't matter. Of course, these three species have behavioral repertoires which are as different as their anatomies. But once you have allowed for differences in the ways they make contact with the environment, and in the ways they act upon the environment, what remains of their behavior shows astonishingly similar properties (Skinner, 1956, pp. 230–231).

And finally, Tolman on "everything important":

> I believe that everything important in psychology . . . can be investigated in essence through the continued experimental and theoretical analysis of the determiners of rat behavior at a choice point in a maze (Tolman, 1938, p. 34).

In the past few years, the general process view has increasingly come under attack. This chapter will discuss some of the reasons for questioning the generality of the laws of learning. First, we shall consider data on animal learning that have resisted being fit into the traditional categories. Second, we shall take up the problem of generalizing from animals to humans: to what extent do the principles of conditioning discovered in the animal learning laboratory help us understand human behavior?

BIOLOGICAL DETERMINANTS OF LEARNING

For all their experience with animal learning, very few psychologists have ever seriously attempted to put their knowledge to practical use training animals. The husband and wife team of Keller and Marian Breland, however, was an exception. While working in B. F. Skinner's laboratory, the Brelands became acquainted with the power of the shaping technique. They soon graduated from shaping pigeons to peck keys to a more lucrative application: training chicken acts for state and county fairs. These acts were popular with the fair-going public, and General Mills, Inc., which used them as advertising for its feeds, was pleased with the publicity they received. Soon the Brelands were branching out, training animals not only for fairs, but for window displays, for circus acts, and for parts on television and in the movies. They decided to pursue a nonacademic career, training animals for profit.

In 1951, in an article in the *American Psychologist*, the Brelands discussed the initial success of their business. They claimed no special problems in applying the shaping technique to the behavior of a variety of animals, and predicted a brilliant future for a whole new field of applied psychology, which they called "behavioral engineering." They saw the laws of animal learning—in particular those set out in Skinner's *Behavior of Organisms*—as having general application, regardless of the species of animal or the particular behavior involved.

Ten years later, after training some 6,000 animals representing 38 different species, their message had changed. In an article entitled "The Misbehavior of Organisms," published in the same journal, the Brelands described a number of puzzling failures of animals to behave according to psychological theory. In one example, a chicken was trained to pull a loop on a solenoid-operated bat, knocking a small baseball out into a miniature baseball field. If the ball rolled past the toy players and hit the back fence, a feeder mechanism delivered food near first base. Thus, whenever the chicken managed to knock the ball far enough, it ran down the first-base line for its reward. A four-foot long cage with the bat mechanism at one end and the feeder at the other was used in initial training. When the chickens had been highly trained on this task, the cage was removed. This change had an astonishing effect. As soon as the ball started to roll, the birds would jump onto the playing field and chase the ball wildly, pecking it in every direction. The behavior, which had never occurred during training, persisted despite the fact that it prevented the chicken from obtaining food.

In another example, pigs were trained to pick up large wooden "dollars," carry them several feet, and drop them into a large piggy bank. They were put on a ratio schedule, with reinforcement delivered only after four or five coins had been deposited in the bank. The pigs learned this easily, but with additional training the behavior began to break down. The animals would eagerly run and pick up a coin, but then would drop it, root it on the ground, pick it up and toss it into the air, and drop it and root it some more. Despite the fact that this behavior delayed the reinforcement, the behavior became more and more frequent, and increasing the pig's hunger only seemed to make the problem worse.

How can such violations of the laws of conditioning be understood? Breland and Breland (1961) suggest that these instances and others like them can best be explained by resurrecting one of the concepts discarded by behaviorism—the concept of instinct. The animals are apparently drifting into the "natural," or instinctive, food-getting behaviors of their species, despite the reinforcement contingencies set up by the trainer. An adequate understanding of animal behavior, apparently, cannot consider only learning—it must take into account how learning interacts with the animal's instincts, or *species-specific behaviors*.

Behaviorism and Ethology

The concept of instinct, as we saw earlier, was drummed out of psychology primarily because it had been applied to human behavior in an indiscriminate way. One effect of the behaviorist revolution was that instinct was discarded as an unscientific notion, inappropriate for explaining either animal or human behavior. The concept did not die out in all scientific circles, however. In Europe, during the 1920s, 1930s, and 1940s, a small group of zoologists began studying the behavior of animals in their natural habitats and explaining their observations in terms of instinct—that is, genetically determined patterns of behavior. These zoologists called their special field of study *ethology*. The most prominent of the early ethologists were Karl Von Frisch, Konrad Lorenz, and Niko Tinbergen, who in 1973 were jointly awarded the Nobel Prize for Physiology and Medicine in recognition of their pioneering work on animal behavior.

The approach of European ethology to the study of animal behavior stood in stark contrast to that of American behaviorism. Behaviorists tried to isolate their animals as much as possible from extraneous influences, raising them in the laboratory in order to restrict early experience, controlling their motivation, and testing them in experimental apparatus where stimuli could be precisely controlled and behavior was rigidly constrained. Their preoccupation with learning—particularly classical and instrumental conditioning—was consistent with this approach to research. Ethologists, on the other hand, wanted to study the behavior of animals in their natural environments, in order to understand how the behavior helps each species and subspecies to adapt to its particular ecological niche. They thought of behavior, like bodily form, as molded by evolutionary pressure. Accordingly, they emphasized the genetic inheritance of behavior patterns and showed much less concern with the role of learning. The study of behavior, for an ethologist, always began with naturalistic observation. Experiments were done only to resolve questions that naturalistic observation could not settle. The experiments attempted, in many respects, to mimic the "real world."

For years behaviorism and ethology went their separate ways, each scarcely acknowledging the existence of the other. To the ethologist, the behaviorists' practice of studying an arbitrary response of an animal in a highly unnatural experimental environment, giving no consideration to the function of that behavior in the animal's natural surroundings, was absurd. It seemed doomed to produce trivial results, yielding no knowledge of lasting value. To the behaviorist, the ethologists' naturalistic approach and poorly controlled experiments seemed hopelessly unscientific. Their use of the concept of instinct was subjected to the same criticisms that had been used against it earlier as an explanation of human behavior. Instinct seemed to be just a name for something that was not understood—a pseudoexplanation that would bring to a premature end the empirical study of the causes of behavior. The bias within behaviorism against the idea of instinctive or inborn behavior was so strong that some American psychologists contended that even the simple reflexes present in the newborn may be learned. Lehrman (1953) made the unlikely argument that coordination of the pecking reflex in newly hatched chicks could have been learned in the embryo, through associations that were formed among movements of the neck muscles as they were passively moved in unison by the beating heart. The discovery of a learned component or an alleged learning component in any so-called instinctive behavior pattern was treated by learning psychologists as justification for their rejection of ethology and confirmation of their extreme environmentalist point of view.

Why were the ethologists so much more willing than American behaviorists to invoke the concept of instinct? First, there is the fact that ethology developed on the European continent, where the rationalist school of philosophy thrived. Unlike British empiricism, which stressed that all knowledge comes from experience, rationalism accepted the doctrine of innate ideas. For a tradition that accepts innate ideas, innate behavior patterns would not seem controversial at all. Second, there is the fact that ethology grew out of zoology. Zoologists are trained to emphasize differences between species, and to consider the genetic determinants of those differences. Thus, the shaping of genetic differences by the environmental history of the species is emphasized far more than the shaping of behavior by the environmental history of a living individual.

Imprinting

The different approaches of ethology and behaviorism can be seen in the example of *imprinting*. Casual observations of imprinting may be as old as man's domestication of animals, but apparently the first published report was the 1873 article by D. A. Spalding in a popular magazine; and Konrad Lorenz was the first to study this phenomenon systematically and to give it its name. A new-born animal, in the absence of its mother, may approach and snuggle against an animate or inanimate object that looks nothing like the mother, particularly if the object moves; and as a result of this early experience, the animal may direct social behavior toward the object throughout its life. There is usually a very limited age span—called the *critical period*—during which this learning can occur, and the learned attachment is nearly irreversible. Lorenz called this special kind of learning "imprinting." His and most other experiments on the phenomenon have been done with chicks and ducklings, although other baby animals such as calves and lambs display a similar tendency (remember "Mary's little lamb" of nursery rhyme fame). The adaptive function of imprinting is probably to enable the animal to recognize its mother and other members of its own species. Lorenz (1952) reported that baby ducklings that had been imprinted on Lorenz himself would waddle after him rather than follow their own mother, and that male birds imprinted on humans would, when mature, court human beings rather than females of their own species.

How can imprinting best be explained? Lorenz accounted for imprinting by assuming that as the nervous system developed, it passed through a special stage during which imprinting could occur. The beginning and end of this stage were assumed to be genetically determined and not influenced by experience. "It was as though a window opened on the external world and then closed again. While the window was open the young animal was affected by certain types of experience, at other times it was not" (Bateson, 1973, p. 103). This special learning mechanism, of course, evolved because of its adaptive significance for the species.

Imprinting, being a form of learning, was not as easy as other ethological findings for behaviorists to ignore. Its most puzzling characteristic is the critical period. Consider how the critical period is handled in a learning-theory account of imprinting offered by Moltz (1960).

Moltz made two assumptions about the newly hatched bird that seemed consistent with his observations: first, that the baby bird is unemotional—that is, shows little fear; and second, that its visual system is especially sensitive to movement. During the earliest period, Moltz assumed, a moving object will become associated with the low anxiety state through classical conditioning (an S–R bond). At a slightly later stage, fear develops; and at the same time, locomotor ability (the ability to walk and run) develops. During this stage, Moltz assumes, moving objects associated with low anxiety during the first stage have the power to decrease anxiety or fear—and a decrease in the fear drive will reinforce any habit that precedes it. Thus if the fearful bird approaches the moving object to which it was exposed during the first stage, the fear will be reduced, and the behavior will be reinforced. In this way the bird learns to follow a moving object. Finally, Moltz assumed that as the bird becomes older still, anxiety becomes less easily aroused, and so approach to the imprinted stimulus is no longer so easily reinforced. Here Moltz has explained the "critical period" not by assuming a specialized learning mechanism which turns on and then off, as Lorenz theorized, but by assuming a developmental increase and then decrease in anxiety. Moltz's imprinting theory does not require a special learning mechanism, governed by special laws—only a developmental change in emotionality. The conditioning laws assumed in his theory were ones most behaviorists would find acceptable.

Moltz's (1960) attempt to explain imprinting in familiar learning theory terms did not survive for long (see Moltz, 1963), but it is a good illustration of a behavioristic attempt to deal with ethological findings. Current work on imprinting continues to search for underlying mechanisms, as Moltz did. Some theorists, like Moltz, attempt to explain imprinting in terms of the time-honored laws of classical and instrumental conditioning (for example, Hoffman and Ratner, 1973);

others are more receptive to the notion that imprinting may be a form of learning with its own special laws (see Bateson, 1973).

Taste Aversion Learning

To the student of animal learning using standard experimental paradigms, standard laboratory apparatus, and the standard laboratory rat or pigeon, the implications of ethological research for learning theory were not obvious at first. Research using unfamiliar methods and unfamiliar organisms, published in unfamiliar journals (often in unfamiliar languages), was easy to ignore. When the biological determinants of learning were eventually forced on the attention of learning theorists, it was by experiments using standard experimental methods and the standard white rat. The experiments were concerned with learned taste aversion.

Wild rats that survive a poisoning attempt will thereafter refuse to touch the poisoned bait. This has been known for some time, but its implications for learning theory were recognized only recently, when John Garcia and his colleagues began investigating the phenomenon in the laboratory. Garcia and Koelling (1966) conducted four experiments all having the same basic design: In stage one, white rats drank flavored water from an apparatus that flashed a light and produced a loud click whenever they licked the water spout. The stimulus complex present during drinking had two components of interest to the investigators: a gustatory ("tasty" water) CS and an audio-visual ("bright-noisy" water) CS. These stimuli were paired with a UCS, which was different in the four experiments. In one experiment, the UCS was X-radiation, administered during 20-minute periods while the animal drank. In another, it was the chemical lithium chloride, present in the drinking water. Being exposed to X-rays and drinking lithium chloride, in the dosages used, resulted in delayed onset of gastrointestinal disturbance and nausea. In the other two experiments, the UCS was electric shock to the feet. In stage two of all four experiments, after recovering from effects of the UCS, the rats were allowed to drink water. To determine whether conditioning had occurred to the gustatory and audio-visual components of the CS, the rats were tested separately with either the "tasty" or the "bright-noisy" water, and the amount drunk was measured. The rats made sick during stage one, either by X-rays or by the drug, avoided the gustatory CS, but not the audio-visual one. Those that had received electric shock in stage one avoided the audio-visual CS, but not the gustatory one. It seems that learning was selective. Electric shock was associated with light and sound, while sickness was associated with taste. It was almost as though pain made the animal think, "it must have been something I could hear or see," while sickness made it think, "it must have been something I ate."

Note an important point about this finding: it appears to be a violation of the general process view of learning. The gustatory CS was associated with sickness and not with shock, while the audio-visual CS was associated with shock and not with sickness. The laws of learning apparently depend on the particular combination of CS and UCS involved. The finding suggests a specialized learning mechanism. Linking sickness with taste would be of survival value for a rat; but linking sickness with flashes and clicks would not be. It could be that a learning mechanism has evolved to assure that the appropriate connection is made.

Another experiment, by Garcia, Ervin, and Koelling (1966), demonstrated an even more remarkable fact: that taste aversion learning occurs over quite long CS–UCS delays. In this study, six groups of rats were used. In stage one, each group drank saccharin-flavored water. In stage two, this was followed by an injection of a sickness-producing drug either 30, 45, 75, 120, or 180 minutes later, for five groups, and the animals were then given time to recover from the sickness. A control group was given no injection during stage two. In stage three, the rats were allowed to drink saccharin water, and their fluid intake was measured. The results are shown in Figure 7.1. Apparently, the rats trained with a CS–UCS delay of as long as 75 minutes learned to avoid drinking the saccharin water; only the 2- and 3-hour delay groups drank about the same amount as the no-UCS control.

This ability to associate events over delays of many minutes is astonishing, given the laws of conditioning established with responses such as the GSR, the eye blink, and leg flexion. These responses show optimal conditioning with a CS–UCS interval of $\frac{1}{2}$ second, and little or no conditioning with intervals of 2 seconds or greater (see Kimble, 1961, pp. 155–160). Only the trace conditioning and temporal conditioning procedures, discussed in Chapter 5, show learning over delays of minutes, and these procedures require extensive and painstaking training of the animal. Indeed, taste aversion learning appears to violate the law of contiguity, which has been an unquestioned principle of learning from the writings of the British associationists to the

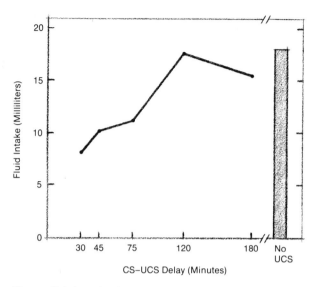

Figure 7.1 Acquired taste aversion in rats. Fluid intake following treatments with various CS–injection delays. "No UCS" denotes control group. [Adapted from Garcia, Ervin, and Koelling, 1966.]

present day. To define "contiguous occurrence" as "at the same time, give or take 75 minutes" is stretching the meaning of the term too far.

Garcia's findings on taste aversion learning in rats—particularly those showing learning over long delays—were not immediately accepted by other investigators. *The Journal of Comparative and Physiological Psychology, Science,* and *The Psychological Review* refused to publish his initial papers. One researcher (quoted by Seligman and Hager, 1972) stated publicly that the findings were "no more likely than birdshit in a cuckoo clock." Subsequent research, however, has confirmed the original results; and additional discoveries have been made about special associative abilities in taste aversion learning.

If a rat samples several foods before becoming sick, the tendency will be to associate sickness with the most recent one. This result is implied by the delay gradient shown in Figure 7.1. But there are exceptions to this rule. In particular, it has been shown that a rat that eats both a novel food and a familiar food prior to illness is more likely to avoid the novel than the familiar food on a later test. This occurs regardless of the order in which the two foods were eaten (Revusky and Bedarf, 1967). Roll and Smith (1972) have shown that rats learn taste aversions even when under deep anaesthesia. In stage one of their study, rats were allowed to drink saccharin water. Immediately after, they were anaesthetized. In stage two, 60 minutes after drinking the solution, half the anaesthetized rats were irradiated with X-rays and the other half were not. The rats were kept under anaesthesia for 8 hours, and were then allowed to recover from effects of the radiation and anaesthetic. In stage three, they were allowed to choose either plain water or saccharin solution to drink. The irradiated animals much preferred plain water, while the controls preferred the saccharin solution. It would seem that rats associate illness with flavor even when they are unconscious.

Rozin and Kalat (1971) have proposed that learned taste aversions may underlie what have been called *specific hungers*. It has been known for many years that rats and other animals can control their own diets, eating foods that contain important nutrients and avoiding those that do not. It was once believed that rats must have many innate hunger drives, each specific to a particular nutrient. Rozin and Kalat, however, produced evidence that the decline in health of an animal that has been eating a deficient diet leads to a learned aversion to that diet. Thus, they hypothesize that the balanced diet is chosen not because it tastes particularly good, but because the deficient diets have come to taste bad.

A practical application of taste aversion learning has been proposed by Carl Gustavson, at the University of Utah. For years, sheep ranchers and environmentalists have been at odds over the problem of loss of sheep to predators—especially coyotes. One way to save both the sheep and the coyotes may be to teach the coyotes not to kill and eat the sheep. Gustavson, Garcia, Hankins, and Rusiniak (1974) propose letting the coyotes eat sheep carcasses laced with lithium chloride, to develop a specific aversion to sheep. Their initial tests have been promising; after two such meals the coyotes tested would not attack a lamb, and in some cases they actively avoided it. Similar proposals have been made for protecting crops from destructive pests. Allowing birds to feed on chemically treated cherries, for example, might save orchards millions of dollars each year.

The adaptive value of many of the findings surrounding taste aversion learning in rats is obvious. In nature (unlike the laboratory), sickness is most likely to be brought on by food; to avoid a repetition of poisoning, the rat should avoid eating the same food again. For a rat, which forages at night, taste would be the most reliable cue in making such a discrimination. If a rat has made a meal on two substances, a novel one it has never eaten before and a familiar one it has eaten safely many times, then any subsequent sickness was probably caused by the novel food. And since most poisons encountered in nature act slowly, food aversion learning must operate over fairly long CS–UCS delays.

In humans, food aversion may be acquired in much the same way. It is not unusual, in our society, for a young person drinking alcohol for the first time to overindulge. If nausea results, for a long time afterward the person may find the smell and taste of the particular beverage he drank to be aversive. Likewise, a bout with "stomach flu" sometimes produces a distaste for a food eaten prior to the illness— particularly if the food was an unfamiliar one. Despite these apparent similarities between humans and rats, one should recognize that food aversion learning could differ considerably among species, depending upon the particular species' ecological niche.

A striking demonstration of this fact was provided by Wilcoxin, Dragoin, and Kral (1971). In nature, birds learn to avoid eating the toxic monarch butterfly, apparently on sight. This suggests that certain birds, unlike rats, may be predisposed to associate sickness with visual cues. Wilcoxin and his co-workers tested this hypothesis in an experiment using both rats and quail. Both species were given the same experimental treatment. In stage one they were given blue, sour water to drink. In stage two, a half hour later, a sickness-producing drug was administered. In stage three, half the animals of each species were allowed to drink blue water and half to drink sour water, and fluid intake was measured. The rats avoided drinking the sour water but showed no aversion to blue water. This finding, of course, is consistent with previous work. The result for quail, however, was the opposite. The quail avoided drinking blue water, but drank clear sour water as much as they had before being given the drug.

It would be hard to come up with a more obvious contradiction to the general process view of learning. If one wants to predict how closely one event must follow another in time in order to become associated, one must know what the first event is, what the second event is, and what organism is involved. It is significant, also, that these relationships can apparently be predicted from a careful consideration of how the organism relates to its natural environment, and how that environment might have led to the evolution of predispositions to learn certain relationships rather than others.

Instinct in the Learning Laboratory

The sudden realization that biological determinants of learning exist has led learning psychologists to begin reading the literature on ethology, and to begin analyzing the standard laboratory animal in the standard laboratory task in terms of the function of the animal's behavior in its natural surroundings. In the process, new findings have emerged and old findings have taken on new significance.

Many investigators have noted that a hungry rat in a T-maze will tend to alternate turning left and right from trial to trial, even when food is found only at the end of one of the two paths. Is this because a wild rat, foraging for food, is more likely to find it in a new location than in a location where it recently consumed all the available food? Hogan (1973) has demonstrated long-delay operant conditioning in 3-day-old chicks. First, the chicks were allowed to peck sand for 10 minutes; 2 hours later they were force-fed a food-water mixture. After another $1\frac{1}{2}$ hours, their rate of pecking sand was measured and found to have increased significantly. Is this because animals learn what to eat, and the choice must be affected by the slow process of digestion? Bregman (1934) attempted to replicate and extend the Watson and Rayner findings of fear conditioning in infants, and discovered that while an animal would function as an effective CS, an object such as a block of wood or a curtain would not. Is this because babies are genetically predisposed to fear animate objects but not inanimate ones? And some phobias, such as the fear of snakes or of being in a high place, are common among human adults, while others, such as the fear of scissors or forks, are extremely rare. Is this because the dangers posed by snakes and high places were part of the precivilization environment in which we evolved? It is difficult to train a cat to press a lever for food; the cat will crouch before the empty feeder mechanism in anticipation, but will not approach the lever. Is the cat's natural food-getting behavior in conflict with the habit it is supposed to learn? It is easy to teach a rat to run or jump to avoid a shock, but teaching a rat to press a lever for the same reward requires special training procedures. Is this because running and jumping are natural defense responses of the rat, while "freezing," another natural response, interferes with lever-pressing (see Bolles, 1970)? It is very difficult to teach a pigeon to peck a key to turn off a shock, but very easy to teach it to peck the key for food. Is this because pecking is part of a pigeon's natural food-getting behavior but not part of its escape behavior?

The example of key-pecking for food by pigeons is an especially interesting one. Skinner and his followers have used it as a prime example of operant conditioning. However, as was mentioned in Chapter 4, the phenomenon known as *autoshaping* shows that key-pecking is easily conditioned using classical procedures. Repeated pairings of a lighted key and food soon bring a pigeon to peck the lighted key. Notice that this procedure involves a CS–UCS, not a response–reinforcer relationship, and so conforms to the classical or Pavlovian conditioning paradigm. Indeed, key-pecking in such a situation is apparently so natural for a pigeon that one cannot eliminate it by removing any possibility of response–reinforcer pairings. Williams and Williams (1969) paired a lighted key with food, but omitted the food whenever the pigeon pecked the key. Thus the key-peck was never rewarded, and the CS–UCS pairing occurred only when the pecking response was not made first. Despite the negative consequence of key-pecking, the hungry pigeons continued to peck, albeit at a low rate. It has been shown that even when the bird does not have access to the key, repeated pairings of the lighted key and food result in conditioning. Given access to the lighted key after observing such pairings, the pigeon will immediately approach and peck it (Moore, 1973).

Further evidence that autoshaping is classical conditioning comes from examination of the topography, or form, of the response. Jenkins and Moore (1973) trained pigeons that were both hungry and thirsty by using two keys—the left one paired with water and the right one with food. They recorded the key-pecks on film, and some of their photographs have been redrawn in Figure 7.2. When pigeons pecked the right key (right half of figure) their beaks were open, as they must be to pick up food. When they pecked the left key (left half of figure) their beaks were nearly closed, and further observations showed that they licked with their tongues much as they do when drinking water. In pigeons trained with the operant procedure, with water or food reward, pecks resemble those that Jenkins and Moore obtained with autoshaping. Wasserman (1973) has shown autoshaping of key-pecks for a heat reinforcer. Baby chicks were placed in a cold chamber, and a lighted key was repeatedly paired with onset of a heat lamp. The

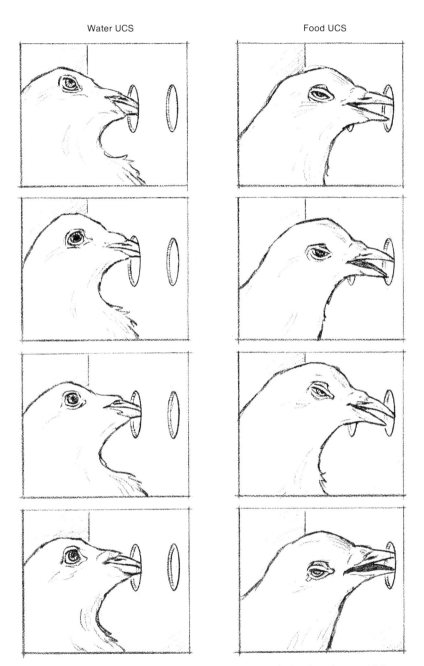

Water UCS   Food UCS

Figure 7.2 "Topography" of autoshaped key-pecks in the pigeon. [After Jenkins and Moore, 1973. Copyright 1973 by the Society for the Experimental Analysis of Behavior, Inc.]

chicks soon began to peck the key. The form of the key-peck gradually came to resemble snuggling. Baby chicks will approach, peck, and snuggle against a mother hen to initiate brooding (Hogan, 1974).

The research on autoshaping has come as a distinct embarrassment to Skinnerian researchers. Experimenters claim that it is much easier to get a pigeon to peck a key if you simply wait until it looks toward the key and then pair illumination of the key with food (the autoshaping procedure) than if you reinforce closer and closer approximations to the desired response (the operant "shaping" procedure). Moore (1973) argues that much of what Skinner and other workers have investigated over the years under the heading of operant conditioning has really been classical conditioning in the form of autoshaping. It has also been claimed that the stereotyped behavior seen in the "superstition" experiment, which Skinner attributed to the accidental pairing of an arbitrary response with reinforcement, is really species-specific food-seeking behavior, produced through classical temporal conditioning (Staddon and Simmelhag, 1971).

Learning in Ethology

Other examples of biological determinants of learning have come from ethological research. Marler (1970) has studied song development in the white-crowned sparrow, and has postulated a specialized learning mechanism to explain his findings. The song of the white-crowned sparrow varies somewhat from area to area, forming local "dialects." Marler's research shows that the young male birds learn the local dialect by hearing it during a critical period from 10 to 50 days after hatching. This is about 8 months before they come into song. If the bird is exposed to the song of another species, or to no song at all, during this early critical period, it later sings only a very degraded version of the song of its own species. If it is exposed to a particular dialect during this time, it later sings that version of the song, regardless of the song of its parents. Marler suggests that a kind of auditory "template" is formed during the critical period, and that exposure to the song fills in the details of the template that are not genetically determined. Later, when the bird comes into song, it gradually learns to produce a version closely matching the template that was formed earlier. This theory is supported by the fact that deafening the bird before it comes into song, and thus depriving it of auditory feedback to compare with the template, prevents the early exposure to a particular dialect from having its effect. A bird deafened before coming into song never learns to sing properly; one deafened afterwards, however, continues to sing normally.

Another even more remarkable learning ability has been shown to play a role in migratory activity of the indigo bunting, studied by Emlen (1975). Indigo buntings, like many other birds, fly south in the fall and north in the spring. By testing the birds in a planetarium, in small cages with transparent tops, Emlen showed that they oriented themselves with respect to the star pattern of the nighttime sky. By systematically blocking out different parts of the sky, Emlen determined that the constellations closest to Polaris (the North Star) were the ones they used for orientation. In the fall the birds oriented away from northern constellations that were visible; in the spring they oriented toward them. Apparently, the birds possess a "star map" of a limited part of the sky, which they use in migration.

Is this star map learned or innate? There are reasons to suppose it might be learned, since the stellar orientation of the Earth's axis changes—13,000 years ago Polaris was 43° away from north, and in another 13,000 years it will be 43° away again. A genetically fixed star map, therefore, would have to slowly evolve to take these changes into account. To determine whether the star map was innate or learned, Emlen raised nestling indigo buntings by hand. Some birds were not exposed to the night sky; others were exposed to the night sky in the planetarium, rotating, as usual, around Polaris; still others were exposed to the planetarium sky modified to rotate around the star Betelgeuse. When the birds were tested in the fall, those that had not seen the night sky did not orient themselves consistently; those previously exposed to the normal sky oriented away from Polaris; and those that had seen the stars rotate around Betelgeuse oriented away from Betelgeuse. Apparently, these birds are genetically programmed to learn the star patterns around the sky's axis of rotation, and to use that information in their later migratory behavior.

The Challenge to Learning Theory

These examples, and others as well, have assaulted learning theory in an unending barrage. There has hardly been time to stop and assess the damage done. Evidence for the biological determinants of learning is overwhelming, but what does it all mean? Can the general process view of learning be salvaged at all?

Seligman (1970) has proposed that this problem can be handled by assuming that every behavior falls at some point on a dimension of *preparedness*. At one end of this dimension are those behaviors that appear with no learning whatever. Such behaviors are what can be called instincts. Near this end of the dimension are "prepared" behaviors, which appear with a minimum of experience. In the middle of the preparedness scale are behaviors that are "unprepared"; these behaviors can be learned with moderate difficulty. Seligman proposes that most laboratory learning tasks fall in this middle range. Toward the other end are behaviors for which the organism is "contraprepared"; that is, the animal's biology is such that these behaviors are difficult or impossible to learn.

Seligman's hypothesis is that such a dimension may be of considerable predictive value, if it can be shown that the laws of learning vary in a systematic way as one moves up and down the scale. He suggests, for example, that as one moves from the prepared to the contraprepared end of the dimension, one might find that (a) the number of trials necessary for learning increases, (b) the maximum temporal separation of events which will produce learning decreases, (c) the degree of generalization decreases, and (d) resistance to extinction decreases.

As soon as the problem is phrased in terms of ease of learning, however, it becomes clear that the general process view should be able to deal with some of the relevant findings. Learning theorists have always assumed that some stimuli are more learnable than others, if only because certain properties such as movement, intensity, or uniqueness make them more noticeable or "salient." Likewise, it is obvious that some responses should be easier than others to learn simply because they are easier to make. And most learning theorists have made use of the notion of competing responses. The cat that cannot be trained to press a lever for food and the pigeon that fails to learn to peck a key to escape shock could be demonstrating interference by innate (UCS–UCR) behaviors that prevent the desired response from occurring. But it is clear that such considerations will not handle all the findings regarding biological determinants of learning. The Garcia and Koelling (1966) finding that an audio-visual CS is associated with shock and a gustatory CS with sickness cannot be explained just in terms of the quality of the CS or the animal's reaction to the UCS.

Another approach is to assume that the general process view is basically correct, but incomplete. Testa (1975) found that the effectiveness of classical conditioning using a light CS and an air-blast UCS depended on the sources of the two stimuli (from the ceiling or floor of the rat's cage) and on the temporal patterns of the two stimuli (steady or rapidly pulsed). The best conditioning occurred when the CS and UCS had similar locations and temporal patterns. Testa suggests that, in addition to temporal contiguity, *spatial contiguity* and *similarity* be adopted as basic principles of associative learning. This modification might, as Testa argues, account for taste aversion learning in the rat.

But neither Testa's proposal nor Seligman's preparedness hypothesis seems capable of handling all the data. Both proposals suggest that the laws of conditioning for all highly prepared behaviors should be essentially the same. But in what sense are the laws of song learning in the white-crowned sparrow and star-map learning in the indigo bunting similar to each other, or to those of taste aversion learning in the rat? The complexities of these phenomena suggest, not a general learning mechanism, but special mechanisms that have evolved to serve particular adaptive functions in each species' relationship to its environment.

The challenge to learning theory seems to be this: Must *all* forms of learning be thought of as reflecting special learning mechanisms, or can the forms of learning that appear peculiar, such as star-map learning in migratory birds, be considered special cases, leaving the general process view of learning intact to deal with the vast bulk of learned behavior? This is a problem that ethologists and learning theorists will probably struggle with for some time to come.

THE EVOLUTION OF INTELLIGENCE

A somewhat different challenge has been hurled at American learning theorists by Gregory Razran (1971). Born in Russia and educated in the United States, Razran has maintained contact with both the Western and the Soviet psychological traditions. Psychology in the Soviet Union has firm roots in physiology (see the discussion of Pavlov in Chapter 3) and has always had an evolutionary flavor conspicuously lacking in American theories. In his book *Mind in Evolution*, subtitled, "An East–West Synthesis of Learned Behavior and Cognition," Razran chides behaviorists and cognitivists alike:

The main establishment of present-day American psychology is sharply severed into two antagonist, yet in one sense allied, camps: unevolutionary conditioners, for whom the minds of worms and men are the minds of rats, and unevolutionary cognitionists, to whom the minds of worms and rats are the minds of men (Razran, 1971, p. 5).

His point is well taken. American learning theorists have ignored differences not only among species that are at about the same phylogenetic or evolutionary level, but also among species of obviously different levels. B. F. Skinner has earned notoriety with his assumption that complex human behavior can be understood in terms of principles derived from the behavior of a pigeon in a box; and more than one attempt has been made to apply Hullian theory to human thought, language, personality, or social behavior (for example, Dollard and Miller, 1950). As for Tolman's theory, one can readily believe that learning in humans and apes involves expectancies and cognitive maps (and if one accepts the experimental evidence, one may believe this of rats as well)—but what about worms, or even fish?

Razran's Learning Hierarchy

Razran's view is that different types of learning, of increasing complexity, have evolved along with the nervous system. His major effort, in which he reviews over 1,500 publications in Russian, English, and German, is to identify the various types and relate each to the evolutionary stage at which it first appears. The types of learning form a hierarchy, and each type is assumed to (a) evolve out of the simpler types below it, and (b) coexist with the simpler types in all species above the phylogenetic level at which it first emerged.

Razran identifies four "superlevels" of learning, each including more than one identifiable subtype (1971, pp. 310–311). Beginning with the simplest type of learning, the superlevels are as follows:

A. *Reactive.* This category includes habituation and sensitization, which some investigators are reluctant to classify as learning at all. Habituation occurs at all phylogenetic levels, even appearing in the protozoa (one-celled animals). Sensitization is first found in coelenterates (simple, many-celled animals such as the jellyfish).

B. *Associative.* Razran discusses three types of associative learning. One is inhibitory conditioning—learning not to repeat an act which is punished—which he considers the most primitive form of associative learning. Such learning has been demonstrated in coelenterates. The second is classical or Pavlovian conditioning, which has been demonstrated in animals as simple as worms. The third is instrumental or operant conditioning, which appears first in lower vertebrates (fish) and in some insects. (Both fish and insects are thought to have evolved out of wormlike creatures, but they represent different branches of the evolutionary tree.)

C. *Integrative.* This level of learning is considered particularly important by Razran, who equates it with "perception." In essence, it is the ability to combine different sensations into a single perceived stimulus. One sublevel of integrative learning is sensory preconditioning (S–S learning). Another is configuring, which is learning to respond to two or more sensations in combination and to not respond to them separately. Configuring could be demonstrated in dogs by using two stimuli, say a bell (CS_1) and a light (CS_2). The combination $CS_1 + CS_2$ is followed by food; CS_1 alone and CS_2 alone are never followed by food. If the dog learns to salivate to $CS_1 + CS_2$ and to not salivate to either component alone, configuring is shown. According to Razran's review of the literature, the capacity for sensory preconditioning and configuring forms a dividing line between higher and lower vertebrates. These phenomena can be shown with birds and mammals, but are difficult or impossible to demonstrate in fish, amphibians, and reptiles.

If integration of sensations (S–S learning) is possible only in higher vertebrates, as Razran contends, then Tolman's theory could not apply to learning in lower vertebrates. Unlike birds and mammals, fish and reptiles may be fated to live as S–R mechanisms. More will be said on this matter in a moment.

D. *Symbolic.* The highest level of learning in Razran's system is associated with language, and is almost exclusively human. The capacity to use arbitrary symbols is necessary not only for communication, but also for abstract thought. The symbolic level is assumed to dominate the perceptual level, and the perceptual level to dominate the associative. Thus conditioning, in humans, can be influenced by symbolic thought.

Let us return to Razran's view regarding the learning abilities of higher and lower vertebrates. The comparative psychologist M. E. Bitterman has studied the learning of species of different phylogenetic levels, and has arrived at conclusions that complement and extend those of Razran. Bitterman and his colleagues have compared the effects of various manipulations on learning in fish, turtles, rats, and pigeons. One such experiment was the reward-shift experiment discussed in the previous chapter. Recall that a rat trained with a large reward and switched to a small one slows its running as soon as the switch has been discovered—a finding at variance with the "strong law of effect" embodied in the 1943 version of Hull's theory. The strong law of effect assumes that the only function of a reinforcer is to strengthen the just-exercised habit, and that the degree of strengthening is proportional to the size of the reward. A switch from a large reward to a small one will slow down the rate of learning, but cannot reverse it. Thus, the strong law of effect does not predict that the animal will slow down. Bitterman's surprising result is that fish and turtles, unlike rats and pigeons, behave as the strong law of effect says they should. A fish trained to swim for 40 worms swims faster than one trained with only 4. But if the reward is switched from 40 worms to 4, it continues to swim as rapidly as before. A similar result has been obtained for reward shift with turtles (see Bitterman, 1975). This suggests that the complete rejection of reinforcement theories, based primarily on experiments with rats, was premature. The elegant and plausible adaptive mechanism postulated by Hull and other S–R reinforcement theorists may actually exist, but in animals phylogenetically simpler than the rat.

Another such finding discussed by Bitterman (1975) concerns the partial-reinforcement effect. Simple S–R reinforcement theories predict that 100-percent reinforcement will produce a stronger habit than will partial reinforcement, and that the habit will therefore take longer to extinguish. This outcome, too, is found in fish and turtles (providing the trials are widely spaced)—but not in rats and pigeons. Again, the suggestion is that whatever conclusion one makes about learning in mammals and birds, S–R reinforcement theory may be valid for lower vertebrates.

Still other evidence suggests that damage to particular brain structures may make a mammal behave like one of its more primitive ancestors. Damage to a structure called the hippocampus is known to retard learning in humans. Primarily because of this fact, numerous experiments have been done with rats in an attempt to determine exactly what role the hippocampus plays in learning. However, removal of the hippocampus from a rat's brain has been found to affect the animal's performance in learning tasks in ways that are difficult to understand. Hirsch (1974) has reviewed the literature on the role of the hippocampus in rat learning, including many experiments similar in design to those described in Chapter 6. His thesis, essentially, is that removal of the hippocampus changes the animal from a Tolmanian rat, which behaves according to its expectancies, into a Hullian rat, which learns according to S–R reinforcement principles. Much the same conclusions have been reached by O'Keefe and Nadel (1974), who hypothesize that the hippocampus is the location of Tolman's cognitive map.

In relating such speculations to the work of Bitterman, one might be tempted to conclude that removal of the hippocampus, in effect, "turned the rat into a reptile." A safer conclusion would be that S–R reinforcement theory is not "wrong," but just describes a more primitive kind of learning than that normally exhibited by the intact, higher vertebrates that have provided the bulk of our data on learning. The learning mechanism described by S–R reinforcement theory may be present in all vertebrates, but may be dominated by a more powerful expectancy mechanism in organisms as phylogenetically advanced as the rat.

Brain Size

Razran's conclusion about the relative learning abilities of higher and lower vertebrates also receives support from a very different kind of evidence. In a book entitled *Evolution of the Brain and Intelligence*, Jerison (1973) has compared the brain sizes of many vertebrate species, both living and extinct, and has drawn from these data conclusions about the evolution of the mind.

It is reasonable to suppose that the more neurons there are in a brain, the greater is its information-processing capacity. Brain size, then, should be related to intelligence. But one cannot use brain size alone to estimate the intelligence of a species, since the larger the body is the more sensory input and motor output must be integrated by the brain just to keep the animal functioning. Brain size should increase with body size for that reason alone.

A graph relating brain weight to body weight among vertebrates is shown in Figure 7.3. Because there are many more small vertebrate species than large ones, and because the differences between small animals are much smaller than those between large ones, the figure is drawn using logarithmic coordinates. It is derived from data presented by Jerison, representing over 200 species, including fossil rep-

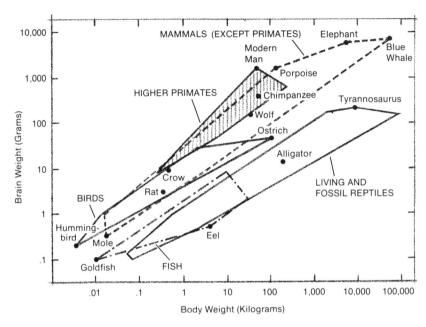

Figure 7.3 Brain weight as a function of body weight for various vertebrates. [Adapted from Jerison, 1973.]

tiles. (Estimates of brain weight of fossil animals were derived from casts of the insides of the skulls.) Points representing several familiar species are labelled in the figure. The five enclosed areas—for fish, reptiles, birds, mammals, and higher primates—were constructed by drawing the smallest possible perimeter figure around all members of a particular class. The general increase in brain weight with body weight is apparent from the figure. It is also apparent that there is a clean separation between the higher and lower vertebrates; the areas for fish and reptiles fall below and do not overlap with those for birds and mammals. Notice that this difference in brain weight is really much larger than the logarithmic scale makes it appear: The typical higher vertebrate has a brain perhaps ten times as large as that of a lower vertebrate of about the same body size.

From examination of fossils, Jerison (1973) has concluded that the increases in brain size of birds and mammals were due to different selective pressures. That for birds apparently took place rapidly; that for mammals much more slowly. He presents a most interesting hypothesis about the evolution of brain size in mammals. In essence, it is that early mammals adapted to nocturnal life, rather than competing for daytime ecological niches with the dominant reptiles, by developing a perceptual system in which the sensory modalities of sight, hearing, touch, and smell were integrated, providing a unified representation of the environment. It is just such a system that would be required for integrative learning such as configuring, which Razran (1971) attributes to higher, but not lower, vertebrates.

The striking increase in brain size with the evolution of modern man is also documented by Jerison (1973). This increase, like the one separating lower and higher vertebrates, corresponds to one of Razran's dividing lines: The capacity for symbolic learning separates humans from their furred and feathered relatives. Just as communication among sensory modalities may have led to evolution of a larger brain in mammals, perhaps communication among individuals led to the increased brain size of man. Possessing language, early humans must have had a tremendous advantage over their competitors. Not only could they exchange detailed information while hunting, they could also share with each other past experiences and future plans. Selective pressure, in such a situation, would favor those with greater linguistic skills and with greater capacity to store and use the information language can carry.

CONDITIONING, LANGUAGE, AND THOUGHT

Most of the major figures in the history of learning theory, such as Thorndike, Watson, Hull, Tolman, and Skinner, felt that by studying learning in simpler organisms they would come to understand learning in humans. Often this belief led them to apply directly to humans conditioning principles discovered using cats, rats, or pigeons, with little regard for unique human qualities. As we have seen in this chapter, there are reasons to be skeptical of attempts to extrapolate from these animals to man—not only because the human ecological niche is different from that of a cat, rat, or pigeon, but also because *Homo sapiens* has achieved a higher evolutionary level than other animals. Jerison (1973) estimates that the human brain contains some 8.5 billion "extra" neurons, over and above those required of a "basic" mammal of the same body size. In comparison, the chimpanzee, our closest living relative, has around 3.3 billion "extra" neurons. The extra brain power of humans has been put to spectacular uses: language, the ability to make and use tools, and a complex social structure. Above all, human behavior is vastly more flexible than that of any other animal. It is hard to believe, considering these accomplishments, that no principles are involved in human learning beyond those governing learning in rodents and birds.

The position taken here follows Razran (and Pavlov, before him) in assuming that human evolution marked the emergence of new learning principles, associated with the development of language. These higher forms of learning can (and usually do) control human behavior, even in situations tailored for classical and instrumental conditioning. If this position is correct, then the direct implications of conditioning principles for human behavior are limited indeed. Behavioristic theories, then, will inevitably prove inadequate for understanding human behavior. Only some form of cognitive theory, which assumes that behavior is controlled by mental events, can succeed. We saw in the last chapter that cognitive theory has proved better able to cope with the behavior of rats. Surely this must be even more true of the behavior of humans.

There are those who would disagree on both counts. Skinner, and many other behaviorists with applied interests, have claimed that conditioning principles can be applied to complex human behavior essentially unchanged. They have further claimed that such behavior can be understood without reference to mental events (for example, Skinner, 1971). The proof of their assertions lies in the vast and growing literature on "behavior modification." Since the claims of Skinner and his followers are diametrically opposed to the position taken in this book, some space must be devoted to an examination of the evidence they present. Our purpose is not to survey all the supposed applications of conditioning principles to human behavior, or to dwell on related questions of the effectiveness of these techniques or of the ethics of their use. It is simply to determine what they tell us about the nature of human learning. Can human behavior be predicted using principles of animal conditioning, with little or no modification? Can it be explained without reference to mental events? Let us see.

Programmed Instruction

One of the more dramatic ventures of conditioning principles into the "real world" began with a talk by Skinner, published in the *Harvard Education Review* in 1954. In it, Skinner put his reputation as an authority on learning behind a proposal that techniques of operant conditioning be applied to the classroom. The task of education, he said, was not much different from that of the experimenter in the operant conditioning laboratory. It was to bring behavior under the control of appropriate stimuli. For example, the verbal behavior involved in counting, or saying "odd," "even," or "prime" could be considered as responses to a spoken or written number. From his vantage point, he saw many things wrong with the way teachers tried to establish such behavior in their students. For one thing, teachers tended to use punishment (for example, low grades or trips to the principal's office) rather than positive reinforcement. For another, reinforcement was far too infrequent. When it did occur, it was probably too late:

> The contingencies [the teacher] provides are far from optimal. It can easily be demonstrated that, unless explicit mediating behavior has been set up, the lapse of only a few seconds between response and reinforcement destroys most of the effect. In a typical classroom, nevertheless, long periods of time customarily elapse. The teacher may walk up and down the aisle, for example, while the class is working on a sheet of problems, pausing here and there to say right or wrong. Many seconds or minutes intervene between the child's response and the teacher's reinforcement. In many cases—for example when papers are taken home to be corrected—as much as 24 hours may intervene. It is surprising that this system has any effect whatsoever (Skinner, 1954, pp. 90–91).

A far better system could be devised, Skinner said. It would have several important properties: (a) it would provide immediate positive reinforcement of each response, (b) it would require the student to emit the desired behavior (writing an answer instead of choosing an alternative on a multiple-choice test), (c) it would allow the student to proceed at his own pace, and (d) it would carefully control the sequence of stimuli to which the student is exposed—thus keeping errors to a minimum and shaping closer and closer approximations to the final complex behavior desired.

As with lower organisms in the laboratory, Skinner said, all this could best be accomplished using a machine. He advocated adoption of the "teaching machine," invented in the 1920s by S. L. Pressey at Ohio State University, but never accepted by educators. In Skinner's scheme, teaching machines would play the role of a good tutor, by presenting material and administering reinforcement according to a carefully thought out sequence of stimulus frames called a program. As a result of such developments, Skinner foresaw vast changes in the field of education:

> We are on the threshold of an exciting and revolutionary period, in which the scientific study of man will be put to work in man's best interests. Education must play its part. It must accept the fact that a sweeping revision of educational practices is possible and inevitable (Skinner, 1954, p. 97).

It is quite obvious that Skinner's revolution has not come about. This has not been because of a lack of interest on the part of psychologists or educators. Research on *programmed instruction,* as it is called, proceeded apace. The effectiveness of programmed instruction was evaluated by conducting experiments in the classroom, and different types of programs were developed and compared. It was soon discovered (to the dismay of manufacturers of teaching machines) that the cost of programmed instruction could be brought down by using a programmed text rather than a machine. Programmed textbooks have become fairly common, but one certainly could not say that programmed instruction has revolutionized education.

The reason does not lie in the inertia of the educational establishment; it lies in the fact that programmed instruction is not much better (and in some ways worse) than traditional teaching methods (Hilgard and Bower, 1966). Most of the advantages Skinner saw in the technique have turned out to be less important than he thought. Carefully sequenced programs are not always superior to random presentation of frames; allowing the student to make errors is not necessarily harmful; immediate reinforcement (knowledge of results) may be no better than delayed reinforcement; and requiring the student to emit an overt response can be helpful or harmful, depending on the subject matter. In spelling, as one might suppose, overt responding helps. In other subjects, however, written responses may take so much time that they interfere with learning more than they help. In addition, some experimental studies of human learning using techniques to be described in the next chapter have shown delayed reinforcement to be more effective than immediate reinforcement, and overt responding to be less effective than studying silently (Cook, 1963).

Thus we see that variables that are important in the operant conditioning of rats and pigeons may be of little importance in human education. Skinner himself noted that children do learn in the classroom—a fact he found "surprising." It is only surprising, however, if one assumes that the laws of human and animal learning are the same.

Behavior Control

Problems of discipline, as well as instruction, have invited application of operant techniques in the classroom. Consider an "extension of the principles of the experimental analysis of behavior" described by Sulzbacher and Houser (1968). A class of mentally retarded children was repeatedly disrupted by a gesture the article refers to as the "naughty finger." The teacher set out to eliminate this disruption using behavior modification. After recording the "baseline" or pre-treatment rate of occurrence of the gesture for 9 days, the teacher began the tenth day with the following instruction:

> From now on there will be a special ten minute recess at the end of the day. However, if I see the naughty finger or hear about it, I will flip down one of these cards, and you will have one minute less of recess whenever this happens. Remember, every time I flip down one of these cards, all of you lose a minute from your recess (Sulzbacher and Houser, 1966, p. 88).

After the contingency had been in effect for 18 days, the teacher told the children it no longer held. Occurrence of the naughty finger was measured for 9 more days after this. The data are shown in Figure 7.4.

How do these results relate to operant conditioning? Recall that Skinner's (1938) law of operant conditioning specifies that the response occurs, is reinforced, and consequently increases in frequency. The desired response, in this case, can be defined as *not* making the gesture. Notice, however, that the frequency of the desired response changed before reinforcement ever occurred; that is, the extra recess came at the *end* of day 10, after the behavior had already dramatically changed. (Extinction, on day 28, was less dramatic, but that change also seems to have occurred before the absence of the contingency was experienced.) What happened here was not operant conditioning. Something made the behavior change even *before* it could be reinforced—and that something, obviously, was the verbal instruction.

Other examples of the effectiveness of verbal instruction are easy to find in the literature on behavior modification. A method called *con-*

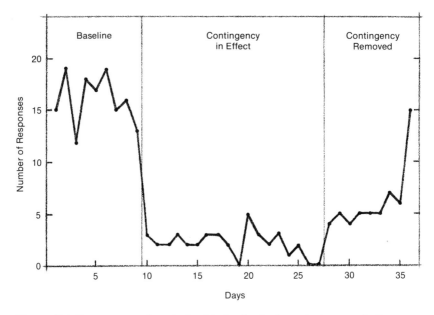

Figure 7.4 Occurrence of undesired behavior before, during, and after contingency. [After Sulzbacher and Houser, 1968. Copyright 1968 by the American Association on Mental Deficiency.]

tingency contracting, used in the classroom, has the teacher manipulate an individual student's study habits by entering into an agreement or "contract" with the student, specifying which activities will lead to which rewards. A student fascinated by history but poor in mathematics, for example, might be allowed to read history for a specified time if and only if he correctly completes his homework assignment in arithmetic. (Note that this is an application of the "Premack principle," discussed in Chapter 6.) Alternative reinforcing events might be playing chess, painting, or talking with a friend. The important point is that the terms of the contract must be specified clearly and the contingencies followed exactly as agreed upon. In contingency contracting, obviously, it is the verbal agreement that affects the child's behavior. The promised reinforcer does not occur until after the child has done his part. It is, indeed, the *promise* that changes the behavior, not the reinforcer itself. Contingency contracting, therefore, does not fit the definition of operant conditioning.

Another supposed application of operant conditioning principles, used in a variety of institutions such as schools, mental hospitals, prisons, and reform schools, is the *token economy* (Ayllon and Azrin, 1968). The basic idea is that tokens—or perhaps just points—are awarded for the behaviors desired by those in charge. These rewards (usually referred to in the behavior modification literature as "secondary positive reinforcers") can then be used by the inmate or student to purchase other, more desirable rewards or privileges, which may be time watching television, use of the machine shop, candy, cigarettes, library privileges, a day in town, and so on, depending on the exact situation in which the system is being used. A set of explicit rules is laid out, specifying the reinforcement contingencies—which activities will earn tokens, and how many tokens each is worth—together with a list of available rewards or privileges and their token costs.

Token economies have been found very effective in most settings where they have been put into use. As is the case with contingency contracting, however, theoretical discussions of the system have often been misleading. Again, the behavior is clearly controlled by verbal statements. Persons under a token economy regimen do not have to have their behavior carefully shaped, or to discover what behavior will lead to reward, as does a rat in a Skinner box—if that were so, it is doubtful whether the system would work. Behavior is guided by verbal descriptions of the complex activities that will earn tokens and by the verbal promise of what the tokens will buy.

Operant conditioning and the token economy are similar, of course, in that both involve reinforcement contingencies. But the processes by which behavior is acquired in the two cases are obviously quite different, and ignoring these profound differences can only prevent us from understanding the uniqueness of human behavior. For an organism to do what will have beneficial consequences is of obvious value, and it would not be surprising if nature had evolved several different ways in which this could be accomplished—some more efficient than others. The similarities between animal and human learning should not blind us to their differences.

How can the control of human behavior by linguistic stimuli such as spoken or written instructions be understood? The assertion that "a subtle and complex history of reinforcement has generated a special kind of stimulus control" (Skinner, 1974, p. 106) does not seem to throw any light on this matter. At a minimum, it appears that one must assume (a) that human behavior is guided by ideas, and (b) that these ideas can be communicated from one mind to another through symbols. The facts of human behavior seem to require a cognitive approach.

Therapy

Let us consider another applied area: clinical psychology. In the 1960s, at the same time that adherence to behavioristic doctrine was on the decline in experimental psychology, its popularity among clinical psychologists increased dramatically. A small but growing group of psychologists and psychiatrists were battling for the acceptance of *behavior therapy* techniques by a reluctant, tradition-bound profession. The most common techniques of psychotherapy—most notably those of Freudian psychoanalysis—required the patient, or "client," to introspect and talk to the therapist in lengthy sessions designed to uncover repressed memories purported to be the cause of his problems. The theoretical underpinninnings of many of the techniques were complex and obscure (one might even say "occult") and their predictions regarding direct observations, ambiguous. Little effort had been made to verify that the therapeutic methods worked—and what evidence there was suggested that psychotherapy was no more beneficial than no treatment at all (for example, Eysenck, 1952).

In contrast, behavior therapists claimed that their methods (a) dealt with current problem behavior itself, rather than with the past cause assumed to underlie it, (b) assumed that most maladaptive behaviors were learned, (c) were based on well-established principles of learning, (d) could be adapted to the client's problem, (e) set specific, well-defined goals of treatment, and (f) had been empirically validated and found to be effective (Rimm and Masters, 1974). An additional claim was that the methods of behavior therapy were behavioristic, and therefore more scientifically respectable than the older cognitively based talk therapies.

Perhaps the most successful behavior therapy technique has been Joseph Wolpe's *systematic desensitization,* which was mentioned in Chapter 3 in connection with Watson's work on fear conditioning in children. The basic rationale—as in the method that Mary Cover Jones found successful in eliminating the infant Peter's fear of rabbits (Jones, 1924)—is that of counterconditioning: to condition the stimulus to a response incompatible with the response one wants to eliminate. Wolpe and others have used the technique primarily to deal with phobias and general anxiety.

A patient, or client, visiting Wolpe for relief of anxiety would typically be treated as follows (Wolpe, 1958; Wolpe and Lazarus, 1968). First, the therapist inquires about the patient's problems, and reassures the patient that they can be cured through systematic desensitization. He may, if appropriate, use his authority as therapist to correct mistaken beliefs that the patient holds (for example, that masturbation is harmful) or even to change the patient's moral values. He describes the desensitization procedure to the patient, to be sure the patient understands the rationale for the treatment he will be going through. Next, the patient is asked to list the things and situations that cause him fear or anxiety, and to indicate on an anxiety scale the degree of unpleasantness evoked by each of them. The therapist discusses the items on the list with the patient to make sure he understands them, and this information, together with other evidence from the patient's life history, is used to construct a "fear hierarchy" in which situations are ranked in order of their tendency to arouse anxiety.

Actual treatment begins with instruction on muscle relaxation. The patient is told to tense and relax various muscle groups, and eventually to relax all the muscles simultaneously. Once relaxed, he is instructed to imagine the thing or situation ranked the least fear-arousing in his fear hierarchy. The purpose of this is to pair the feared stimulus with deep muscle relaxation, a response presumably incompatible with fear. If the imagined scene elicits anxiety, the patient is to signal by lifting his finger, whereupon the therapist will tell him to stop imagining the scene. Once the patient has been successful with that scene, he is told to imagine the next higher situation in the hierarchy. At the therapist's instruction, the patient moves up through all the situations in the hierarchy, until he has succeeded in imagining each without experiencing fear. Supposedly, counterconditioning has succeeded in eliminating the anxiety previously aroused by each situation by replacing it with conditioned relaxation.

Wolpe (1958) goes to great pains to ground this technique in behaviorism. He defines anxiety in a purely objective way, as a response complex made up of raised blood pressure, rapid breathing, dryness of the mouth, muscle tension, and palmar sweating. And the therapeutic procedure is seen as an application of the principles of classical conditioning. A paper by E. A. Locke (1971), however, takes issue with the claim that the systematic desensitization procedure is behavioristic. Locke points out that although Wolpe defines anxiety in an objective way, in practice he measures it by asking the patient to introspect. This is true of the initial diagnostic interview, in which the patient describes fear-arousing situations, the therapy procedure itself ("raise your finger if you feel anxious") and the post-therapy evaluation of success. The discussions to make sure the therapist understands the patient's problem, to make sure the patient understands the procedure and really believes it will help him, and to convince the patient that certaion prior beliefs or moral values are wrong, all imply a belief that mental states can be communicated from one mind to another through language. The instruction to relax assumes that conscious ideas can control behavior; the instruction to imagine a scene assumes that images can be generated at will; and the analogy between the therapy procedure and the classical conditioning situation implies that mental images have a status equal to that of an external, observable stimulus. In short, systematic desensitization is a cognitive therapy throughout. Any superiority it has over other methods of treating anxiety cannot be due to its supposed behavioristic nature.

Apparently, systematic desensitization is effective—the question is, why? Research evaluating the importance of various components of Wolpe's procedure suggests that neither relaxation nor slow progression through the fear hierarchy is important, but that practice at imagining fear-arousing situations is (Wilkins, 1971). (Perhaps the patient learns from this practice that he has some control over his mental images and controlling them allows him to better control anxiety.) Research has also shown that it is important that the patient expect the procedure to work—the beneficial effects of the technique are not automatic.

One should not infer from this discussion that all those who work with behavior modification and behavior therapy consider themselves behaviorists. As more and more workers have decided that the assumptions of behaviorism are inadequate for dealing with complex human behavior, cognitive theory has become increasingly popular in these fields. This change in emphasis will be discussed in more detail in Chapter 13.

Conditioning in Humans

Contrary to what many "behavior modifiers" have been taught to believe, the effects on humans of the pairing of a CS and UCS, or of reinforcing a response, are not automatic. As Pavlov pointed out, the human capacity for symbolic thought can alter the laws of conditioning. Let us consider three experimental demonstrations of this fact.

The first is a study using the classical conditioning paradigm, conducted by Grings, Schell, and Carey (1973). Each volunteer subject was seated before a panel on which two lights, one red and one green, were mounted. His right forearm was attached to a shock generator which produced ½-second bursts of 55-volt direct current. His left hand was wired to a device that measured GSR (palmar sweating), a UCR to shock. At the beginning of stage one of the experiment, the subjects were told: "The shock will follow the red light. The other light will not be followed by shock." Thus the shock was the UCS, the red light the CS+, and the green light the CS–. (For half the subjects the green light was the CS+ and the red light the CS–.) Thirty trials were administered, 15 CS+ and 15 CS–, but 6 of the CS+ trials did not include shock. The purpose of these trials was to test for the GSR in the absence of the shock. In stage two, the subjects were told that the relationships were now reversed. The light that had been the CS+ became the CS–, and the old CS– became the CS+. Again, 30 trials were given, just as in stage one. Events were carefully arranged so that the first occurrence of the new CS+ in stage two was a test trial, not followed by shock.

The results are shown in Figure 7.5. Notice that in stage one the GSR to the CS+ was higher than that to the CS–, as one would expect. But the responses to the red and green lights were dramatically reversed by the verbal instruction. On the very first trial of stage two, before the new contingency could be experienced, the former CS– produced a full-fledged GSR; and "extinction" of the response to the former CS+ was equally sudden. In this experiment there was no evidence for automatic S–R conditioning at all. The GSR apparently was determined solely by the subjects' verbally induced expectations.

The second experiment, by Kaufman, Baron, and Kopp (1966), used an operant conditioning paradigm. The experiment was designed to investigate the effects of verbal instructions on the operant responses of subjects (college students) under different schedules of reinforcement. The subjects pushed a button which occasionally turned on a green light, which, in turn, allowed them to make a choice in another task in which they could earn money. The subjects thought the money-making task was the important one, but the experimenters were interested in their operant, button-pushing behavior. For all sub-

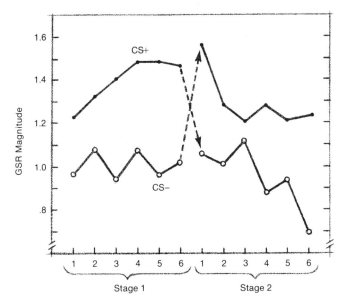

Figure 7.5 GSR magnitudes in classical conditioning, as influenced by verbal instructions. [Adapted from Grings, Schell, and Carey, 1973.]

jects a variable interval 1-minute reinforcement schedule related the button press to the green light; that is, the button would not turn on the light for some interval after it last had done so, and this interval varied, averaging 1 minute (see Chapter 4 for a discussion of reinforcement schedules). The manipulation of interest was the verbal instruction. One group of subjects was given only minimal instructions, and told nothing about the relationship between the button and green light. Another group was given a correct description of the schedule relating the button and light (the VI-1 group). Another was given a false description, of a variable-ratio 150 schedule (the VR-150 group). Still another was given a description of a fixed-interval 1-minute schedule (the FI-1 group). Each subject served in the experiment for a total of 3 hours, in 30-minute sessions spread out over a 2-week period.

The average response rates in the final 30-minute session (after 150 minutes on the task) were as follows: minimal instruction group, 44 per minute; VI-1 group, 41 per minute; VR-150 group, 275 per minute; FI-1 group, 7 per minute. Even after all subjects had been exposed to the same schedule for more than 2 hours, the response rates of the groups were markedly different. Apparently the beliefs established by the verbal instructions were more powerful determinants of the subjects' behavior than was the actual reinforcement contingency to which they were exposed.

The third example deals with reinforcement of a simple verbal response. Fingerman and Levine (1974) had college students attempt to solve seven tasks. In each, the subject went through a deck of cards, half bearing the letter sequence "A B", and the other half "B A". For each stimulus card, the subject was to call out either "A" or "B", and according to a predetermined rule, the experimenter responded either "correct" or "wrong." If the subject could discover the rule, he could always make the correct response. The rules for the first six tasks were sequential ones, which increased in complexity. Thus, in the first task, the subject was to say the letter on the right for two trials, then the one on the left for two trials, and so on (RRLL). An example of application of this rule over a 15-card sequence is shown in column one of Figure 7.6. By the sixth task, the rule was so complex that it could not be described simply, and it repeated only after 10 trials (LLRLRRRLRR). See the second column of the figure for an example.

In the seventh task, the rule was extremely simple: "A" was always correct and "B" was always wrong. The third column in the figure illustrates this task. If one believes that reinforcement automatically strengthens the previous response, then one should expect the seventh task to be learned in just a few trials—the subject should very quickly be saying "A" exclusively. But that is not what happened. Only 11 percent of the subjects were able to solve the seventh problem in 60 trials. (One of these subjects said she suspected that the experimenter might try to trick her.) The other 89 percent chose "A" only about half the time throughout the 60 trials, showing no effect of reinforcement on response rate. At the end, the subjects who had not solved the problem were given a questionnaire on which they were asked to pick the solution to the problem from among six alternatives, including "I said 'correct' on this last problem whenever you said 'A'." Not one subject picked this alternative.

The point of the experiment, of course, was to "trick" the subjects into thinking the solution to the seventh problem must be a sequential one. Fingerman and Levine's theory is that behavior in such a situation is controlled by a strategy of producing and testing hypotheses

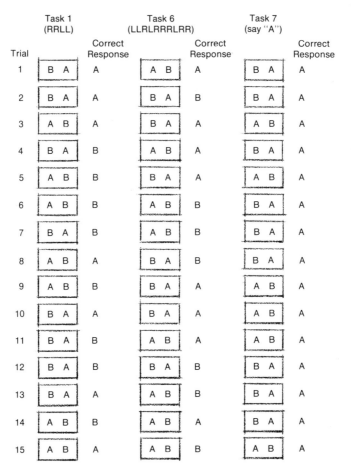

Trial	Task 1 (RRLL)	Correct Response	Task 6 (LLRLRRRLRR)	Correct Response	Task 7 (say "A")	Correct Response
1	B A	A	A B	A	B A	A
2	B A	A	B A	B	B A	A
3	A B	A	B A	A	A B	A
4	B A	B	A B	A	B A	A
5	A B	B	B A	A	A B	A
6	A B	B	A B	B	B A	A
7	B A	B	A B	B	B A	A
8	A B	A	B A	B	B A	A
9	A B	B	B A	A	A B	A
10	B A	A	B A	A	A B	A
11	B A	B	A B	A	A B	A
12	B A	B	B A	B	B A	A
13	B A	A	A B	B	B A	A
14	A B	B	A B	A	B A	A
15	A B	A	A B	B	A B	A

Figure 7.6 Sequence of events in three of the tasks used by Fingerman and Levine (1974).

about the rule the experimenter is using. If "'A' is always correct" is not one of the hypotheses the subject considers, even such a simple problem will not be solved.

In the three examples just given, we see why caution must be used in applying principles of animal conditioning to humans. The symbolic representation of the task, whether produced by the experimenter or spontaneously generated by the subject, exerts stronger control over the subject's behavior than does the CS–UCS or response–reinforcer contingency. Independent evidence for this conclusion comes from other sources, as well (for example, Dulany, 1968).

This is not to say that true classical and instrumental conditioning never occur in humans—they apparently do, although the conditions for clearly demonstrating them are difficult to arrange. Beh and Barratt (1965) obtained classical conditioning in sleeping subjects. During a drug-induced sleep, a low tone (CS+) was paired with shock to the finger, while a high tone (CS−) was not. The shock UCS was not strong enough to awaken the subjects, but it did elicit the pattern called the "K complex" in their EEG records. During sleep, the K complex was conditioned to the low tone and extinguished, and after the subjects awakened it showed evidence of spontaneous recovery. Hefferline, Keenan, and Harford (1959) obtained operant conditioning in subjects who were unaware of the reinforcement contingency. The subjects listened to taped music, which was interrupted by a loud, 60-cycle hum. Although they did not realize it, they could turn off the hum by twitching a tiny muscle in the thumb. The rate of the muscle twitch increased, and when the contingency was removed, the response extinguished. The subjects were astonished to learn afterward that the aversive hum had been under their control. Apparently, true conditioning is best demonstrated in human subjects when they are not thinking about the contingencies involved.

Given the conclusion that the subject's internal representation of the situation can strongly influence the effects of actual contingencies, it is not surprising that Skinner's application of operant principles to programmed instruction failed to trigger the educational revolution he foresaw. And it is not surprising that the most successful techniques of behavior modification make use of cognitive principles, even though they may not be explicitly recognized as such. To many readers, this point may seem intuitively obvious. But it needs to be made, and to be given experimental support, for two reasons. First, implicit, intuitive understanding is not the same as explicit, scientific understanding. What is "intuitively obvious" is not necessarily true. Second, it shows that the widely publicized claims behaviorists have made about the causes of human behavior (as controversial outside psychology as within) are incomplete, if not entirely incorrect.

Language in Apes

This discussion of the relationships among conditioning, language, and thought would not be complete without reference to the fascinating research that has been done on language learning in chimpanzees. It is fitting that the search for the origins of human language should include work on chimpanzees. Genetic analysis shows that the chimp is a very close relative of man; the "genetic distance" between chimp and man is even less than that between chimp and gorilla (King and Wilson, 1975).

Language learning in chimps has been studied in several laboratories. Early attempts to teach apes to speak were a failure, apparently because apes lack the necessary vocal apparatus (see Kellogg, 1968). Allen and Beatrice Gardner, working at the University of Nevada, sidestepped this difficulty by using a sign language of the deaf, instead of vocal speech. In American Sign Language (Aslan), the configurations and movements of the hands represent words (not letters, as in "finger-spelling"), and grammatical structures are different from those of English. Gardner and Gardner (1969) raised an eleven-month-old chimpanzee named Washoe among experimenters who communicated with her (and with each other, in her presence) only by sign. In four years, Washoe acquired an Aslan vocabulary of more than 130 words, which she chained together in primitive sentences. More recent work, in which chimps have been raised among signers from birth, show promise of even greater success (Garner and Gardner, 1975a).

Other approaches have been taken by David Premack, at the University of California at Santa Barbara, and Duane Rumbaugh, at Georgia State University. Premack trained a chimp named Sarah to read and write sentences and answer questions using colored plastic forms as words. Rumbaugh and his co-workers trained a chimp named Lana to communicate with the experimenters and with a computer by means of a special keyboard. Both Premack and Rumbaugh have found that chimps can construct sentences according to simple grammatical rules.

The initial stages of teaching language to an ape may make use of operant conditioning principles. Premack (1971), for example, taught Sarah the meanings of her first plastic words by rewarding her with an object (for example, an apple) whenever she placed the corresponding "word" on a slate. Teaching a chimp sign language may require, in addition to reward, showing the animal how to make the sign or molding her hand into the appropriate form. It would seem a mistake, however, to assume that the more complex language behavior chimps show is simply a matter of chaining together operant responses in the manner studied by Skinner (see Chapter 5). Chimps use language creatively, to say things that they have not said before and that have never been said to them. Response chains are stereotyped, while the use of language by chimpanzees is inventive.

Roger Fouts (1974), who originally worked on the Gardners' Project Washoe and has since taught sign language to several other chimpanzees, describes the animals' combination of signs into new words. Washoe, for example, referred to brazil nuts as *rock berry*, and to ducks as *water birds*. Washoe even invented swearing. The word *dirty*, learned in the context of "dirty" diapers, was applied to a monkey that had threatened her *(dirty monkey)* and to Fouts, when he refused to comply with one of her requests *(dirty Roger)*. Another female chimp, Lucy, called radishes *cry hurt food* and referred to watermelon as *drink fruit*.

Premack and Premack (1972) taught the chimp Sarah the concepts *interrogative* (question mark), *same* and *different, no* (not), *color-of, shape-of, size-of, name-of,* and even *if–then*. The *if–then* concept was taught using complex sentences such as:

(1) *Sarah take apple*
     if–then
     Mary give chocolate Sarah

and

(2) *Sarah take banana*
     if–then
     Mary no give chocolate Sarah.

Sarah showed apparent understanding by taking the apple, in the case of (1), and not taking the banana, in the case of (2). To prove that the animal understands such concepts, of course, one must show that it responds appropriately to problems that were not used in training. According to the Premacks, Sarah's behavior meets this criterion.

Can the ability of chimps to use language be explained without reference to mental events? Premack (1970) has concluded that it cannot. Let us consider two examples that seem to require a cognitive interpretation. The first example concerns Sarah's use of the concept *color-of* (Premack and Premack, 1972). After this concept had been well learned, Sarah was first introduced to the word *brown* in the following sentence:

(3) *Brown color-of chocolate.*

Sarah was familiar with the words *color-of* and *chocolate,* but the word *brown* was new to her. (None of the three plastic words, incidentally, was colored brown, and actual chocolate was not present when Sarah was shown the sentence.) It would seem that if the meaning of *brown* is learned in such a situation, the learning must be mediated by ideas. As a test for learning, Sarah was later shown four colored disks (one of which was brown), and was told, *take brown*. She chose the correct color. Apparently, the word *chocolate* in sentence (3) had generated a mental image of chocolate, including its color. By associating the imagined color with the word, Sarah learned the meaning of *brown*.

The second example involves inventive use of the concept *name-of* by the chimpanzee Lana (Rumbaugh, Gill, von Glasersfeld, Warner, and Pisani, 1975). Lana had been taught to use her special computer keyboard to make requests using grammatical sentences such as:

Please machine give coffee.

and

Please Tim tickle Lana.

(Lana was especially fond of coffee, and all young chimps apparently love being tickled.) She had also been taught the concept *name-of*, so that she could answer correctly when shown an object and asked:

? What name-of this.

She had never, however, been taught to ask for the name of an object.

One morning Tim (the experimenter) was sitting in front of Lana's cage with two objects she knew the names of (a can and a bowl, both empty) and one she did not (a box, full of M&M candies). The following conversation (all recorded by the computer) ensued:

Lana: Tim give Lana this can. (11:36 AM)
Tim: Yes. (And Tim gave her the empty can, though apparently she wanted the box with the M&Ms.)
Lana: ? Tim give Lana this can. (11:42 AM)
Tim: No can. (Which meant that Tim did not have the can to give her as it had just been given to her.)
Lana: ? Tim give Lana this bowl. (11:43 AM)
Tim: Yes. (And Tim gave the empty bowl to her.)
Lana: ? Shelley (sentence unfinished) (11:43 AM)
Tim: No Shelley. (Shelley, the technician, was not present.)

> *Lana:* ? Tim give Lana this bowl. (Before Tim could answer, she continued. . . .) (11:44 AM)
> *Lana:* ? Tim give Lana name-of this. (11:45 AM)
> *Tim:* Box name-of this. (Thereby giving her the name of the vessel which she apparently wanted.)
> *Lana:* Yes. (11:46 AM)
> *Lana:* ? Tim give Lana this box. (11:47 AM)
> *Tim:* Yes. (Whereupon Tim gave it to her, and she immediately ripped it open and extracted the M&M candies.) [Rumbaugh et al., 1975, p. 368.]

Here, Lana spontaneously asks for the name of an object, even though she has never been trained to do so. It is difficult to escape the conclusion that some fairly complex reasoning lay behind her request. She must have realized that in order to obtain the candies she had to learn the name of the container they were in, and somehow guessed that she could request information in much the same way that she could request a concrete reward. (The experimenters, of course, had asked Lana for the names of things when they taught her the concept *name-of*.) To be sure, one should not put complete trust in anecdotes such as this. Randomly emitted behavior can, by accident, appear intelligent. Thorndike's (1898) warning that the protagonist of a smart-cat anecdote can become "representative of the cat-mind in all the books" applies equally to chimps. It is important, therefore, that definite conclusions about the mental abilities of apes await repeated, systematic observation of the behavior on which the conclusions are based.

Do educated chimps such as Washoe, Sarah, and Lana really possess language? The answer to this question depends on how language is defined. Apparently, chimps can use creatively the symbol systems they have been taught, and they seem able to use them to discuss the properties of objects that are not present (for example, in Sarah's case, the color of chocolate). The Gardners have shown that Washoe's ability to answer who-what-where questions appropriately (for example, *Roger* in reply to *Who me?*, or *out* in reply to *Where we go?*) is comparable to that of human children (Gardner and Gardner, 1975b).

A number of linguists and psycholinguists, most notably the linguist Noam Chomsky, have taken a rationalist position with regard to human language. They argue that the human capacity for language is not due simply to the large number of neurons in the human brain, but rather reflects a unique learning ability peculiar to the human species. Of course it is obvious that language is learned, but their proposal is that it is learned by a genetically programmed "language-acquisition device" which (like the supposed star-map learning device of the indigo bunting) operates according to its own laws. Evidence for the existence of such a device is diverse: the left hemisphere of the human brain is specialized for language; there appears to be a critical period in early childhood during which language learning is easier than at a later age; and children learn language with no special training from adults (language learning is highly "prepared"). The most remarkable property of this hypothetical device is an ability to infer the grammatical rules underlying the particular natural language to which the child has been exposed. This is presumably done by generating hypotheses about the nature of the rule system, and using sentences produced by adults to confirm or reject the hypotheses. (Of course, the child is not necessarily conscious of this activity.) Once the rules have been acquired, the child can produce sentences which use the rules in innumerable grammatically correct combinations, including many the child has never actually heard.

Fodor, Bever, and Garrett (1974, pp. 440–462) have argued that it is precisely this ability to combine the rules in new but grammatically correct ways that chimpanzees do not have. Further research may tell us whether or not this assertion is correct. Whatever the eventual decision turns out to be, there is no question but that language is more "natural" for humans than for apes. But if a special-purpose, innate language mechanism did evolve in the brain of early man, it must have evolved out of something. The work with chimpanzees suggests that their ability to reason, and to use symbols to stand for objects, actions, and relations is highly developed. It must have been just such a general intellectual ability that served as the foundation upon which human linguistic ability was built.

If the principles of human learning are different in important respects from those of learning in animals, as they seem to be, then an understanding of human learning must be based primarily on the study of humans. At this point, then, we shift our emphasis. In the next few chapters we shall explore methods, theories, and disputes in the field of human memory.

8

Experimental Procedures
in Human Memory

In Chapter 2 we saw how Hermann Ebbinghaus proved, contrary to the view prevailing at the time, that human learning and memory could be studied in an experimental and objective way. Ebbinghaus's pioneering investigations used one basic method: a list of items (stimuli) was read aloud, at a fast rate, until they could be recited from memory in order, without error or hesitation. The measure of difficulty was the number of repetitions or trials needed to master the list, and the measure of retention was the savings score, which compared the number of trials required to learn the list initially with the number needed to relearn it at a later time. Today, the particular experimental task Ebbinghaus developed is referred to as *serial recall*, because it requires the subject to recall the stimuli in a particular serial order; and the method he devised to measure retention is called *relearning*. But there are many ways of having human subjects learn material and many ways of testing their memory, and it was not long after Ebbinghaus's work became known that other objective experimental procedures began to appear. Neither the serial-recall task nor the relearning measure of retention is used much today. They have been replaced by a wide variety of experimental techniques, the most common of which are discussed in this chapter.

RECALL TASKS

A recall task is one that requires the subject to produce items from memory. The "items" are usually verbal materials, such as nonsense syllables, words, or sentences. Inasmuch as most human subjects are much better at writing or speaking than they are at drawing pictures or imitating sounds, the use of verbal materials makes it easier for the experimenter to "know what the subject meant" and to score recall unambiguously as either "right" or "wrong."

The three most frequently used recall tasks are serial learning, paired associates, and free recall. We shall discuss each of these in turn.

Serial Learning

The *serial-learning task* evolved directly out of the serial-recall task of Ebbinghaus. The basic difference is that in serial learning the subject does not try to recite the entire list at one time; instead, he is presented each stimulus of the list in turn, and tries to say the next stimulus aloud. Because the subject's job is to try to give each item of the serial list before it is presented to him, this technique is sometimes called the *anticipation procedure*.

A typical serial list of nonsense syllables is shown in Figure 8.1. The stimuli shown in the middle column are presented one at a time, at a fixed rate (say, 3 seconds each). During the presentation of each stimulus the subject must do two things: (a) try to memorize the current item, and (b) try to anticipate and say the next item in the list.

In order to leave the experimenter's hands and attention free to record the subject's responses, serial-learning experiments are usually conducted with the aid of a machine. Slide projectors, tape recorders, or (today) computers may serve this function; but by far the greatest number of serial-learning experiments have been done using a device called a *memory drum*. This apparatus consists of a shield with a hole or window behind which a paper loop is moved in stepwise fashion by a motor-driven metal drum. The subject thus sees one stimulus move into the window and stop for a fixed amount of time, to be replaced by the next stimulus in the list, and so on. A typical memory drum is shown in Figure 8.2.

Ordinarily, the experimental subject will be tested on the list, trial after trial, until he is able to anticipate each item without error. If,

Serial Position	Stimulus	Correct Response
0	XXX	"hig"
1	HIG	"wug"
2	WUG	"kyr"
3	KYR	"ciz"
4	CIZ	"peh"
5	PEH	"luj"
6	LUJ	"naj"
7	NAJ	"bep"
8	BEP	"ral"
9	RAL	"vif"
10	VIF	"fup"
11	FUP	"daq"
12	DAQ	_____

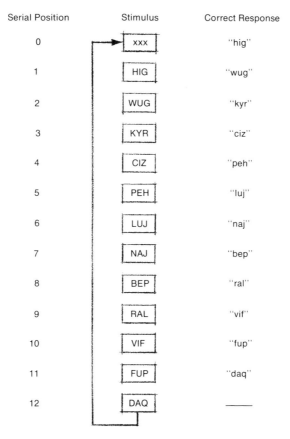

Figure 8.1 The anticipation procedure in serial learning.

following this, the experimenter tallies on the data sheet the errors made in anticipating each item, it becomes quite apparent that the items in different serial positions are not equally difficult to learn. Stimuli at the beginning of the list are learned quickly; those at the end produce more errors; and those near the middle are the most difficult of all. The point of maximum difficulty lies just past the middle of the list. Figure 8.3 shows how the number of errors varies with serial position. In this experiment, two groups of subjects learned a 12-item list of nonsense syllables. The lists were presented to one group at a rate of 2 seconds per syllable and to the other group at a rate of 4 seconds per syllable. Naturally, the subjects who had 4 sec-

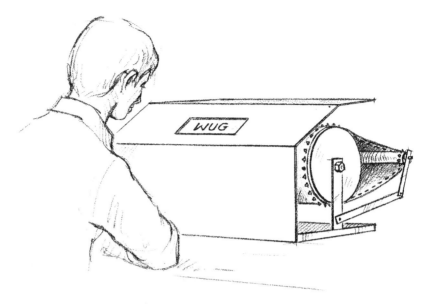

Figure 8.2 A memory drum.

onds per item learned the list with fewer total errors, and this is shown by the separation of the two curves in the top panel of the figure. It may appear that the shapes of the two curves are different. However, if the overall difference in difficulty is taken into account, by determining the percentage of all the errors made that occurred at a particular serial position, it becomes clear that the forms of the curves are essentially the same. This is shown in the bottom panel of the figure. A paper by McCrary and Hunter (1953) showed, surprisingly, that the form of the serial-position curve is independent of many variables that affect the overall difficulties of serial lists. A list of words, for example, is much easier to learn than is a list of nonsense syllables. But if overall difficulty is taken into account, as it was in the bottom panel of Figure 8.3, the serial-position curves look the same.

The typical graph, or "function," relating errors to serial position is known as the *serial-position effect*. It has been of considerable theoretical interest, partly because it is such a robust (or reliable) finding. One might imagine that the serial-position effect is just a product of aritificial laboratory conditions, and of no practical significance. However, Jensen (1962) has shown that essentially the same relationship holds between spelling errors and letter position within a word. Misspellings

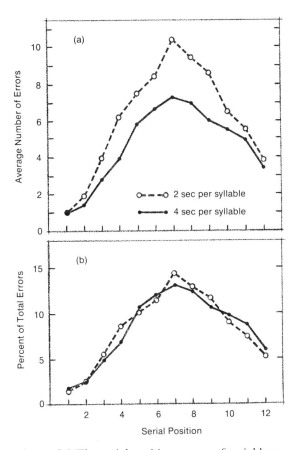

Figure 8.3 The serial-position curves of serial learning, for two rates of presentation, plotted as: (a) number of errors; (b) percent errors. [After McCrary and Hunter, 1953. Copyright 1953 by the American Association for the Advancement of Science.]

are much more frequent in the middle of a word than they are near the beginning or end. The detection of typographical errors by proofreaders bears a similar relationship to letter position. Apparently, then, one of the principles that applies to the learning of serial lists of nonsense syllables also applies to the learning of the "serial lists" of letters we call words.

An interesting exception to the McCrary and Hunter generalization about the form of the serial-position curve is what is called the *isolation*

effect, or *von Restorff effect* (after Hedwig von Restorff, whose experiments will be discussed in the next chapter). The phenomenon is this:
If a stimulus item in a serial list is made distinctive—or "isolated" from
the others—it is learned more easily than it would be otherwise. As an
example, consider two conditions of a larger experiment conducted by
McLaughlin (1966). Subjects learned 15-syllable serial lists, presented
at a 3-second rate. In the control condition, all 15 syllables were typed
in black, lower-case letters. In the experimental or isolated condition,
all syllables were black and lower case except the one in position 8.
This syllable was typed in red capital letters. The effect of this manipulation on the serial-position curve can be seen in Figure 8.4. The arrow
indicates the point corresponding to the isolated item. The effect is the
same if one black syllable is embedded in a list of red ones; so it is
clearly the distinctiveness of the isolated item, not just its color per se,
that makes it more easily learned.

Paired Associates

As we just saw, the subject learning a serial list must attempt to do two
things during each stimulus exposure: (a) memorize the current

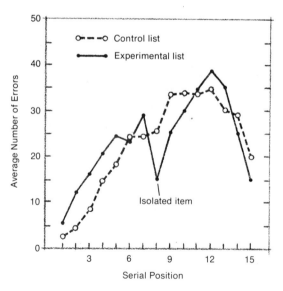

Figure 8.4 The isolation, or "von Restorff," effect.
[Adapted from McLaughlin, 1966.]

stimulus so that it can be correctly anticipated in future trials, and (b) correctly anticipate the next stimulus on the list. Put another way, each item in the list serves two functions: it is the "response" to the preceding item, and the "stimulus" for the next one. Because of the double function served by each item, serial learning has been viewed as difficult to analyze theoretically. A variable such as meaningfulness, which affects the difficulty of a serial list, could do so by influencing an item's response function, its stimulus function, or both. The two roles an item plays are said to be *confounded* in the serial-learning task, because they cannot be separated experimentally.

The *paired-associates* task is one that eliminates this confounding. In this task, items are learned in pairs. Each pair consists of a *stimulus term* and a *response term*. (Both are stimuli, really—the words "stimulus" and "response" have been borrowed from the conditioning literature, and used, here, in a somewhat inappropriate way.) The stimulus term of a pair is a cue for the subject to recall the response term. The paired-associates procedure was introduced to psychology by Mary W. Calkins, in two papers appearing in 1894 and 1896. Although the advantages of the paired-associates task were not recognized at first, by the 1950s this task had replaced serial learning as the technique most commonly used to study human learning and memory.

Procedures. Two arrangements of study and test presentations have been used with paired associates: the *anticipation* method, and the *study–test* method. The anticipation method works much like the serial-learning method of the same name. A pair is presented in two stages: first the stimulus term is shown alone, and the subject is to try to anticipate the corresponding response term; then the complete pair—both stimulus and response terms—is shown. The subject's attempted recall is thus either confirmed (some would say, "reinforced") or disconfirmed almost immediately. After all pairs have been presented in this way, the procedure is repeated, but with the pairs in a different order. Each presentation of the entire list is called a trial. The anticipation method is illustrated, for a list of ten pairs of words, in Figure 8.5.

In the study–test method, the subject first studies all the pairs in the list, and then is tested on all the pairs in the list. The study phase may be paced at, say, a 3-second rate, and the test phase may be unpaced, allowing the subject as much time as he needs to recall each response. In the test phase, the stimulus terms are presented in an order differ-

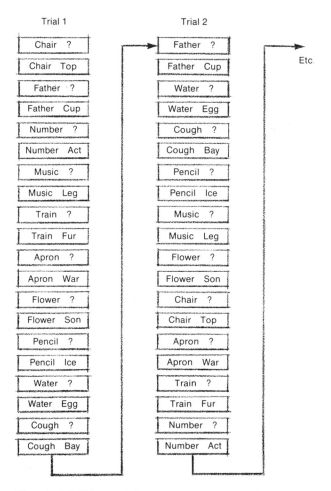

Figure 8.5 The anticipation procedure of presenting paired associates.

ent from that in which the pairs were studied. The study–test method is illustrated in Figure 8.6.

Which procedure produces the most efficient learning? One might expect the anticipation method to be better, since "reinforcement" or knowledge of results comes immediately after the subject's response, while in the study–test method it is usually delayed for 30 seconds or so. The evidence, however, suggests that the two methods are about equally effective. If either has an edge over the other, it is the study–test method (see Hall, 1971). Since the effects of delayed reinforcement are quite different in conditioning studies, this is another situation in which the analogy between animal conditioning and human verbal learning breaks down.

Similarity. One of the most powerful variables affecting paired-associates learning is *stimulus similarity*. Having stimulus terms that are very similar to one another can either aid learning or interfere with it, depending upon how the stimulus and response terms are paired. Suppose there are five names of trees in a list, and five names of

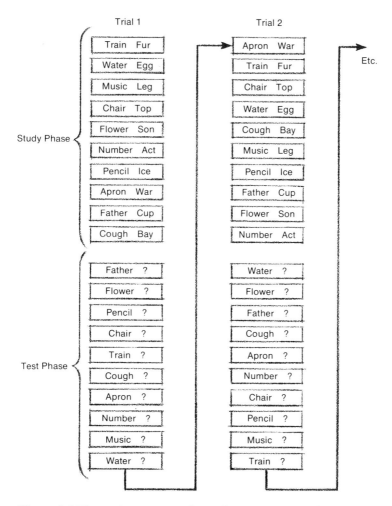

Figure 8.6 The study–test procedure of presenting paired associates.

presidents. Suppose further that all the tree names are paired with the response WUK, while all the presidents are paired with DAX. Since the similar items are treated the same (paired with the same response), the list will be very easy to learn. In fact the paired-associates task, in this case, has degenerated into one of learning a simple rule that sorts the stimulus terms into two categories. Such a task is usually referred to as *concept identification,* because all the subject has to do in order to respond correctly is to identify the "concept" or rule relating the stimuli to the two response items.

When stimulus and response terms are paired randomly, by contrast, stimulus similarity interferes with learning. Consider an experiment by Hintzman (1969b) in which college students learned paired associates of high and low stimulus similarity. Each list consisted of eight pairs. The stimulus terms were three-consonant combinations, or "trigrams" (for example, KGP), and the response terms were single digits. Four of the trigrams were made up of only five different letters and were therefore highly similar to one another, while the other four trigrams had no letters in common and so were quite distinct. The eight pairs were learned by the anticipation procedure, with the high-similarity and low-similarity items randomly intermixed. Recall

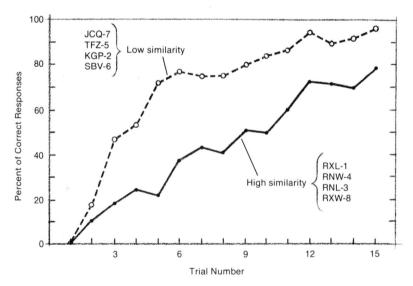

Figure 8.7 Effect of stimulus similarity on acquisition of a paired-associates list.

scores for the two sets of pairs were computed separately on each trial. Figure 8.7 shows the two learning curves, together with examples of the high-similarity and low-similarity pairs. As is evident from the graph, the low-similarity pairs were learned much more rapidly than the high-similarity pairs. More extreme manipulations of similarity (for example, using just three letters to construct all stimulus and response terms of the list) can make a paired-associates list almost impossible to learn.

Meaningfulness and Concreteness. As we saw in Chapter 2, when Ebbinghaus (1885) compared the difficulty of learning a poem with the difficulty of learning a list of nonsense syllables, he found the poem much easier to learn. Since then, many studies of effects of *meaningfulness* on learning have been done, but most have used paired associates, rather than serial recall.

Nonsense syllables, as Ebbinghaus realized, differ in how nonsensical they are. Some syllables—for example, MON, WEV, TER, and DUC—very quickly remind people of ordinary words. Syllables that do so reliably, over a large sample of subjects, are said to be of "high meaningfulness," or high *m*. Others, such as BOH, KAZ, JEP, and POZ, do not remind us of words so easily, and so are of medium *m*. Still other syllables, such as XIJ, KYH, GYQ, and DAQ, seldom remind people of actual words, and are said to be of low *m*. Three-consonant trigrams, like nonsense syllables, vary in meaningfulness. DRK, SLW, and JFK are highly meaningful, while QJF and ZXJ are not.

The measurement of meaningfulness and assessment of its effect on paired-associates learning has occupied a number of investigators (for a thorough discussion see Underwood and Schulz, 1960). For present purposes, it is sufficient to say that more meaningful materials are more easily learned, and that the meaningfulness of the response member of a pair is a more important determinant of ease of learning than is that of the stimulus member. The greater effect of response meaningfulness is probably due to the fact that the subject must produce the response term from memory, while he does not have to do so with the stimulus term.

All familiar words are meaningful, but like nonsense syllables and three-consonant trigrams, they vary in how easy they are to learn in the paired-associates task. Paivio, Yuille, and Rogers (1969) have shown that word *concreteness* is an important determinant of difficulty.

Concrete words (for example, elephant, grass, magazine, and tom-ahawk) are more easily associated than are abstract words (for example, history, profession, anxiety, and virtue). A currently popular explanation of the effect of concreteness holds that concrete words arouse vivid mental images, while abstract words do not, and that imagery makes associations easier to learn. The effects of imagery on memory will be discussed in Chapter 9.

Transfer. One could think of the effects of meaningfulness and concreteness on learning as examples of the transfer of past learning to the present task. The degree to which a syllable reminds us of a word, and the ease with which the referent of a word can be pictured, both depend on previously acquired information about words and what they stand for. Properly speaking, therefore, meaningfulness and concreteness are not properties of syllables and words: they refer to relationships between these stimuli and information in our memories. It should be apparent that the ability to transfer past learning to new situations is a most important characteristic of the human mind. Without it, neither personal experience nor education would be of much adaptive value. (Imagine not being able to multiply numbers outside your fourth-grade classroom.)

While the transfer of past learning can be observed in the effects of meaningfulness and concreteness, it is impossible to study the transfer process itself if the original learning did not take place under experimental control. We do not know when a given subject first learned the word "tomahawk"—whether it was in a story or on a spelling test, whether it was paired with a picture or not, how many times the subject has read, heard, or spoken the word, or when it was encountered most recently. If one wants to test a hypothesis about the effects of such factors on transfer, one cannot adequately do so without producing the original learning experience in the laboratory, where it can be carefully controlled. The paired-associates task lends itself particularly well to the experimental analysis of the *transfer of training,* and has been used extensively for this purpose.

Let us suppose we want to measure the effect of one association on the learning of another. We might do this by having subjects learn two successive paired-associates lists. Each pair in the first list (List 1) bears a special relation to a pair in the second (List 2), and what we want to do is assess the influence of the List 1 pairing on the learning of the corresponding pair in List 2. Logically, there are three possibilities: (a) the first association may aid the learning of the second (*positive transfer),* (b) the first association may impair the learning of the second *(negative transfer),* or (c) the first association may have no effect on the learning of the second *(zero transfer).* To determine the direction and amount of transfer, we need to compare the learning of a List 2 pair when it is related to a pair in List 1 with the learning of the same pair when it is not related to a pair in List 1. The condition in which the pairs in List 1 and List 2 are unrelated is our control condition, with which the possible transfer conditions are to be compared.

Consider Figure 8.8. This figure illustrates four common "transfer

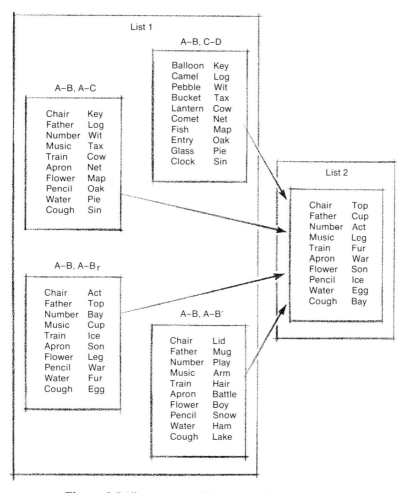

Figure 8.8 Illustrations of four transfer paradigms.

paradigms." Each paradigm has been given a label that describes how the List 1 pairs and List 2 pairs are related. The same List 2 is used to illustrate all paradigms, since what we want to measure are differences in List 2 learning due solely to the effects of transfer. The four paradigms thus differ only with respect to List 1.

The topmost condition is the control condition. It is labeled A–B, C–D, to indicate that neither the stimulus nor the response term of a given List 1 pair is repeated in List 2. Moving counterclockwise in the figure, the next paradigm is labeled A–B, A–C. This indicates that List 2 uses the same stimulus terms as does List 1, but that they are paired with a new set of response terms—for example, *chair–key* in List 1 becomes *chair–top* in List 2. The A–B, A–C paradigm generally leads to a moderate degree of negative transfer. That is, List 2 is learned slightly more slowly in the A–B, A–C paradigm than in the A–B, C–D control.

In the A–B, $A–B_r$ paradigm, the same stimulus terms and response terms are used in both lists—but in List 2 they are re-paired (thus the subscript r in $A–B_r$). In Figure 8.8, for example, the elements of *chair–act,* in List 1, become parts of the pairs *chair–top* and *number–act* in List 2. The A–B, $A–B_r$ paradigm leads to massive negative transfer. That is, List 2 in the A–B, $A–B_r$ paradigm is learned much more slowly than in the A–B, C–D control.

In the A–B, A–B′ ("A B prime") paradigm, the List 1 and List 2 response terms paired with each stimulus term are somewhat similar. Thus *chair–lid* in List 1 becomes *chair–top* in List 2, and *pencil–snow* becomes *pencil–ice*. In this paradigm, positive transfer is obtained. That is, List 2 in the A–B, A–B′ paradigm is learned more rapidly than in the A–B, C–D control.

The effects of these paradigms on transfer of training can be summarized in two rules: (a) The *degree* of transfer between List 1 and List 2 increases with similarity among the elements of the two lists. (Thus, negative transfer is stronger in the A–B, $A–B_r$ paradigm than in A–B, A–C.) (b) The *direction* of transfer depends on the compatibility of the stimulus–response pairings in the two lists. If pairings are compatible (as in A–B, A–B′), transfer will be positive; if they are incompatible (as in A–B, A–C and A–B, $A–B_r$), it will be negative.

The four transfer paradigms shown in Figure 8.8 are also used to study forgetting. Suppose the subject learns List 1 and then List 2, and then is tested on List 1. Subjects given the A–B, A–C and the A–B, $A-B_r$ arrangements show more forgetting of List 1 than do subjects in the control condition. This is called *retroactive interference*. Subjects in the A–B, A–B' paradigm often show less forgetting of List 1 than do control subjects. Here memory for List 1 seems to have been enhanced by List 2, a phenomenon called *retroactive facilitation*. More will be said about the study of forgetting in Chapter 10.

Free Recall

In 1894, the same year that Calkins published the first paired-associates experiment, a paper entitled "An Experimental Study of Memory," by E. A. Kirkpatrick, appeared. Among other innovations introduced in that paper was what is now called the *free-recall* task. School pupils ranging from primary to college age were tested in the classroom, in three conditions. In one, a list of words was written on the blackboard, one at a time, and erased after a brief exposure. In the second, the same number of words was read aloud to the class. In the third, instead of words, actual objects were shown to the class. In each condition, the subject's task was the same: to write down as many of the stimulus items as he could remember, in any order he wished. Kirkpatrick found that objects were remembered much better than words, but that it made little difference whether the mode of presentation of words was visual or auditory.

The task which Kirkpatrick devised is called "free recall" because the subject is free to recall the items in *any order* he wishes. This may seem like a simple and very natural task to use to study memory, but free recall saw little further use in memory research until the late 1950s. Today it may surpass even the paired-associates procedure in popularity among memory investigators, and the long period during which free recall was virtually ignored is difficult for its present-day advocates to comprehend.

One reason free recall was little used for so many years was that it did not fit in with the tradition of associationism. The serial-learning and paired-associates tasks seem to lend themselves to the study of associations—in the one case associations linking members of a series, and in the other case associations between the members of a pair. But in free recall it is not clear just what role associations would play, because the order of recall does not have to correspond to the order of presentation. Hermann Ebbinghaus himself refused to put his authority behind the free-recall technique (Ebbinghaus, 1911). He agreed that it appeared to be very practical, because it lent itself easily to mass experimentation (subjects do not have to be tested individually, as with some of the other methods). But from a theoretical standpoint, he saw little value in it. It was, he said, "crude and superficial." Some modern investigators echo Ebbinghaus's view. The experimenter's lack of control over the order in which items are recalled makes the method less useful, for many purposes, than other experimental techniques.

There are three general facts about free recall that should be noted here. The first is that free recall, like serial learning, has a characteristic serial-position curve. The *serial-position curve of free recall* is illustrated in Figure 8.9. (It is customary with free recall to plot this curve in terms of correct responses, rather than errors, and this is why it is shaped like a U rather than an inverted U.) The data in Figure 8.9 come from an experiment by Deese and Kaufman (1957), who read lists of words aloud to their subjects at a 1-second rate, and then asked for free recall. Some lists were 10 words long and others were 32 words long. The graph plots the percentage of items recalled as a function of "input position"—that is, position in the list as it was originally read to the subject. For both list lengths, it can be seen that words

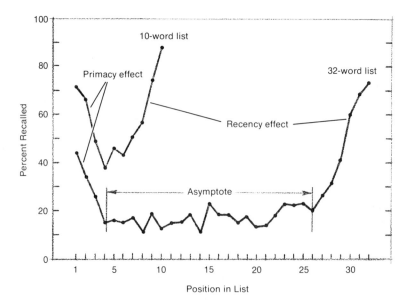

Figure 8.9 Serial-position curves of free recall. [Adapted from Deese and Kaufman, 1957.]

near the end of the list were most easily recalled, with the last word recalled best of all. Superior recall of the last few items is called the *recency effect*. It can also be seen that items from near the beginning of the list were recalled well, although not as well as those near the end. This phenomenon is called the *primacy effect*. There is little more to the curve for the 10-word list than primacy and recency effects, because the list was so short; but data from the 32-word list reveals another significant feature—a flat section, showing that recall of items in the middle of the list was not affected much by serial position. This section of the curve is usually called the *asymptote*. On the average, the order in which items in different serial positions are recalled corresponds to the probability of recall. That is, subjects tend to recall the last items first, followed by items from the beginning, and finally items from the middle of the list.

The second general fact is that although there are no restrictions on recall order, the actual order in which items are recalled shows some structure. This was first demonstrated by Bousfield (1953). Bousfield presented to subjects a list of 60 nouns which fell into 4 different categories: animals (for example, giraffe, chipmunk, badger, camel), male names (for example, Gerald, Wallace, Owen, Simon), professions (for example, milkman, broker, chemist, dancer), and vegetables (for example, parsnip, garlic, spinach, mushroom). The 60 nouns were presented in a thoroughly random order; however, the order of recall was not random. Subjects tended to recall items from the same categories together—a phenomenon Bousfield called *clustering*. If recall order were random, one would expect a word to be followed by another word from the same category slightly under 25 percent of the time. In fact, this happened about 45 percent of the time—far too frequently to be attributed to chance.

Even a list of words supposedly unrelated to one another will not be recalled in random order. Tulving (1962) demonstrated this in a *multitrial free-recall* experiment—that is, one in which the same list is presented more than once. He presented a 16-word list to subjects 16 times, each time with the words arranged in a new order. After each trial the subjects were given a written free-recall test. Tulving found that the order in which a given subject wrote down the words on one trial tended to be related to the order in which he wrote them down on the last. That is, even though the words were supposedly "unrelated," and the presentation order changed randomly from one trial to the next, subjects imposed on the recall a consistent order of their own.

Tulving (1962) called this phenomenon *subjective organization,* and noted that "a list of completely *unrelated* words is probably as fictional as is a truly nonsensical nonsense syllable" (p. 352). Creating order out of chaos seems to be part of the learning process.

The third general fact about free recall is that ordinarily it does not exhaust the subject's memory of the list. Kirkpatrick (1894) demonstrated this by following the free-recall test with a recognition-memory test. The recognition test consisted of a mixture of some words that had been in the free-recall list and other words that had not, and the subjects were asked to sort the words into these two categories. Kirkpatrick noted that many words that had not been recalled were subsequently recognized as having been in the list. This phenomenon illustrates a rule that holds over a wide range of conditions: that recognition is easier than recall.

The fact that free recall does not exhaust the subject's memory can also be shown with a *cued-recall* test. Here, the subject is given a word related to one of the items he failed to free recall. For example, if "lily" was a word he did not produce, he might be given the word "flower" as a hint or cue. Cued recall, like recognition, often succeeds where free recall has failed.

JUDGMENT TASKS

In judgment tasks, unlike recall tasks, the subject does not have to produce items from memory. Items are presented to the subject in the test phase—just as they were in the study phase—and he is required to make some determination about the previous occurrence of each, according to special instructions he has been given. For example, he might be asked to judge whether each item was in the preceding list, or how many times it occurred, or how long ago it last appeared. Judgment tasks have the advantage that they are not restricted to verbal materials, and do not depend on the subject's ability to draw, mimic, or describe in detail the to-be-remembered events. The tasks can be used equally well with nonsense materials, words, sentences, pictures, sounds, and even odors.

The most familiar task that falls into this category is the recognition-memory task, but a number of other judgment tasks have also been used to study memory, and we shall discuss several of them, as well.

Recognition Memory

An experiment on *recognition memory* is generally done in two stages. In stage one, the subject is presented with a list of stimulus items. In stage two, he is presented with another set of items—some repeated from stage one and some that are new—and he is asked to identify the ones that were in the previous list. (Notice that this kind of test, despite its name, is *not* a test of what we commonly call "recognition." When you say you "recognize" a face or a word, you mean it is familiar to you. In a recognition-memory experiment, all the stimuli may be familiar— for example, common words. The subject's job is to tell which ones occurred in the list, not to tell which ones are familiar to him.) In addition to judging whether a particular item was or was not in the list, the subject may be asked to give a numerical *confidence rating,* to indicate how certain he is that the judgment is correct.

Research on recognition memory has paralleled interest in cognitivism. Some important early research was done in the decade between 1900 and 1930, but there was relatively little work on recognition memory for the next thirty years, apparently because the task does not lend itself easily to an analysis in terms of S–R bonds. The use of the method has accelerated, however, from 1960 to the present day.

There are two basic ways of conducting tests of recognition memory. One is similar to the "true–false" test format everyone becomes familiar with in school. Test items are presented one at a time—some *targets* from the memorized list and some *lures* or distractors, not from the list—and the subject responds either "yes" or "no" to each, depending upon whether he recognizes it as coming from the list. This technique is called the *yes–no* procedure. The other technique is similar to the "multiple-choice" test format. The subject is presented with two or more items at a time. One item in each set is a target and the others are lures, and he is to pick one and only one of them as having been in the list. This technique is called the *n-alternative forced-choice* procedure, where *n* is the number of items from which the subject must choose. It is generally conceded that the method of testing recognition memory that is theoretically simplest is the two-alternative forced-choice test. Each test set consists of one target and one lure, and the subject is to decide which is which.

The most striking fact about recognition-memory tasks, when compared with recall, is what they reveal about memory capacity. Let us consider a well-known study by Shepard (1967). Shepard had subjects go through a long sequence of stimuli, each at his own rate, and then gave them a forced-choice recognition test, on 68 pairs of items (one target and one lure per pair). For one group of subjects the original list consisted of 540 words. For another group, it consisted of 612 sentences (for example, "A dead dog is no use for hunting ducks"). For a third group it consisted of 612 pictures, taken mainly from advertisements in magazines. The average percentage of correct recognition judgments for the three types of material were: words, 88 percent; sentences, 89 percent; pictures, 97 percent. If subjects had responded randomly, of course, they would have gotten only 50 percent correct. Retention of words and sentences was remarkably good—but that of pictures was phenomenal.

Other investigators have confirmed and extended Shepard's finding. Standing (1973) showed subjects 10,000 pictures, one at a time, at a 5-second rate. In order to minimize fatigue, he presented 2,000 a day for 5 days. Immediately after the fifth session, he gave a forced-choice test on 160 target-and-lure pairs. The subjects chose the correct alternatives 83 percent of the time. Nickerson (1968) studied the retention of pictures over intervals as long as one year. Initially, the subjects studied 200 pictures, some presented once and others presented twice. Retention was measured by a yes–no test, with a mixture of 100 targets and 100 lures. The performance of subjects thus tested after a year was equivalent to 60 percent correct on a two-alternative forced-choice test for the pictures that had originally been seen once, and 72 percent correct for those that had been seen twice. While 60 percent correct is only 10 percent above chance, and would be considered very poor performance on an immediate test, it is most impressive after an interval of a year.

Recall tests, in essence, ask the subject "What was it?" and recognition-memory tests ask "Was it this?" These questions, basic though they are to the study of memory, do not do justice to the ability of humans to describe their past experience. But the recognition-memory task may be modified in several ways, by instructing the subject to tell not only *whether* the test item occurred, but also *how* it occurred. Usually, the subject is asked to make a judgment about a single aspect of the item's presentation during the experiment. This general statement encompasses all the "memory-judgment" tasks that we turn to next.

List Discrimination

Consider the following question: Can a subject, after seeing two lists of words, remember in *which* list a given word appeared? The appropriate task is not hard to design. After both lists have been shown, present all the words on a test, requiring the subject to assign each to either List 1 or List 2. This task is called *list discrimination*. The ability of subjects to tell what particular list a given item occurred in probably plays a role in most experiments in which more than one list must be learned and retained. Among other variables affecting list discrimination performance is the time interval separating the lists. The longer the interval, the better is the discrimination.

Memory for Recency

Such a finding raises a related question: How well can subjects remember how long ago an item occurred? A classic study on this question was done by Yntema and Trask (1963). These researchers had subjects go through a deck of cards, some of which contained single words, and some of which contained word pairs. When a single word occurred, the subject was simply to study it; when a pair occurred, he was to tell which of the two words had occurred more recently. The task was thus one of *recency discrimination*. The outcome of the study was straightforward, and can be described in two rules: (1) the further apart in time two events occurred, the easier it is for one to identify the more recent of the two; and (2) the longer ago the two events occurred, the harder it is to tell which was more recent.

An alternative to recency discrimination is the *recency judgment* task, in which a sequence of single items is presented, and for each, the subject gives a numerical judgment of how many items have intervened since he saw it last. Subjects tend to overjudge short intervals and to underjudge long ones. This is illustrated in panel (a) of Figure 8.10, a graph taken from a study by Hinrichs and Buschke (1968). The broken diagonal line in the figure shows what the data would look like if recency judgments were perfect.

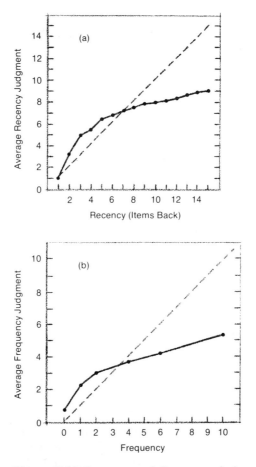

Figure 8.10 Recency and frequency judgments. [Panel (a) after Hinrichs and Buschke, 1968. Copyright 1968 by the American Psychological Association. Reprinted by permission. Panel (b) data from Hintzman, 1969a.]

Memory for Frequency

Another aspect of memory that can be studied using memory judgments is discrimination of frequency, or number of presentations. As with recency, there are two basic tasks that can be used: (a) *frequency discrimination,* in which the subject is shown two items and asked to choose the one that had the greater frequency in the list; and (b) *frequency judgments,* in which the subject is shown a single item and gives a numerical judgment of how many times he thinks it occurred. In an experiment by Hintzman (1969a), subjects saw a 320-word list, presented by a slide projector at a 3-second rate. In the list were words that occurred 1, 2, 4, 6, or 10 times. Then the subjects were given a sheet of paper which listed all the words intermixed with some new ones which had not appeared in the list. After each word, the subjects were told to write a numerical frequency judgment. The results, shown in panel (b) of Figure 8.10, looked very much like those for recency judgments: subjects tended to overjudge low values and underjudge high ones. Frequency judgments, like recognition judgments, are more accurate for pictures than for words.

Memory for Modality

Still another application of the method of memory judgments is to study memory for sensory modality. The *modality judgment* task is illustrated by an experiment by Hintzman, Block, and Inskeep (1972). A tape recorder was synchronized with a slide projector to present words to either the auditory or visual modality, at a 3-second rate. Subjects were presented with 8 lists of 18 words each, and within each list, 9 of the words (randomly selected) were visual and 9 auditory. Following each list the subjects were asked to free recall the words. After the recall test on the eighth and last list, an unexpected modality judgment test was given. There were 160 words presented on the test. For each one, the subject was to indicate either "new," "auditory," or "visual." Subjects correctly recognized about 77 percent of the old words. Of those they recognized, they were able to correctly judge the presentation modality of 74 percent. Chance performance here would be 50 percent correct—so considering the number of words involved and the fact that subjects did not expect a modality judgment test, presentation modality was remembered fairly well.

SHORT-TERM MEMORY TASKS

The terms *short-term memory* and *immediate memory* are generally used to refer to retention over intervals of seconds, rather than minutes, hours, or days. Interest in short-term memory has followed a historical course similar to that of interest in free recall and recognition. During the period dominated by behaviorism, most of the experiments of early cognitivists on short-term memory were forgotten. Then, around 1960, interest in short-term memory was rekindled. Investigators began to adapt the procedures they were familiar with to this exciting "new" topic. In some cases, the tasks they invented bore more than minor resemblance to methods developed between 1890 and 1930. A short-term memory task that did not have to be reinvented, however, was the *memory span*, which was preserved as part of some intelligence tests, and was therefore familiar to psychologists. In this section, several methods of testing short-term memory are discussed. We begin with the memory span.

Memory Span

The memory-span task, as was noted in Chapter 2, is a variation on the serial-recall task invented by Ebbinghaus. The purpose of this task is to determine how many items the subject can repeat back in correct order immediately after a single exposure. An individual subject's memory span may vary somewhat, depending on the type of materials used. For this reason, the measure is sometimes referred to as the "digit span," "letter span," "word span," and so on, to indicate more precisely how it was measured. The digit span is the version most often used in intelligence testing. The person administering the test reads a list of digits in a monotonous tone at a 1-second rate, and the subject attempts to repeat the series back. A number of such tests are given using lists of different lengths. It is unlikely, of course, that any subject will fail on all lists of one length (say 8) and succeed in repeating all shorter lists (7 and less). For this reason, one must resort to a statistical procedure to measure the memory span.

The data in Figure 8.11 are from a study by Oberly (1928). An individual subject was given lists of digits ranging from 2 to 14 items long, and his ability to repeat the lists back without error was measured. As can be seen, lists of 4 or fewer digits were remembered perfectly, while lists of 14 were never repeated successfully. For list lengths between 4 and 14, performance varied, gradually declining as the list length increased. The memory span is usually (but not always) defined as the list length that can be correctly repeated 50 percent of the time. There was no list length that fell at exactly 50 percent for Oberly's subject, so the memory span is determined by finding the point at which the function crosses 50 percent, and reading the corresponding value from the x-axis of the graph. This procedure is illustrated by the arrows in Figure 8.11. The digit span of the subject whose data are shown was about 8.7.

The memory span changes with age. Digit span is about 2 items for two-year-olds, and increases to about 6 by age ten. For college-age subjects it is around 8. It remains fairly constant at this value for adults, but declines in old age. Contrary to popular belief, the memory span is not fixed. It can be increased somewhat by practice, for subjects of any age.

Two further versions of the memory-span task will be mentioned here without detailed discussion. One is the *backward span,* in which the subject's task is to repeat the presented list in backward order. The other is what is called the *missing scan.* Here the subject is presented with all the items but one from a particular set—say all the digits between 1 and 12 *except* 8. He is to tell what the missing item was (Buschke, 1963). The backward span is somewhat harder than the forward memory task; the missing scan is somewhat easier.

The Distractor Task

Another variation on the serial-recall task used in studying short-term memory is what is sometimes called the *distractor task.* The basic idea is to divert the subject's attention from the to-be-remembered material

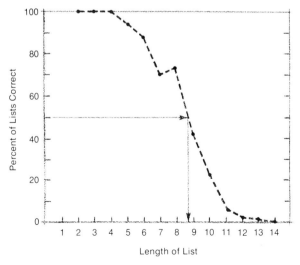

Figure 8.11 Digit span data from an individual subject. [Adapted from Oberly, 1928.]

during the retention interval in order to keep him from rehearsing it to himself. Studies of the effects of distraction on immediate memory were done before the year 1900—apparently independently—by Bigham (1894), W. G. Smith (1895), and T. L. Smith (1896). However, present-day versions of the distractor task originated—again independently—with experiments by J. Brown (1958) and Peterson and Peterson (1959). For this reason it is often referred to as the *Brown-Peterson task.*

We shall use the Peterson and Peterson experiment to illustrate the distractor task. These investigators tested memory for three-letter combinations, or trigrams, following retention intervals of varying length, filled with backward counting. An example of the sequence of events on one trial is given at the top of Figure 8.12. First the experimenter read aloud the trigram the subject was to remember, and then gave a three-digit number. The subject repeated the number and began counting backward by three's at a 1-second rate paced by a metronome. When a certain amount of time had elapsed since the trigram had been given (6 seconds in this example) a red light flashed

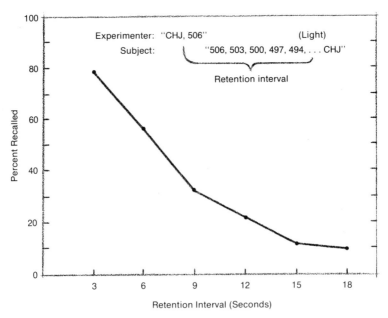

Figure 8.12 Trigram recall after various intervals filled with backward counting. [Data from Peterson and Peterson, 1959.]

on, indicating to the subject that he was to stop counting and recall the trigram. The length of the retention interval could not be predicted by the subject, because on different trials the light could flash at any of six different times, from 3 to 18 seconds after presentation of the trigram.

Figure 8.12 plots the percentage of trigrams recalled correctly (with all letters in their proper order) as a function of the retention interval. As can be seen, performance dropped precipitously as the interval became longer. Nearly 80 percent of the trigrams were correct after 3 seconds of backward counting, but after 18 seconds recall had dropped to less than 10 percent.

Counting backward is not the only distraction that can be used to prevent subjects from rehearsing, of course, and different distractions might have different effects on retention. This is a possibility we shall return to in Chapter 10.

The Probe Task

Still another task used to study short-term retention is the *probe task*. This method bears some similarity to the anticipation procedure in serial learning. A list of stimuli (usually letters or digits) is presented, followed immediately by a single item from the list. The subject's job is to respond to the test item with the item that followed it in the list. The test stimulus is often referred to as a "memory probe"—hence the name "probe task."

The experimenter, of course, can probe for any position in the list (except the first, which has no preceding item), and the subject does not know beforehand which it will be, so he must pay attention to the entire sequence. Consider, as an example, the events shown at the top of Figure 8.13. Here the subject has been given a 12-item list, and is probed for position 4. He gives the correct response. After subjects have been tested on many sequences, each probed for recall of a single item, an average recall curve can be constructed. One could plot percentage correct as a function of serial position—however it is customary to reverse the x-axis of the graph, so that recall is shown as a function of the number of items between the to-be-recalled item and the end of the list. This is just the number of intervening items, and intervening items can be thought of as distractors, just as counting backward was a distractor in the Peterson and Peterson experiment. The curve plotted in Figure 8.13 shows the outcome of one condition of a probe-task experiment conducted by Waugh and Norman (1965).

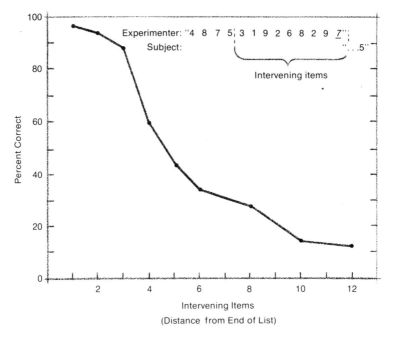

Figure 8.13 Digit recall in the probe task as a function of intervening items. [After Waugh and Norman, 1965. Copyright 1965 by the American Psychological Association. Reprinted by permission.]

In this condition, the digits were presented at a rate of 1 second per item. The retention curve does not look much different from that of the Peterson and Peterson study (Figure 8.12).

CONTINUOUS TASKS

In the distractor task and probe task, an item is presented, the subject is occupied with another task during the retention interval, and then memory for the item is tested. As a purely practical matter, these procedures are useful only for studying retention over short intervals. Suppose you wanted to study the course of forgetting over 10 minutes rather than 10 seconds. It simply would not do to make the subject count backward by three's at a 1-second rate for such a long stretch of time—not only because he would find it extremely tedious, but also because the data obtained would not be worth the effort (or cost) expended. An hour's work for only 6 observations is terribly inefficient. And then again, what if you wanted to study the course of forgetting over an hour? Ebbinghaus, as we saw, studied forgetting over a range of intervals from 19 minutes to 31 days. But he learned (and then relearned) 13-syllable lists, and it would be impossible to study very short retention intervals with that method because even one run through the list would take longer than the desired interval. Can a single task be devised to study retention over intervals ranging from scant seconds to an hour or more?

Memory researchers have solved this problem by allowing the retention interval for a given item to span both the presentation and testing of other items. In this way, stimuli can be presented in a continuous stream. Each stimulus is either a presentation of a new item to be tested later on, or a test of an item presented previously. Such tasks, called *continuous tasks,* allow a large range of retention intevals to be studied in the same experiment under the same conditions. The recency-discrimination and recency-judgment tasks described earlier in this chapter are examples of continuous tasks. There are two others, however, that are more commonly used. Both are natural adaptations of standard tasks to the requirements of continuous presentation. They are *continuous recognition-memory* and *continuous paired-associates learning.*

An excellent example of the range of retention intervals one can study using a continuous task comes from a continuous recognition experiment by Begg and Wickelgren (1974). These researchers had subjects go through a long series of fairly simple sentences (for example, "He cut himself while he was shaving"), spending $7\frac{1}{2}$ seconds on each one. For each sentence a subject was to indicate "same," if he had seen it some time before in the series, or "different," if he had not seen it before. Thus, the first time a particular sentence was encountered the correct response was "different," and the second time the correct response was "same." Subjects were tested on a total of 6,720 sentences, in 4 sessions, on 4 successive days. Each session was $3\frac{1}{2}$ hours long, and the numbers of items intervening between the first and second presentations of sentences ranged from 0 to 960. These values correspond to retention intervals of from (approximately) 0 seconds to 120 minutes, or 2 hours. (If sentences had been repeated from one day to another, of course, longer intervals could have been obtained— but the experimenters would not have had control over subjects' intervening activity.)

The percentage of correct "same" responses to a repetition of a sentence is plotted as a function of intervening sentences in Figure 8.14. Since a wide range of retention intervals was used, with small differences among the short ones and large differences among the long ones, the horizontal scale of the figure is logarithmic. Two scales are provided, one marked off in terms of intervening items and the other marked off in terms of time. Here we can observe forgetting from 0 to 7,200 seconds, under fairly constant conditions, within the same experiment. (Notice that the decrease in percent recognized over the first $7\frac{1}{2}$ seconds was about the same as that over the last hour.)

The conduct of a continuous paired-associates experiment is similar to that of continuous recognition memory. The first time a pair occurs, the subject studies the stimulus and response terms together. The second time, the stimulus appears alone, and the subject attempts to recall the response. Intervening between the study and test presentations of that pair can be many study and test trials on other pairs. Thus the retention intervals investigated can be varied over a wide range.

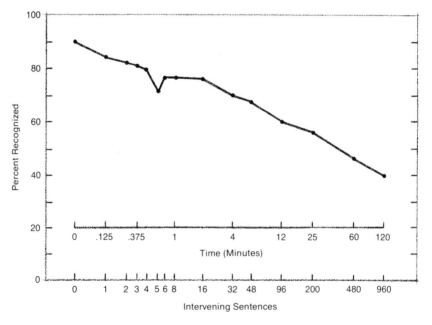

Figure 8.14 Recognition memory for sentences in a continuous task. [Data from Begg and Wickelgren, 1974.]

A COMPARISON OF PROCEDURES

In this chapter we have examined a number of different experimental procedures used to study human memory. Because human behavior is so flexible, the variety of tasks that can be used to study human memory is immense. But if all such tasks are studying the same process, one should expect similar manipulations to have similar effects on performance in all of them. Let us look briefly at the differences and similarities among the various memory tasks.

Differences Among Tasks

First, the differences. One, of course, lies in the retention intervals over which memory can be studied. Serial learning, paired-associates tasks (both anticipation and study–test procedures), the standard recognition-memory tasks, and most other judgment tasks involve the presentation of a fairly long list of items, followed by a test on several or all of the items in the list. Such tasks are suitable for investigating retention intervals of several minutes to many days, but cannot be used, without modification, to study short-term memory. Special short-term memory tasks such as the memory span and the distractor and probe tasks can be used with short retention intervals, but allow the retention of only one item (or very short sequence of items) to be tested at a time. For this reason they are not practical for studies of retention over periods of several minutes or longer. Continuous tasks, as we saw, can be used to study retention over a range of intervals from seconds to hours. In free recall, one might examine the probability of recalling an item as a function of its distance from the end of the list, and thus include a range of retention intervals from seconds to several minutes. The "recency effect" in free recall, in fact, is similar to the short-term retention functions obtained with the distractor and probe tasks. However, the experimenter has no control over when the subject recalls a particular item, and so his control over the actual retention interval is only very crude.

Another way in which the tasks differ is in the completeness of the "retrieval cue" the experimenter supplies on the retention test. In free recall, the distractor task, and the memory span, the subject knows he is to recall the last list of items (words, letters, digits) presented—but he is given no more information than that. In several tasks the subject is given a particular cue to help him recall a particular item. In serial learning and the probe task, the cue is the item that immediately preceded the to-be-remembered item in the list. In paired associates, the cue is the stimulus term that was previously paired with the response. In recognition-memory and other memory judgment tasks, the item itself is the cue given on the test. The subject must make a judgment about it—whether it was in a particular list, how long ago it occurred, how many times it occurred, and so on. Although it is hard to rank-order tasks that are so different from one another on a scale of difficulty, in general the more complete is the cue given the subject on the test, the better is the subject's memory performance. Thus, free recall falls near one end of the difficulty scale, and recognition memory falls near the other.

Similarities Among Tasks

Despite these differences, the effects of certain manipulations in the various tasks are strikingly similar. For example, pictures tend to be remembered better than words. If memory for the word "ball," for example, is compared with memory for a drawing of a ball, the drawing is better recalled in free recall. This is so even though, in free recall, the subject must give the word (for example, "ball") on the test. Likewise, concrete words are generally better remembered than abstract words, regardless of the task.

Meaningfulness also seems to affect performance in all tasks in the same way. Words are remembered better than nonsense syllables or trigrams, and more meaningful syllables and trigrams are better remembered than less meaningful ones. This has been shown in serial learning, paired associates, free recall, recognition memory, the distractor task, and the memory span.

Similarity also appears to be consistent in its effects—although as was indicated earlier, it interacts with compatibility. In the discussion of paired-associates transfer paradigms, we noted that the A–B, A–C and A–B, A–B$_r$ paradigms produce negative transfer, while transfer in the A–B, A–B$'$ paradigm is positive. Lists 1 and 2 are similar in all three cases, but in the first two, similar items must be treated differently, while in the third they are to be treated the same. As a general rule, similarity hurts learning and memory when similar items are to be treated differently, and aids when they are to be treated the same. Thus, if similar stimulus terms are paired with different responses in the same paired-associates list, performance suffers; if they are paired with the same response it is helped. If the similar items in a recognition test were all in the list, and thus all require the "yes" response, performance is high. If some appeared in the list and some did not, recognition memory suffers. In free recall, having several words with similar meanings in a list helps performance, because all are to be treated the same (recalled). In short-term memory tasks and in serial learning, where order of recall is important, similarity hurts performance because the similar items must be produced in different positions. The *kind* of similarity that is important may differ depending on the task (see Chapter 10), but the rule regarding similarity and compatibility seems to be fairly general.

The isolation, or von Restorff, effect occurs in many different tasks. An item that is distinctive is better recognized, more quickly associated with another item, and recalled better (and earlier) in free recall. It seems to benefit over both short and long retention intervals.

Finally, the effect of presentation rate is fairly constant over memory tasks. The faster material is presented, and thus the less time the subject is given to spend on each item, the poorer performance becomes. There may be exceptions to this rule in the memory-span and probe tasks—but in those tasks any manipulation of presentation rate is also a manipulation of retention interval, because the time taken up by intervening items varies with rate. We shall return to this point, also, in Chapter 10.

9

Theoretical Approaches
to Human Memory

Hermann Ebbinghaus, as we saw in Chapter 2, was a cognitivist. His theoretical orientation sprang directly from the philosophical work of the British empiricists. Successively or simultaneously occurring ideas were assumed to become associated, so that at a later time one of the ideas occurring alone would call up the other. Ebbinghaus's goal was to study experimentally the strengthening of these associations with practice and their weakening with time. The early experimental work that followed Ebbinghaus saw the inventions of the paired-associates, free-recall, and recognition-memory tasks, and the beginnings of a promising interest in short-term memory. Observations were basically objective—although combinations of objective and subjective observations were sometimes used. Theoretical concepts were mentalistic. Researchers interpreted their observations in terms of the strengthening and weakening of ideas or of associations between ideas, the existence of mental images, the waxing and waning of attention, and so on. A kind of free-wheeling cognitivism prevailed, in which it was assumed that the theoretical concepts being used were generally understood, even though they were vaguely defined.

While present-day memory theory retains much of the mentalistic flavor of the work of the early cognitivists, it has been heavily influenced by concepts imported from outside the field of memory. There have been three main sources of these imports: First, the behaviorist revolution brought with it S–R theories, which made the assumption that human learning and memory could best be understood in terms of analogies with conditioning. Second, the Gestalt psychologists, who saw memory and perception as manifestations of the same underlying processes, attempted to explain memory in terms of analogies with phenomena of perception. Third, and most important in determining the character of current memory theory, the development of computer technology has led to an information-processing approach to learning and memory, which assumes that the brain or mind can best be understood in terms of a computer analogy. In this chapter, we shall discuss each of these three influences in turn.

S–R THEORY: THE CONDITIONING ANALOGY

During the era of behaviorism's predominance in the field of learning, those investigating human learning and memory looked to theories of animal conditioning for inspiration. Most learning researchers believed that a single set of principles could be found that would hold for both animal and human learning. *The Psychology of Human Learning,* by McGeoch and Irion (1952), was the standard textbook and authoritative reference work in its area for many years. At the beginning of that book's Chapter 3, the authors expressed the general attitude as follows:

> Since the results of Pavlov's (1927) work have become generally known, there has been an enormous amount of research activity in the field of conditioned response learning. There are a number of reasons for the popularity of this approach to the study of learning. From the standpoint of this book, the most important of these is that conditioning techniques permit the relatively precise determination of various relationships which we can assume to be fundamentally true of the learning process in general (McGeoch and Irion, 1952, p. 63).

Probably the most influential advocate of this S–R orientation was Clark Hull. His early experimental and theoretical work was concerned not only with conditioning, but also with the rote learning of serial lists of nonsense syllables. Hull, Hovland, Ross, Hall, Perkins, and Fitch (1940) published a mathematical theory of human rote learning three years before Hull's influential *Principles of Behavior,* which dealt primarily with animal conditioning, was to appear.

Basic to the conditioning analogy is the following notion. In learning a serial list of nonsense syllables by the anticipation procedure, the subject must come to say each syllable before it appears—that is, when the preceding syllable is in the window of the memory drum. If two successive items are YAV and FID, for example, he must learn to say "fid" when he sees YAV. It is easy to identify elements of this procedure with elements of classical conditioning. Assume that FID is the UCS for saying "fid." YAV precedes FID repeatedly, and so could be considered the CS of the classical conditioning paradigm. Indeed, the subject's task is to say "fid" when shown YAV, and so learning to do so might be thought of as a case of classical conditioning. In serial learning, then, the subject may learn to anticipate the next syllable in the list in the same way a dog learns to salivate in anticipation of food. In either case, the formation of a simple S–R association could underlie the learning process. Thus, many of the learning principles uncovered in classical conditioning experiments might be expected to hold for human rote learning, as well.

As was mentioned in the last chapter, serial learning is rather complex from an S–R point of view, because each item in the list serves both as a UCS (for the response that is supposed to anticipate it) and as a CS (for the item that is to follow). For S–R theorists, therefore, paired-associates learning (using the anticipation procedure) has been the preferred experimental task. Here, the stimulus term of each pair presumably corresponds to the CS of classical conditioning, and the response term to the UCS. The CS and UCS roles, therefore, are not confounded.

What reasons might one have for believing that the analogy between rote learning and classical conditioning is valid? There are several. First, the learning curves which plot performance as a function of trial number have a similar form in classical conditioning and rote learning. In both cases, performance improves fairly rapidly over the first several trials, and then less rapidly as it approaches its maximum. Second, in classical conditioning, the latency of the response to the CS continues to decrease with practice, and this is also true of response latencies in the paired-associates and serial-learning tasks. Third, in classical conditioning, backward conditioning is difficult (perhaps impossible) to obtain. In paired associates, if a subject masters the pair VAX–POK in the standard way and is then given the response term (POK) and asked to produce the stimulus term from memory, performance is far from perfect. Such a test of *backward recall* seems analogous to a test for backward conditioning. Many theorists have assumed that when a pair is learned, two associations are set up—a forward association (VAX–POK) and a backward association (POK–

VAX). The forward association is usually assumed to be the stronger of the two, as the conditioning analogy would lead one to expect.

An S–R Theory of Serial Learning

The biggest problem facing any theory of serial learning is accounting for the serial-position effect, which was described in the last chapter (see Figure 8.3). The difficulty of explaining this phenomenon lies not so much in the fact that the beginning and end of the list are relatively easy to learn as in the fact that the serial-position curve is not symmetrical; that is, the point of maximum difficulty lies just past the middle of the list.

Of several attempts to account for the serial-position curve in terms of S–R bonds, the one by Ribback and Underwood (1950) is perhaps the most interesting. Starting with the fact that subjects learn the items at the two ends of the list first, these authors proposed that a serial list is learned by building up two chains of S–R associations—one starting at the beginning of the list and one starting at the end. With repeated trials, the first chain grows forward and the second grows backward, and the list is mastered when the two chains meet.

Why does the point of maximum difficulty lie past the middle of the list? Ribback and Underwood proposed that this is because forward chaining is faster than backward chaining. In a given number of trials, the fast learning process encompasses more syllables than the slow one does. Therefore, the point at which the two processes meet (which is, of course, the last position learned) will fall somewhere past the middle of the list. While Ribback and Underwood showed experimentally that backward chaining is indeed slower than forward chaining, as they hypothesized, they offered no explanation of why this should be so. An obvious explanation is that forward chaining is based on forward associations and backward chaining on backward associations. If backward associations are assumed to be acquired more slowly than forward associations, the form of the serial-position curve is explained.

Gibson's Generalization–Differentiation Theory

A very influential analysis of rote learning, based upon the conditioning analogy, was presented in 1940 by Eleanor Gibson. Her thesis was that many phenomena of serial and paired-associates learning could be understood in terms of *stimulus generalization* and *differentiation,* two concepts that had originated in the work of Pavlov and his colleagues (see Chapter 3).

Gibson's theoretical use of generalization and differentiation can best be seen in her explanation of effects of stimulus similarity on learning. Consider a mixed high- and low-similarity paired-associates list (for example, the list of trigram-digit pairs shown in Figure 8.7). It is assumed that each time a pair is presented, the corresponding S–R bond is strengthened. But the tendency to give a particular response R also generalizes to other stimuli similar to S. Figure 9.1a shows the

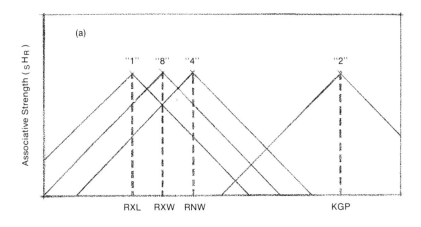

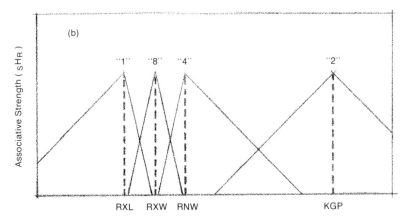

Figure 9.1 Generalization of response tendencies among stimulus trigrams according to Gibson's theory, (a) before and (b) after discrimination training.

generalization of response tendencies among four S–R pairs. Consider the stimulus term RXL. When it is shown to the subject, three habits of greater than zero strength come into play. The strongest is the tendency to say, correctly, "1." But the response "8" is also likely to occur, because it is associated with RXW, which is similar to RXL; and there is also some tendency to give "4." Only the response "2," which is associated with a very dissimilar trigram, has no tendency to occur.

The figure shows all four S–R habits to be of equal strength, but of course that is an oversimplification. Strong habits could dominate correct but weak habits, through generalization. And if Hull's concept of oscillation is added, allowing the four response tendencies to fluctuate in strength over time, the theory predicts many errors of confusion among the high-similarity items of the list. In contrast, low-similarity items such as KGP–2 will be learned rapidly, because no competing response tendencies are present.

Given generalization gradients such as those shown in Figure 9.1a, how does a subject ever learn a list of highly similar items? Gibson postulated a process of differentiation, in which incorrect response tendencies are extinguished. This narrows the generalization gradients, as is shown in Figure 9.1b. Differentiation, Gibson assumed, requires (a) that the incorrect responses be elicited, and (b) that they not be reinforced. Because extinction takes many trials to become complete, lists of highly similar items are difficult to learn.

Gibson (1940) explored a number of other applications of the generalization–differentiation theory to phenomena of paired-associates learning. Why is an isolated item easier to learn than nonisolated items (the von Restorff effect)? Since the isolated item is distinctive, there is little generalization between it and the other items in the list. The phenomenon is thus easily explained. Why are meaningful materials easier to learn than nonsense materials? Meaningful items, she assumed, have acquired unique responses in the past—thus the process of differentiation, which narrows the generalization gradients, has already occurred. Nonsense items, by contrast, must be differentiated from one another for the first time as the list is being learned. Gibson also explained positive and negative transfer, fairly successfully, in terms of generalization between the stimuli of List 1 and those of List 2.

One failure of Gibson's theory should be mentioned. Having identified the differentiation process with extinction of incorrect response tendencies, she naturally assumed that spontaneous recovery could occur. Over time, then, the tendency to confuse similar items should increase; that is, the narrowed generalization gradients should gradually become wider. A straightforward prediction of this analysis is that high-similarity lists, once mastered, should be forgotten more quickly than low-similarity lists. Experiments have failed to confirm this prediction (Underwood, 1961). Highly similar items are certainly harder than distinctive items to learn; but the evidence is that once they have been learned, high- and low-similarity lists are forgotten at the same rate.

The Extinction–Recovery Theory of Forgetting

Perhaps the most influential application of the conditioning analogy has been in the analysis of forgetting. There are two phenomena the analogy has been used to explain: *retroactive interference* (RI), and *proactive interference* (PI). Both refer to the forgetting of "target" information due to the learning of other information that is related to it. Retroactive interference is forgetting caused by information learned *after* the target information was learned. Proactive interference is forgetting caused by information that was learned *before* the target information was acquired.

A common experimental paradigm for studying retroactive interference uses the paired-associates task, with an experimental and a control group, as follows:

Condition	*Stage 1*	*Stage 2*	*Stage 3*
Experimental:	Learn A–B	Learn A–C	Recall A–B
Control:	Learn A–B	Learn C–D	Recall A–B

Notice that the two lists learned by the experimental group are related (the A–B, A–C paradigm), while those learned by the control group are not. If subjects in the experimental group perform more poorly in stage three than those in the control group—as they typically do—retroactive interference has been demonstrated.

The paradigm most used to study proactive interference is similar to that for retroactive interference:

Condition	*Stage 1*	*Stage 2*	*Stage 3*	*Stage 4*
Experimental:	Learn A–B	Learn A–C	Rest	Recall A–C
Control:	Learn B–D	Learn A–C	Rest	Recall A–C

If the experimental group recalls A-C more poorly than the control group in stage four, proactive interference has been demonstrated. Note two ways in which this paradigm differs from that of retroactive interference. First, the subject is tested for retention of List 2, rather than List 1. This follows directly from the definition of proactive interference. Second, a rest period or delay is inserted between the original learning of A-C and the retention test. This delay is necessary, because in stage two, learning is usually carried to mastery of the list. On an immediate test, therefore, performance would be perfect in both the experimental and control conditions, and there would be no measurable proactive interference. In fact, proactive interference grows over time. The difference in recall between the experimental and control groups increases as the retention interval for A-C increases.

S-R theory accounts for the facts of retroactive and proactive interference by analogy with *extinction* and *spontaneous recovery*. The extinction-recovery model was developed by several investigators— among them Eleanor Gibson (1940), Arthur Melton (Melton and Irwin, 1940), and B. J. Underwood (1948). It is often given the label, "the interference theory of forgetting." Its basic assumptions are two: (a) During the learning of the second of two lists bearing an A-B, A-C relationship, the A-B associations become extinguished or "unlearned." (Since they are replaced by A-C associations, it also would be appropriate to call this process "counterconditioning.") Retroactive interference, therefore, is seen as due to extinction of A-B habits during A-C learning. (b) Following the learning of List 2, the extinguished A-B associations spontaneously recover, gradually coming to interfere with recall of A-C. Thus, proactive interference is seen, in the conditioning analogy, as due to recovery of extinguished List 1 habits. The hypothetical processes underlying retroactive and proactive interference are illustrated in Figure 9.2.

While the extinction-recovery theory of forgetting has been very influential in memory research, the evidence, as it currently stands, is not altogether favorable. Something akin to unlearning of List 1 pairs during List 2 acquisition apparently does occur, but there is a question whether List 2 learning causes associations to be unlearned (as S-R theory assumes), or response terms to be "blocked," or stimulus terms to be interpreted in a different way. Furthermore, spontaneous recovery of the "unlearned" List 1 information has been difficult to show, and when it does appear, seems too small to explain the large

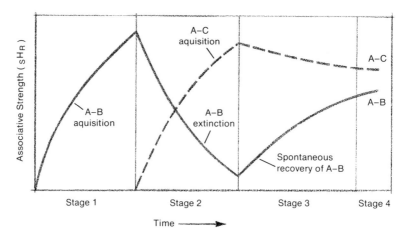

Figure 9.2 Changes in associative strength with practice and time according to the extinction–recovery theory of forgetting. Retroactive interference is typically measured at the beginning of stage 3, and proactive interference during stage 4.

amounts of proactive interference that are often obtained. More will be said about the causes of forgetting in Chapter 11.

GESTALT THEORY: THE PERCEPTION ANALOGY

The Gestalt psychology movement was begun in Germany by Max Wertheimer. In 1910 two young psychologists, Wolfgang Köhler and Kurt Koffka, came under Wertheimer's influence, and over the next three decades they became Gestalt psychology's chief proponents. Gestalt principles were derived chiefly from the study of perception, and it is in that context that American psychologists first learned of them. But the English translations of books by Koffka (1924) and Köhler (1925) greatly expanded the American perspective of Gestalt psychology; and Köhler's *Gestalt Psychology* (1929) and Koffka's *Principles of Gestalt Psychology* (1935), both originally published in English, expanded it still further. Eventually, Wertheimer, Koffka, and Köhler all took academic positions in America, partly to escape the oppressive political climate in Germany.

The teachings of the Gestalt psychologists with regard to learning and memory were slow to be appreciated. There were several reasons for this. One was that Gestalt psychology had a strongly cognitive orientation. Subjective observations were accepted—particularly in the study of perception—and explanations were strongly mentalistic. Some respectability was gained by claiming that the subjective experience is "structurally identical" with the underlying brain process. This principle—called *psychophysical isomorphism* (meaning that the psychological and physical processes have the same form)—allowed them to assume that subjective observations could reveal the structure of the underlying physical processes. But the principle of isomorphism did little to attract behaviorist psychologists to the cognitivist teachings of the Gestaltists.

A second reason that American psychologists found Gestalt psychology difficult to accept was that, in keeping with its continental origins, Gestalt psychology was rationalistic. Certain aspects of experience, it was assumed, were primarily determined by the basic physical structure of the brain and the nature of the neural processes occurring in it, and could not be altered by learning. The physical laws of organization governing these processes were assumed to govern our experience—particularly our experience of space and time.

A third way in which Gestalt psychology contrasted with the dominant American view was in its rejection of associationism. "Association," the Gestalt psychologists held, could be explained in terms of Gestalt principles of organization. Contiguity was not sufficient for the formation of associations, since contiguity alone was not sufficient for organization. In order for learning to occur, other conditions had to be met, as well.

Memory was seen by the Gestalt theorists as continuous with perception. Thus, if one looks at an object and then looks away, the effect of viewing the object continues to exist in the brain as a direct copy of the original experience. This residue of the perceptual process was called the *memory trace*. The term has come into general use today, but it is important to realize that the Gestalt psychologists meant something quite specific by it. The brain process underlying perception was assumed to be "isomorphic" to the perceptual experience itself, and the memory trace to be the residue of that process. One implication of this view is that there should be *modalities of memory*, just as there are modalities of perception. A visual experience gives rise to a memory trace in the visual areas of the brain, an auditory one to a trace in the auditory areas, and so on. A second implication, which is especially important, is that the laws of organization that apply to perception should also apply to memory.

In its approach to perception, Gestalt psychology emphasized the "holistic" properties of experience. The whole is greater than the sum of its parts, because it has an additional property that derives from their arrangement, or configuration. Figure 9.3 illustrates this point. The elements making up the three patterns are quite different—yet the similarity of the three patterns is compelling. The elements of each are arranged to form a triangle, and it is this holistic form that makes the experiences produced by the three patterns alike. The German word for form, pattern, or configuration is "Gestalt." This is the key concept from which the Gestalt school takes its name.

Gestalt laws apply to auditory, as well as visual, experience. A familiar tune can be played in different keys, by different instruments, at different tempos, and still be recognized as the same tune. All the elements are different; it is the relationships among the elements—that is, their overall configuration or Gestalt—that remains the same.

Gestalt Laws of Organization

The most important problem of perception, from the Gestalt point of view, is to discover the laws according to which perceptual elements are grouped, or organized, into a whole. Some of the *laws of organization* the Gestaltists discussed are as follows:

Similarity.   Elements that have one or more properties in common will tend to be grouped together. In Figure 9.4a, for example, the

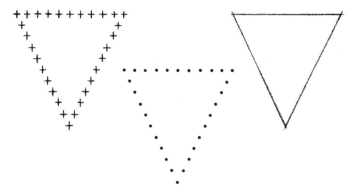

Figure 9.3 The configuration of elements determines how they are perceived.

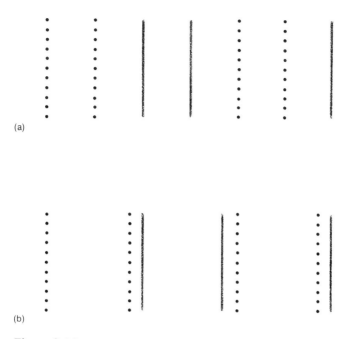

Figure 9.4 Demonstrations of the Gestalt laws of similarity (a) and proximity (b).

columns seem to pair off naturally. Dot columns are seen as going together, and solid lines as going together, even though all the columns are evenly spaced. The principle of similarity helps to organize both our visual and our auditory worlds. When we look at a cluttered desk, widely separated patches of its surface are seen as belonging to the same object because of their similar color and texture. When we listen to a conversation in a noisy room, the pitch and timbre of a person's voice help us pick it out from the others.

Proximity. Items tend to be grouped according to their proximity (or nearness) to one another. Proximity can win out over similarity, as in Figure 9.4b. We can, with effort or practice, see the similar columns in pairs, but the immediate impression is one of pairs consisting of a dot column and a straight line. The law of proximity operates in audition, as well as in vision. Tap with your finger the rhythm: tap-tap-tap (pause), tap-tap-tap (pause), and so on. The taps occurring in close succession are heard as a cluster, with each cluster separated from the next by a long pause. Thus temporal, as well as spatial, proximity tends to determine the organization of experience. Such auditory experiences, since they are extended over time, necessarily involve memory.

Good Form.   The perceptual field tends to be organized into "good forms" or "good Gestalts," that is, patterns that are *simple, regular,* and *symmetric.* The prime example of a good form is the circle. Squares and equilateral triangles are others. The Gestalt psychologists felt that the tendency toward perception of good forms reflected the dynamics of the underlying brain processes, which naturally organized themselves into simple, regular, and symmetric structures.

Good Continuation.   The principle of "good continuation" states that elements will tend to be grouped together if they appear to continue or complete a lawful pattern. Figure 9.5 shows two examples of good continuation. In panel (a) a chain of line segments connected by right angles appears to be superimposed on a chain connected by obtuse angles, although logically the pattern could be seen in other ways (for example, five-sided figures with their corners touching). In panel (b) we tend to see a circle with a gap, rather than a pinched letter C. If the figure is flashed very briefly, the gap may not even be noticed. The tendency to complete, or close, the gaps in such forms is called *closure.* The principles of good continuation and good form are closely related to each other.

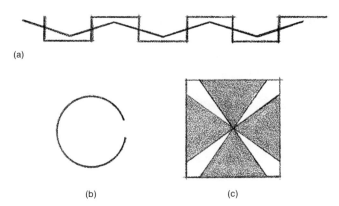

(a)

(b)   (c)

Figure 9.5 The principles of good continuation (a), closure (b), and figure–ground organization (c).

Figure and Ground.   The perceptual world tends to be organized into figures, which have form or shape, and backgrounds, which do not. Sometimes the figure–ground organization of a pattern is so ambiguous that it will spontaneously alternate between one interpretation and another. Figure 9.5c, for example, can be seen either as an X or as a plus. When either figure appears, the elements of the other seem to be formless empty space.

How are Gestalt principles, developed in perception, applied to memory? This has been done in two ways. The first derives from the fact that the memory trace was assumed to have the same form as the perceptual experience that produced it, and therefore to be subject to the same laws of spatial organization. The second derives form the conjecture that the laws of temporal organization and spatial organization are essentially the same. If events spread out in time (such as notes played by a violin) become organized according to Gestalt principles, then the principles must necessarily apply to memory, because it is only in memory that the past events continue to exist. We shall discuss separately the applications to memory of principles of spatial organization and temporal organization.

Spatial Organization and Memory

Association, from the Gestalt point of view, is a matter of organization. Two elements, A and B, become associated when they become parts of a unified whole. The laws of organization, therefore, should apply to "associative" learning. One implication of this notion has been explored by Asch and his colleagues in several experiments (summarized in Asch, 1969). The basic idea behind each of them was to compare associative learning in two situations: one in which the elements to be associated appear to form a single Gestalt (the unitary condition) and one in which they are spatially separated (the paired condition). Several examples are shown in Figure 9.6. The stimuli were mostly geometric forms, but also included nonsense words. Retention tests were of several varieties—recognition memory, paired-associates recall, and free recall. Across experiments, the unitary versus paired manipulation had consistent effects: retention was about twice as good following unitary presentation as it was following paired presentation.

If learning an association between two elements A and B is the same as organizing them into a single Gestalt, then the failure to achieve

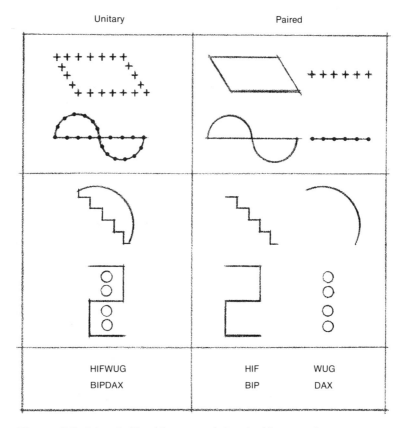

Figure 9.6 Stimuli like those used in Asch's experiments. [Adapted from Asch, 1969.]

such an organization is the failure to achieve associative learning. Thus, it is possible, from the Gestalt point of view, for repeated study of a pair to produce no learning whatever, because the unitary organization has failed to occur. For example, a subject studying a long list of word pairs may see "cigar–horse" for several trials without making a connection. Then on one trial, a unifying image occurs to him—he pictures to himself a horse smoking a cigar. From that point on, he has the necessary association. The "sudden learning" predicted by Gestalt theory is in contrast to the gradual build-up of associative strength predicted by S–R theories such as Hull's.

The Gestalt notion that the memory trace is a copy of the perceptual experience suggests a possible cause of forgetting: The same forces that determine the spatial organization of perception may work on the memory trace over time. If this is true, then the memory trace should change in the direction of a "good Gestalt." Traces of complex patterns should become more simple and regular; traces of asymmetric ones should become symmetric; traces of open or incomplete figures should become closed. This hypothesis is sometimes called the *autonomous trace change* theory of forgetting, because memory traces are assumed to change qualitatively, on their own, independently of the subject's activities. Wulf (1922) tested this hypothesis by showing subjects four figures and having them draw the figures after retention intervals of 30 seconds, 24 hours, 1 week, and 2 months. He found that successive reproductions changed in the expected ways. Unfortunately, Wulf's experimental procedure was open to a number of criticisms. One was that the subjects were tested several times, and may, on the later tests, have been remembering their earlier drawings instead of the figures they had originally been shown. Another was that simple, regular features may have just been easier to draw. More adequate experiments, giving recognition-memory tests rather than recall tests, and testing each subject only at one retention interval, have failed to support the autonomous trace change hypothesis. (For a review of research done on this problem, see Riley, 1963.)

Temporal Organization and Memory

The observation that many of the Gestalt laws of spatial organization apply also to the organization of events in time led Gestalt psychologists to propose a fascinating hypothesis. The principle of psychophysical isomorphism stated that the laws of spatial organization of perceptual experience were the laws of spatial organization of the underlying brain processes. If this is the case, and if the laws of temporal organization are the same as those of spatial organization, then time must be represented spatially in the brain.

This notion was developed most explicitly by Koffka (1935). He proposed that as events are perceived, their traces are laid down in the brain by a continuously moving excitatory process. The result was a temporal record of experience somewhat like a tape recording, which Koffka called the *trace column*. The spatial organization of traces in the column, being subject to the same innate forces that determine visual experience, should reflect the principles of proximity, similarity, good continuation, and so on.

The extension of Gestalt laws to temporal organization suggests several hypotheses. Consider the learning of a serial list of nonsense syllables. From the time of Ebbinghaus, it was assumed that in learning such a list one forms a chain of associations. The Gestalt view, by contrast, suggests that the syllables are elements of a larger Gestalt: the whole list. The organization of a serial list is somewhat like that of a straight line, in that it has a simple kind of symmetry, and its most salient landmarks are the beginning and the end. The most distinguishable characteristic of any point is its distance from the beginning or the end of the list. Viewing a serial list as a Gestalt suggests that each syllable is linked, not to the preceding and following items, but rather to a *position in the list*. Notice that this hypothesis seems to lead in a natural way to an explanation of the serial-position effect of serial learning. Endpoints are the most distinctive positions in the list, and as one moves away from one of these landmarks, precise locations become more and more difficult to specify. More errors may occur in middle positions because those positions are less discriminable, making middle syllables harder to place correctly. (This hypothesis does not explain why the peak of the serial-position error curve falls beyond the middle of the list, but it can be modified to do so; see Murdock, 1960.)

So we have two quite different theories of serial learning: the traditional *associative chaining* theory and the *ordinal position* theory, drived from Gestalt theory. What evidence might help us choose between them?

The associative chaining theory makes an obvious prediction: If learning a serial list involves the formation of associations between adjacent items, then these associations should transfer to the learning of an appropriately constructed paired-associates list. Young (1962) conducted several experiments testing this prediction, only one of which will be described here.

In stage one of this experiment, subjects learned a serial list of 14 adjectives by the anticipation procedure. To ensure that any associations between successive words would be very strong, Young had each subject master the list and then continue for 10 trials of overlearning. In stage two, the subjects learned a paired-associates list made up of 14 adjective pairs. Half of these were transfer pairs, taken directly from the serial list learned in stage one by pairing the adjective in each odd-numbered position with the one following it. The other half were control pairs, made up of new adjectives that had not appeared in stage one. The design of the experiment is illustrated by the lists shown in Figure 9.7. Young's experiment showed no transfer from serial to paired-associates learning. In learning the paired associates list in stage two, subjects made an average of 49.6 correct responses on the transfer pairs and 51.9 correct responses on the control pairs. These values are nearly identical—a result apparently inconsistent with the associative chaining hypothesis, which predicts much better performance on the transfer than on the control pairs.

Young's dissertation included several experiments that were in conflict with the associative chaining account of serial learning. But the chaining hypothesis was so deeply ingrained in the thinking of learning theorists that he had difficulty getting his dissertation published. The initial reaction of journal editors was to disbelieve the results. Notice, however, that even if Young's finding is accepted, it can be interpreted in several ways. It suggests that what is learned in serial learning is different from what is learned in the paired-associates task, but it does not tell us what the difference is. It might be the case, for example, that serial learning does involve item-to-item associations,

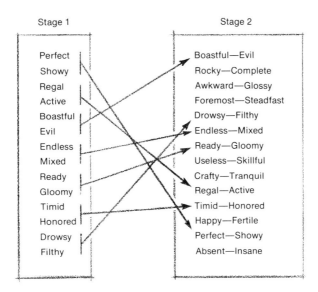

Figure 9.7 Adjective serial and paired-associates lists like those used in Young's (1960) transfer experiments.

but that paired-associates learning involves a different process, such as organizing the two items into a unified Gestalt.

Direct support for the ordinal-position hypothesis comes from a transfer experiment by Ebenholtz (1963). Ebenholtz showed that subjects can use the analogy between space and time in a way the Gestalt theory predicts. Subjects learned lists of 10 nonsense syllables. There were two tasks: a standard serial-learning task, in which the syllables were seen in a fixed serial order, and a spatial-position learning task, in which each syllable appeared in a different location in space. In the spatial task, 10 windows were arranged in a vertical column in front of the subject. Whenever a red patch appeared in a window, the subject was to anticipate the syllable that would replace it. A given syllable always appeared in the same window—but the temporal order in which the syllables were shown was random. Thus the subject's task was not to learn *when* each syllable would appear, but rather *where* it would appear.

Half of the subjects in Ebenholtz's experiment were given the serial learning task in stage one and the spatial learning task in stage two; the other half did the tasks in the reverse order. The manipulation of most interest concerned the relationship between serial position, in one task, and spatial position, in the other. The same ten syllables were used in both tasks. For half the subjects, the serial and spatial positions of the syllables were consistent; that is, the ordering in the serial task corresponded to the top-down ordering in the spatial task. For the other half of the subjects, the positions of the syllables in the two tasks were inconsistent. Transfer, from one task to the other, can be seen in the number of errors committed during learning in stage two. Figure 9.8 shows that, for both tasks, there was considerable benefit from the consistent relationship between spatial and temporal orderings. This is what Gestalt theory would lead one to expect.

Actually, the experimental evidence regarding what is learned in serial learning is mixed, and the issues have not all been resolved (see Young, 1968). Some evidence favors the serial chaining hypothesis, and some favors the ordinal position hypothesis. The truth may be that the cues subjects use in serial learning are complex, and that both hypotheses are partly correct.

It was the application of Gestalt laws to temporal organization in memory that predicted the isolation, or von Restorff, effect. In the top row of Figure 9.9 are ten forms—nine very similar and one quite distinct. The rounded form stands out from the others, much as a

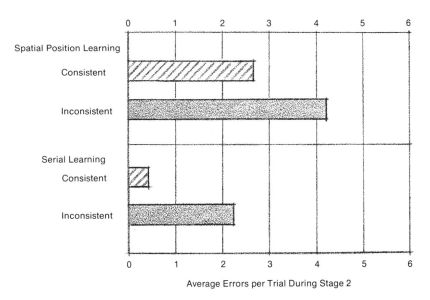

Figure 9.8 Results of Ebenholtz's transfer experiment. [Data from Ebenholtz, 1963.]

figure against a ground. Because of their similarity, the triangles group together into a homogeneous set to which the rounded form does not belong. Von Restorff (1933) reasoned that the same should happen in memory, with the similar and dissimilar stimulus items distributed over time. She experimented with several tasks and several types of materials. One of her experiments used lists like those shown in the second and third rows of Figure 9.9. Following presentation,

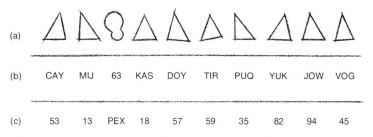

Figure 9.9 The "isolation" effect: (a) in a spatial array of visual forms; (b) and (c) in free-recall lists like those used by von Restorff (1933).

subjects spent 10 minutes reading, and were then tested for free recall of the items in the list. In both types of list, the isolated item was recalled best. The isolated number was recalled 2.4 times as often as one of the syllables from the same list; the isolated syllable was recalled 4.4 times as often as the numbers that surrounded it.

Gestalt theory attributes the isolation effect to a process called "trace aggregation." The similar stimuli are assumed to be grouped together, forming an aggregate, in which some of their individuality is lost. The fifth triangle in Figure 9.9a is seen as "one of those triangles," at the expense of being considered as a particular triangle, distinct in subtle ways from the rest. Likewise, the syllables in 9.9b and the numbers in 9.9c, according to the Gestalt interpretation, form aggregates (in memory) in which their individuality is lost.

"Trace aggregation" is a vague concept, but one that seems to turn up again and again in memory theory, under different names. "Merging," "crowding," "diffusion," and "loss of differentiation" are some of the apparent aliases under which trace aggregation has been used to account for isolation effects, effects of similarity on learning, and retroactive and proactive interference. Just how the Gestalt concept of trace aggregation differs from Gibson's concept of stimulus generalization is not clear. It may be that the conditioning and perception analogies have produced explanations of similarity effects which are essentially the same.

INFORMATION-PROCESSING THEORY: THE COMPUTER ANALOGY

Computers are useful to psychologists in many ways. Used to control the presentation of stimuli and to record subjects' responses, they afford a degree of flexibility and precision that is not possible when experiments are run "by hand." Used in data analysis, they allow huge quantities of data to be manipulated quickly, accurately, and at a minimum expense. In these practical respects, psychology has been affected by computers just as has industry. But in psychology, computer technology has also had a more profound impact. The computer is a "machine that thinks," and as such, it provides psychology with a powerful theoretical tool. The analogy between the human brain or mind and the computer has drastically altered the nature of psychological theories.

The computer is an information-processing machine, which takes in, or "inputs," information from peripheral sensing devices such as a card reader or keyboard terminal, codes it internally and stores it for later use, retrieves it, compares it with other information, makes decisions based on these comparisons, transforms the information according to complex rules, and produces the results of the transformations as "output." Why would one claim that such a machine thinks? For one thing, it can perform many jobs which done by humans, require thought. For another, many of the internal operations of the computer seem to parallel mental processes we observe in our own minds when we introspect.

Given the contrast previously drawn between mechanistic and mentalistic explanations of behavior, a "machine that thinks" may seem like a contradiction in terms. But it is just this marriage of two seemingly irreconcilable traditions that gives the computer analogy its great appeal. Mechanistic theories of psychological processes can be logical and precise, but generally lack intuitive plausibility. Mentalistic theories can be intuitively plausible, but typically suffer from vagueness. Information-processing theories, based on the computer analogy, are able to combine these virtues of the behaviorist and cognitivist traditions. The same process can be viewed either as a mental act or as a mechanical operation. Neither view destroys the virtues of the other.

The information-processing theorist may or may not actually use a computer in his theoretical work. He may write a program embodying the assumptions of his theory, and then run the program on a computer to see whether it behaves in the same way as the organism he is trying to understand. Such activity is called *computer simulation,* and in principle (aside from the use of the computer itself), it is no different from the hypothetico-deductive method advocated by Clark Hull. Alternatively, the theorist may wish to avoid bothering with all the irrelevant details of a running program that are not part of his theory, and use what he knows about computers as a source of ideas about how things might be done by the brain. An example is the TOTE unit concept of Miller, Galanter, and Pribram (1960), discussed in Chapter 6. This second form of theoretical activity has become so commonplace that theorists may hardly realize that their ideas are based on the computer analogy. But a comparison of present-day theories with those of, say, twenty years ago shows just how deeply the computer analogy has permeated psychological theory.

One of the first psychologists to advocate an information-processing approach to psychology was Kenneth Craik, a brilliant young British psychologist who, during World War II, became familiar with the primitive electronics technology of that time. In a book entitled *The Nature of Explanation,* Craik (1943) argued that the brain should be viewed as a complex machine that has the ability to construct internal models of external reality. It is the working of such models, he said, that we call thought; and it is through them that we predict and "explain" or understand external events. Craik did not have at his disposal the powerful computer metaphor that seems so natural to us today, but he asked the reader to imagine the brain as analogous with a symbol-manipulating machine—similar to a mechanical calculator but vastly more powerful. He tried to show how a machine might be built that would exhibit certain perceptual phenomena (for example, shape constancy), but the machine analogies available to him were clearly limited.

In the 1950s and 1960s, computer technology and the theory behind it grew, and computers became increasingly familiar tools of psychological research. The natural outgrowth of this familiarity was the tendency of psychologists to view the brain as in information-processing machine. Two influential early examples are found in the work of Noam Chomsky (1957), on linguistics, and Donald Broadbent (1958), on attention.

Chomsky's (1957) argument, which almost singlehandedly overthrew the prevailing behaviorist approach to linguistics, was that the linguist, rather than trying to describe a language directly, should try to describe the "device" that generates the language. The description of the device was to be a *generative grammar*—that is, a set of formal rules for generating the sentences of the language. Such rules might be of the following form: a sentence consists of a noun phrase plus a verb phrase; a noun phrase must have a noun or pronoun; a noun may be preceded by an adjective; and so on. Specifying a generative grammar of this type is essentially the same as writing a computer program for producing sentences. Most importantly, the grammar can be thought of not only as a linguistic theory, of the language itself, but also as a psychological theory, of the language user. The linguist, in discovering the grammar of a language, is presumably discovering the rules a speaker of that language follows when he generates sentences.

Broadbent's (1958) contribution, though less revolutionary than Chomsky's, has been very influential. Broadbent proposed an information-processing theory of attention. This theory assumed that much more information is available to our senses than the brain can deal with at one time; that is, the brain is a "limited capacity channel." Thus, there must be preliminary selection, with some information passed on into the channel for further processing, and the rest ignored. The device Broadbent proposed to accomplish this selection he called a *filter*. The filter could be set to allow some types of stimuli into the limited capacity channel (for example, sounds having the pitch and timbre of the voice to which you are listening) and to screen others out. Broadbent's filter theory provided the initial thrust for a great deal of research on attention that is still going on today.

Characteristics of Information-Processing Theory

Information-processing theories take on a variety of forms. There is no single characteristic they all share. But they do have in common the notion that the brain is an information-processing device similar to a computer—and the computers with which theorists are most familiar are general-purpose, electronic digital computers. Several characteristics of these machines have become common elements of recent theories in cognitive psychology. None of these is a *necessary* element of an information-processing theory—the theorist is free to make any combination of assumptions he wishes. But because of the computer analogy, theorists are *predisposed* to make certain assumptions about how the brain works. Some of the more widespread predispositions that characterize the information-processing approach to psychological theory are as follows:

All-or-None Storage.   In the memory of a digital computer, a particular bit of information is either present or not present. The "state" of the memory location is either 0 or 1; there are no intermediate states. Thus, the computer analogy predisposes theorists to think of learning and forgetting as all-or-none processes, rather than as changes that occur gradually with practice or with the passage of time. The distinction here is between *all-or-none* processes, suggested by the computer analogy, and *incremental,* or gradual, processes, suggested by conditioning theories such as Hull's.

Propositional Representation.   In a digital computer, elementary information is represented by arbitrary symbols, and complex information by "symbol strings." Information is also represented by symbol strings in natural language, mathematics, and formal logic. Symbol strings can be used to state propositions. If we want to represent the fact that a red square is inside a blue circle, for example, the appropriate symbol strings of the computer language and their equivalents in English might be as shown in Figure 9.10a. The computer analogy suggests that the brain might store all information internally in the form of such *propositional representations,* or symbol strings.

Alternatively, the brain might store some information in *analogue representations.* An analogue representation is one in which relations among elements in the representation mimic relations among elements of the thing represented. Thus, relations in the representation allow one to draw inferences "by analogy" about relations in the other domain. Some common analogue representations are maps and globes, slide rules, clock faces (those with hands), mercury thermometers, and graphs (for example, any of those in this book). In psychology, the "cognitive map" hypothesized by Tolman is an analogue representation; and the Gestalt psychologists, as we just saw,

(a)

Symbolic (Propositional) Representations

Computer	English
SQUARE (A)	A is a square
CIRCLE (B)	B is a circle
RED (A)	A is red
BLUE (B)	B is blue
INSIDE (A,B)	A is inside B

(b)

Analogue Representation

Figure 9.10 Symbolic (propositional) and analogue representations of "The red square is inside the blue circle."

proposed that both spatial and temporal relations among events were stored internally in analogue form. Mental images are, presumably, analogue representations, since they preserve many properties of the corresponding perceptual events. An analogue representation of the fact that a red square is inside a blue circle, to return to our previous example, is shown in Figure 9.10b. Since digital computers represent all information internally in the form of symbol strings, information-processing theorists generally find analogue representations difficult to deal with—they prefer to assume that information is represented in the brain in propositional form.

Multiple Memory Stores.   Most digital computers have several memory "stores," rather than just one. The properties of a given memory store depend on the function it serves. If a symbol string is input (read in) one symbol at a time, and the string is to be processed as a whole, each symbol must be held briefly while the remaining members of the string are being read. Likewise, if a string is to be output (written) one symbol at a time, the entire string must be held briefly while this operation is performed. Memory stores that will hold a small number of symbols while operations are performed on them are called "buffer stores," or "registers." The part of a computer that does the actual symbol manipulation specified in the program is called the "central processing unit." It consists, in part, of a network of registers where symbol strings are stored temporarily while operations are performed on them. This network is sometimes called a *working memory*. The working memory is flexible—that is, it can be organized differently depending on the demands of the task—and information in it can be retrieved quickly. But it has a strictly limited capacity, and the information in it is easily lost (as, for example, where there is a temporary interruption of electrical power). Finally, most computers have one or more "auxiliary memories" of much larger capacity (for example, magnetic tape), where information can be stored when not in use. These auxiliary stores are permanent, but access to them is slow, and locating information in them may require a time-consuming search.

The influence of the computer analogy can be clearly seen in an assumption common among current memory theories: that the human information-processing system includes several memory stores. Typically, three types of stores are postulated: (a) *sensory registers,* in which sensory information is held very briefly (about $\frac{1}{4}$ second in the case of vision, perhaps 2 seconds for audition); (b) a single *short-*

term store of limited capacity and short duration, corresponding to the working memory of the computer; and (c) a permanent *long-term store* of large capacity and slow access. Memory theories postulating distinct short-term and long-term stores are sometimes called "duplex," or "two-process," theories. They have been so influential that much of Chapter 11 will be devoted to examining the eivdence for and against them.

Serial Processing. When a digital computer executes a program, it follows each instruction in turn, performing the required operations one at a time. Each step must be finished before the next one can begin. Such a process, consisting of a series of subprocesses, is called a *serial process*. The time taken by a serial process is the sum of the times taken by its component operations. Thus, if one knows what the component operations are and how long each takes, he should be able to predict accurately how much time the entire process will take.

Serial processing is to be contrasted with parallel processing. In a *parallel process*, two or more operations can go on at the same time. If the final output must await completion of each of the component operations, then the slowest operation determines how long the entire process will take. If the final output can be based on any one of the component operations alone, then the fastest operation determines how long the process takes. Of course, a complex process could be made up of a number of component operations, some occurring in serial fashion and some going on in parallel (see Figure 9.11).

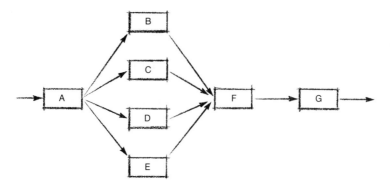

Figure 9.11 A mixed serial and parallel process. Operations *B, C, D,* and *E* occur in parallel (simultaneously), and in series with *A, F,* and *G.*

The computer analogy suggests that the brain be thought of as a serial processing device. This is a powerful assumption, since it can be used to make fairly precise predictions about how long a mental process should take. In a reaction-time experiment, the subject can be given a simple task thought to consist of two or more component operations occurring in series, and the time to make the correct response can be measured. The observed reaction time can then be compared with predictions of a mathematical model which postulates a particular combination of underlying operations, whose times sum to determine the total reaction time.

Hardware Versus Software.   The behavior of a computer—that is, the relationship between its input and output—is determined by its program. Programs can be rewritten, or one program can be substituted for another, and it is this flexibility that makes the computer a general-purpose symbol-manipulating machine. Programs are referred to as *software*. Other characteristics of the computer are "wired in," and cannot be changed by the programmer. The number of memory stores and their capacities and access times are examples. Such structural characteristics of the computer are its *hardware*. The computer hardware imposes limitations on the software. The program must not require more memory capacity than is available, for example, or perform operations in a way that requires an unreasonable amount of time.

Information-processing theorists often make a similar distinction in discussing human memory. We have, first of all, certain capacity limitations, and processes that are required, or "obligatory," because of the structure of the brain. These correspond to the hardware of the computer. Second, we have strategies we have developed for processing information. These strategies are sometimes called *control processes* (Atkinson and Shiffrin, 1968). They are "optional," in the sense that we can choose which of them to use. This choice may be determined in part by what we know about our capacity limitations. In other words, our software may be tailored to make optimal use of our hardware, which we can do nothing to change.

The computer analogy is sometimes used to argue that psychology can never be reduced to physiology. The argument is that no matter how much one knew about a computer's hardware, he would be unable to predict the computer's behavior in any significant way unless he also knew its program. If, in the study of human behavior, experimental psychology is essentially the study of software and physiological psychology the study of hardware, the analogy suggests that the former discipline cannot really be understood in terms of the latter. The extent to which human behavior is or is not "wired in" is not known, but the computer analogy tends to suggest that it is mostly learned.

The biases just described do not define a single, coherent theoretical position. Often, certain assumptions borrowed from the computer analogy are combined with assumptions from S–R or Gestalt psychology. Nevertheless, some relatively pure examples of information-processing theory can be found. Let us consider three of them as illustrations of the information-processing approach.

A Computer Model of Serial Learning

A theory of serial learning, proposed by Feigenbaum and Simon (1962), was one of the earliest information-processing theories of human learning. Feigenbaum and Simon proposed to explain the bowed serial-position curve with the following set of postulates:

> *Postulate 1. Serial mechanism.* The central processing mechanism operates serially and is capable of doing only one thing at a time. Thus, if many things demand processing activity from the central processing mechanism, they must share the total processing time available. . . .

> *Postulate 2. Average unit processing time per syllable.* The fixation of an item on a serial list requires the execution of a sequence of information processes that requires, for a given set of experimental conditions, a definite amount of processing time per syllable. . . .

> *Postulate 3. Immediate memory.* There exists in the central processing mechanism an immediate memory of limited size capable of storing information temporarily; and all access to an item by the learning process must be through the immediate memory. . . . This memory is assumed to hold 2 syllables (6 letters) (Feigenbaum and Simon, 1962, p. 310).

Postulates 1 through 3 refer to the hardware aspects of the memory system: the learning mechanism is a serial process, requiring a fixed amount of time to learn each syllable of the list, operating on information held in a register of limited capacity. Postulate 4, by contrast, describes the control process or strategies (that is, the software) of the system:

> *Postulate 4. Anchor points.* . . . Subjects learning the syllables of a serial list will reduce the demands on memory by treating the ends of the list as "anchor points," and by learning the syllables in an orderly sequence, starting from these anchor points and working toward the middle (Feigenbaum and Simon, 1962, p. 310).

It is further assumed that the subjects adopt a strategy of first learning the first two syllables, and then switching attention to another anchor point. This can either be the last syllable in the list, or the third, which becomes an anchor point by virtue of being adjacent to an already learned syllable. This procedure continues until the two chains of syllables, one starting at the beginning of the list and the other starting at the end, meet somewhere in the middle. When that happens, the list has been mastered.

Notice that this theory is quite similar to the S–R theory of Ribback and Underwood (1950) in using forward and backward chaining to account for the bowed shape of the serial-position curve. The two theories explain the location of the point of maximum difficulty in different ways, however. In the Ribback and Underwood theory, the forward and backward chains were learned at different rates. In the present theory, the point of maximum difficulty is displaced past the middle of the list because the subject always learns the first and second syllables first. The last syllable may not be learned until trial two or three. Thus, the forward and backward chains are learned at the same rate, but the forward chain has a head start.

Discrimination Net Theory

Our second illustration is a theory of the effect of stimulus similarity on paired-associates learning. Recall that Gibson (1940) explained the greater difficulty of high-similarity items in terms of the generalization of S–R habits. The information-processing theory we shall consider is based, instead, on a structure called a *discrimination net*. Discrimination net theory was applied to paired-associates learning by Simon and Feigenbaum (1964), in a computer simulation model called EPAM (for Elementary Perceiver and Memorizer). We shall consider here a simpler version of the model, developed by Hintzman (1968).

A discrimination net is a "sorting tree" which classifies stimuli by asking a series of questions about them. Figure 9.12a illustrates a discrimination net that has partially learned the five-pair list shown in the inset of the figure. A stimulus term is sorted by beginning at the top of the net, asking the question indicated in the circle, and following the descending path corresponding to the answer to that question. When a terminal point is reached, the response term is found and output. In sorting JCQ, for example: (a) the first-letter position is tested for R, (b) the negative branch is taken, (c) the first-letter position is tested for J, (d) the positive branch is followed, and (e) the response "7" is retrieved. Since this response is correct, no change is required in the net.

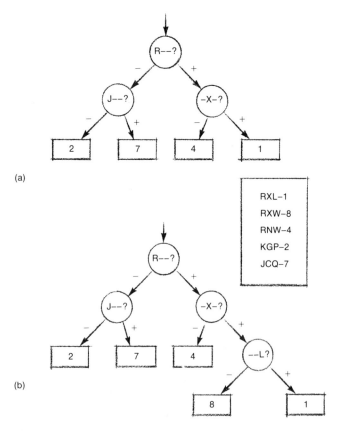

Figure 9.12 Learning in a discrimination net. The five-pair list is shown in the inset. In (a), RXW and RXL are confused. In (b), they are not.

But suppose, instead, that RXW is sorted through the net. The first position is tested for R and the second for X, and both outcomes are positive, leading to the response "1." This is an error; the correct response should be "8." The discrimination net in Figure 9.12a confuses RXL and RXW, because they have letters in common. New learning is necessary to resolve the difficulty, and this takes the form of additions to the net, as shown in Figure 9.12b. Once this change has been made, the third position of any trigram beginning with RX will always be tested for L. A positive answer leads to the response "1," and a negative answer to "8." The discrimination net will now perform perfectly on the five-pair list.

Discrimination net theory explains the effect of stimulus similarity on learning in this way: The more elements two stimuli have in common, the more information must be examined in order to sort them into different categories. The incorporation of this information into the sorting tree requires time and effort. Therefore, it takes longer to learn to discriminate between similar than between dissimilar stimuli. (For other testable predictions of discrimination net theory, see Hintzman, 1968.)

Memory Scanning

Our third illustration of information-processing theory comes from the work of Sternberg on short-term recognition memory. An early experiment using what has come to be called the "Sternberg paradigm" was conducted as follows (Sternberg, 1966): There were eight subjects, each tested for 144 trials. On each trial, a subject was shown a list of from one to six digits, presented at a 1.2-second rate. The length of the list, from one to six, is called the memory set size. Two seconds later there was a warning signal, and a test digit was shown. On half the trials, the test digit was from the preceding list, and on half it was not. The subject responded by pressing one of two levers—the "yes" lever if the digit was from the list and the "no" lever if it was not. He was asked to respond as quickly as possible, and his response latency, or reaction time, was measured.

Subjects were correct on more than 98 percent of the trials. Their average reaction times are plotted as a function of the memory set size (S) in Figure 9.13. "Yes" and "no" responses are shown separately. Two essential features of these data should be noted. First, "yes" and "no" reaction times were about the same. Second, as the set size in-

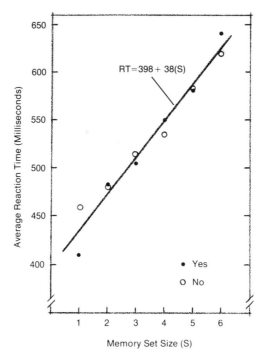

Figure 9.13 Reaction times in the memory scanning task. [After Sternberg, 1966. Copyright 1966 by the American Association for the Advancement of Science.]

creased, reaction time also increased, in what appears to be a linear (straight-line) fashion. Indeed, the straight line shown in the figure fits the data closely. Its equation says that reaction time can be predicted by starting with 398 milliseconds, and adding 38 milliseconds for each item in the memory set. It does not differentiate between "yes" and "no" responses in predicting reaction time.

The outcome of this experiment suggested to Sternberg that short-term recognition memory is accomplished by a process he called "serial, exhaustive scanning." The basic idea is this: On each trial it takes the subject a certain amount of time to perceive the test digit and to press a lever, and these times do not depend on the memory set size. They account for the constant 398 milliseconds in the equation of Figure 9.13. The additional time is taken up by memory scanning. The subject compares the test digit with each digit (in memory) that was in the list. The time to "scan" each memory digit is 38 milliseconds, and the digits are scanned one at a time. This accounts for the linear increase in reaction time as a function of size of the memory set. Finally, it is assumed that once memory scanning is initiated, it does not stop until the entire list has been scanned. Thus, if the first digit scanned matches the test item, the high-speed scanning process does not terminate. It continues through the entire list, and only then signals whether or not the test digit was found; that is, scanning "exhausts" the contents of the list. This assumption accounts for the fact that the "yes" reaction times increased at the same rate as the "no" reaction times.

Sternberg has conducted many experiments on memory scanning, and has continued to hold the view that it is a serial, exhaustive process (for example, Sternberg, 1975). It is worth noting, however, that this is not the only possible explanation of his findings. A parallel retrieval process (one that simultaneously examines all digits in the memory set) could produce an increasing reaction-time function— particulary if it is assumed that the more digits there are in the list, the lower are the strengths of their memory traces. Sternberg's theory, it appears, borrows from the computer analogy not only the notion of serial processing, but the all-or-none storage assumption, as well.

CONCLUSION

As earlier chapters indicated, the fundamental difference between behaviorism and cognitivism is in degree of interest in mental events. Behaviorism rejects mentalistic explanations of behavior, preferring mechanical analogies instead. The S–R approach to memory is essentially a behaviorist one. Cognitivism, in contrast, sees mental events as the causes of behavior. The Gestalt approach to memory theory, relying heavily on intuitions about conscious perceptual experience, is strongly cognitivist in orientation. The information–processing approach, based on the computer analogy, provides a synthesis of mechanistic and mentalistic accounts of behavior. Its ability to combine the rigor of behavioristic theory with the intuitive plausibility of cognitivism, we have argued, is why it has had such a powerful impact on the field.

As a result of the cognitivist renaissance being witnessed today, psychologists have become nearly as fond of the term "information-processing psychology" as they once were of the term "behaviorism."

Indeed, some writers use the term so broadly that it includes almost all work on attention, memory, and cognitive processes being done today. The truth is, however, that there is much in current cognitive theories of memory that comes from the Gestalt and S–R traditions. By no means can all the concepts in use be traced to the computer analogy.

A theorist may assume, for example, that some information is stored in memory in analogue form—that the relative sizes of animals are represented by the sizes of their visual images, or that the dates of important historical events are represented as points on a line. Such notions derive directly from the Gestalt tradition. They can be fitted into an information-processing framework only with difficulty (for example, Pylyshyn, 1973). A theorist may also assume that the links between internal representations vary in strength, depending on the recency and frequency of use, or that cues encountered in the environment can trigger habitual mental processes automatically, regardless of the subject's intention to ignore them. Such assumptions derive more from S–R theory than they do from the computer analogy.

The point is that while the computer analogy has produced certain "theoretical predispositions," as we have called them, it does not rigidly constrain the assumptions a theorist may make. Many current memory theories are amalgamations of S–R, Gestalt, and information-processing principles, and cannot be fit unambiguously into one of the three categories. This fact should become obvious in the chapters ahead.

Logically, any memory theory—whether based on S–R, Gestalt, or information-processing principles—must divide the history of a memory trace into three phases: (a) one in which it is acquired through experience, (b) one in which it is passively retained for a period of time, and (c) one in which it is revived and used in some way. Usually, these three phases are referred to as *encoding, storage,* and *retrieval.* The next chapter examines each of these phases in some detail.

I O

An Overview of Human Memory: Encoding, Storage, and Retrieval

This chapter is concerned with the three main phases in the history of a memory trace: encoding, storage, and retrieval. *Encoding* refers to the formation, or acquisition, of the memory trace—that is, putting information into memory. *Storage* refers to the holding, or retention, of the encoded information while it is not being used. *Retrieval* refers to the regeneration and use of the information at the end of the retention interval. In principle, it is impossible to study any one of these phases in isolation, for every objective manifestation of memory must include all three. The failure of encoding, storage, or retrieval will result in a failure to remember. It is possible, however, for an experimenter to "hold constant" the factors that determine two of the phases and manipulate only those involved in the third. Thus, although encoding, storage, and retrieval are confounded in many memory experiments, their effects can be separated in experiments that have been carefully designed.

We shall examine the three phases in the order in which they naturally occur.

ENCODING

The encoding into memory of everyday events seems to require no special effort on our part. Most of us can recall what we had for breakfast this morning or what we talked about with a friend yesterday, even though we made no attempt to commit the information to memory at the time. The effectiveness of encoding varies, however. Some experiences are remembered much better than others, and certain kinds of information (for example, chemical formulae, proper names, and historical dates) are notoriously difficult to learn. Let us consider some of the factors involved in encoding information into memory.

Arousal

Anecdotal evidence suggests that how well an event will be remembered depends partly on our level of alertness, or physiological arousal, at the time the event occurs. Events experienced under the influence of alcohol or marijuana are remembered less well than those experienced under more normal circumstances; and events associated with a high level of alertness, such as a near auto accident or an exciting play in a sporting event, are remembered especially well. Experimental evidence supports such observations and suggests that the effect of arousal is on the initial strength of encoding. Alcohol depresses activity of the brain, and its effects on memory seem to be on the initial degree of learning (Wickelgren, 1975); and stimulants such as caffeine and strychnine, which increase brain activity, enhance learning in animals (for example, Lashley, 1917).

Learning ability, like arousal, fluctuates in a cyclical fashion during each 24-hour period. Ebbinghaus (1885) conducted his experiments during three daily time periods: 10 to 11 AM, 11 AM to 12 noon, and 6 to 8 PM. His learning was most efficient between 11 AM and noon; it was poorest between 6 and 8 PM. At least one other study confirms that late morning is the optimal time of day for learning. Blake (1967) measured the digit spans of thirty subjects, at five different times during the day. The data, shown in Figure 10.1, indicate that memory span peaks in late morning and declines throughout the afternoon. (This is in contrast to most motor skills tasks, for which performance peaks in late afternoon. Why learning ability behaves differently from these other skills is not understood.) The curve shown in Figure 10.1 suggests that the poorest time for encoding new information into memory should be during the night. Certainly, the recall of dreams is notoriously poor. And it is not unusual for someone to be awakened from a nightmare or a bout of sleepwalking, interact briefly with another person, and return to sleep, only to be unable to remember anything of the entire incident the next morning.

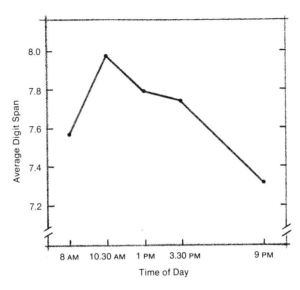

Figure 10.1 Memory span as a function of time of day. [Data from Blake, 1967.]

Our level of arousal is lowest of all, of course, when we are actually asleep. Nevertheless, many persons believe that our ability to learn while sleeping is considerable. A small industry has even grown up, promising to make useful the time we "waste" sleeping, by providing us with pillow speakers, tape players, and foreign language tapes. (Imagine awakening after a refreshing sleep, confident that you possess more useful knowledge than you had eight hours ago.)

Does "sleep learning" work? We saw in Chapter 7 that classical conditioning apparently is possible during sleep. But what about higher-level learning, such as acquiring the vocabulary of a foreign language? A classic study on sleep learning done by Emmons and Simon (1956) provides little basis for optimism. Emmons and Simon told their nine male subjects that a list of ten words would be presented repeatedly while they were asleep, and that they should try to learn them. As the subjects slept, their EEG records were monitored, and the taped list of words was played over and over again to each subject. If a subject's EEG record showed signs that he was awakening, the tape player was stopped, and note was made of the last word played. Whenever a subject awoke he was immediately asked to repeat any word he had just heard.

To one subject, who was a light sleeper, the list was played 16 times. To another, who was not easily awakened, it was played 81 times. The average number of repetitions of the list for all subjects was 46. In the morning, the subjects were allowed to dress and wash, and were then given a recognition-memory test, consisting of the 10 target words mixed in with 40 lures. They were told to pick out the 10 words that had been presented during the night. By chance, subjects would guess correctly 20 percent of the time on such a test. These subjects were right just 24.4 percent of the time. They recognized 33.4 percent of the words that had been presented just before periods of waking; when these items were removed, overall performance dropped below 20 percent. These results suggest that sleep learning is very inefficient, if it is possible at all. There may be some learning of material presented during the night, but most of the learning that does occur very likely takes place during intervals of waking; and even that learning is probably not very good (see review by Aarons, 1976).

Intentional and Incidental Learning

Although it is clear that information is often encoded into memory without any special effort on our part (as when we recall what we had for breakfast this morning), it seems intuitively as though such learning is less effective than that done under the intention to learn. This suggests that we may be able to turn the encoding mechanism on and off (or up and down) at will. Research on this question compares *intentional learning* with unintentional or *incidental learning*.

What role does the intention to learn play in encoding? The conclusions of investigators concerned with this problem have been fairly consistent, and contrary to what intuitive judgment suggests. Consider, as an example, an experiment done by Hyde and Jenkins (1969). In this experiment, all the subjects were read a 24-word list, at a rate of one word every 2 seconds, and were then asked to recall the words (the free recall task). There were seven different groups of subjects, each receiving different instructions prior to presentation of the list. In all other respects the groups were treated the same. One group (the recall group) was given intentional-learning instructions. These subjects were simply told that they would be asked to recall the words after presentation of the list. Three of the groups were not told they would have to recall the words. They were given "orienting tasks," which did not require retention of the words. One group rated each word, as it was read, on the "pleasantness–unpleasantness" dimension. The second group indicated whether or not the word contained an "E." The third group estimated the number of letters in the word. Three remaining groups were given mixed intentional and incidental instructions. They were required to perform one of the three orienting tasks, but in addition were told they would have to recall the words.

Recall percentages for subjects given the seven different instruction combinations are shown in Figure 10.2. Several conclusions can be drawn from these data: First, learning was as effective when words were rated on the pleasantness scale as when subjects were told to learn the words. Second, the other two orienting tasks—detecting E's and estimating the number of letters—produced poor learning of the words. Third, when combined with the intentional-learning instruction, the inefficient orienting tasks interfered with learning. This can be seen by comparing the bottom two bars of the figure with the top one. Apparently, the intention to learn, per se, is not particularly

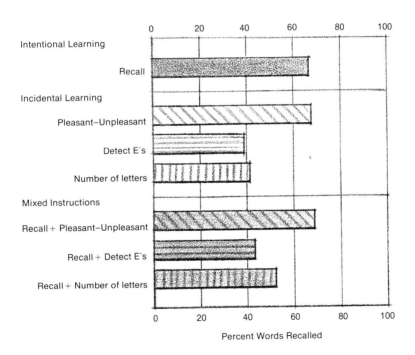

Figure 10.2 Free-recall performance of subjects given words under various "orienting" instructions. [Data from Hyde and Jenkins, 1969.]

important in encoding. What is important is attending to the material and thinking about it in a particular way. A pleasantness–unpleasantness rating requires subjects to think about the meaning of the word. Detecting E's and estimating number of letters require them to think about structural features of the word. The latter two tasks apparently interfere with the processing of meaning that is necessary for good recall. Incidental learning can be as effective as intentional learning, if one can get the subject to attend to the material in the right way.

Types of Memory Code

The Hyde and Jenkins study just described tells us something more. Information can be encoded in memory in qualitatively different ways, and the form of encoding, or *memory code,* affects performance on a memory test. The Gestalt psychologists proposed that stimulation of the different sensory modalities produced different types of memory codes, and this idea is in favor today. Theorists distinguish a number of different types of memory codes, among them: *visual* (an item is represented in memory by its visual appearance), *acoustic* (an item is represented by its sound or name), *haptic* (an item is represented by how it feels to the touch), and *semantic* (an item is represented by its meaning). Much research has been aimed at uncovering the types of internal memory codes that subjects use, and determining when and how they transform one type of code into another. The ultimate goal of this research is to describe the "software" with which the human brain communicates with the outside world and, internally, with itself.

The introspectionists thought they could observe internal memory codes directly. Modern cognitive psychology, however, requires that mental events be inferred from objective measures of behavior. How can one determine the type of internal representation being used from objective observations of subjects' behavior? There are a number of ways this is done. Let us consider some of them briefly.

1. *Transfer* experiments are sometimes used to infer the type of memory code underlying performance in a task. The serial-learning and paired-associates tasks lend themselves especially well to transfer studies. For example, in the A–B, A–B′ illustration of Figure 8.8, LID and TOP are dissimilar both visually and acoustically, but they have similar meanings. Positive transfer from CHAIR–LID in List 1, to CHAIR–TOP, in List 2, therefore, can be taken as evidence for a semantic code. Notice that the observation does not rule out visual or

acoustic codes, since a subject could encode an item in more than one form. Positive transfer shows that the semantic code exists, but does not prove that other types of code are absent.

2. *Selective interference* experiments provide a second type of evidence regarding the type of memory code used. Such experiments are based on the fact that both proactive and retroactive interference increase with similarity. In a retroactive interference experiment, a subject encodes information into memory, is engaged in one of several tasks, and then is tested for retention of the original information. One group of subjects, for example, might listen closely to music during the retention interval, while another group might examine pictures. If listening interferes with retention more than looking at pictures, the experimenter might infer that subjects encoded the information in acoustic form. If looking at pictures interferes more, he might infer that a visual code was used.

3. *Clustering* in free recall is sometimes used to make inferences about the memory code. For example, if HALF, LAUGH, and STAFF are frequently recalled as one cluster, and FEIGN, PANE, and GRAIN as another, despite the visual and semantic differences among the clustered words, the experimenter might infer that an acoustic memory code was used.

4. *Retrieval latency* is commonly thought to provide information about the nature of the memory code. The basic idea is that the more closely the perceptual experience produced by the retrieval cue matches the form of the memory trace, the more quickly the required information will be retrieved. The letter "A" can be presented in either upper case or lower case. Acoustically and semantically, "A" and "*a*" are essentially the same. Therefore, if a letter is recognized as old more quickly when the original and test presentations match (A and A, or *a* and *a*) than when they are visually different (A and *a*, or *a* and A), it is concluded that subjects used a visual memory code of the letter in making the match (for example, Posner and Mitchell, 1967).

5. *Recall confusions* provide still another kind of evidence regarding the nature of the memory code. In a memory-span task, for example, a subject may frequently write down T in place of P, or 5 in place of 9. Such errors, among items with similar-sounding names, suggest an acoustic memory code. Confusion between E and F or 6 and 9, on the other hand, would suggest that the memory code is visual.

6. *False-recognition* experiments are based on a similar principle, but rather than waiting for subjects to spontaneously produce confusions in recall, the experimenter encourages confusions by using carefully

chosen lures on a recognition-memory test. The lures are chosen to be similar to the target items in specific ways (acoustically, visually, semantically), and their effectiveness is assumed to reveal the nature of the underlying memory code. After studying a word list including the word LAKE, for example, a strong tendency to incorrectly accept RAKE as "old" would suggest an acoustic memory code; a tendency to call BAY "old" would suggest the memory code was semantic.

Chunking

The ability to transform information from one type of internal code to another underlies many cognitive skills. A most important fact about this ability is that it allows us to integrate complex information into single "ideas." That is, several encodings of one level can be represented by a single encoding of a higher level. The process of integrating several encodings into one is called *chunking;* and the higher-level units formed in this way are called *chunks* (Miller, 1956). The chunking process is primarily based on past experience; that is, our ability to integrate information into a chunk depends on the familiarity of the chunk itself. For this reason, chunking can be considered an example of positive transfer.

Chunking has a dramatic effect on memory capacity. This is well illustrated by an experiment by Murdock (1961). The experimental procedure was essentially the same as that of the distractor task experiment of Peterson and Peterson (1959): on each trail the subject heard the material he was to recall, counted backward by three's for a predetermined amount of time, and then attempted recall. There were three conditions in Murdock's experiment. In one, the to-be-remembered materials were three-consonant trigrams, as they had been in the original Peterson study (for example, PTK). In another, they were single three-letter words (for example, HAT); and in the third, they were three-word combinations (for example, EAR-MAN-BED). The short-term retention curves of Murdock's subjects are shown in Figure 10.3. Notice that the curve for consonant trigrams closely matches that of Peterson and Peterson (Figure 8.12). The forgetting of three-word combinations was about the same as that of the trigrams. However, there was little apparent forgetting, in 18 seconds, of the single words.

At first glance, these data may not seem particularly striking—but notice that in both the single-word condition and the trigram condi-

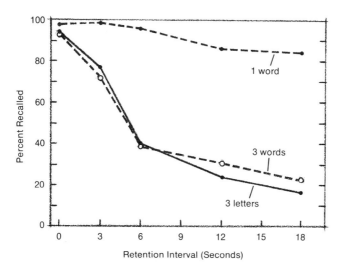

Figure 10.3 Percentages of 3-letter words, 3-letter combinations, and 3-word combinations recalled after various intervals of counting backward. [Data from Murdock, 1961.]

tion, three-letter combinations had to be remembered. Murdock's subjects, however, remembered the three-letter words much better than the trigrams. And they recalled nine-letter combinations (in the three-word condition) as well as they could recall three unrelated letters. A word is a familiar unit—a chunk; and through chunking, a subject's memory for strings of letters can be greatly increased.

A more dramatic demonstration than Murdock's can easily be arranged. Consider Figure 10.4. In panel (a) are two rows of figures made up of straight and curved line segments. If one were shown these rows and asked to reproduce them, he would undoubtedly find the second easier than the first. Yet the figures in the first row are no more complex than those in the second. The critical difference is that each figure in the second row is a familiar unit—a chunk—which we identify as a letter. By recalling the sequence of letter names we are able to reproduce the entire pattern of line segments fairly accurately. In panel (b) are two rows of letter clusters. Again, the upper row is much more difficult to remember than the lower one. This is so even though both rows contain exactly the same letters. Each letter cluster in the lower row is a familiar unit, or chunk, that we identify as a word. In panel (c) are two sets of word strings. The word strings in the first set are harder to recall than those in the second set. Again, it is be-

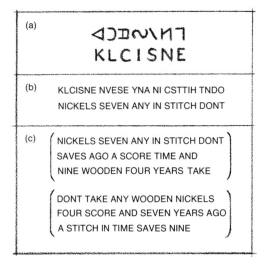

Figure 10.4 Effects of chunking on memory. Familiar materials (bottom of each panel) are easier to encode than unfamiliar materials (top of each panel). This holds for combinations of line segments (a), letters (b), and words (c).

cause each word string in the second set is a familiar unit, or chunk—in this case a common saying, or cliché.

Each of these transformations—from line segments to letters, from letters to words, and from words to common phrases—increases our capacity to remember. Indeed, one can read the three clichés in the bottom of Figure 10.4, look away, and reproduce with fair accuracy an incredibly complex pattern of line segments—an ability that would astonish the nonreader. The chunks we are referring to are not familiar patterns, of course, to people who cannot read. Reading is a complex skill acquired through years of training and maintained by frequent practice. While there is much about reading that still is not understood, it is clear that the ability to deal with information in higher-order meaningful units, or chunks, is an important part of this remarkable cognitive skill.

Chunking may be equally important in other kinds of complex skills, such as chess playing. Pioneering work on chess skill by the Dutch psychologist de Groot (1965), and more recent work by Chase and Simon (1973), suggest that this is indeed so. De Groot had weak chess players and chess masters give subjective reports of their analyses and strategies while playing. He found little difference in how the two classes of players analyzed a chess position in deciding on the next move. A short-term memory task, however, revealed a striking difference between players of different levels. This difference was explored further by Chase and Simon.

Consider the following experiment by Chase and Simon (1973). The subjects were a beginning chess player, a class A player, and a master. They were given 5 seconds to view a chess board with 24 pieces arranged on it, and then were asked to reconstruct the pattern of pieces on another board. When the 24 pieces were randomly arranged on the board, performance of the three subjects was about the same, with the master doing slightly worse than the weaker players. When the pattern of pieces was a position from an actual chess game between advanced players, however, the outcome was quite different. After one exposure of the board, the beginner correctly placed about 18 percent of the pieces, the class A player about 34 percent, and the master about 62 percent.

Chase and Simon theorize that the difference in performance can be attributed to the ability to recognize familiar configureations of pieces, or chunks, and they offer a considerable amount of evidence in support of this hypothesis. It may be that a large part of the chess master's superior skill derives in a rather simple way from his more extensive experience. The more games one has played and studied, and the greater their variety, the more different ways one has of chunking the relative positions of pieces on the board. Thus, the master may see relationships (and therefore possibilities) that the weaker player is likely to miss.

The transformations from one level of encoding to another that are involved in chunking are largely automatic. They take place with little effort, and neither the reader nor the chess master is aware of just what it is he is doing. But the automatic encoding of such complex information requires much previous practice. Chunks are *familiar* units. How do we go about encoding complex information into memory when it is not already familiar?

Mnemonic Devices

Faced with the task of memorizing detailed and unfamiliar information, we seem to have only two alternatives: either learn it "by rote"—

study it over and over again until it becomes familiar through sheer repetition—or transform it into a different type of memory code that is easier to work with. Over the centuries many persons, discouraged with the tedium of rote repetition and seeking to make learning more efficient, have invented a variety of memory aids. These generally involve transformations from difficult-to-work-with memory codes to more efficient ones. The art of applying these memory aids is called *mnemonics.* Those who use them (especially professionally) are called *mnemonists,* and the techniques themselves are called *mnemonic devices.*

Mnemonic devices data back at least to the ancient Greeks. Poets, historians, and orators were taught to memorize lengthy passages through the "method of loci." They imagined moving through a familiar series of architectural or geographical locations (the loci), and systematically associated each to-be-remembered topic with a location, by means of visual imagery. Later, topics could be recalled in their proper order by mentally "visiting" each location in turn and retrieving the associated image. Other examples of mnemonic devices familiar to every schoolchild take the form of rhymes—for example, "In fourteen hundred and ninety-two, Columbus sailed the ocean blue," and "Thirty days has September. . . ." It is a curious fact that psychologists, although always vaguely aware of the existence of mnemonic devices, did not bring them under intense laboratory investigation until the late 1960s. This new interest was partly due to the reawakening of interest in cognitivism. But in addition, many psychologists, discouraged by the lack of "relevance" of learning research, saw the analysis of mnemonic devices as a way to make a positive contribution to educational practice.

The mnemonic devices that have been invented are many and varied. A number of them, like the method of loci, use visual imagery. Some, as we have seen, use rhymes to impose structure on the material. Others transform the information into a more meaningful form. One way to do this is to use an elaborate coding system that has been so thoroughly learned that it is almost as automatic as reading. A system invented in 1634 by Pietro Herigon, for example, assigns consonant sounds to the ten digits, and thus allows one to memorize a number such as a date from history by pronouncing it as a word or phrase (Norman, 1976, pp. 142–148).

A popular mnemonic device that includes all three of these components—visual imagery, rhyme, and meaningful transformations—is the "one-is-a-bun mnemonic," otherwise known as the *peg-word system*. This method can be used to easily link concepts to the digits 1 through 10 (and it can be expanded, with some effort, to include the numbers 1 through 100). The first step is to learn thoroughly an association between each of the first 10 digits and a concrete noun. This association allows a relatively meaningless number to be transformed quickly into a meaningful word. To aid in this initial learning, the nouns are chosen to rhyme with the digits. Thus, one learns:

1 is a bun	6 is sticks
2 is a shoe	7 is heaven
3 is a tree	8 is a gate
4 is a door	9 is wine
5 is a hive	10 is a hen

Once these transformations have been mastered, other concepts can be associated with the "peg words" through visual imagery. Thus, in learning the pairing 8–APPLE, I imagine an iron gate with an apple impaled on one of its vertical spikes. To learn 3–MASK, I imagine a tree with masks hanging from its branches, and so on. When associations are not made directly, but use intervening ideas (such as the peg words, which in this system intervene between numbers and words) they are said to be "mediate" (as opposed to immediate or direct) associations. The process of learning through indirect associations, therefore, is called *mediation*, and the intervening links (for example, the peg words) are called *mediators*.

The peg-word system can be adapted to a variety of uses. By successively cuing oneself with the digits in order, one can recall a sequence of topics in the order they are to be covered in a speech, or guarantee that all the items on an important shopping list have been purchased. One can also respond appropriately to number cues given out of order ("Who was the seventh president of the United States?") or give the numerical ranking of an arbitrarily chosen item ("Where does Calcutta rank in population among cities of the world?")

To the experimental psychologist, the analysis of a mnemonic device must begin with one obvious question: Does it work? Research done in the past decade shows that mnemonics work remarkably well. Consider one of the first investigations of the peg-word system, by

Bugelski (1968). Subjects in the experimental group first learned the one-is-a-bun rhyme, and then were given six different paired-associates lists to learn. In each one, the stimulus terms were the digits 1 through 10, and the responses were 10 concrete nouns (different nouns for each list). The experimental subjects were told to form visual images linking the nouns with the peg words they had previously learned. Control subjects were not taught the rhyme, and they were told nothing about the use of visual imagery. Both groups learned the same six lists of digit–noun pairs. Each subject studied each list once, and was tested on it immediately after. He was also given a delayed test, for retention of all six lists. On the delayed test, he was asked to give all the "number 1" words, all the "number 2" words, and so on.

The results of Bugelski's experiment are shown in Figure 10.5. The peg-word mnemonic produced better recall on both the immediate and the delayed test. On the delayed test, in fact, nearly twice as many words were correctly recalled with the mnemonic than without it. Other studies have confirmed Bugelski's conclusion, and have shown that the key component of the peg-word system (as of the method of loci) is the instruction to form a visual image.

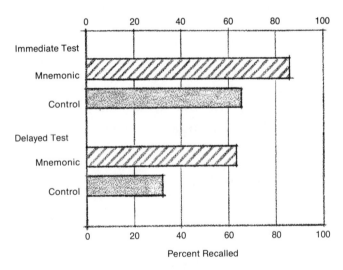

Figure 10.5 Effect of the peg-word mnemonic on immediate and delayed recall. [Data from Bugelski, 1968.]

Visual Imagery

Why does visual imagery improve associative recall? Several explanations have been proposed. One proposal is the *dual-coding theory* (Paivio, 1969, 1971). This hypothesis holds that two types of memory code—verbal and visual—are involved. It may be further assumed that verbal codes are located in the left hemisphere of the brain, which is known to be specialized for language, and visual codes in the right hemisphere, which may be specialized for spatial tasks (for example, Dimond and Beaumont, 1974). Such physiological speculation, however, is optional. The basic notion of the dual-coding theory is that without imagery instructions only a verbal code is formed, but with imagery instructions the subject produces both the verbal code and a visual code of the item. Simply stated, the assumption is that two different memory codes lead to better recall than one.

A second explanation is suggested by Gestalt theory: if the visual image depicts the objects interacting, then a single, unitary trace, or Gestalt, is formed. Instructions to form visual images, according to this account, facilitate associative learning by encouraging the subject to form interacting, unitary representations.

Still a third possibility is that the effect of visual imagery on associative learning is simply a special case of the effect of similarity. Visual images may be so distinct from one another that they seldom become confused, and that property of images may underlie their effects on memory. Indeed, the ancient Greeks believed that bizarre images were more effective memory aids than commonplace ones, and this suggests that similarity may be of crucial importance.

What aspects of visual imagery account for its effects on paired-associates learning? Bower (1970) found that subjects instructed to imagine the two objects in separate pictures were not better at associative recall than subjects simply instructed to say the word pair aloud. Recall was much better, however, when the objects were imagined in an interactive scene.

In a related investigation, Wollen, Weber, and Lowry (1972) investigated the joint effects on paired-associates learning of bizarreness and interaction. To control the bizarreness of their subject's images, they presented them directly, in the form of pictures. A list of nine paired associates was presented in different ways to several groups of subjects. The four groups of most interest had different combinations of noninteractive versus interactive and nonbizarre versus bizarre scenes.

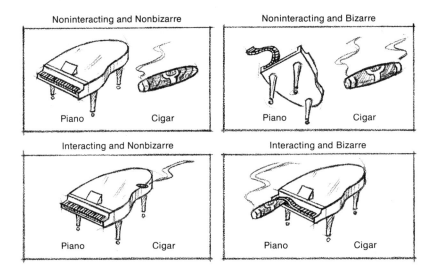

Figure 10.6 Stimulus pairs varying in interaction and bizarreness. [After Wollen, Weber, and Lowry, 1972. Copyright 1972 by Academic Press, Inc.]

The four ways of depicting pairs are illustrated in Figure 10.6. Following one presentation of the list, subjects were shown the stimulus words and required to give the appropriate response terms. Correct recall percentages for the four conditions of interest are shown in

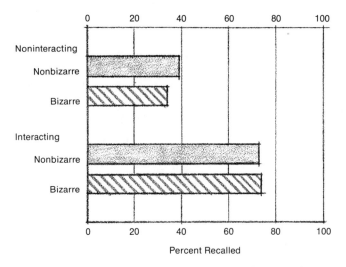

Figure 10.7 Paired-associates recall, from the experiment by Wollen, Weber, and Lowry (1972).

Figure 10.7. The result was clear-cut. Interaction strongly affected recall, while bizarreness had no effect.

Thus, the present evidence seems to favor the Gestalt interpretation of imagery effects on associative learning. Imagining separate objects should establish a visual code in addition to a verbal code, but this has little effect on recall. Likewise, bizarreness or distinctiveness of the image is of little, if any, value. The enhancement of recall seems to depend on the interactive, or unitary, nature of the image, just as the Gestalt theory predicts.

STORAGE

If an event occurs which the subject later recognizes or recalls, we infer that a memory trace was encoded, survived for a certain amount of time, and was retrieved. The storage phase—this period the trace must endure if it is to be retrieved—is passive. That is, during the storage phase there is no evidence, either subjective or objective, that the trace exists. It lies hidden, waiting to be aroused by an appropriate internal or external stimulus (a retrieval cue). The appropriate cue, however, may never occur.

The storage phase is passive, but this does not mean that it is psychologically uninteresting. It has been suggested that memory traces in storage undergo changes of various kinds. For example, Chapter 9 discussed Wulf's hypothesis that the memory trace undergoes autonomous change in the direction of a "good Gestalt." It has also been proposed that memory traces pass through a sequence of states, differing from each other in a number of ways. Such proposals adopt the multiple memory store view suggested by the computer analogy, and typically distinguish between two "processes"—a short-term store and a long-term store. The validity of the two-process assumption is a matter of current debate, and we shall put off its discussion until the next chapter, where it can be given the space it deserves.

The Permanent Memory Hypothesis

Another question regarding the storage phase is whether or not anything is ever "really forgotten." Now it is quite obvious that we are often unable to remember things we could remember at an earlier time, and in this sense the answer to the question is obviously "yes."

But in another sense the answer is indeterminate, since a failure to remember could be due simply to a failure to retrieve. The trace could be *available* in memory, but *inaccessible* to retrieval. Theoretically, it is useful to distinguish between *true forgetting*, in which the memory trace is eroded, degraded, or destroyed, and *retrieval failure*, in which it has become inaccessible, even though its completeness, potency, or strength may be unchanged. The hypothesis that all forgetting is due to retrieval failure is often illustrated by the "junk box" analogy. When searching for an object in an unorganized junk box, we are easily able to find those things on top (which were placed there recently), but must make a longer search for objects put there some time ago. Sometimes, we may give up before the sought-after item is found, concluding that it is no longer in the box.

Before even considering the relevant data, we can see a number of reasons for thinking that true forgetting does occur. Throughout our adult lives, brain cells die and are not replaced. Even those that survive undergo continual change. There is a constant "turnover" of the chemicals that make them up, just as there is in other parts of the body. And as we deal with our changing environment, it seems likely that we encode many new experiences by modifying trace structures originally developed to deal with old ones. Despite such considerations, several individuals have proposed that true forgetting does not occur, and that all retention loss can be explained as retrieval failure. This hypothesis we shall call the *permanent memory hypothesis*. What is the evidence regarding the permanence of memory?

Recall, Recognition, and Relearning

First, it must be admitted that many cases of apparent forgetting are due to retrieval failure. Experiments in which a free-recall test is followed by a test of cued recall or of recognition memory demonstrate this fact clearly. Many items can be remembered, on such tests, that were inaccessible to free recall. Tulving (1974) has used such demonstrations to argue in favor of the permanent memory hypothesis. Since we know that *some* forgetting is due to retrieval failure, he argues, why not assume that *all* forgetting is of this type? This argument, of course, is indirect. To demonstrate that the permanent memory hypothesis is correct, one must show that there are circumstances under which memories of events long since "forgotten" can be remembered with the clarity of events of the recent past.

Experiments that both control the conditions of learning and also study retention over intervals of years are extremely rare. One such rarity is a study by Burtt (1941), on memory for infantile experiences. When his son was 15 months old, Burtt read him passages from Sophocles, in the original Greek. Each passage was 22 lines long, and was read aloud to the child 90 times, over a period of three months. By the age of 3, when this unusual treatment ended, the child had been exposed to 21 such passages. At the age of $8\frac{1}{2}$, the boy was asked to rote memorize 10 passages from Sophocles. The child was not told that 7 of the passages were ones he had heard earlier. The other 3 passages were new. Burtt repeated this procedure, using the 14 remaining original passages, when the boy was 14 and 18 years old. Since both new and old passages of comparable difficulty were memorized at each age, Burtt was able, by computing a savings score, to measure how well the old passages were retained. At the age of $8\frac{1}{2}$ years, savings were 27 percent; at 14, they were 8 percent; and at 18 they were only 1 percent—not significantly different from zero. Thus, even the savings score—the most sensitive measure of retention we have—was unable to detect evidence of the infantile experience after the passage of 15 years. The result is certainly contrary to the permanent memory hypothesis.

The evidence most often offered as support for permanent memory comes from two sources: reports of Wilder Penfield on effects of electrical stimulation of the brain, and studies of hyponotic age regression. Let us next turn to Penfield's work.

Penfield's Observations

Wilder Penfield is a renowned brain surgeon who, over the years, has performed many operations on patients suffering from especially serious cases of epilepsy. A frequent cause of epilepsy is an area of abnormal brain tissue called an "epileptic focus," in which abnormal synchronous electrical activity occurs. In serious cases, the epileptic focus can drive the electrical activity of the rest of the brain, causing convulsions and loss of consciousness—an epileptic fit. In debilitating cases of epilepsy, the patient's condition can often be improved by removal of the epileptic focus. This was the operation Penfield performed.

Before removing brain tissue, Penfield attempted to locate important functions such as speech, by stimulating various points on the exposed surface of the cortex with weak electrical current. The patient was conscious during this procedure (since the brain itself has no pain receptors, only local anaesthesia had to be used). Thus the patient could report his subjective experiences; and in addition, tell-tale disruptions in his speech could be noted. During one such exploratory probing, in 1933, a patient reported an astonishing memory experience Penfield refers to as a "flashback." Since then, Penfield's electrical probes have elicited many such reports. The following excerpt, from the case of patient M.M., is an example. A point on the right temporal lobe is stimulated (the numbers are labels given to the points stimulated just prior to each report):

> 11—"I heard something familiar, I do not know what it was."
>
> 11—(repeated without warning)—"Yes, Sir, I think I heard a mother calling her little boy somewhere. It seemed to be something that happened years ago." When asked to explain, she said, "It was somebody in the neighborhood where I live." She added that it seemed that she herself "was somewhere close enough to hear."
>
> Warning without stimulation—"Nothing."
>
> 11 repeated—"Yes, I hear the same familiar sounds, it seems to be a woman calling, the same lady. That was not in the neighborhood. It seemed to be at the lumber yard." Then she added reflectively, "I've never been around the lumber yard much."
>
> This was an incident of childhood which she could never have recalled without the aid of the stimulating electrode. Actually she could not "remember" it but she knew at once, with no suggestion from us, that she must have experienced it sometime. The same incident was evoked again by another stimulation at approximately the same point. Then at a different point, 12, she had another experience but of a similar character. The ticket 12 was displaced before its position was recorded.
>
> 12—"Yes, I heard voices down along the river somewhere—a man's voice and a woman's voice calling."
>
> When she was asked how she could tell that the calling had been "along the river," she said, "I think I saw the river." When asked what river it was, she said, "I don't know. It seems to be one I was visiting when I was a child."
>
> Warning without stimulation—"Nothing."
>
> Three minutes later without warning stimulation was carried out again, probably near 13. While the electrode was held in place, she exclaimed: "Yes, I hear voices. It is late at night, around the carnival somewhere—some sort of travelling circus."

Then, after removal of the electrode: "I just saw lots of big wagons that they use to haul animals in."

These simple re-enactments of experience had auditory and visual elements in them.

Eleven minutes later, stimulation was carried out without warning at a point just posterior to 11—"I seemed to hear little voices then," she said, "the voices of people calling from building to building somewhere—I do not know where it is but it is very familiar to me. I cannot see the buildings now but they seem to be run-down buildings."

14 (just posterior to 15)—This stimulation caused her to say: "The whole operation now seems familiar."

Warning without stimulation—"Nothing."

15—"Just a tiny flash of familiarity and a feeling that I knew everything that was going to happen in the near future." Then she added, "as though I had been through all this before and thought I knew exactly what you were going to do next."

At point 17, an electrode, covered with an insulating coat except at its tip, was inserted to different depths and the current switched on so as to stimulate in various buried portions of the first temporal convolution and uncus.

17c (1 cm deep)—"Oh, I had the same very, very familiar memory, in an office somewhere. I could see the desks. I was there and someone was calling me, a man leaning on a desk with a pencil in his hand" (Penfield, 1955, pp. 54–55).

From such reports, Penfield draws far-reaching conclusions: "It is evident that the brain of every man contains an unchanging ganglionic record of successive experience," he says. It is a "permanent record of the stream of consciousness," which includes "all those things of which the individual was once aware."

But there are at least two serious objections to Penfield's conclusions. First, the experiences produced by electrical stimulation are not always reported as memories. Sometimes the patient reports a dream or hallucination. At other times, he reports only a feeling of familiarity, or what is called the *déjà vu* experience—the feeling that what is happening has all happened before. (To epileptic patients, the *déjà vu* experience is often a warning of an impending attack.) Now if electrical stimulation were occasionally to produce both these elements together—a dream or hallucination *and* the feeling of familiarity—it would naturally give rise to the kind of report that Penfield interprets as a revived memory. There is never any independent verification of the reported "memories"—nothing to indicate the experience is really an event from the patient's past. There is only the subject's statement that it seems familiar, and therefore must be something that happened at an earlier time.

The second objection is that such reports have not been obtained from non-epileptic patients. Only stimulation of the temporal lobes gives rise to "flashbacks," and then, apparently, only when the temporal lobe is the site of an epileptic focus. Thus, even if it could be established that the reported "flashbacks" were true memories, the most reasonable conclusion would be that permanent memory occurs in abnormal brain tissue. (Perhaps electrical activity in the area surrounding an epileptic focus repeatedly reactivates memories, preventing the normal process of decay.) In his conclusion that every person possesses a permanent record of the stream of consciousness, Penfield obviously has gone far beyond the evidence he presents.

Hypnotic Age Regression

The phenomenon of *hypnotic age regression,* in which the hypnotic subject is progressively taken backward in time, to "re-live" previous experiences, is often cited as evidence for permanent memory. Most memory theorists tend to dismiss this subject because of the aura of sensationalism and mysticism that surrounds it. There have even been reports of hypnotic subjects being regressed backward in time to "previous lives." Less fantastic are claims of regression backward to birth and earlier, to life in the womb; but the crude perceptual abilities of human infants at birth and their extremely limited ability to learn (Sameroff, 1971) make such reports implausible.

There have been many reports of subjects, regressed to an earlier age, exhibiting long-forgotten skills (for example, singing a song learned in childhood, or translating from a foreign language studied in school). Typically, in such cases the subject denies having the ability while in the waking state, both before and after the hypnotic session in which the skill is revealed. Such demonstrations cannot be taken as strong evidence for permanent memory, for two reasons. First, there is no way to tell whether the skill is performed *as well as* it was at the earlier age (showing that a manipulation can improve recall is not equivalent to proving that memory is permanent). Second, the uncritical acceptance of the subject's waking statement that he cannot perform the skill ignores the well-established (but often underestimated) human tendency to lie.

Hypnotists are often convinced that a regressed subject is actually "re-living" an earlier experience by the performance he puts on. A man regressed to the age of four may talk in a high-pitched voice, deny the ability to write or tell time, and even throw a temper tantrum. He will describe events from his life in great detail. But Rubenstein and Newman (1954) projected individuals who were good regression subjects ten years into the future, and found their performance equally convincing. (One medical student, for example, described in detail the abdominal surgery he was performing; and a young girl portrayed grief at the recent death of her child.) Good hypnotic subjects will go to great lengths to comply with the hypnotist's requests, and this apparently includes constructing realistic scenarios and acting them out. Reports by regressed subjects may contain a mixture of memory and imagination—in what proportions, it is difficult to say.

What is needed is some objective way to verify statements made by age-regressed subjects. True (1949) reported regressing fifty college-age subjects to ages ten, seven, and four, each time asking a subject to give the day of the week of Christmas, and of his birthday. True checked their answers with a 200-year calendar. The success rates he reported were remarkably high, averaging 81 percent correct. Such accuracy, on information that is ordinarily forgotten quite rapidly, is what is needed to give strong support to the permanent memory hypothesis. Unfortunately, the high rate of success True claimed for subjects regressed to four (76 percent and 62 percent for Christmas and birthdays, respectively) has led to suspicion about his results. It seems unlikely that four-year-olds are so aware of the day of the week, even on a special day like Christmas. Even more serious has been the failure of other investigators, using the same test, to obtain better than chance performance from regressed subjects (for a review, see Barber, 1962). It has been suggested that some of True's subjects, who were tested over a period of many months, may have discussed the experiment with each other and figured out the answers in advance.

Perhaps the most ambitious study of age regression is one conducted by Reiff and Scheerer (1959). These investigators regressed five highly suggestible subjects to ages ten, seven, and four, observing their performance on a number of tasks and comparing it with that of waking controls, who has been instructed to behave as though they were the target age. The behavior of the hypnotically regressed subjects was much more childlike than that of the controls. (When offered a lollipop while making mud pies, for example, the regressed subjects would accept, while the controls insisted on washing their hands first.)

An attempt to assess the accuracy of recall was made by having both regressed and control subjects give the names of teachers and classmates from the second and fifth grades. The answers were verified against school records. The regressed subjects were much better at such recall than the controls, who tended simply to say, "I don't know." What may be the most remarkable feature of the Reiff and Scheerer investigation was the extremely poor performance of the control subjects. The description of their behavior on the various tasks suggests that they thought the whole experiment silly, and did not try very hard. Hypnotized but not regressed controls would probably have done better. Indeed, not only were the control subjects not hypnotized, they were not even hypnotically susceptible. Since susceptiable and unsusceptible subjects could differ in a number of ways (for example, the tendency to rehearse childhood memories while daydreaming), the Reiff and Scheerer (1959) study must be considered too poorly controlled to be definitive.

What can we conclude about the permanent memory hypothesis? The notion that every past experience is stored in memory, waiting to be recaptured by an electrical probe or a hypnotic suggestion is a tantalizing one. The evidence that has been offered as favoring the hypothesis, however, is weak. Both Penfield's observations and the phenomena surrounding hypnotic age regression are open to other, less fantastic explanations. And the study of retention of infantile memories by Burtt (1941), using the highly sensitive relearning measure, found no retention of infantile experiences after an interval of fifteen years. The most reasonable conclusion regarding the permanent memory hypothesis, at the present time, is that it is probably incorrect.

Storage and Rehearsal

A final point about the storage phase of memory is that it is difficult to isolate experimentally. The storage phase is supposed to be passive—a period during which the subject is not thinking about (rehearsing) the to-be-remembered material. *Rehearsal* can be defined as the retrieval and re-encoding of information during the retention interval. If one wants to learn what changes the memory trace undergoes in storage, one must somehow make sure the information is not rehearsed. Otherwise, any changes inferred might be due, not to storage, but to encoding or retrieval. This problem is fairly obvious in the study of short-term retention, and that is why retention intervals are routinely filled with rehearsal-preventing "distractor" tasks. But rehearsal can also be a problem in studies of long-term retention. As a simple example, consider your ability to remember the name of your first-grade teacher. If this memory really thirteen (or so) years old? On rare occasions you may have thought about it during the intervening years. Thus, the memory trace retrieved today may be the relatively fresh product of one or more rehearsals. And several successive retrievals, elaborations, and re-encodings could drastically change the nature of the trace. Just a few opportunities to check remembered information against recorded facts are enough to demonstrate that some of our memories are not accurate, even when we feel sure that they are.

RETRIEVAL

Given that a memory trace has survived the passage of time and is available in storage, how is contact made with the trace so that it can be revived and the information put to use? The two key factors here seem to be: (a) the strength of the trace, and (b) its relationship to the retrieval cue. Let us consider some of the evidence concerning the process of retrieval.

Automatic Retrieval

Retrieval, like encoding, is sometimes automatic, or effortless. This is especially true for information that is very well learned. When we are in a high state of excitement, information that is only moderately well learned may not be retrieved at all. That is why soldiers and firemen must continually drill, and why musicians rehearse their pieces and actors their lines well beyond the point of apparent perfection. Panic and stage fright can prevent retrieval of information if it has not been highly overlearned.

The experimental evidence suggests that we cannot "turn off" retrieval of highly familiar information, even if we want to. One example of automatic retrieval is found in the *Stroop effect,* named after its discoverer, J. R. Stroop (1935). The task used by Stroop required that the subject look at a sequence of words printed in color, naming aloud as quickly as possible the color of the ink in which each word was printed. The Stroop effect is this: If the word itself is the name of a color (for example, GREEN written in blue ink) subjects take longer to respond than if it is not (for example, GIRL written in blue ink). Since the interference with color naming is selective—that is, it happens only with color-related words—it must be that the meanings of the words are being retrieved. Subjects in the Stroop task are aware of the difficulty caused by color-related words (they sometimes inadvertently say the word itself rather than naming the color of the ink), but apparently cannot prevent it. Even with extended practice on the task, the difference in response times between color words and noncolor words persists.

Winkelman and Schmidt (1974) demonstrated a similar effect in a mental arithmetic task. Subjects were shown simple addition statements such as 5 + 3 = 8, or 6 + 4 = 9, and were required to respond "true" or "false" to each, as quickly as possible. They found that it took subjects longer to respond "false" to an incorrect sum that was the product of the two numbers (for example, 4 + 3 = 12) than to one that was not (for example, 4 + 3 = 11). Apparently, although the subjects were consciously trying only to add, their brains were automatically "looking up" the products as well as the sums. Retrieval of the products from memory made them especially difficult to reject as inappropriate, causing interference with the mental addition task.

Partial Retrieval

But memory retrieval is not always automatic. This fact is illustrated by the *tip-of-the-tongue phenomenon*—a case of partial retrieval, in which we feel that we know a word but are unable to produce it. The experience was aptly described in this introspective account by William James (1890):

> Suppose we try to recall a forgotten name. The state of our consciousness is peculiar. There is a gap therein; but no mere gap. It is a gap that is intensely active. A sort of wraith of the name is in it, beckoning us in a given direction, making us at moments tingle with the sense of our closeness and then letting us sink back without the longed-for term. If wrong names are proposed to us, this singularly definite gap acts immediately so as to negate them. They do not fit into its mould. And the gap of one word does not feel like the gap of another, all empty of content as both might seem necessarily to be when described as gaps (James, 1890, p. 251).

More recently, Brown and McNeill (1966) studied the kinds of information available in the tip-of-the-tongue state. They read to subjects definitions of selected words from the dictionary, and requested recall of the appropriate words. As an example, one definition was: "a navigational instrument used in measuring distances, especially the altitudes of the sun, moon, and stars at sea." Subjects were supposed to respond, in this case, with "sextant." When a tip-of-the-tongue state occurred, the subjects answered a series of questions about the partial information they could retrieve. The questions included the following: (a) How many syllables does the word have? (b) What is its first letter? (c) What other words can you think of that have a similar sound? (d) A similar meaning? (e) Did you have any particular word in mind other than the intended word?

As James said, the gap in consciousness is not empty—it contains a "wraith of the name." Persons unable to produce an intended word have some idea of its length. Estimates by Brown and McNeill's subjects of the number of syllables increased with the actual number of syllables in the word. Their subjects also had a good idea of the first letter of the sought-for word. The first letters of the target words were guessed correctly 57 percent of the time, and 49 percent of the words thought to have similar sounds shared the first letter of the target word. The words thought to be similar also tended to match the correct word on last letters, word length, and pattern of syllabic stress. In the navigational-instrument example, words said to be similar to the target word were: secant, sextet, and sexton.

The unretrieved information, in the tip-of-the-tongue state, is not gone from memory. Sometimes the answer seems to come to us spontaneously, after some "incubation" time. We say, "It will come to me after a while," and turn to other business; and frequently, it does. At other times, a retrieval cue will produce the sought-after word. A particularly useful hint is the first letter of the word. Freedman and Landauer (1966) found that second attempts to recall tip-of-the-tongue items were twice as effective if the first letter was supplied than if it was not. (An interesting finding was that second attempt performance was not significantly impaired when a misleading first-letter cue was given.) Many people learn, on their own, to make use of first-letter cues in tip-of-the-tongue states by running through the alphabet, cuing themselves with each letter in turn.

Of course, the most effective retrieval cue is the word itself. An answer that cannot be recalled is often recognized when actually presented, as on a multiple-choice test. Hart (1965) has shown that subjects are able to predict with some accuracy whether they will be able to recognize unrecalled items on a multiple-choice test. On a six-alternative multiple-choice test, subjects were correct on 78 percent of the items they had said they were certain they knew, and were correct on only 30 percent of the items they said they were certain they did not know (a value still above chance). The "feeling of knowing" that often accompanies the tip-of-the-tongue state has some validity.

The Importance of Retrieval Cues

These experiments on the tip-of-the-tongue phenomenon illustrate the crucial role of retrieval cues in finding stored information. A basic principle of retrieval is that the more closely the information in the retrieval cue matches that in the memory trace, the more successful the attempted retrieval will be. This principle may account for the difference between recall and recognition. A number of different explanations have been given for the superiority of recognition to recall, postulating two different retrieval mechanisms, two different types of memory trace, and so on. But the simplest explanation is that the only difference lies in the completeness of the retrieval cue itself. According to this view, recall and recognition memory are points on a continuum. On a free-recall test, the cues provided are vague and incomplete. On a cued recall test, they are more specific. On a test of recognition memory, they are even more specific than in cued recall.

Tulving and Watkins (1973) did an experiment to demonstrate the continuity of recall and recognition. They presented a list of five-letter words, and then cued the subjects with fragments of the words—fragments consisting of the first two, three, four, or five letters. For each cue, the subjects were told, "write down any word it causes you to remember from the list." They were given six seconds per item to do this. In a control condition, subjects were given a free-recall test. Average performance is shown in Figure 10.8. Most investigators would call retrieval using a two-letter cue (for example, PL—) recall, and retrieval using a five-letter cue (for example, PLANT) recognition. The fact that the results show a gradual increase in performance with the increase in number of letters supplied suggests that there is no sharp line dividing the two kinds of test.

Are retrieval cues *necessary* for memory retrieval? A good case could be made that they are—even in the free-recall task, in which the

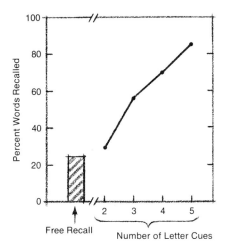

Figure 10.8 Word recall as a function of the number of letter cues. [After Tulving and Watkins, 1973. Copyright 1973, by the Board of Trustees of the University of Illinois.]

experimenter-supplied cues are vague ("recall the words in the last list you saw"). In this task, subjects apparently overcome the lack of specific cues by supplying cues themselves. This may be one reason that related words tend to be recalled together or clustered. In studying a word list, a subject may derive a small set of category names (for example, animals, trees, professions, girl's names). If, at recall, he cues himself with these category names one at a time, then items from the same category will tend to occur together in output.

The concept of the retrieval cue may help explain the common belief that our dreams are related to future events. Sleep researchers tell us that we have from 10 to 20 vivid dreams a night, and that comes to about 5,000 dreams per person, per year. Unless we awaken within a few seconds of a dream's occurrence, the chances are that it will never be recalled. Introspection reveals that on the rare occasions when a dream is recalled the following day, the recall was triggered by a retrieval cue—either in the environment (for example, meeting an acquaintance who appeared in the dream) or in our train of conscious thought. If dream recall depends on the occurrence of an appropriate retrieval cue, then it is no wonder our dreams seem to foretell future events. ("What a coincidence that you called—I dreamed about you just last night!") Only the few dreams that do so will be remembered. The thousands that do not do so sink into oblivion, never to haunt our waking life.

Context and Retrieval

Retrieving information from memory depends not only on the retrieval cue itself, but also on the surrounding context in which the cue appears. It seems that retrieval is most effective when the context at the time of the test is most similar to that at the time of encoding.

Consider a study by Light and Carter-Sobell (1970). These researchers had subjects study a list of sentences, each containing a specific adjective-noun combination. Then, on a recognition-memory test, adjective-noun combinations were presented, and the subjects decided whether the nouns had occurred in the previous list of sentences. The subjects understood that their recognition judgments were to be based on the noun only, and not on the adjective that accompanied it. There were three conditions, differing with respect to the relationship between the study context and the test context: same adjective, same meaning, and different meaning. As an example, for the original sentence, *The child received a bad grade,* the test pair for the same-adjective condition was *bad GRADE;* that for the same-meaning condition was *good GRADE;* and that for the different-meaning condition was *steep GRADE* (the adjective biased a completely different meaning of the noun). Recognition judgments were 70 percent accurate in the first of these conditions, 62 percent accurate in the second, and 58 percent accurate in the third. Chance performance, due to random guessing, would be 50 percent. Clearly, the relationship between study context and test context had a strong influence on the ability to recognize the nouns as "old."

One explanation for the Light and Carter-Sobell finding is fairly obvious. The memory codes subjects used were primarily semantic. A bad grade is different from a good grade, and even more different from a grade that is steep. By biasing different interpretations of the retrieval cue "grade," the adjectives influenced the probability that it would contact the "bad grade" memory trace.

But what about changes in the context that are not associated with the task itself? Introductory psychology texts often tell the student that it is best to learn material in the same room where he will be tested, implying that extraneous stimuli such as sights, sounds, odors, temperatures, and postural cues are somehow incorporated into the traces of the to-be-remembered material itself. There is anecdotal evidence to support this recommendation. There is also some evidence for what is called "state-dependent learning" under drugs. The idea is that it is easier to retrieve information from memory when one's "state of consciousness" is the same as it was when the information was learned than it is when the mental state has changed.

The truth is, however, that such effects are difficult to demonstrate experimentally. They tend to be small, and they frequently fail to replicate. One reason for this may be that the manipulations of context typically are not extreme—changing the room the subject is in, for example, or having him standing up versus sitting down, or mildly intoxicated versus sober. Another reason may be that the tasks usually used are serial learning and paired associates, in which there are specific retrieval cues that are taken from the experimental materials themselves. Tasks that are relatively lacking in specific retrieval cues—such as free recall—may be more suitable for demonstrating effects of extra-task context on retrieval.

Some evidence for this interpretation is found in a recent study by Godden and Baddeley (1975). In this study, scuba divers were presented 36-word lists, under two conditions: either (a) 20 feet under water, in full diving gear, or (b) at the surface, sitting by the water's edge. A free-recall test was administered 4 minutes later, in one of the same two environments (recalled words were written on a waterproof board). Thus, there were 4 combinations of learning and test environments: dry–dry, dry–wet, wet–dry, and wet–wet. Free recall was about 46 percent better when the learning and test environments were the same than it was when they were different. The experiment was not very well controlled, as Godden and Baddeley admit. However, it at least suggests that an extreme context manipulation, together with a task that lacks specific retrieval cues, may produce large and reliable effects of extra-task context on retrieval.

I I

Theoretical Issues in Human Memory

In this chapter, we shall discuss two general issues that are of central interest to memory theorists. The first concerns the distinction between short-term and long-term "memory stores." As it is in storage, does the memory trace undergo some qualitative change, or does it remain essentially the same? That is, does the storage phase consist of one process or two? The second issue, related to the first, concerns the causes of forgetting. Is forgetting the result of time in storage, or of interference from other material that has been learned? Both of these questions were touched on briefly before, but will be given more thorough consideration here.

THE STORAGE PHASE: ONE PROCESS OR TWO?

The distinction between short-term and long-term memory processes is not new. The early philosophical psychologists noted that remembering a long-past event is a quite different experience from remembering an event that just occurred. William James (1890) described the difference in this way:

> An object which is recollected, in the proper sense of that term, is one which has been absent from consciousness altogether, and now revives anew. It is brought back, recalled, fished up, so to speak, from a reservoir in which, with countless other objects, it lay buried and lost from view. But an object of primary memory is not thus brought back; it never was lost; its date was never cut off in consciousness from that of the immediately present moment (James, 1890, pp. 646–647).

312

In what James called *primary memory*, the remembered experience has not yet completely faded from conscious awareness. In what he called *secondary memory*, the remembered event has been absent from conscious awareness for perhaps a very long time, and the act of "recollection" brings it back.

For the behaviorists to accept a distinction between two kinds of memory solely on the basis of introspective reports would have been completely out of character. As one might expect, they ignored it. But in 1949, Donald Hebb presented a physiological theory of behavior—based, at least in part, on objective evidence, and therefore "scientifically respectable"—which renewed interest in the idea. Hebb's (1949) proposal was this: A sensory event immediately gives rise to a pattern of electrical activity in the brain. This pattern of activity reverberates (or repeats) for a short period of time—and during this time, the activity itself constitutes the memory trace of the sensory event. A pattern of activity that continues or is repeated will gradually cause relatively permanent, structural changes in the brain. Thus, if two neurons repeatedly fire in close succession, the tendency for one of them to fire the other is permanently raised. Long after the reverberating pattern of firing has ceased, this structural change remains, and constitutes the lasting memory trace.

It is not hard to see a parallel between the two types of memory described by James and the two types proposed by Hebb. Primary memory and the reverberatory trace are active and temporary. Secondary memory and the structural trace are passive and relatively permanent. Interest in Hebb's neurophysiological speculations was undoubtedly reinforced by this correspondence.

The direct ancestor of current two-process memory theories, however, was not Hebb's physiological theory, but rather the information-processing theory of attention, memory, and performance proposed by Broadbent (1958). Broadbent's theory, illustrated by box-and-arrow diagrams depicting the "flow of information" in the organism, included a sensory memory store in which information decays rapidly, a selective filter which determines which information will receive further processing, a limited-capacity short-term store, and a permanent long-term memory store. It was proposed that information in the sensory and short-term stores would decay with time, unless this was prevented through rehearsal—essentially, "recycling" the information through conscious attention.

Two-process theorists following Broadbent (for example, Atkinson and Shiffrin, 1968; Waugh and Norman, 1965) have added, deleted, and reordered boxes, moved arrows, and changed certain other assumptions—primarily to accommodate the results of innumerable experimental tests. There are often important differences between two-process theories proposed by different individuals, and between those proposed by the same theorist at two different times. Nevertheless, the family resemblances are strong. Let us consider a typical two-process theory. (The following is based primarily on the theory of Atkinson and Shiffrin [1968, 1971], but differs from it in some minor respects.)

A Two-Process Theory

A schematic diagram of a typical two-process theory is shown in Figure 11.1. Stimulus information from the environment is assumed to first enter the *sensory register* of the appropriate modality. In most memory experiments, the sensory register involved is either auditory or visual. Information is assumed to decay from the sensory registers very quickly. From a number of experiments, it has been estimated that visual sensory information disappears in about $\frac{1}{2}$ second, while auditory information lasts perhaps as long as 3 seconds. The information must be attended to and read into the *short-term store* (STS) during this brief time, or it will be lost.

The STS is the working memory. Here, information is held temporarily while it is being rehearsed, elaborated upon, recoded, related to past knowledge, and so on. The STS is typically assumed to have a small, *fixed capacity* of about seven chunks (Miller, 1956). Typically, also, information in the STS is assumed to be subject to fairly rapid decay. If rehearsal is prevented (by having the subject count backward, for example), the information will be lost within about 20 seconds. This value is derived from distractor-task experiments like that of Peterson and Peterson (1959), described in Chapter 9. If the subject is allowed to rehearse freely, information can be maintained in the STS indefinitely; but when rehearsal stops, the information decays.

Information in the STS is continually being copied into a more permanent memory store of vast size, the long-term store (LTS). This copying process, which is not under the subject's voluntary control, is called *consolidation*, because it transforms the information from a temporary to a more permanent form. Consolidation is assumed to be a

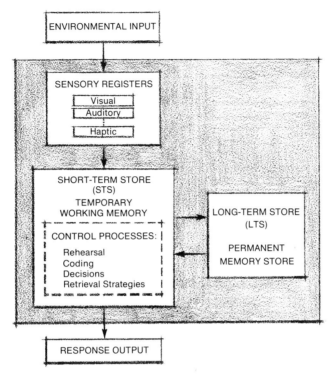

Figure 11.1 A typical two-process model of human memory. [Adapted from Richard C. Atkinson and Richard M. Shiffrin, "The Control of Short-Term Memory." Copyright © 1971 by Scientific American, Inc. All rights reserved.]

rather slow process. Because of this, the LTS trace resulting from the brief stay of an item in the STS may not be complete enough to support recall or even recognition. Building up a sufficient LTS trace, therefore, may require that the item spend a considerable amount of time in the STS. This can be accomplished in two ways: repeated study trials, each of which affords the item some time in the STS; or rehearsal, which maintains the strength of the STS trace and thus prolongs the item's stay.

The STS is assumed to do more than just hold information for short periods. It is in the STS where the *control processes* are performed. In addition to controlling rehearsal and encoding (for example, forming visual images), control processes are assumed to guide the retrieval of information from the LTS and decide when to produce an overt response. In a rough sense, the STS corresponds to what we experience as consciousness. Attending to incoming information, rehearsing and recoding, "searching" for information in the LTS, and deciding what response to give all seem to be conscious, voluntary activities. The LTS, by contrast, is not the site of such activities. It can be likened to a storehouse, where information is kept on file for possible future reference, whether or not it is currently being used.

A common misconception created by diagrams such as Figure 11.1 is that the theorist believes the STS and LTS to be located at different places in the brain. Because of our current ignorance of the workings of the brain, however, it is doubtful that many two-process memory theorists would make such an assertion. Such diagrams are meant to be functional models only. It is assumed that the STS and LTS have distinct properties (for example, different capacities), and that they interact in particular ways in determining behavior. Presumably, different brain processes are involved; and these processes could be spatially separated (for example, the STS in the higher brain stem and the LTS in the cerebral cortex), but they could also occupy the same locations, as the reverberatory and structural traces do in Hebb's theory. Until we know that a two-processes theory is needed to account for behavior, the memory theorist is likely to view such physiological speculation as premature.

The critical eye may already have seen one problem with the model diagrammed in Figure 11.1: it cannot account for the automatic retrieval of information from the LTS. All memory retrieval, according to the diagram, is guided by control processes. The chunking of line segments into letters, and letters into words, depends on past learning (the LTS). But when we read, these chunks are formed without the conscious retrieval effort the model seems to require. Words presented in the Stroop task automatically retrieve their meanings; and simple arithmetic problems automatically "look up" their answers in memory, as we saw in Chapter 10. According to the model, such automatic retrieval should not occur. Some theorists have handled this problem by adding an arrow from the sensory registers directly to the LTS, thus allowing retrieval to bypass the STS. Diagrams such as that in Figure 11.1 have a way of becoming cluttered with boxes and arrows, as the theorist takes more and more experimental findings into account.

What is the evidence for the STS–LTS distinction? Does the evidence require a two-process approach, or can it be explained in some other way? Let us examine some of the most common arguments given on both sides of this issue.

Capacity

A common claim about the STS is that it has a small, fixed capacity. In contrast, the capacity of the LTS is said to be very large—perhaps infinite. This claim about the STS is based primarily on studies of the memory span, which show that most subjects can repeat a maximum of about seven digits, letters, or words in correct order after hearing them once. A famous paper by Miller (1956) suggests "the magical number seven, plus or minus two" as the capacity of immediate memory, measured in chunks. Those who take the computer analogy seriously even assume the capacity of the STS must be a whole number—as though the STS were actually a storage register with a certain number of "slots" or locations to be filled—one chunk per slot.

Several problems with this view have been pointed out. First, as we saw in Figure 8.11, the number of items a subject can recall correctly varies from trial to trial. The "memory span" is an average—a statistical abstraction. Second, as was pointed out in Chapter 8, the memory span improves with practice. Advocates of the fixed-capacity view argue that this is because practice teaches one to form bigger chunks. Third, the memory span varies with the materials that are used. It is slightly smaller for letters than for digits, and smaller still for words. It is smaller for similar-sounding words (for example, INCIDENT, SENTIMENT, RESIDENT, SETTLEMENT, TENEMENT) than for words with dissimilar sounds. It is smaller for abstract than for concrete words, and even smaller for familiar phrases and clichés. To maintain the hypothesis that the STS holds a fixed number of chunks, given such findings, the theorist must assume that the "chunks" are not familiar units, but something else, more abstract (see, for example, Simon, 1974; and Broadbent, 1975). This detracts considerably from the elegance of the theory.

Advocates of the fixed-capacity view point out that the memory span, unlike more permanent learning, is unaffected by presentation rate. Indeed, variations in presentation rate from $\frac{1}{4}$ second per item to 2 seconds per item seem to affect the memory span very little. (Some experiments find that it goes down with increasing rate and some find that it goes up; others find no change.) But in the memory-span task, presentation rate is confounded with retention interval. At a ½-second rate, the first digit of a seven digit list must be retained for only 3 seconds before it can be recalled; at a 2-second rate, it must be retained for 12 seconds. Thus, better learning at the slow rate may be overcome by greater forgetting due to the longer retention interval.

Especially troubling about the capacity argument is the seemingly arbitrary choice of the memory-span task to define STS capacity. The memory span requires immediate serial recall. Why require recall in a particular order? Why recall rather than recognition? Immediate free-recall or recognition-memory tests would produce considerably higher estimates of the capacity of the STS. An alternative method of estimating STS capacity, based on the size of the recency effect in free recall, produces values much smaller than the memory span—usually two to three items.

One might argue that neither the method of estimating STS capacity nor the value obtained is particularly important—what is important is the fact that memory performance after a single presentation is limited. But performance after two or three or even fifty presentations is also limited. Should one conclude, therefore, that the LTS has a limited capacity? The simple fact is, the more study trials we are given, the more we can remember. There seems to be no particular reason to accord special status to what can be retained from a single trial.

Some investigators have attempted to demonstrate the limited capacity of the STS by showing that filling it part way interferes with conscious thought. The idea is that the working memory we use in the memory span task is also used to understand sentences, solve problems, and so on. Baddeley and Hitch (1974), for example, gave subjects a "memory load" of zero, one, or two letters, immediately before presenting a difficult sentence the subjects had to comprehend. The time taken to respond to the sentence was measured, and the letters were then recalled. Contrary to what was predicted, there was no effect of memory load on reaction times to the sentences. Only in other experiments, when the memory load was increased to six items (practically "filling" the STS), did Baddeley and Hitch observe any interference. And it seems likely that this happened because subjects rehearsed the to-be-remembered items while attempting to read the sentences (rehearsal requires retrieval and re-encoding), rather than because of limits on the capacity of working memory. Indeed, Spelke, Hirst, and Neisser (1976) have shown that if subjects are given many days of practice, they can read for comprehension and take written dictation simultaneously, with no deficit on either task. This is certainly not what the hypothesis of a fixed-capacity working memory would predict.

Everything considered, then, the claim that the STS has a fixed capacity and the LTS does not cannot be said to rest on compelling logic or unambiguous data. There seems to be nothing here to convince the skeptic to accept the two-process view.

Coding

A number of investigators have proposed that the STS and LTS might employ two different types of memory code. Let us examine the evidence for and against this assertion.

Although previous investigators of short-term memory had noticed that subjects tended to confuse items having similar-sounding names, the British psychologist R. Conrad was the first to present a clear demonstration of the phenomenon. Conrad's (1964) demonstration compared the results of two experiments: a listening experiment and a recall experiment. In the listening experiment, subjects listened to letter names which were read aloud one at a time, against a background of "white noise." (White noise is so called because, like white light, it is a mixture of all frequencies. It sounds like radio static, or the hiss of escaping steam.) The white noise was loud enough so that the letters could not be heard clearly, and the subject's task was to listen to each letter name and write down what he thought it was. Six letters were used: B, C, P, T, V, F, M, N, S, and X. Whenever a subject misunderstood a letter name, an error was tallied according to the actual stimulus letter and the subject's incorrect response. If the stimulus was P and the subject wrote down V, for example, a P–V confusion was entered in the appropriate place in a table. The result of such an analysis is a *confusion matrix,* which shows how often each confusion is made. The confusion matrix from Conrad's listening experiment is shown in the top half of Figure 11.2. Notice that the letters Conrad used seem to fall into two sets: B, C, P, T, V, and F, M, N, S, X. Errors within these sets are common, while those between the two sets are rare. Within these sets, certain letter pairs are more confusable than others: P–T, B–V, N–M, and F–S were especially frequent confusions. All this corresponds to our intuitive judgments of the similarity of the letter names.

LISTENING CONFUSIONS
Stimulus Letter

Incorrect Response	B	C	P	T	V	F	M	N	S	X
B	–	171	75	84	168	2	11	10	2	2
C	32	–	35	42	20	4	4	5	2	5
P	162	350	–	505	91	11	31	23	5	5
T	143	232	281	–	50	14	12	11	8	5
V	122	61	34	22	–	1	8	11	1	0
F	6	4	2	4	3	–	13	8	336	238
M	10	14	2	3	4	22	–	334	21	9
N	13	21	6	9	20	32	512	–	38	14
S	2	18	2	7	3	488	23	11	–	391
X	1	6	2	2	1	245	2	1	184	–

RECALL CONFUSIONS
Stimulus Letter

Incorrect Response	B	C	P	T	V	F	M	N	S	X
B	–	18	62	5	83	12	9	3	2	0
C	13	–	27	18	55	15	3	12	35	7
P	102	18	–	24	40	15	8	8	7	7
T	30	46	79	–	38	18	14	14	8	10
V	56	32	30	14	–	21	15	11	11	5
F	6	8	14	5	31	–	12	13	131	16
M	12	6	8	5	20	16	–	146	15	5
N	11	7	5	1	19	28	167	–	24	5
S	7	21	11	2	9	37	4	12	–	16
X	3	7	2	2	11	30	10	11	59	–

Figure 11.2 Perceptual confusions between letter names read aloud with a background of white noise (top), and memory confusions between letters presented visually in a memory span task (bottom). [Data from Conrad, 1964.]

Conrad's second experiment used the letter-span task. Six-letter strings were presented visually, one letter at a time, and subjects were then required to write the letters down in their proper order. Again, an error analysis was made. When a subject recalled a letter incorrectly (for example, an X in the position where an S belonged), the error was tallied just as in the listening experiment. The confusion matrix resulting from Conrad's recall experiment is shown in the bottom half of Figure 11.2. Comparison of the two confusion matrices reveals a striking correspondence. The pattern of recall confusions among letters presented visually is very similar to that of listening confusions. What does this mean? An obvious interpretation is that in the recall task subjects transformed the visual letters into an acoustic code—a representation of how the letter names sounds. A fading acoustic trace of, let us say F, would have many features in common with the acoustic trace of S—thus the tendency to confuse the two in memory.

These data can, however, be interpreted in another way. Instead of using an *acoustic code,* based on how the letter name sounds, subjects may transform visual letters into an *articulatory code,* based on how the name is articulated, or produced. (This second hypothesis would have found favor with John B. Watson, who proposed that tiny movements of the vocal apparatus were the basis of thought.) Acoustic and articulatory codes would give rise to similar patterns of confusions, since the sound of a word corresponds closely to how it is produced. Thus, it is difficult, from confusion errors alone, to determine which interpretation is correct.

Several experiments, however, suggest that the memory code that gives rise to these errors is an articulatory code. For example, Conrad (1970) gave a visual letter-span test to "profoundly deaf" English schoolboys. Some of the subjects tended to confuse letters with similar-sounding names, but others did not. The tendency to make these confusions was related not to degree of hearing loss but to speaking ability. That is, the boys with the best speech were the ones who made "acoustic" confusions. These children, presumably, knew how to articulate the letter names but did not know how they sounded. In another study, Glassman (1972) used a biofeedback technique to train subjects to inhibit subvocal activity. Electronic sensors were attached to the "voice box," and a buzzer was triggered whenever muscular activity was detected. The subjects were trained to keep the buzzer from sounding. After this suppression training, the subjects were tested in a short-term memory task. Overall, their memory performance did not differ from that of a control group that was not given suppression training; but they confused similar-sounding items much less often than did the controls. By discouraging articulatory coding, Glassman apparently prevented "acoustic" confusions. These experiments and others suggest that articulatory, rather than acoustic, coding underlies errors in short-term memory.

One can take a neutral stance on the acoustic versus articulatory coding issue, by referring to confusions among similar-sounding items as *phonemic* confusions, and citing them as evidence for *phonemic coding*. (A "phoneme" is the basic unit of sound out of which words are made. The term is used with reference to both the perception and production of speech, and so is neutral with regard to the distinction between acoustic and articulatory codes.)

While the memory-span task typically gives evidence of phonemic coding, other tasks, not adapted to the study of immediate memory, yield results suggesting a very different kind of memory code. Figure 11.3 demonstrates this, with a recognition-memory task. Read through the 20-word study list at the left of the figure, trying to commit each word to memory. Then go through the test words, decid-

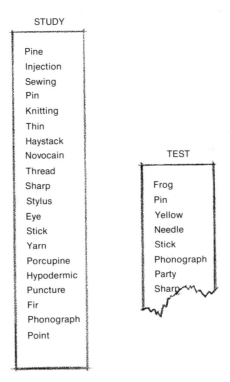

Figure 11.3 Study and recognition-memory test lists for demonstrating semantic confusions.

ing for each of them whether it was in the study list. Then check your decisions against the study list itself. (Follow these instructions before reading further.)

The chances are that you incorrectly decided that the word NEE-DLE had been in the list. In fact, although NEEDLE does not appear in the list, it is associated with every word that does. This example illustrates the *false-recognition* technique of studying memory coding. In this case, the result strongly suggests that the memory code involved was a *semantic code* based on word meanings. When a word is presented in a recognition-memory experiment, either an associated word or a word with a similar meaning is a likely candidate for false recognition on the test. The false recognition of words semantically related to those in the list was discovered by Kirkpatrick (1894), but received little attention until it was rediscovered in the 1960s (Anisfeld and Knapp, 1968; Underwood, 1965).

Now, the different kinds of errors typically found in the memory span and the false recognition paradigms have led some theorists (for example, Baddeley, 1966) to propose that the memory code of the STS is phonemic (either acoustic or articulatory), and the code of the LTS is semantic. That is, the two memory stores might be distinguished on the basis of the type of coding used. If this notion could survive appropriate experimental tests, the value of the STS–LTS distinction would be greatly enhanced. There is good reason, however, to believe that it is wrong.

For one thing, the distinction does not allow for lasting visual memory codes. Once visual information is gone from the sensory register, it should no longer be available. Yet, we know we are good at remembering faces and scenes; and as was pointed out earlier, pictures are generally remembered much better than words. A two-process theorist might counter by denying that his theory applies to faces and scenes. It was derived from experiments on memory for verbal materials: words, digits, letters, and nonsense syllables. When such stimuli are used, he might claim, the visual information lasts only a quarter of a second or so.

But does it? The results of several short-term memory experiments suggest a visual code that lasts for at least several seconds. One such experiment, by Parkinson (1972), used a modification of the familiar distractor task. Rather than having subjects count backward during the retention interval, he had them listen to letter names presented over earphones at a fast rate, and "shadow" them—that is, repeat them aloud. The to-be-remembered items (letter combinations) were presented visually on some trials, and auditorily on others. Recall was tested after either 1 or 20 seconds of shadowing. Parkinson found that the auditorily presented items were recalled best at the 1-second retention interval, but visually presented items were recalled better than auditorily presented items after 20 seconds. The most straightforward interpretation of this result is that visually presented items are represented by visual memory traces, which are less vulnerable to retroactive interference from the activity of shadowing than phonemic traces are.

Demonstrations of modality-specific interference in short-term memory are not new. Bigham (1894) compared effects of two distractor activities—reading, and listening to the experimenter read—on memory for visually and auditorily presented materials. Retroactive interference was greater when the presentation and distractor modalities were the same than when they were different. And another forgotten study, by Nagge (1935), extended the conclusion to long-term memory. In stage one of Nagge's experiment, the subjects learned a serial list of 12 nonsense syllables, presented either visually or auditorily. In stage two, the subjects either rested or learned a second serial list. Presentation of List 2, like List 1, could be either visual or auditory. In stage three, 24 hours later, the subjects relearned List 1, presented in the same modality as it had been originally. Savings scores, shown in Figure 11.4, reveal how the different treatments affected retention. Clearly, List 2 caused more retroactive interference when it was in the same sensory modality as List 1 than it did when the modalities were different. The suggestion, again, is that visual sensory events give rise to long-lasting visual memory traces and auditory events to long-lasting auditory traces, as the Gestalt psychologists proposed.

Other evidence lends support to this conclusion. On a memory judgment test, subjects are fairly accurate at remembering whether a word was originally presented visually or auditorily (see Chapter 9); visually presented words are recognized as "old" more quickly when tested in the original type style than when the type style is changed (Hintzman and Summers, 1973); and a passage printed in upsidedown letters is easier to read if it was read in the same orientation a year earlier than if it was read in the upright orientation (Kolers, 1976). All this evidence suggests that even with verbal materials a

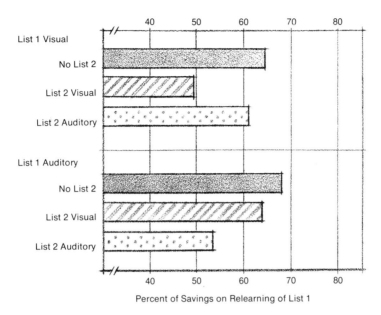

Figure 11.4 Retroactive interference as a function of List 1 and List 2 presentation modalities. [Data from Nagge, 1935.]

visual code stays with us far longer than the $\frac{1}{4}$ second presumably allowed by the visual sensory store.

So much for visual memory. Is auditory memory limited to the 20 seconds or so the STS is assumed to span? This seems implausible. We remember voices, melodies, and so on, over long intervals. While little experimental work has been done on long-term retention of nonverbal sounds, Lawrence and Banks (1973) tested recognition memory for 194 common sounds (for example, running water, baby sneezing, tapdance routine), and found that it was quite good after an interval of about an hour.

Again, however, the two-process theorist might object that his theory only applies to verbal materials. But there is contrary evidence from studies of verbal materials, too. Craik and Kirsner (1974) tested subjects in a continuous-recognition experiment, with auditory presentation of words. The words were spoken at a 4-second rate, some by a female and some by a male voice. When a given word occurred the second time, it was spoken either by the same voice that had given it originally, or by the other voice. Figure 11.5 shows that recognition memory was more accurate when a word was repeated by the same voice than when the voice was changed. This was so even after 32 items (over 2 minutes, which is beyond the hypothesized range of the STS) had intervened.

So visual and phonemic memory codes last longer than the two-process theory assumes. What about semantic information? Can word meanings be encoded in the STS? Again, an intuitive argument suggests that they can be. Otherwise, how could we construct the meaning of a passage when we read? But again, since intuitive arguments can be misleading, let us turn to experimental evidence.

A recognition memory-experiment by Shulman (1972) is relevant here. On each trial, a subject saw a list of 10 words, presented at a $\frac{1}{2}$-second rate. Immediately after, he was shown a test word, together with one of two instructions: (a) the letter I, indicating that he was to judge whether the test word was identical to one in the list (recognition memory); or (b) the letter M, indicating that he was to judge whether the test word had the same meaning as one in the list (for example, TALK, when SPEAK was in the list). Subjects made correct identity

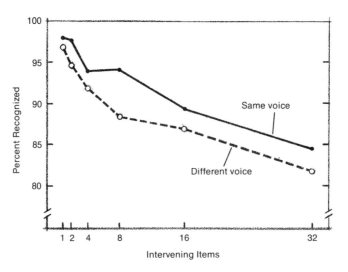

Figure 11.5 Recognition performance for words originally presented and tested in the same voice or different voices. [After Craik and Kirsner, 1974. Copyright 1974 by Experimental Psychology Society.]

judgments 89 percent of the time, and were able to make correct meaning judgments 67 percent of the time. The latter figure suggests that they had short-term semantic codes. Further evidence for semantic coding appeared in the identity task, as false recognitions. Test words that were synonyms of presented words (for example, TALK and SPEAK) were incorrectly judged as "old" 19 percent of the time, compared with 11 percent for words that were not synonyms of those in the list. It is apparent that, if a distinct STS does exist, it must include semantic information.

But the fact remains that phonemic confusions are more typical of short-term memory experiments, and semantic confusions are more typical of experiments on long-term retention. How should this be explained? Craik and Lockhart (1972) propose that the idea of multiple memory stores be abandoned, and replaced with a *depth of processing* framework. The basic notion is that when a stimulus is perceived, it can be processed to varying levels, from the "shallow" analysis of sensory features, such as angles, colors, and loudness, through intermediate levels such as naming, to "deep" elaboration in terms of images and meaningful associations with past experience. Craik and Lockhart assume that memory traces corresponding to the different levels of processing differ in their persistence; that is, the greater the depth of processing, the stronger, or longer lasting, is the resulting trace. In this view, subjects in short-term memory experiments tend to make phonemic confusions because the relatively meaningless materials, fast presentation rates, and short retention intervals encourage them to concentrate on naming the stimulus items; subjects in long-term memory experiments tend to confuse semantically similar items because meaningful materials, slow rates, and long retention intervals encourage "deep" semantic encoding. Thus, different types of errors may reflect the flexibility of subjects' control processes, rather than fixed characteristics of distinct short- and long-term stores.

Forgetting Rate

Information in the STS is assumed to be forgotten much more rapidly than information in the LTS—indeed, this is the primary distinction between the two stores. Of course, we know from retention curves that the rate of forgetting is greater immediately after presentation than it is later on, but this fact alone does not establish that two processes are involved. The assumption of dramatically different STS and LTS forgetting rates requires a rather abrupt change in the retention function, at the point where the STS trace disappears.

Most psychologists who have argued for this abrupt change have cited as evidence the effect of a distractor task on the serial-position curve of free recall. A classic study of this effect was done by Postman and Phillips (1965). These researchers presented subjects with word lists 10, 20, or 30 items long, and had them recall the words either immediately or after 15 seconds or 30 seconds of counting backward. The results of four of their conditions are shown in Figure 11.6. The primary effect of the distractor task, it is plain, was to eliminate the recency effect. When 30 seconds of mental activity separated presentation and recall, the last few items in the list were recalled no better than those in the middle, along the asymptote section of the curve.

These data have been interpreted by two-process theorists in the following way: Immediately after studying a list, the subject holds the last few items in his STS. If he is given an immediate recall test, he will first recall the items from the STS, and then retrieve earlier items, from his LTS. (Remember, from Chapter 8, that in free recall the last items in are typically the first items out.) If the subject is not given an immediate test, however, but is occupied with a distractor task for a sufficient time, the STS traces will be lost. All subsequent recall will come from the LTS. Thus, the recency effect, in the serial-position curve of free recall, is attributed to immediate recall from the STS; and the primacy effect and asymptote are attributed to information that has consolidated in the LTS. (The primacy effect is given no special importance—it is simply attributed to the fact that the first few items in the list have more opportunities to be rehearsed.)

There are several difficulties with this account of the serial-position curve of free recall. First, it has been found that the recency effect develops as subjects become practiced at the free-recall task. This suggests that the "last in, first out" recall order is determined by control processes, or strategies gradually learned by the subject, rather than by the structure of the memory system itself. Second, the experimenter cannot be sure subjects have encoded items in different positions in the same way. They may, for example, adopt a strategy of encoding the last few items in a phonemic rather than a semantic code, making them less resistant to forgetting than earlier items in the list. Third, despite two-process theorists' claim that the distractor task only

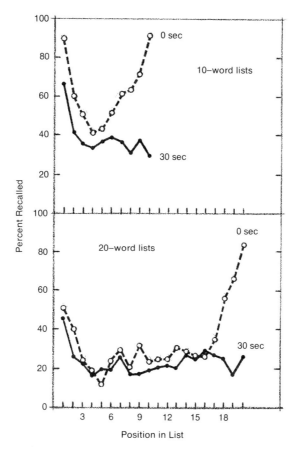

Figure 11.6 Serial-position curves of free recall, following 0 and 30 seconds of counting backward. [Adapted from Postman and Phillips, 1965.]

affects the recency portion of the curve, an effect on recall of earlier items is often evident. In Figure 11.6, for example, the primacy and asymptote portions of the curves are somewhat depressed in the 30-second distractor conditions—although, to be sure, the effect on the recency portion is greater. Fourth, in free recall the retention intervals of individual items are poorly controlled. When recall is immediate, the last items are typically the first recalled. The "last in, first out" strategy denies items in early positions the opportunity to be the first items recalled. When recall is delayed (for example, the 30-second conditions), the first items recalled tend to be the *first* items in the list, which means the most recent item must be held in memory longer than 30 seconds—perhaps for 60 seconds or so—before it has an opportunity to be recalled. Subjects have freedom, in the free-recall task, to shuffle retention intervals of individual items around in whatever haphazard way they wish. Finally, under certain conditions, recency effects can be obtained in free recall even when 30 seconds of distracting activity follows presentation of the list (Bjork and Whitten, 1974).

To determine whether the abrupt change in forgetting rate predicted by the two-process theory exists, we must use tasks that are better controlled than free recall. In addition, we should consider as wide a range of retention intervals as is practical, to learn whether there is more than one such abrupt change. In a number of experiments, W. A. Wickelgren has carefully examined forgetting rates over retention intervals from seconds to minutes, hours to days, and days to years. Where relatively short intervals were involved, the experiments typically used the continuous recognition paradigm, the virtues of which were described in Chapter 8. In order to understand Wickelgren's findings, we must first be more precise about what the term "rate of forgetting" means.

Mathematically, a quantity that decreases at a constant rate is described by an *exponential decay curve*. Simply described, such a curve has the following property: if it takes the quantity t seconds to decay to half its initial value, then in the next t seconds it will decay half the remaining amount (to one-fourth the initial value), and so on. In other words, for any time interval of a given length, the amount of decay is a fixed fraction of the value at the beginning of that interval. Figure 11.7 shows three exponential decay curves. Curve b has a decay rate 4 times that of c; curve a has a rate 20 times that of c; but all three curves have the same exponential form. For each curve, the rate of decay is the same throughout its length. Many processes in nature—chemical reactions, for example, and radioactive decay—follow such functions. It is reasonable, therefore, to assume that forgetting might do so, as well.

In his early investigations, Wickelgren studied forgetting over intervals ranging from 0 seconds to 3 minutes. He found that a single exponential curve did not adequately fit the data—the rate of forgetting over the shortest intervals was much greater than that between 15 seconds and 3 minutes. He proposed that two traces were involved,

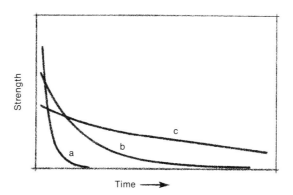

Figure 11.7 Three exponential decay curves. Curve *a* decays 20 times as fast, and curve *b* 4 times as fast, as curve *c*.

one decaying about four times as rapidly as the other. Thus far, the STS–LTS distinction was supported. Subsequent work, however, showed that the slower-decaying of these two traces could not account for retention over longer intervals, of minutes to hours or weeks to years. In fact, the longer the retention interval was, the slower the decay rate appeared to be. In one paper, Wickelgren (1970) postulated four different traces: very-short-term, short-term, intermediate-term, and long-term—and the evidence suggested that one more might have to be added, as well. Clearly, the multi-store approach was getting out of hand.

More recently, a different approach has been tried, which appears more successful (Wickelgren, 1974). Only one trace is assumed. It has two properties: strength and "fragility." Strength determines the accuracy of recognition and recall. Fragility determines the susceptibility of the trace to decay. This property of the trace is assumed to decrease with time. Thus, the strength of the trace continues to decay over longer and longer intervals, but the rate of decay is continuously slowing down. The decay curve is not exponential. Wickelgren reports that a single equation embodying these assumptions fits forgetting curves over intervals ranging from a few seconds to a few years. At present, therefore, it does not look as though data on forgetting rates are particularly good evidence for the distinction between short- and long-term memory stores.

Spacing Effect

A very persistent finding in memory experiments is that retention is affected by the spacing of repetitions. An item presented two times in close succession is not remembered as well as one presented twice with the two presentations spaced further apart. This finding is a general one, obtained in recall, recognition memory, and frequency-judgment tasks, using pictures, words, sentences, nonsense syllables, and letters.

A typical example of the *spacing effect* is shown in Figure 11.8. In this experiment (Hintzman, 1969a), subjects saw a list of 320 words, presented at a rate of 3 seconds per word. In the list were some words that occurred once only, and others that occurred twice. The number of words separating presentations of a repeated item varied from 0 to 16. Following presentation, the subjects judged the number of times each word had occurred in the list. The average frequency judgments, shown in the figure, increased as the spacing between presentations increased from 0 to about 4 items (12 seconds), and then leveled off. Recall and recognition memory are affected by spacing in much the same way.

A two-process theorist could account for the spacing effect in several ways. He could claim that the second presentation of an item, immediately following the first, disrupts the consolidation of the trace

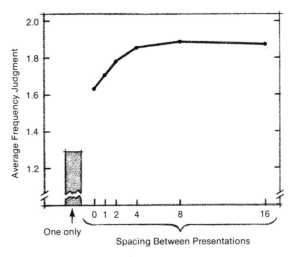

Figure 11.8 Effect of the spacing of two presentations of a word on its remembered frequency. [Adapted from Hintzman, 1969a.]

of the first presentation, thus affecting its strength in the LTS; or that ongoing consolidation of the first presentation prevents consolidation of the second; or that the subject chooses to ignore an item he already has in his STS. All such hypotheses explain the spacing effect in terms of some kind of processing conflict between the first and second presentations—a conflict which is prevented if the second presentation is delayed until the STS activity of the first presentation has disappeared.

While one or another of these accounts of the spacing effect may very well be correct, the phenomenon is not generally regarded as strong evidence for the STS–LTS distinction. The reason is that there are equally plausible explanations of the phenomenon which do not postulate distinct short- and long-term memory stores. (For a discussion of some of the alternative explanations of the spacing effect, see Hintzman, 1974).

Retrograde Amnesia

Our species has always suffered from accidents and has always fought, so it must have been discovered very long ago that a traumatic incident such as a blow to the head can lead to a loss of memory for events experienced shortly before the incident occurred. This phenomenon is called *retrograde amnesia,* which means a loss of memory directed backward in time from the precipitating incident. Retrograde amnesia is often cited as evidence for two-process memory theory. The hypothesis is that the trauma (often causing unconsciousness) disrupts the ongoing activity of the STS, thus preventing adequate consolidation of traces of very recent events. If this hypothesis is correct, then precise measurement of the duration of the "blank" interval in memory should provide independent evidence regarding the time course of the consolidation of STS traces into a more permanent LTS form.

How can one study the duration of retrograde amnesia? Ethics prevent us from conducting experiments in which human subjects are knocked unconscious at selected intervals after studying a nonsense syllable. A similar experiment can be done, however, if the traumatic incident has been prescribed for the subject's benefit by a qualified member of the medical establishment. Although the practice is on the decline, it has been fairly common for patients suffering from depression to be given "electroconvulsive therapy"—a series of administrations of electroconvulsive shock (ECS), which passes through the brain causing convulsions, loss of consciousness, and (apparently) relief from the depression. Cronholm (1969) reports giving patients numbers to remember at various short intervals before an ECS treatment, and testing their recall of the numbers later. As expected, the nearer presentation of a number was to the ECS, the more poorly it was later recalled. This result, however, could be due to differences in the amount of rehearsal, rather than in the degree of consolidation, since rehearsal apparently was not prevented.

Because of the obvious difficulties in studying retrograde amnesia experimentally in humans, most experimental work on the problem has been done using animals. A favorite experimental paradigm in these studies uses a *passive avoidance* procedure—so called because the animal demonstrates memory for an aversive event by *not* making a response that it ordinarily would make. An experiment by Chorover and Schiller (1965) demonstrates the technique. Each rat was placed on a safe platform, surrounded by an electrified grid. Upon stepping off the platform onto the grid the rat received a painful footshock. When placed back on the platform, an animal that remembers the experience will not step off—at least not as quickly as the first time. Step-down latency, therefore, can be used to measure retention. The longer the latency, the better the animal is assumed to remember the footshock.

Chorover and Schiller also administered ECS, delivered through the wires attached to the animals' ears. The ECS was given from $\frac{1}{2}$ second to 30 seconds following the footshock. The retention test was given 24 hours later. The numbers of rats not stepping down within 20 seconds (thus, presumably remembering the footshock) is shown as a function of the footshock–ECS interval in Figure 11.9. Apparently, the tendency for ECS to interfere with memory of the footshock was greater when it occurred soon after the event than if it was delayed. The animals getting ECS after a 30-second delay performed no differently from control animals that had received no ECS at all. The time course of consolidation that one would infer from Figure 11.9 agrees nicely with what two-process memory theorists would predict.

Unfortunately, other research has cast doubt on the meaning of this seemingly simple finding. First, the time course of the apparent consolidation process has been found to vary from a few seconds to several hours, depending on details of the experiment such as the difficulty of the task and the amount of current used as ECS. Second, the retrograde amnesia apparently is not present shortly after ECS admin-

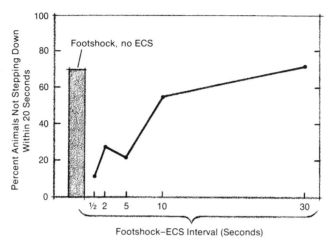

Figure 11.9 Passive avoidance of footshock as a function of the interval between footshock and ECS during training. [Adapted from Chorover and Schiller, 1965.]

istration, but instead develops over a period of several hours. It is as though the effect of the ECS were, not to directly cause the memory trace to be forgotten, but to make it more susceptible to forgetting. (Curiously enough, the retrograde amnesia may not appear even over a 24-hour period, if the rat is kept in the dark during the interval.) Third, various drugs injected into the brain also produce retrograde amnesia—but the duration of the amnesic period can be as short as brief seconds or as long as several days, depending on the drug, the dosage, and the retention interval. Some drugs interact with ECS in producing amnesic effects (for a more detailed discussion of the consolidation literature, see Deutsch and Deutsch, 1973). Finally, it has been shown that the apparently forgotten experience of the footshock can be recovered, by giving the subject relevant retrieval cues—a finding known as the *reminder effect*. A footshock, not given in the test apparatus, will serve as such a reminder. It may be sufficient to simply give the animal several test trials, without footshock. Quartermain, McEwen, and Azmitia (1972) found that such test trials, one per day on four successive days, were enough to bring the performance of amnesic animals up to the level of the no-ECS controls.

The relevance of this tangle of results for two-process memory theory is difficult to assess. Indeed, experiments on rats may be irrelevant—human memory might very well involve distinct short-term and long-term mechanisms even if memory in rats did not. As uncontrolled as they are, therefore, naturalistic observations of the recall of patients recovering from head injury or ECS therapy may be the best available source of data on retrograde amnesia in humans.

Russell and Nathan (1946) summarized a large number of clinical observations of retrograde amnesia resulting from concussion. In such cases, the doctor tries to assess the extent of the amnesia in an interview. In severe cases of head injury, interviews may be conducted several times during the patient's hospital stay. The extent of the blank period can sometimes be estimated fairly exactly. Following an automobile or motorcycle accident, for example, the last thing the victim can recall may be passing a particular house. Knowing the distance from the house to the accident scene, and the approximate rate of travel, one can calculate the corresponding time interval.

Russell and Nathan claimed that concussion almost invariably results in some memory loss, extending backward in time from the concussion. The extent is variable, however, ranging from a few seconds to many years. Only very rarely does the patient recall the impact itself (a blinding flash or a ringing in the ears). Most interesting is the observation that the period of amnesia shrinks. As the patient recovers, his memories return, with the older ones returning first. Eventually, most of the forgotten information recovers, leaving a permanent retrograde amnesia which is usually of less than a minute's duration, but may be as long as several days.

It is always possible that information obtained from clinical interviews may be biased by the interviewer's expectations. Is it true, for example, that more recent memories are the most easily lost and the last to return? Or could it be just that memories of less important events (for example, seeing a particular house) are disrupted more easily than those of more important events (for example, getting married)?

Squire, Slater, and Chase (1975) used an objective test to measure retrograde amnesia following administration of ECS treatments for depression. The test concerned memory for "prime-time" television programs that had been cancelled because of poor ratings. Programs were sampled, using a method designed to eliminate bias, from the years 1957 through 1972. The format of the test was a four-alternative forced choice. (A typical question was: Which of the following was a TV show? (a) Carbine Caravan, (b) The New Breed, (c)

Breakfast with Bernie, (d) Horse Trader's Hour.) Testing was done in early 1974. Sixteen patients were administered one form of the test before their first ECS treatment and another, of equal difficulty, one hour after their fifth treatment. The data are shown in Figure 11.10. Apparently, ECS disrupted recent memories ($1\frac{1}{2}$ to $2\frac{1}{2}$ years old) more than earlier ones, as Russell and Nathan's clinical observations would lead one to expect. Squire, Slater, and Chase also found objective evidence that the period of retrograde amnesia shrinks. They read-ministered the test 1 to 2 weeks later, and found that memory for the more recent programs had almost fully recovered (to 60 percent). All this tends to confirm Russell and Nathan's (1946) observations con-cerning retrograde amnesia.

How does all this relate to the distinction between the STS and LTS? Certainly, the observation that most concussion victims suffer a per-manent loss of memory for events occurring less than a minute before the injury is consistent with two-process theory. But this might be explained in other ways: the events may sometimes be unavailable because the person was daydreaming at the time—indeed, such a lapse in attention may have caused the accident. And there is the troublesome fact that the permanent amnesia sometimes extends over

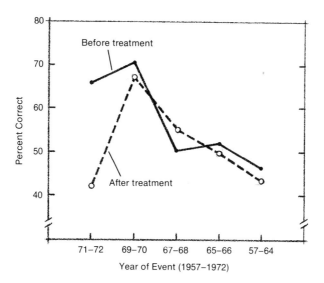

Figure 11.10 Effect of ECS on memory for television programs from various years. [After Squire, Slater, and Chase, 1975. Copyright 1975 by the American Associa-tion for the Advancement of Science.]

several hours, or even days. The consolidation postulated by two-process theorists is over with in several seconds. Finally, the temporary amnesia, at first extending back for as long as several years and then shrinking, with the older memories returning first, is a major puzzle for two-process theories. [Wickelgren's (1974) notion that the fragility of a memory trace decreases with time might be used to account for the fact that the more recent memories are most susceptible to disruption, but this theory contains no ready explanation of why memories recover at all.] Two-process theories that assume a relatively brief period of consolidation receive as much contradiction from the retrograde amnesia literature as they receive support.

Prolonged Anterograde Amnesia

To many investigators, the most convincing evidence for two-process memory theory comes from instances of severe memory disturbance associated with brain damage. Patients exhibiting this disturbance are found in several categories (Barbizet, 1970): some are victims of war wounds or traffic accidents; others have suffered from brain tumors, strokes, or encephalitis (inflammation of the brain brought on by diseases such as mumps or typhoid). Most of the available cases, however, are chronic alcoholics, whose brain damage apparently was brought on, not by alcohol itself, but by an associated vitamin deficiency. The pattern of symptoms exhibited by this latter class of patients is often referred to as *Korsakoff's syndrome,* after a doctor who described it in 1889. Of even greater theoretical importance is a tiny group of patients whose memory problems were brought on not by "natural" causes but by the surgeon's knife. An operation involving partial removal of the hippocampus on both sides of the brain was undertaken to relieve a variety of problems, including chronic schizophrenia and debilitating epilepsy. Once its effects on memory were discovered, the technique was largely abandoned, so not many such patients exist; and because of their mental disturbance, few of the existing ones are suitable experimental subjects. One, however, has probably provided more memory data than any other individual subject since Ebbinghaus. He is referred to in the memory and neurology literature by his initials: H. M.

Patients in these categories may differ somewhat, but the form of the brain damage and its effects on behavior are quite similar. The brain damage almost invariably is in one or more related structures in the midbrain, referred to collectively as the "circuit of Papez." This circuit includes, among other structures, the hippocampus (which attaches to the temporal lobe) and the mammillary bodies. The effects on behavior are simply described as a *prolonged anterograde amnesia.* (Anterograde amnesia, unlike retrograde amnesia, extends *forward* in time from the precipitating incident—in other words, it is an inability to permanently learn new information.)

The profound effect of such an inability on a person's life is well illustrated by the case of H. M., who underwent his operation in 1953, at the age of 27, for epilepsy, and whose condition has changed little in the intervening years (see Milner, Corkin, and Teuber, 1968). Following the operation,

> His language was normal and so was his verbal span. He suffered, however, from such a gradual forgetting that he retained practically nothing of the events of his current life. For instance, six months after his operation, his family moved into another house in the same street; he could never remember the new address and always returned to the old house. His parents moved again a few years later, and, although he seemed to know that he had moved, he could not remember the address. He could not remember where things belonged; he mowed the lawn regularly, but had to ask his mother each time where the mower was kept. He did the same puzzles day after day and reread the same magazines. He did not recognize or know the names of his neighbors, and invariably treated them as strangers. . . .
>
> When he learned of the death of an uncle of whom he was very fond, he became very moved, but forgot about it immediately and showed the same emotion each time he received the same news.
>
> He managed to retain three figures for about fifteen minutes, provided he were not interrupted by anything and was able to repeat them mentally.
>
> He had a retrograde amnesia covering approximately the year prior to his operation; on the other hand, twelve years after the latter he had preserved almost intact his store of earlier memories, and was inclined to repeat the same anecdote several times to the same person without being aware of the repetition (Barbizet, 1970, p. 60).

The symptoms exhibited by such patients may vary somewhat, but summaries often emphasize three points: (a) The recall of events that occurred prior to the brain damage, for example during childhood, is unimpaired. (b) The patient is incapable of permanent new learning. New information is rapidly forgotten unless he is able to rehearse. (c) Verbal skills, intelligence, and the memory span are unimpaired.

It is easy to see why these cases of brain damage are of great interest to two-process theorists. Here we have people who have normal memory spans—hence, encoding into and retrieval from the STS must be intact. They remember events from before the brain damage occurred—thus, retrieval from the LTS is intact. If they are incapable of permanent new learning, it must be the *consolidation* process that is faulty. The symptoms can be explained simply: these people have lost the ability to copy information from the STS into the LTS. It is difficult to see how any other kind of theory could explain their symptoms.

But each point in the summary of their symptoms might be questioned. Let us examine some of the evidence. First, is it true that memory for events prior to the brain damage is intact? Until recently, this belief rested largely on clinical interviews, with little objective evidence to back it up. An objective test, however, was made by Marslen-Wilson and Teuber (1975). These investigators asked subjects to identify public figures from news photographs taken from five different decades, ranging from the 1920s through the 1960s. Among their subjects were H. M., a group of Korsakoff patients, and a group of normal subjects. The ability of these subjects to identify the photographs is shown in Figure 11.11. H. M. and the Korsakoffs remembered events from the remote past as well as did the normal controls. But they were markedly worse on events from the 1950s and 1960s. This result is consistent with clinical descriptions, and also with the conclusion that it is new learning, rather than LTM retrieval, that is impaired.

Notice that according to the passage from Barbizet quoted above, H. M. had not only prolonged anterograde amnesia, but also retrograde amnesia, for events occurring a year or so before the operation. This seems to contradict the assertion that it is only consolidation that is impaired, since two-process theories typically assume that consolidation is over in less than a minute. Why, then, should H. M. have retrograde amnesia extending back for more than a year? This observation may not pose as much of a problem for the two-process theory as it at first appears. For months before his operation, H. M. was probably heavily drugged. His epilepsy was severe, and at the time of the operation, was growing worse; and the epileptic focus was in the

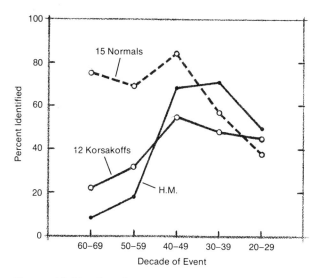

Figure 11.11 Identification of photographs of public figures by H. M., Korsakoff patients, and normal subjects. [Data from Marslen-Wilson and Teuber, 1975.]

hippocampal region of the brain, which is known to be associated with learning. It seems likely, therefore, that H. M.'s ability to learn was disrupted to some extent even before his operation.

Is it true that these amnesic patients are incapable of new learning? Strictly speaking, no. The problem varies in degree. Korsakoff patients can learn to identify fragmented pictures and words, and to learn paired associates made up of closely related words (for example, TABLE–CHAIR). But they do worse on these tasks than normal control subjects do. Even H. M., whose memory disturbance is profound, is able to learn perceptual motor skills—again, however, his learning is slower than that of normals. He sometimes remembers particularly important events for a day or so, and recalled President Kennedy's assassination several years after it happened. If the retrieval cues are adequate, H. M.'s memory may even be made to appear quite good. Given prompts including occupations, initials, first names, and so on, he was able to identify 80 percent of the public figures from 1960 to 1969 that he did so poorly on from the photographs alone (see Figure 11.11). Korsakoffs got 83 percent and normals 100 percent with prompts (Marslen-Wilson and Teuber, 1975).

Clearly, then, these amnesic patients have not completely lost the ability to learn. It has even been suggested that their learning ability is intact, and that their only problem is retrieval; or that the incoming information is encoded but is not properly organized. A two-process theorist, however, can handle these observations by assuming that the consolidation process, while not entirely lost, is severely damaged. LTS traces are formed—but they are usually so weak that they are very difficult to retrieve.

Finally, is it true that the immediate retention of amnesic patients is normal? The evidence for this conclusion appears weak. A distractor-task experiment by Cermak, Butters, and Goodglass (1971) found Korsakoff patients to be much worse than either normals or non-amnesic alcoholic controls. Three-consonant trigrams were used, which subjects did *not* have to recall in the correct order. The retention curves are shown in Figure 11.12. Within just three seconds of presentation, the Korsakoff patients were able to recall less than the controls.

In the memory-span task, Drachman and Arbit (1966) found the average digit span of five patients with hippocampal lesions (including H. M.) to be 7.0, compared to 8.3 for the controls. H. M.'s, span, often said to be "normal," was put at 6—quite low for someone of his high intelligence. Six amnesic patients tested by Baddeley and Warrington

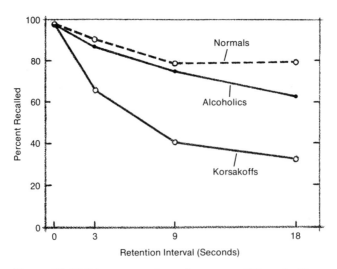

Figure 11.12 Distractor-task performance of Korsakoff patients and controls. [Adapted from Cermak, Butters, and Goodglass, 1971.]

(1970) had an average digit span of only 5.7. Such data will not convince the skeptic that the memory span of amnesics is unimpaired.

The phenomenon of prolonged anterograde amnesia may be the best existing evidence for the two-process memory theory, but it is not as convincing as two-process theorists have claimed. There are two main problems: First, amnesic patients remember some things that happened during the period of anterograde amnesia, particularly when appropriate retrieval cues are provided. Thus, it is clear that their ability to learn has not been completely destroyed. Second, it has not been established that the immediate memory of amnesiacs is normal. It may be that their initial encoding is impaired, or the new traces they form are simply subject to rapid decay. Thus, it is not yet clear that their problem cannot be explained as well by a one-process as by a two-process theory of memory.

Conclusion

Does the storage phase of memory consist of one process or two? As we have seen, a great variety of phenomena have been interpreted as support for the two-process view. To the skeptic, however (and ideally a scientist should treat all theories with some skepticism), no single kind of evidence that has been offered so far is entirely convincing. But shouldn't the variety of evidence be given some weight? This aspect of the question can be looked at in two ways. On the one hand, a person might argue that the two-process view should be accepted because it accounts for so many diverse phenomena in a simple, integrated way. On the other hand, he might criticize psychologists for becoming too enthusiastic over an unproven idea, trying to hang too many phenomena on an elaborate theoretical framework that is poorly constructed and without adequate support. Two-process theory, not long ago accepted by most memory theorists, has had a recent decline in popularity. The issue is far from settled, however; and as we have seen, it is complex. We can expect it to continue to occupy investigators for some time to come.

WHAT CAUSES FORGETTING?

The question of why we forget is a central one for memory theory. Earlier, we touched on two hypotheses that have been offered to account for forgetting—the autonomous trace change hypothesis, derived from Gestalt theory, and the permanent memory hypothesis, which holds that all forgetting is due to retrieval failure, and that true forgetting does not occur. Here, we shall examine in a more systematic fashion the general question of what causes forgetting. It is particularly instructive to view this issue in historical perspective, as it offers some clear instances of the reincarnation of long-dead theoretical ideas in a seemingly new form.

The Law of Disuse

If a hundred citizens were stopped on a street corner and asked why we forget, the chances are that the large majority would attribute forgetting to the passage of time. That intuition is apparently shared by psychologists. Prior to the 1930s, virtually every philosopher or psychologist who wrote about forgetting stated some version of what was called the *law of disuse*. The basic notion was that a habit (or memory trace) that is not used, or exercised, tends to fade away. Thorndike expressed the law formally, in terms of S–R bonds:

> When a modifiable connection is *not* made between a situation and a response during a length of time, that connection's strength is decreased (Thorndike, 1914, p. 4).

Learning theorists, however, were primarily interested in acquisition. Few paid much attention to forgetting until the appearance in 1932 of a paper by John A. McGeoch, attacking the law of disuse.

McGeoch (1932) attacked the law of disuse from several directions. In the first place, he said, it really says nothing about the cause of forgetting. "Time, in and of itself, does nothing." The only role of time is to provide an opportunity for the true causes of forgetting to operate. In seeking the causes of forgetting, therefore, we must consider what happens during the retention interval. In the second place, he said, there are clear exceptions to the law of disuse. Extinction occurs when a habit is being exercised, and spontaneous recovery when it is not. This is the opposite of what the law of disuse predicts. In the third place, he argued, even when forgetting is correlated with time there are other manipulations that can be shown to have a more powerful effect. These are the manipulations shown experimentally to produce retroactive interference. The simplest way to explain forgetting, then, would be to attribute it all to retroactive interference, caused by activity during the retention interval.

The Interference Theory

A number of studies, at the time of McGeoch's paper, had shown that a second list learned during the retention interval of List 1 caused List 1 to be partly forgotten, and that the amount of forgetting depended on the similarity of the materials in the two lists. McGeoch, however, wanted to argue that substantial retroactive interference could result from everyday activity. He based this claim on the results of experiments comparing retention over periods of sleep and waking. The classic study on this topic, done by Jenkins and Dallenbach (1924) found that lists of nonsense syllables learned just before going to sleep were forgotten less rapidly over an 8-hour period than were lists learned at the beginning of the day. It is possible that the retiring subjects, having nothing better to do while waiting to fall asleep, rehearsed the lists. It is also possible that memory traces decay faster during the daytime (when metabolic rate is high) than at night. Neither alternative explanation for the sleep findings was considered, however. McGeoch's explanation was that the mental activity during the day produced more retroactive interference than sleep did. Apparently, psychologists found McGeoch's arguments thoroughly persuasive, because, for the next twenty-five years, retroactive interference was considered the primary—if not the only—cause of forgetting. When this hypothesis was eventually questioned, the challenger was not disuse, but proactive interference, produced by previously learned material.

Although the basic phenomenon of proactive interference had been known for years, it was considered a minor factor in forgetting until an influential paper by B. J. Underwood (1957) appeared. Prior to that time, it was routine in experiments on human learning and memory to use the same subjects over and over again in different conditions—a practice this paper showed to be a grave error. Underwood had puzzled over several published experiments in which subjects learned a list to mastery and then attempted to recall it 24 hours later. During the 24 hours, no other lists were learned. Percentages recalled were wildly different in the various experiments, ranging from as high as 82 percent to as low as 12 percent. Since the retention intervals always spanned 24 hours of routine daily activity, something other than disuse or retroactive interference must have caused these differences in recall. What Underwood discovered was that retention was closely related to the number of lists the subjects had learned previously in the same experiment. When the list being tested was the first, recall was around 75 percent correct. When there had been 20 previous lists, recall was below 20 percent. The relationship between recall and number of previous lists, for 14 of the studies Underwood examined, is shown in Figure 11.13.

Underwood's paper argued that the major cause of forgetting in most experiments was not retroactive interference, as McGeoch had claimed, but proactive interference, from similar material that had been learned previously. The task remained of tying retroactive and proactive interference together in a single comprehensive *interference theory of forgetting*. The theory that was developed was based on the conditioning analogy (for example, Underwood and Postman, 1960).

A key experimental demonstration underlying interference theory was conducted by Barnes and Underwood (1959). It was directly concerned with retroactive interference, and only indirectly with proac-

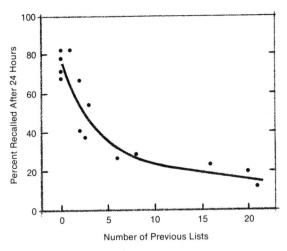

Figure 11.13 Recall after 24 hours in 14 different studies, plotted as a function of the number of previous lists learned. [After Underwood, 1957. Copyright 1957 by the American Psychological Association. Reprinted by permission.]

tive interference. Originally, McGeoch (1932) had attributed retroactive interference to "response competition"—what we have called retrieval confusion. The basic idea was that after a subject learns two lists—say, paired-associates lists bearing an A–B, A–C relationship—he remembers associations from both lists, but does not know which one to give. The confusion over whether B or C is from List 1 causes errors. Over the years, however, evidence had accumulated suggesting that more than retrieval confusion might be involved—that, in fact, learning A–C might cause the destruction, or *unlearning*, of the previously learned A–B. Barnes and Underwood (1959) demonstrated this unlearning process rather directly. They had subjects learn two lists having an A–B, A–C relationship, and interrupted the subjects at various points during List 2 learning to give them a special test (called an MMFR test). On this test, the stimulus terms (A) were listed on a sheet, each with two empty blank spaces underneath. The subject was told to write down *both* responses (B and C) for each stimulus, if he could. This test is important because it avoids retrieval confusion. It does not matter whether the subject knows whether B or C came from the first list, since making that discrimination is not part of his task.

The recall of List 1 and List 2 responses, at various points during the learning of List 2, is shown in Figure 11.14. Clearly the MMFR test, for which retrieval confusion is irrelevant, does not eliminate all retroactive interference. The more trials subjects had on A–C, the less well they recalled A–B. As A–C was learned, A–B was being (partially) unlearned.

As it stood in 1959, the interference theory of forgetting explained retroactive and proactive interference as outlined in Chapter 9. Retroactive interference was assumed to be due partly to retrieval interference and partly to unlearning. In keeping with the conditioning analogy, unlearning was equated with extinction, and extinguished bonds were assumed to be capable of spontaneous recovery. As time passed following A–C learning, the extinguished A–B associations were assumed to recover, eventually causing retrieval confusion during attempts to recall A–C. Spontaneous recovery was thus held to explain proactive interference. In a paper written for a conference held in 1959, Postman (1961) was able to claim: "Interference theory occupies an unchallenged position as the major significant analysis of the process of forgetting." To most memory researchers, the law of disuse was a mere historical curiosity.

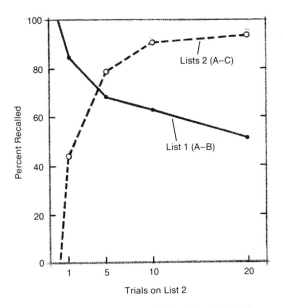

Figure 11.14 Percentages of List 1 and List 2 responses correctly recalled as a function of practice on List 2. [After Barns and Underwood, 1959. Copyright 1959 by the American Psychological Association. Reprinted by permission.]

Forgetting in Short-Term Memory

At about this time, however, the study of short-term retention was experiencing a rebirth, marked by the publication of experiments using the distractor task (Brown, 1958; Peterson and Peterson, 1959). The question of what caused the rapid forgetting found with the distractor procedure was an intriguing one. Intuitively, it seems that when we want to remember something—say a telephone number—for a short time, we must rehearse it or the memory will quickly fade away. Such intuitive considerations led Brown (1958) to propose that forgetting over intervals of a few seconds is due to *time-dependent decay*. It was assumed that decay of a memory trace could be forestalled by rehearsal, but as soon as rehearsal was prevented by a distractor activity such as counting backward, rapid decay would set in.

The decay theory of short-term forgetting became fairly popular. It was, of course, just a restatement of the discredited (and by this time largely forgotten) law of disuse. If Thorndike's "modifiable S–R connection" is replaced by "memory trace," and "making" (or exercising) the connection by "rehearsing" the trace, the law of disuse becomes the principle of time-dependent decay. Champions of decay theory, however, did not advocate that interference theory be abandoned— they argued instead that this was one more piece of evidence for a two-process theory. Forgetting in the STS, in their view, was due to time-dependent decay, while forgetting in the LTS was due to interference.

Interference theorists, having once banished disuse from forgetting theory, saw as a challenge its return in this thinly disguised form. But could either proactive or retroactive interference play a role in the distractor task?

Keppel and Underwood (1962) set out to show that proactive interference was involved. Peterson and Peterson (1959) had tested their subjects over and over again, on one trigram after another. Perhaps the rapid forgetting they found was caused by proactive interference from previously presented items. If this were so, the more previous tests there had been, the more rapid forgetting would be. The Keppel and Underwood study supported this conjecture. In one of their experiments, for example, each subject was tested six different times for recall of visually presented trigrams, following either 3 seconds or 18 seconds of backward counting. Performance is plotted as a function of the item tested in Figure 11.15. While recall after the 3-second interval was not affected appreciably by the number of previous items, recall after 18 seconds obviously was. Apparently, the more previous items had been presented, the faster the current item was forgotten. This is exactly what the hypothesis of proactive interference predicts.

Does the proactive interference found in short-term memory experiments obey the same laws as proactive interference in long-term retention? One variable known to affect the latter is similarity. Experiments demonstrating an effect of similarity in short-term memory have been done by Wickens and his colleagues. One of their findings will illustrate the basic technique. Wickens and Clark (1968) showed subjects three-word combinations, had them count backward by three's for 15 seconds, and then requested recall. This was done for five successive tests. The meanings of the three words presented for a given test had either been judged to be of high "potency" (for example, STEEL, MOUNTAIN, SCIENCE, COLLEGE, OFFICER) or low "potency" (for example, KISS, VOICE, BEAUTIFUL, BABY, FLOWER, DREAM). Roughly speaking, high-potency words refer to

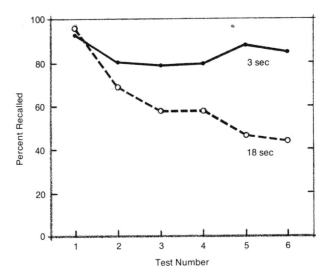

Figure 11.15 Recall after 3 and 18 seconds of distractor activity, as a function of test number. [After Keppel and Underwood, 1962. Copyright 1962 by Academic Press, Inc.]

concepts that are "hard," and low-potency words to concepts that are "soft." In one condition, the words presented on all five tests were drawn from the same one of these two categories (for example, low-potency words on all five tests). In the other, they were drawn from the same category for the first four tests, but were drawn from the other category on the fifth. As Figure 11.16 shows, the shift from high- to low-potency words (and vice versa) on the fifth test eliminated much of the interference the previous items had produced. Subjects who experienced the shift forgot considerably less on Test 5 than those who did not. This phenomenon is called *release from proactive interference.* Many types of shifts in to-be-remembered materials have this effect (see Wickens, 1970). It shows that proactive interference in short-term memory, as in long-term memory, is determined by the similarity of the materials.

One other finding concerning proactive interference in short-term retention, however, could not be anticipated from what was known from studies of long-term memory. Loess and Waugh (1967), using the distractor task, found that the time between successive tests was an

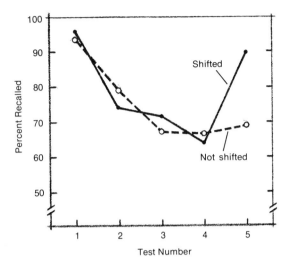

Figure 11.16 Short-term recall in the "release from proactive interference" paradigm. [After Wickens and Clark, 1968. Copyright 1968 by the American Psychological Association. Reprinted by permission.]

important factor. They gave subjects rest periods between tests, varying from 0 seconds to 5 minutes in duration. When the rest intervals were short, proactive interference built up rapidly. When they were as long as 2 minutes, no proactive interference was evident. The extinction–recovery theory of interference predicts no such effect.

Can an equivalent phenomenon be demonstrated in long-term memory? The answer is yes. Underwood and Freund (1968) had subjects learn two paired-associates lists having an A–B, A–C relationship. Half the subjects learned both lists on Thursday, and half learned List 1 on Monday and List 2 on Thursday. All were tested the following day for retention of List 2. The amount of proactive interference was considerably greater for the subjects who had learned A–B and A–C on the same day than it was for those who had learned the two lists spaced three days apart. Apparently, the effect on proactive interference of the temporal spacing of memorized materials is essentially the same, whether short or long intervals are involved. The laws of proactive interference do not appear to necessitate an STS–LTS distinction.

Retroactive interference also plays a role in short-term retention. A number of experiments have shown that the difficulty of the distractor task is directly related to the rate of forgetting; and it has also been demonstrated that the more similar the distractor task activity is to the processing required by the to-be-remembered stimuli, the more rapidly those stimuli are forgotten. The experiments referred to earlier, by Parkinson (1972) and by Nagge (1935; see Figure 11.4)—suggest that effects of similarity on retroactive interference are essentially the same in long-term and short-term retention.

Causes of Interference

A memory theorist is not likely to be completely satisfied with the conclusion that both proactive and retroactive interference cause forgetting, in both short-term and long-term retention. The reason is that proactive and retroactive interference are not explanations of forgetting. They are statements of empirical laws, relating certain experimental manipulations to certain effects on behavior. Memory theorists are interested in discovering underlying mechanisms that will explain the empirical laws. Why do similar materials interfere more than dissimilar materials? Why does proactive interference increase over time? Why does it decrease as a function of temporal separation? An adequate theory will account for all these findings. The extinction–recovery theory, as we have seen, explains some facts but not others. It does not explain, for example, why proactive interference is greater when List 1 and List 2 were learned on the same day than when they were widely separated in time. And it is hard to see how the S–R conditioning analogy applies to the differential effects of shadowing on memory for auditory and visual stimuli, as found by Parkinson (1972).

To determine exactly why interference occurs has been the aim of many memory experiments, and it has proved to be exceedingly difficult. To understand why, one must consider some of the possible mechanisms that might be at work.

Consider retroactive interference. Suppose, (a) X is learned; (b) Y, which is similar to X, is learned; and (c) recall of X is tested and found to be poor relative to recall in a proper control condition in which Y was not learned. What are the ways Y could have produced this effect? There are several:

1. *Permanent unlearning*—The activity of learning Y partly destroys the memory trace of X.

2. *Temporary inhibition*—The activity of learning Y makes the memory trace of X temporarily inaccessible, but the trace recovers with time.

3. *"Acid bath" hypothesis*—Highly similar memory traces "eat away" at each other for as long as they coexist in storage (Posner and Konick, 1966).

4. *Retrieval confusion*—The subject retrieves both X and Y, but cannot discriminate their recencies, to determine which one occurred first.

5. *Blocking*—The subject retrieves Y, which he knows is incorrect, but this prevents or delays retrieval of X.

6. *Altered cues*—The subject establishes retrieval cues during the learning of Y which are inappropriate for X. These persist into the recall test. (Suppose X is the pair BALL–WIG and Y is the pair BALL–PARROT. In learning X, the subject thinks of a girl wearing a wig at a dance (ball); in learning Y he thinks of a parrot sitting on a ball. On the recall test for X, he continues to give the second meaning to BALL.)

Now, consider proactive interference. Suppose following the learning of X and Y we test for recall of Y, and find it poorer than in an appropriate control condition lacking X. There are several ways X might interfere with Y:

1. *Initial strength*—When learning Y, the subject thinks about X, because of the similarity. The initial strength of the trace of Y, because of this distraction, is low.

2. *Encoding quality*—Because he previously learned X, the subject may encode Y in a qualitatively different way than he would have otherwise. The code used may be less durable (for example, phonemic, rather than semantic).

3. *"Acid bath"*—The traces of X and Y eat away at each other in storage.

4. *Retrieval confusion*—X and Y are both retrieved but the subject cannot tell which occurred more recently.

5. *Blocking*—X is retrieved, and temporarily blocks the retrieval of Y.

6. *Permanent unlearning*—The subject anticipates a retention test, and rehearses X after Y is learned. This rehearsal tends to destroy the trace of Y. (Evidence that some proactive interference may be due to unlearning—basically a retroactive interference mechanism—has been presented by Houston, 1969).

The possible interference mechanisms just outlined have all been proposed at one time or another by various investigators; the list, however, is not necessarily complete. To the reader, some of them may seem very much alike, and in fact it is not always easy to design experiments that will discriminate among them. If only one of the proposed mechanisms were at work, it probably would not be too difficult to determine which it was; but the evidence suggests that the causes of proactive and retroactive interference are complex. Several of the proposed mechanisms may be at work. The task of determining the causes of interference is likely to continue to occupy researchers for many years.

A Re-evaluation of the Law of Disuse

Although experiments on both short- and long-term retention have demonstrated that interference is a potent cause of forgetting, our discussion of forgetting must return again to disuse; for the interference theorists have not proved that time-dependent decay does not occur. Their argument has been that the effectiveness of interference is beyond dispute, and that a pure interference theory of forgetting is more parsimonious than a theory that admits both interference and decay. There are reasons, however, to believe that an adequate theory of forgetting may have to include both factors.

Studies of long-term retention have always found some forgetting in the conditions in which no proactive or retroactive interference was deliberately induced. The evidence for proactive interference assembled by Underwood (1957) and displayed in Figure 11.13, for example, shows that 24-hour recall of the first list learned was about 75 percent correct. What caused the 25 percent retention loss? It could be proactive and retroactive interference from nonexperimental sources, but no one has been able to provide solid support for this hypothesis. One could just as easily attribute it to time-dependent decay. Also, there is the question of why a List 1 learned just prior to List 2 causes more proactive interference than one learned three days earlier

(Underwood and Freund, 1968). One possibility is that a substantial amount of forgetting of List 1 occurs over three days, reducing its potential for interference. A similar explanation can be given for the fact that when tests in the distractor task are separated by as long as two minutes, no proactive interference is evident (Loess and Waugh, 1967). Two minutes may be enough time for substantial decay of the prior items, eliminating them as a cause of interference.

Experiments on short-term retention have been specifically designed to find evidence for time-dependent decay. One study by Waugh and Norman (1965) used the probe task, in which a string of digits is heard, followed by a probe digit which cues the subject to respond with the next digit in the list (see Chapter 8). Waugh and Norman presented digit strings at two different rates: either 1 second per item or $\frac{1}{4}$ second per item—four times as fast. They hoped to determine whether forgetting in the probe task was basically a function of time or of the number of intervening items. In the $\frac{1}{4}$-second condition, retention intervals were much shorter, so if forgetting were primarily a matter of time-dependent decay, the amount forgotten in this condition would be expected to be much less. Percent recalled is plotted as a function of number of intervening items in Figure 11.17. The similarity of the 1-second and $\frac{1}{4}$-second curves convinced Waugh and Norman that decay was not a factor in short-term retention.

The procedure used by Waugh and Norman, however, confounds presentation rate and retention interval. It is possible that greater forgetting was produced in the 1-second condition, but was balanced by better initial learning. Indeed, the differences between the two curves are exactly as this hypothesis predicts. The 1-second retention curve starts out higher than the $\frac{1}{4}$-second curve, suggesting better learning, and ends up below, suggesting greater decay.

Reitman (1974) approached the question of whether decay is a factor in short-term retention in a different way. She used the distractor task, choosing for one of her conditions a distractor activity that was demanding, but did not require verbal processing of any kind. The idea was to come as close as possible to a "perfect mental vacuum" during the retention interval, while still keeping the subject too busy to rehearse. The distractor activity she used was signal detection: the subject listened continuously for a very weak tone, pressing a button each time it was heard. On each test, the subject saw a five-word combination, and then either (a) tried to recall the words immediately, or else (b) engaged in signal detection activity for 15 seconds, and then

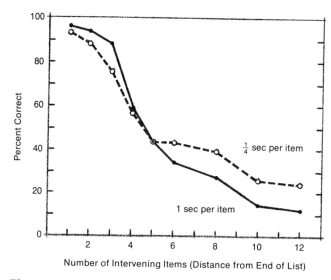

Figure 11.17 Recall in the probe task, with digits presented at fast and slow rates. [After Waugh and Norman, 1965. Copyright 1965 by the American Psychological Association. Reprinted by permission.]

attempted to recall the words. Compared with immediate recall, performance after the 15 seconds of tone detection showed an average retention loss of 12 percent. Subjects who admitted trying to rehearse the words during tone detection showed a loss of 7 percent; those who claimed they had not rehearsed showed a loss of 15 percent. Although small, this degree of forgetting convinced Reitman that decay was indeed a factor in forgetting over short intervals of time. It should be pointed out, however, that proactive interference cannot be completely ruled out. Intervals separating successive tests, in Reitman's study, were within the range where proactive interference has been found.

Conclusion

There is no convincing evidence, at this time, that the causes of forgetting over short and long retention intervals are different. Most of the forgetting studied in memory experiments can be classified as either proactive or retroactive interference. The mechanisms underlying these two types of forgetting are not yet well understood. While inter-ference theorists claim that all forgetting can be explained without reference to disuse (or time-dependent decay), there are some reasons to question this conclusion. The law of disuse, long in dispute, may yet take a place alongside interference as a necessary principle in a com-plete and adequate theory of forgetting.

12

How Much Do We Know
About Memory?

In Chapter 7, we asked how much light had been thrown on the nature of learning by standard laboratory investigations of classical and instrumental conditioning. We saw that there are many reasons to question the generality of laws of learning discovered using one or two animal species in a handful of different experimental paradigms. Here, the same question is faced, but in a slightly different form. How much do standard laboratory investigations of human memory tell us about human memory in general? Are the laws of memory for visually presented nonsense syllables or words the same as those for sounds, for faces, for visual scenes, for motor skills, for odors, for information read in a textbook, or for the plot of a motion picture? Is memory in children essentially the same as that in the standard experimental subject, the college sophomore? Do members of different cultures remember in the same way?

These are just a few of the legitimate questions that could be asked. We will not be able to consider them all in this chapter, but we will discuss the more prominent doubts that have been raised by persons conducting memory research.

MODALITIES OF MEMORY

Could the laws of memory differ for different types of memory codes? It does not seem unreasonable to think that they might. The brain includes many patches of neural tissue apparently specialized to deal with particular kinds of information. If, among their other functions, these patches of neural tissue retain information over time, then one might well imagine that different types of memory codes could be governed by somewhat different laws. Craik and Lockhart (1972), in their proposal that the two-process view of memory be replaced by a levels-of-processing framework, suggested one such difference—that the rate of forgetting is much faster for memory codes produced by "shallow" processing (for example, sensory codes) than for memory codes produced by "deep" processing (for example, semantic codes).

Sometimes what appears to be a difference between two modalities may actually be a good illustration of a general principle, rather than an exception to it. For example, we have seen that the shadowing task interferes less with memory for letters presented visually than for letters spoken aloud by the experimenter. Shadowing and counting backward interfere even less with motor memory—for example, a kinesthetic memory of a hand movement. But while verbal activity does not interfere with retention of a hand movement, other hand movements during the retention interval do. Such findings can all be considered illustrations of the general principle that the degree of retroactive interference increases with the similarity of the to-be-remembered information and the interfering material. Rather than forcing us to abandon the idea that the laws of memory are the same for all modalities, such findings give it added support.

Other differences among modalities may simply reflect the kind of information for which the modality is specialized. It is often said that the visual modality is best at encoding spatial information (left versus right, above versus below, and so on), while the auditory modality is best at encoding temporal-order information (before versus after, first, second, third, and so on). This is a worthwhile observation, but it is just one of the less obvious differences among modalities. No one would be surprised by the conclusion that vision is specialized for encoding color, audition for pitch, olfaction for odors, touch for pressure, and so on. Different sensory modalities encode different kinds of information, and the associated memory modalities, if they exist, retain them. When we ask whether the laws of memory differ for different modalities, we mean to exclude such differences, for if they are included the general question becomes rather pointless.

Excluding similarity effects, then, and differences in the kinds of information the different modalities encode, let us consider evidence suggesting that the laws of memory may differ for different modalities.

Memory for Pictures

It is often proposed that memory for pictures differs from that for verbal materials. We have seen that pictures are typically remembered much better than words—and this has suggested to some that entirely different mechanisms are involved. But it may just be that words are more similar to one another than are pictures. Indeed, one can make recognition memory for pictures extremely poor just by making the new "lures" very similar to the old "targets."

Another possible difference between memory for pictures and memory for words is that words can be rehearsed, while pictures cannot. Shaffer and Shiffrin (1972) showed subjects a long list of pictures, exposing each for 0.2, 0.5, 1.0, 2.0, or 4.0 seconds, and following each with a blank period of 1.0, 2.0, or 4.0 seconds during which the subject was told to think about (that is, rehearse) the previous slide. Presentation of the list was followed by a recognition-memory test. The surprising result was that, while the duration of exposure of a picture affected memory, the length of the blank rehearsal period following the picture did not. The investigators concluded that there is "no analogue of verbal rehearsal in the visual memory system that can be applied to moderately complex visual stimuli." Other researchers, however, have disputed this conclusion, and the issue is not yet resolved. At present, the hypothesis that rehearsability differentiates verbal from visual memory codes must be considered unproved.

Memory for Odors

If one is looking for a memory modality that might behave differently from audition and vision, a likely candidate is olfaction (smell). The olfactory areas of the brain are among the most primitive and are tied in structurally with the areas involved in emotion. Introspective reports suggest that odors sometimes act as retrieval cues for traces of events experienced as long ago as early childhood. There has been very little objective experimental work on olfactory memory—but the little that has been done has produced intriguing results.

Engen and Ross (1973) performed a recognition-memory experiment in which subjects first sniffed 48 substances that had widely different odors, giving familiarity and pleasantness judgments for each one. A recognition-memory test was then given, either immediately, or 1, 7, or 30 days later. In addition, the experimenters managed to locate 15 or the 37 subjects a year later, to give another test using odors that had not been tested previously. A two-alternative forced-choice test was used—that is, pairs of odors were presented, one old and one new, and the subjects were to choose the one that had been presented before. The results are shown in Figure 12.1. For comparison, recognition-memory data for pictures, obtained by Shepard (1967), are also shown. The horizontal (time) scale of the graph is logarithmic.

As can be seen, memory for odors was rather poor, but well above the chance level of 50 percent correct. Most remarkably, there was little if any forgetting of the odors over a very long time span. Picture memory in the Shepard study, by contrast, was very good at first but eventually dropped below that for odors. While there are a number of differences between these two experiments that make comparison hazardous, the fact is that the rate of forgetting of odors was far slower than anyone doing work on memory for pictures, words, or nonsense syllables would have guessed.

A second intriguing result reported by Engen and Ross was that odors subjects labeled as "familiar" were remembered only slightly

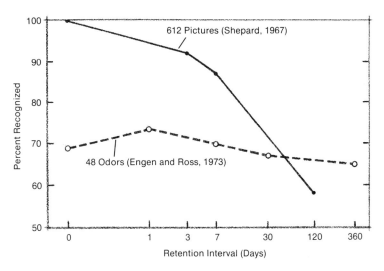

Figure 12.1 Retention of pictures and of odors over long intervals. [Data from Engen and Ross, 1973, and Shepard, 1967.]

better than those they called "unfamiliar." This is in striking contrast
to the effect of familiarity on memory for visual and auditory stimuli.
We saw in Chapter 10 that our capacity to remember a stimulus generally increases with familiarity—apparently because we become more
and more able to deal with the stimulus as a single meaningful unit, or
chunk. It may be that odors are such primitive, unitary stimuli that
the concept of chunking just does not apply. Indeed, it may eventually
be found that olfactory memory differs from memory for other types
of information in a number of ways.

Memory for Motor Skills

Another modality of memory we might expect to differ from memory
for auditory or visual materials is memory for motor skills. Unlike
olfactory memory, motor memory has been the subject of much research; for skilled performance is not only of theoretical interest to
psychologists—it is also of practical interest to those who design indus-
trial equipment, to those who train drivers and pilots, and to coaches
and athletes.

It is difficult to study in the laboratory complex skills such as flying
an aircraft or playing basketball. Most experimental work, therefore,
has been done on simple movements such as those required by the
pursuit rotor, shown in Figure 12.2. This device is very much like a
phonograph turntable. Located on the rotating plate is a small metal-
lic disk. The subject's job is to keep the hand-held stylus in contact
with the disk. To do this, he must move the stylus in a nearly perfect
circle, at a fixed speed. "Time on target" can be recorded on a clock,
which moves only when an electrical circuit between the stylus and
disk target is completed. Until fairly recently, the pursuit rotor was the
most popular apparatus for studying motor skills. Currently, however, much research is aimed at investigating even simpler
movements. Short-term motor memory is often studied by having the
subject move a lever horizontally from a starting position until it hits a
stop. The lever is then returned to the starting position, and after a
short retention interval the subject attempts to reproduce the movement, with the stop removed. Lever, stop, hand, and arm are hidden
from view, so that visual memory is not involved.

For a few years, experiments seemed to indicate that short-term
motor memory was not subject to retroactive or proactive interference. Retroactive interference is obtained, however, if the distractor

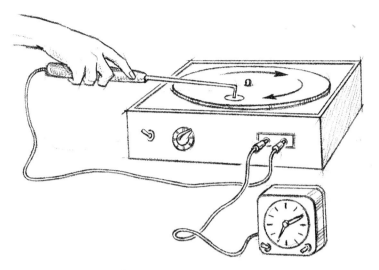

Figure 12.2 A pursuit rotor.

activity filling the retention interval involves hand movements, rather than mental activity. And if the interval between movements is short enough and both movements have to be remembered, proactive interference occurs, as well. Thus, with regard to interference effects, motor memory seems to be much like memory for verbal materials.

A peculiar phenomenon that can be produced reliably in studies of motor skill learning is *reminiscence*. This term refers to an improvement in performance, rather than a decline, over a retention interval in which practice, or rehearsal, does not occur. A good example of reminiscence is seen in a pursuit rotor experiment by Grice and Reynolds (1952). In this experiment, a trial was defined as a 30-second period of practice at tracking the disk. (For all subjects, trials were separated by brief 10-second periods of rest.) There were several groups of subjects in the experiment; the average performance of two groups, shown in the top panel of Figure 12.3, illustrates the phenomenon of reminiscence. In stage one of the experiment, both groups were given 15 trials of practice on the pursuit rotor, using their left hands. In stage two, they were given 15 more trials of practice, exactly as in stage one; but for one group stage two followed stage one immediately (with only the usual 10-second rest), while for the other group, stage two occurred following a 10-minute delay. As can be

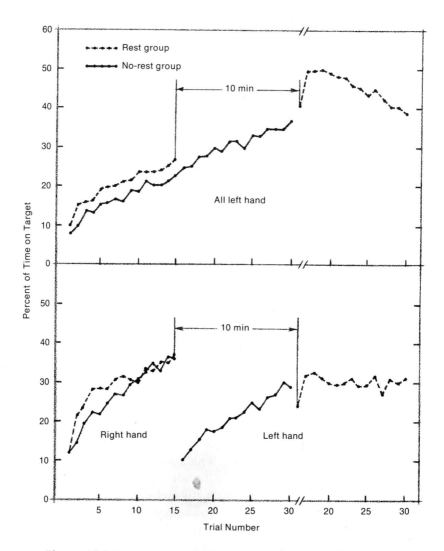

Figure 12.3 Reminiscence in the pursuit rotor task. Top: same hand in stages one and two. Bottom: different hands in stages one and two. [Adapted from Grice and Reynolds, 1952.]

seen from the graph, the subjects who were given the 10-minute rest improved considerably over the interval, from 27 percent to 50 percent time on target. In fact, the rest was apparently just as beneficial to them as the extra 15 trials of practice was to the subjects who had stage two immediately after stage one.

One might assume that reminiscence shown by the group given a prolonged rest is simply due to recovery from fatigue. Indeed, the fact that that group's performance declined from trial 18 to trial 30 in stage two suggests that the fatigue was gradually building back up. Another fact that is consistent with a fatigue interpretation is that *distributed practice* (with long intertrial intervals) leads to better motor skill learning than does *massed practice*. When trials are widely spaced, performance should not be impaired by fatigue. Clark Hull's theory, described in Chapter 5, accounts for reminiscence with a fatigue-like concept: Reactive inhibition (I_R) builds up each time the response R is made. This temporary inhibition can dissipate with time. When it does, we can actually observe an increase in performance over a rest interval. Hull's explanation of reminiscence and his account of spontaneous recovery are essentially the same.

We know, however, that reminiscence cannot be attributed simply to muscle fatigue and recovery. This can readily be inferred from the performance of two other groups of subjects in the Grice and Reynolds study, shown in the bottom panel of Figure 12.3. These subjects were treated the same as those whose data appear in the top panel, except for one important detail. In stage one they practiced tracking with their right hands and in stage two they switched to their left hands. Notice that the group that had a 10-minute rest period performed much better initially than did the group that switched hands without being allowed an extended break. Thus, reminiscence transferred from one hand to another. Whatever causes reminiscence, we may conclude, does not reside in the muscles themselves. If it involves some kind of fatigue, this fatigue must be a state of the central nervous system, not of the muscles. Reminiscence, then, is not the same as recovering from "writer's cramp."

Does reminiscence occur in other kinds of memory tasks? The answer to this question seems to be "no," but it cannot be given with complete confidence. Many studies of reminiscence in memory for poems, and for serial lists of nonsense syllables and words, were published prior to World War II, but most of these studies lacked crucial experimental controls. Sometimes the subject was given combined study and test trials, over and over again, at different intervals after the end of the original learning session. Since each of these trials provided a learning experience, it is not surprising that performance sometimes improved. In other studies, there was no control for rehearsal, and this, too, might lead to an apparent improvement in memory. When such factors as these are controlled, reminiscence in memory for verbal materials is difficult or impossible to show. In memory for motor skills, in contrast, reminiscence is a powerful and reliable effect.

There is another way in which motor skill learning differs from other varieties of human learning. In Chapter 6 we discussed animal experiments on sensory preconditioning and on latent learning. These experiments seemed to show that—at least for higher vertebrates such as rats, pigeons, and dogs—classical conditioning and instrumental conditioning can occur without reinforcement. In Chapter 7 we examined the role of reinforcement in certain human learning situations and concluded, again, that it does not have the automatic strengthening effect assumed by reinforcement theorists such as Thorndike, Hull, and Skinner. Motor skill learning, however, may be an exception. It is difficult to see how motor skills could be acquired without feedback regarding the consequences of the response that was made. Feedback (or *knowledge of results*) seems to play the role in motor skill learning that was assigned to reinforcement in the traditional reinforcement theories of learning.

Why should reinforcement be necessary for one kind of learning but not for another? Let us consider for a moment why this might be the case.

If a subject is learning a list of pairs of English words, his task is to be able, when tested, to say a response term when shown the stimulus term with which it was paired. But the subject already knows how to pronounce the words—this is a highly learned motor skill he brings into the experiment with him. All he needs to learn during the experiment is what words go together—and this information is all in the stimulus materials themselves. All the subject must do is study the pairs. He can do this silently, never emitting a response and never being told "right" or "wrong" or "close but not quite good enough."

In motor skill learning, in contrast, what the subject must know is how close the result of his action is to the outcome he wanted to produce. One cannot become a skilled speaker of French, an automobile driver, pool player, archer, or pole vaulter, simply by observing the behavior of those who have mastered the skill—even though this may be a great help; ultimately, it is absolutely necessary that he be able to compare the consequences of his own behavior with the desired result. Successful movements can be retained and unsuccessful ones eliminated only if one knows which are successful and which are not.

It was just such considerations that led Thorndike to conclude that the law of effect was valid for learning in humans as well as in animals. In one experiment, Thorndike (1932) blindfolded himself and then tried to draw a 4-inch line. After hundreds of attempts, without being able to compare the produced line with a standard, and without ever being told "good" or "too long" or "too short" he was no better at drawing 4-inch lines than he was at the beginning. Reinforcement, or knowledge of results, is necessary for improvement on such tasks. Thorndike's error was to generalize this conclusion to *all* kinds of human learning. The learning of motor skills apparently differs from other varieties of human learning in several ways; the necessity of reinforcement is one of them.

EPISODIC AND GENERIC MEMORY

The psychology of memory, born of philosophy and weaned in the laboratory, parted abruptly with its parent discipline when the behaviorist movement began. The philosophy of memory and the psychology of memory were no longer on speaking terms. After a long separation, however, the wayward offspring finds its views becoming more like those of its parent. Communication is at least possible. But does the philosophy of memory know anything it would be worthwhile for psychology to learn?

A distinction between two kinds of memory that is currently attracting attention in psychology was apparently first made by the philosopher Henri Bergson (1911), on the basis of introspective evidence. Bergson distinguished between "pure memory" and "habit memory". The former involves remembrance of one's own past experiences and the latter does not. Since Bergson, other philosophers have made essentially the same distinction, using different terms. A recent book by D. Locke (1971), for example, uses the terms "personal memory" and "factual memory." Although the distinction has appeared in fields related to psychology, most memory psychologists first encountered it in a paper by Tulving (1972), which introduced the terms "episodic memory" and "semantic memory." Tulving's terminology has been widely adopted—however, "semantic memory" seems too narrow, as it suggests a concern only with the meanings of words. The terms *episodic memory* and *generic memory* better capture the essence of the distinction, and these are the labels that will be used here.

Some of the terms that have been applied to the two types of memory by different writers are listed in Figure 12.4. The labels themselves tell a great deal about the distinction being made. Episodic memory records episodes from one's own past—events that were personally experienced. Information retrieved from episodic memory, therefore, is autobiographical. A remembrance of an event usually includes temporal information, which tells us roughly how long ago the event occurred, and often includes images—primarily visual and auditory—producing the impression that to remember an event is, in some sense, to re-experience it. Generic memory, by contrast, contains what we usually refer to as knowledge: well-learned facts, not only about the meanings of words, but also about grammatical rules, abstract concepts, mathematics, geography, people's names and faces, the uses of objects, professional knowledge, and so on. Information retrieved from generic memory is not autobiographical, in the sense of being an experiential record of an event from one's past. Details of

Field and Author	Episodic Memory	Generic Memory
Philosophy		
Bergson (1911)	True memory	Habit memory
Ayer (1956)	Event memory	Habit memory
D. Locke (1971)	Personal memory	Factual memory
Literature		
Koestler (1967)	Picture-strip memory	Abstractive memory
Neurology		
Penfield (1975)	Experiential record	Concepts
Psychiatry		
Schactel (1947)	Autobiographical memory	Practical memory
Reiff and Scheerer (1959)	Remembrances	Memoria
Psychology		
Tulving (1972)	Episodic memory	Semantic memory
Piaget and Inhelder (1973)	Memory in the strict sense	Memory in the wider sense

Figure 12.4 Terms used by various authors to distinguish between episodic memory and generic memory.

personal experience surrounding the learning of the information have been lost. Only the abstract, generic information remains. In describing episodic memory, we often say, "I remember . . .," but in describing generic memory we say, "I remember (or I know) *that*. . . ." Thus, I remember having breakfast this morning; but I remember *that* 3 times 8 is 24. I remember the assassination of President Kennedy (that is, when and where I was when I first learned about it), but I remember *that* President Garfield was assassinated, too. In recalling from generic memory, there is no experience of personal involvement. Not all instances of recall are pure cases of either episodic memory or generic memory, of course—elements of both may be present. Still, the distinction between episodic and generic memory is intuitively very compelling. If this were not so, it is doubtful that there would be the widespread agreement evidenced by Figure 12.4.

But is the dichotomy of episodic versus generic memory a useful one for experimental psychology? Tulving (1972) maintains that it is. Most memory experiments, he claims, tap episodic memory. When an experimenter says to a subject, "Remember that list of words I showed you yesterday? I want you to write down as many of those words as you can recall," autobiographical and temporal information are being used as retrieval cues for a specific episode in the subject's past. This is quite different from asking "How many legs does a donkey have?", "What is five times seven?", or "What is the capital of France?" Such knowledge is generally well learned, and not associated with a particular experience from one's own past. Thus, it could very well be that our traditional experimental paradigms have misled us. In attempting to discover and explain the laws of behavior in standard memory experiments, we may have concentrated on episodic memory, and unwittingly ignored our knowledge of abstract concepts and their relations to one another. The laws of learning and forgetting in episodic memory and generic memory may not be the same.

The Organization of Generic Memory

This is not to say that psychologists have ignored generic memory entirely. One way it has been studied is with the well-known *word association technique,* which was invented by Sir Francis Galton, even before Ebbinghaus's experiments were published (Galton, 1879–1880). There are two basic types of word-association test: *free association,* in which the subject responds to the stimulus word with the first word that comes to mind; and *controlled association,* in which he responds with a word related to it in a particular way (for example, its opposite). In either case, response latencies can be measured and frequency counts can be made to determine how much the associations given by different subjects agree (Kent and Rosanoff, 1910). Early memory researchers saw the word association task as a technique for mapping out the associative structure of natural concepts in memory. More recently, generic, or "semantic," memory has been studied with other types of tasks. In what is called the *semantic decision task,* for example, the subject answers as quickly as possible a question about the relationship between two concepts (for example, "Do gorillas have ears?", or "Is a python a bird?"). Subjects' reaction times in answering such questions are then used to test theories about how knowledge is organized in memory (for example, Collins and Quillian, 1969).

While experiments on the organization of natural concepts in generic memory have their place, their usefulness is limited by the experimenter's lack of control over what the subject knows and how well he knows it. When were the pertinent facts learned (if they were)? How often and how recently were they rehearsed? The experimenter usually does not know. Furthermore, given the complex interrelationships among natural concepts in memory, there may be several different ways of arriving at the same answer. A subject might decide that gorillas have ears because (a) he has noticed, in pictures, that they have; (b) he knows they are animals, and thinks that most animals have ears; (c) he knows they are mammals, and believes that all mammals have ears; (d) he knows they physically resemble humans. Similarly, a subject might decide a python is not a bird because (a) he knows it is a reptile and that reptiles and birds are mutually exclusive categories; (b) he thinks it is cold and slimy and that birds are usually warm and fluffy; (c) he knows it cannot fly, and thinks (incorrectly) that all birds can fly; (d) he knows it cannot fly and thinks that the only nonflying birds are dodos, ostriches, and penguins; (e) his image of a python looks nothing like his image of, say, a robin (see Collins and Loftus, 1975).

Given the complexity of the average subject's real-world knowledge and the obvious fact that different subjects come into an experiment with different backgrounds, it would be surprising if performance on word-association or semantic-decision tasks were to produce simple, general conclusions about memory organization and retrieval. It is just such problems that Ebbinghaus tried so hard to avoid. It seems likely that in the future, careful work on generic memory will tend to make use of "artificial" concepts learned in the laboratory, where the frequency and recency of exposure to the concepts, and the number or variety of their interrelationships can be carefully controlled.

Repetition in Episodic and Generic Memory

The distinction between episodic memory and generic memory will be of lasting value in psychology only if the two types of memory can be shown to obey different laws. This, in turn, requires that the distinction be made on objective, rather than purely subjective, grounds. It also requires that the theorist specify just how epsiodic and generic memory interact. They obviously must do so: abstract concepts are derived somehow from specific experiences; and general knowledge, in turn, determines what specific experiences are like.

One way in which the laws of episodic and generic memory might differ is in the effects of repetition. We know very well that repetition improves retention. But exactly how it does this is still something of a puzzle. There are two basic hypotheses about how repetition produces its effects on memory. One of these, the *strength hypothesis,* proposes that when an item is repeated, the corresponding memory trace increases in potency or strength. Strong memory traces are assumed to be more easily retrieved and more long-lasting than weak ones—thus, the more frequently an item occurs, the better it is remembered. The second explanation of the effect of repetition is the *multiple-trace hypothesis,* which makes the assumption that each occurrence of an item is a unique event, and is encoded as such in memory. Thus, the more times an item is presented, the more traces of the item there will be in memory. Finding at least one trace of an item is easier the more traces there are. Thus the speed and accuracy of retrieval will increase with repetition. (Notice that the multiple-trace hypothesis seems to be implied by Koffka's "trace column" theory, discussed in Chapter 9.)

The crucial difference between these two hypotheses lies in what they say about the representation of individual events. According to the strength hypothesis, each presentation of an item simply adds an increment to the overall strength of the appropriate memory trace. Since each presentation of the item has the same effect, the identifiability of the individual presentations is lost. According to the multiple-trace hypothesis, each presentation produces its own memory trace. Since presentations are individually represented in memory, their identifiability is preserved.

But how could one show experimentally whether subjects remember several individual presentations instead of a single strong memory trace? Hintzman and Block (1971) tried to get subjects to differentiate among individual traces of the same item on the basis of temporal information. As we saw in Chapter 8, subjects can discriminate and judge the recencies of items. If the multiple-trace hypothesis is true, subjects may be able to do the same with the recencies of different occurrences of the same item. In one experiment, Hintzman and Block (1971) showed subjects two lists of words, separated by 5 minutes spent working on an unrelated task. Many words that occurred in List 1 also occurred in List 2. Each word was presented either 0, 2, or 5 times in List 1 and, also, either 0, 2, or 5 times in List 2. Thus, there were nine different conditions altogether, with individual words occurring 2 times in List 1 and 5 times in List 2, 0 times in List 1 and 2 times in List 2, and so on. Under instructions to simply try to remember the words, subjects studied both lists. Then they were given a combined list discrimination and frequency judgment test. All the words were listed on the test form, and after each one the subjects were told to write two judgments: one for the number of times the word occurred in List 1 and one for the number of times it occurred in List 2.

The average frequency judgments, shown in Figure 12.5, demonstrate that subjects were fairly good at discriminating the List 1 and List 2 frequencies of the same word. That is, the judgments were primarily determined by the word's frequency in the list being judged, and only slightly by its frequency in the other list. This is important because it is not predicted by the strength hypothesis. If all a subject had to go on was the overall strength of the trace of the word, he would not know how the word's overall frequency had been divided up between the two lists. Another experiment showed that subjects can make the same sort of discrimination within a single list. Subjects can remember whether a word occurred two times near the middle of the list, or once near the beginning and once near the end, and so on. Such results are predicted by the multiple-trace hypothesis; but they are not what would be expected if the effect of repetition were simply to increase the overall strength of a single memory trace.

Now, how much generality should be attached to this conclusion? Is

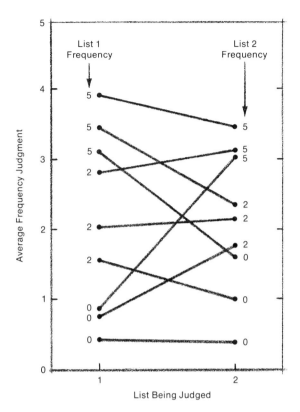

Figure 12.5 Judgments of the List 1 and List 2 frequencies of words that occurred various numbers of times in the two lists. Actual List 1 and List 2 frequencies are given by the numbers alongside the data points. [After Hintzman and Block, 1971. Copyright 1971 by the American Psychological Association. Reprinted by permission.]

the strength hypothesis wrong? IBM changes from a meaningless trigram to a chunk through repeated exposure. Is this because repetition produces many memory traces of IBM? It seems, in this case, as though the strength hypothesis is a more reasonable explanation of how repetition has its effect; likewise for the familiarity of a friend's face and the knowledge that three is the square root of nine. Perhaps the episodic versus generic memory distinction will help here. The Hintzman and Block experiment certainly had to do with episodic memory, since the use of temporal information was such an important part of the task. When we speak of the familiarity of a word, a face, or a fact, on the other hand, we refer primarily to generic memory. It may be that repetition produces multiple traces in episodic memory, but strengthens traces in generic memory. This seems eminently reasonable, since episodic memory is said to deal with concrete, individual events and generic memory with more abstract, general concepts. Traces in generic memory must be based on individual experiences, but with their individual characteristics stripped away. Can we find experimental evidence that traces of abstract concepts are strengthened by the presentation of individual instances?

A series of experiments by Posner and Keele appears to demonstrate such an effect. These investigators first had subjects learn to classify random dot patterns. Examples of such stimuli are shown in Figure 12.6. The patterns subjects classified were random distortions of "prototype" patterns, such as those shown in the top row of the figure. The distortions were generated by moving each dot a randomly determined distance and direction from its position in the prototype. Three distortions of the prototype B are shown in the bottom row of the figure.

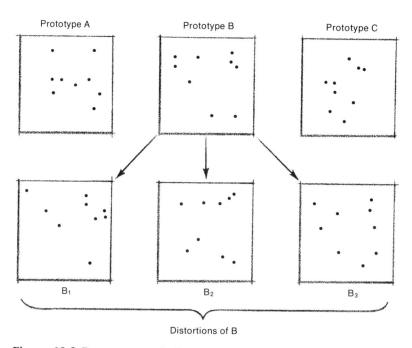

Figure 12.6 Dot patterns similar to those used by Posner and Keele (1970). The bottom row shows three distortions of the same prototype pattern.

In stage one of their experiment, Posner and Keele (1970) had subjects learn to classify distortions of three prototypes, much like those shown in the figure, into the three corresponding categories (A, B, and C). During this stage, however, the subjects were never shown the prototypes themselves; they were not even told such patterns existed. During stage two, the subjects were given additional dot patterns, to classify into the same three categories. These patterns included (a) old distortions, which the subjects had learned to classify during stage one; (b) new distortions of the A, B, and C prototypes; and (c) the three prototypes themselves, which the subjects had never seen. The new distortions were just as similar to the old distortions the subjects had learned as were the prototypes themselves. This stage-two test was given to half the subjects immediately after stage one, and to the other half following a one-week delay.

Two findings are important: First, subjects were better at classifying the prototypes than they were at classifying the new distortions. This suggests that in learning to classify the old distortions, the subjects had abstracted out the "most representative" pattern for each category, which corresponds to the pattern from which the distortions were generated. Second, the ability to classify prototypes declined less over the one-week interval than did the ability to classify the old distortions (see Figure 12.7). This suggests that the abstract idea derived from the individual instances is more long lasting than the traces of the individual instances themselves. It is as though the episodic memory traces, for specific patterns, were disappearing, while the generic memory traces, of the abstract concepts, remained.

Further work on the learning of abstract concepts has confirmed these findings using materials other than dot patterns. Franks and Bransford (1971) found that prototypes were classified better than distortions the subjects had actually seen, even when the test occurred immediately after stage one. Apparently, presentation of many instances of a category produces an abstract representation of the category—derived from the individual instances, but not identical to any of them. Such a single, general memory trace, representing all the items in the category, is what the strength hypothesis would lead one to expect.

These experiments suggest that repetition may affect memory in two ways. It may produce multiple traces, as in the study by Hintzman and Block, and it may increase the strength of a single trace, as suggested by the Posner and Keele results. The distinction between

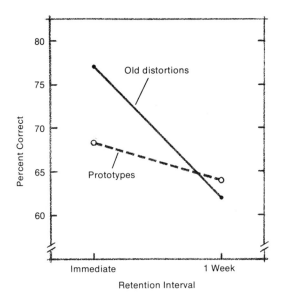

Figure 12.7 Percentages of correct classifications of prototypes and old distortions immediately after learning and following a one-
week delay. [Data from Posner and Keele,
1970.]

episodic and generic memory may help us understand these seemingly contradictory conclusions. The multiple-trace hypothesis may
hold for episodic memory, and the strength hypothesis for generic
memory. This is one way the two kinds of memory proposed by
Bergson and other philosophers may differ from one another.

MEANINGFUL LEARNING

In most research on human learning and memory, the to-be-
remembered material has been relatively meaningless. Often, nonsense syllables, consonant trigrams, numbers, random shapes, or dot
patterns are used. When words or scenic pictures are used as stimuli,
they are typically arranged in a meaningless, random order in a list.
Thus, either the stimuli themselves or the order in which they occur
fail to "make sense" to the subject. They cannot be related easily to
thinks the subject already knows. They do not have the familiarity,

regularity, and predictability of most events encountered in everyday life.

We have seen why relatively meaningless materials are so often used. Ebbinghaus himself set the pattern. He wanted to study new learning, as uncontaminated by pre-existing associations as possible. In deciding to follow Ebbinghaus's lead, however, researchers have made the assumption that the laws of human learning and memory discovered using relatively meaningless materials will hold for meaningful materials, as well. This assumption may not be true.

Ausubel (1963), a prominent educational psychologist, has claimed that the "rote" learning usually studied in the laboratory and the kind of meaningful learning that takes place in the classroom obey different laws. If this is true, then the theories of human memory developed to account for laboratory results will be of little value when applied to everyday problems of learning and memory. As we shall see, cognitive psychologists are becoming more and more interested in the kinds of learning that occur when we hear a lecture, read a book, or hear testimony in a court of law. Their work suggests that meaningful learning, to a certain extent, does involve different principles. But to what degree does meaningful learning differ, and in exactly what ways? Do we really need a completely new theory in order to deal with it? Are principles derived from standard laboratory tasks irrelevant where meaningful learning is concerned?

Many of the phenomena that occur in standard learning tasks also occur with meaningful learning. Overlearning has the same effect on retention of poetry or prose as it has on retention of nonsense syllable lists. The effect of presentation rate is also the same—the more time one spends reading a passage, the better it is remembered. Positive transfer occurs with meaningful learning—the more compatible the new information is with what we already know, the easier it is to acquire. Information is forgotten over time; recognition is better than recall; and the more there is to learn, the longer it takes to learn it. In these respects, meaningful learning presents no surprises.

Forgetting of Meaningful Material

How is meaningful material forgotten? Do the laws of proactive and retroactive interference apply? There apparently is no dispute about proactive interference. Ausubel (1963) attributes nearly all forgetting of meaningful materials to proactive interference—a process he calls "obliterative subsumption," in which the new information gradually merges with the old information to which it relates. Retroactive interference, however, is another matter. Several attempts to demonstrate retroactive interference in memory for prose passages have failed, leading Ausubel to conclude that this is one respect in which the forgetting of meaningful material differs from the forgetting of "rote" material.

Consider a retroactive interference experiment by Ausubel, Stager, and Gaite (1968). In stage one, the experimenters had high school students read a passage on Zen Buddhism. In stage two, the experimental subjects read a passage on Buddhism judged to be highly similar to, but conflicting with, the preceding passage. The control subjects read a passage on drug addiction, in stage two, which was unrelated to the original material. In stage three, all the subjects took a multiple-choice test covering the Zen Buddhism passage. No retroactive interference was found. In fact, the experimental group did somewhat better than the control group—they showed retroactive facilitation.

Anderson and Myrow (1971) have pointed out that such overall facilitation could occur if there were more consistent than inconsistent material in the two passages. If a subject learns a paired-associates list (A–B) and then another in which some of the pairs are consistent with the first (A–B') and others are inconsistent (A–C), the overall effect of List 2 on the retention of List 1 will depend on the mixture of A–B' and A–C pairs in List 2. A predominance of A–B' pairs will lead to overall facilitation; a predominance of A–C pairs will lead to interference. The conflicting information in the passages used in the Ausubel study may have been outweighed by compatible information.

To evaluate this interpretation of the Ausubel, Stager, and Gaite results, Anderson and Myrow had students read two passages—each about an imaginary primitive tribe, describing its religion, climate, agriculture, government, and so on. Corresponding facts in the two passages were categorized as consistent (for example, both tribes were said to make beer out of a kind of squash), neutral (for example boat building was cited as an activity of one tribe, and hunting as an activity of the other), or inconsistent (for example, the basic food of one tribe was said to be rice, and that of the other, wheat). In stage one, both experimental and control subjects read about Tribe A and took a short-answer and multiple-choice test. In stage two, the experimental subjects read about Tribe B, and the control subjects read unrelated material. In stage three, all subjects were tested for knowledge of Tribe A. The outcome was as expected: the experimental group remembered consistent items better than the control group (facilitation) and inconsistent items worse than the control group (interference). In a second experiment, Anderson and Myrow (1971) applied the same analysis to the Zen Buddhism material used by Ausubel, with similar results.

Retroactive interference has been demonstrated with actual classroom materials, as well (for example, Entwisle and Huggins, 1964). Apparently, the phenomenon of retroactive interference does not differentiate standard laboratory experiments from meaningful learning tasks, as Ausubel claimed.

Recent work by Loftus (1975) has demonstrated subtle retroactive interference effects with information even further removed from "rote" learning. The experiments concerned eyewitness testimony for naturalistic events. The interference, in these studies, comes from "leading questions" asked the eyewitness following the witnessed event. In one experiment, Loftus showed college students a videotape of the disruption of a class by 8 demonstrators. Afterward, the subjects filled out questionnaries regarding what they had seen. For half the subjects, one of the questions was, "Was the leader of the 4 demonstrators who entered the classroom a male?", clearly suggesting that the demonstrators had numbered 4. For the other half, the same question was used, but "4" was replaced by "12." One week later, the subjects returned and answered a series of questions, including: "How many demonstrators did you see entering the classroom?" Subjects who had been asked the "4" question gave, on the average, 6.40 demonstrators, while those who had been asked the "12" question gave an average of 8.85. In another experiment, subjects saw a videotape of an automobile accident. Half the subjects were then asked how fast the white sports car was going when it passed the barn, and the others were asked the question with no reference to a barn (no barn, in fact, had appeared in the scene). Returning one week later, 17.3 percent of the subjects who had been asked the leading question reported having seen a barn. Only 2.7 percent of the control subjects did so. These experiments and others show that the memory of eyewitnesses can be biased in subtle ways by questioning. This is just one of the many ways psychological factors might influence testimony in a court of law.

Memory for Orderings

In learning a particular subject matter, one often must know how items within a set rank with respect to some property. An astronomy student, for example, should know the relative distances of planets from the sun. A geography student should know the relative populations of major world cities, and something about the relative areas of states of the United States. Our world knowledge includes many examples of relative orderings: standings of football teams, sizes of universities, conservativism of political candidates, and so on. How is such information represented in memory? Some recent experiments have attempted to answer this question.

An experiment by Potts (1974) will serve as an illustration. The subjects were given paragraphs to read and understand, each describing the ordering of items along some dimension. For example:

> In art class, Sally showed her nature painting to the teacher. Her teacher felt that certain parts of the picture were drawn better than others. The teacher said her tree was better than her grass, her sky was better than her bird, and her bird was better than her tree. Upon hearing this, Sally decided to drop art and major in psychology (Potts, 1974, p. 433).

After a subject indicated he understood the relationships, he was tested by being shown sentences that were either true or false according to the paragraph. The test sentence, "The sky is better than the tree," for example, is true of the preceding paragraph, while the sentence, "The bird is better than the sky," is false. The subject was to respond "true" or "false" by pressing a button, and his reaction time was measured.

Now, a straightforward prediction about performance in this task would be that subjects should be faster on relationships they actually read (for example, "The bird is better than the tree") than on relationships that must be inferred from the information given (for example, "The bird is better than the grass"). The result, however, is just the opposite. The further apart the items are on the dimension being judged, the faster is the reaction time. Thus, the relationships actually shown, between adjacent items, take longest to recall. This is true of "6-term" problems, as well as of "4-term" problems like our example; and it is true whether the end items (for example, the best and worse) are included in the analysis or not (Potts, 1974). The same basic effect has been found with naturally learned information such as number magnitudes ("which number is greater, 6 or 4?") and animal sizes ("which animal is bigger, a mole or a fox?"). The greater the *distance* between the items being judged, the faster the judgment can be made.

This outcome—called the *linear-ordering effect*—seems to disprove one account of how relative orderings might be encoded in memory. The computer analogy suggests that propositions relating adjacent items will be encoded directly into memory (for example, A > B, B > C, C > D), and indirect relationships such as that between A and C will be derived from the stored propositions at the time of retrieval—a process that should require additional time. The data, however, suggest a kind of analogue representation, in which positions on an internal dimension are compared with each other whenever a judgment is made. The closer together the positions are, the more difficult they are to discriminate—hence the longer reaction times.

If this discussion produces a feeling of familiarity, or *déjà vu,* it is not surprising. For although the data are different, the theoretical issues are essentially the same as those surrounding serial learning, discussed in Chapter 9. The Gestalt interpretation of serial learning, we noted then, was that the items in the list were assigned positions on an internal dimension. The serial-position curve arose, according to this hypothesis, because extreme positions were easier to discriminate than positions near the middle. Much of the serial learnig data support this so-called ordinal position hypothesis over the associative chaining hypothesis, which maintains that subjects learn associations linking adjacent items. It seems likely that the linear-ordering effect, which arises in meaningful learning, and the serial-position effect, of "rote" serial learning, are illustrations of the same principle of memory organization.

Learning from Prose

Are the laws of meaningful learning entirely different from those uncovered with relatively meaningless materials? The evidence we have considered so far indicates that such an assertion is too strong. Many of the basic phenomena of human learning discovered using nonsense syllable lists have been found to apply also to the learning of material in prose passages. It is reassuring to know that the thousands of painstaking laboratory experiments done on human learning over the years cannot be rejected as irrelevant to everyday learning simply because meaningless materials were used.

It would be equally improper, however, to conclude that everything relevant to meaningful learning can be discovered using traditional laboratory techniques. The British psychologist Sir Frederic Bartlett, in 1932, published research on memory for prose, suggesting that the encoding and recall of meaningful material involves an active, constructive effort on the part of the learner to relate it to things with which he is familiar. For years, Bartlett's work was largely ignored, for several reasons: it was highly cognitive, at a time when cognitivism was declining in popularity; the experiments were crude; and Bartlett's theory, in which memory functions were said to be carried out by "active, developing patterns" called schemata (singular, *schema*), was, to most, incomprehensible. In recent years, however, psychologists have turned increasingly to the question of how information in prose passages is learned and remembered. Like Bartlett, they have discovered facts that were not anticipated from previous research on learning, and that seem to require theoretical interpretations radically different from those that have gone before. This investigation of the understanding and retention of prose is perhaps modern cognitive psychology's most ambitious and exciting undertaking. The hope is that we will gain, at the practical level, and understanding of the educational process; and at a more philosophical level, and understanding of the nature of knowledge itself. The problems, however, are formidable.

The single most important question to be faced when considering memory for a prose passage (or "connected discourse," as it is often called) is this: How is the information encoded in memory? One might, naively, suppose that since the information is presented in word strings, it is represented in strings of the corresponding ideas in the head. But recent work in linguistics, artificial intelligence, and psychology has made it abundantly clear that this approach will not work. Our *understanding* of a string of words is something quite different from the string of words itself.

Consider an early attempt to program a computer to translate from one language to another. The proposal was quite simple: Each word in the input language would be "looked up" on magnetic tape, and the corresponding word in the output language found. Then, rules relating the grammatical structures of the two languages would juggle the word order appropriately, producing a sentence in the output language. As Raphael (1976) tells us:

> Unfortunately, these experiments failed miserably, producing translations whose meanings differed from the original in all kinds of strange, unexpected ways. For example, when the biblical quotation, "The spirit is willing but the flesh is weak," was translated from English to Russian and then back to English, what came out of the computer was, "the wine is agreeable but the meat has spoiled" (Raphael, 1976, p. 180).

The problem, of course, was that the computer did not "understand" what the original sentence was about, so it had no way of rejecting this particular translation as inappropriate. But the general problem is not peculiar to translation between languages. It crops up with a single language, as well. There are many different ways to express the same idea. Most people would agree that the two sentences:

(1) *A dog is chasing the skunk.*

and

(2) *The skunk is being chased by a dog.*

describe the same situation. They are paraphrases of each other. The complement of *paraphrase* is *ambiguity*. The sentence:

(3) *The missionary is cooking.*

is ambiguous; it can be understood in two different ways. Paraphrase and ambiguity are problems because they show that the order of words in the sentence does not uniquely specify its meaning. Different sentences can have the same meaning, and the same sentence can have two different meanings. Thus, a memory representation must exist in which (1) and (2) are the same, while there must be two quite different representations of (3).

Surface Structure and Deep Structure

Linguists have proposed as a solution to the problems of paraphrase and ambiguity a distinction between the *surface structure* of a sentence, which is its actual appearance (that is, as a word string) and the *deep structure* of the sentence, which represents the way it is understood. Sentences (1) and (2) have different surface structures—DOG is the subject of (1), for example, and SKUNK is the subject of (2)—but they have the same deep structure. DOG is the actor and SKUNK is the recipient of the action in the deep structure underlying both (1) and (2). Sentence (3), on the other hand, has a single surface structure, but two different deep structures. In one, MISSIONARY is the actor; in the other it is what is being acted upon.

The concept of deep structure has proven useful in studies of memory. Apparently, subjects remember the deep structure of a sentence (their understanding of it) much longer than they remember the sentence's surface structure, or grammatical construction. This fact was demonstrated in an experiment by Sachs (1967). Subjects heard passages of connected discourse, presented by a tape recorder. They were tested for retention of one sentence in each passage, but did not know which sentence it would be. A yes–no recognition test was used, with the test sentence either identical to the original sentence or changed. Two types of changed sentences were used—some that preserved the deep structure of the original and some that changed it. For example, one of the original sentences was:

> (4)   *There he met an archaeologist, Howard Carter, who*
> *urged him to join in the search for the tomb of King Tut.*

The changed test sentence that preserved the deep structure of (4) was:

> (5)   *There he met an archaeologist, Howard Carter, who*
> *urged that he join in the search for the tomb of King Tut.*

The test sentence that changed the deep structure was:

> (6)   *There he met an archaeologist, Howard Carter, and*
> *urged him to join in the search for the tomb of King Tut.*

The test sentence could occur at three intervals after the original: either immediately, after 80 further syllables of the same passage (about 27 seconds), or after 160 syllables (about 46 seconds). The overall ability of subjects to correctly identify the changed sentences as new is plotted as a function of intervening material in Figure 12.8. Changes in deep structure were easy to detect at all three intervals. But surface structure changes that did not change the deep structure were identified easily only on an immediate test; at the longer retention intervals, subjects were able to reject them at a rate only slightly better than chance (about 50 percent).

A Theory of Deep Structure

The Sachs experiment and others show clearly that we remember best our *understanding* of a meaningful passage—memory for the actual words is relatively poor. If it is accepted that memory for prose is based primarily on some kind of deep structure encoding, then the next question to be answered is, just what is the deep structure like? Put differently, we are asking how knowledge is represented in memory. This, of course, is one of the central questions with which the philosophical study of the mind originally began.

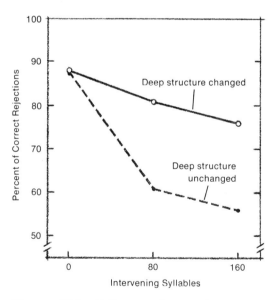

Figure 12.8 Ability to detect changes in sentences which alter or do not alter the deep structure, as a function of intervening syllables. [After Sachs, 1967. Copyright 1967 by Psychonomic Press.]

Since we are asking the same question the early philosophers asked, it seems fair to consider first the answer they gave. Can associations between ideas be the basis of knowledge, as the British empiricists proposed?

Suppose we read and understand the following sentence:

(7)   *The player hit the baseball.*

The kind of representation that the British empiricists might have proposed for this sentence is shown in Figure 12.9. Here, the ideas representing player (A), hit (B), and baseball (C) are interconnected with three associations. Each idea is also assumed to be associated with its corresponding word. This kind of structure cannot represent the understanding of sentence (7); for although it could stand for

(8)   *The baseball was hit by the player,*

which has the same deep structure as (7), it could also represent

(9)   *The baseball hit the player*

and

(10)   *The player was hit by the baseball,*

which do not. If one attempts in such a simple associative network to represent a short episode in which one player hits a baseball, which hits a second player, causing the second player to hit the first, the futility of the approach becomes obvious. It seems clear that the sim-

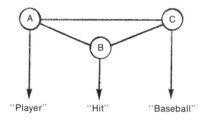

Figure 12.9 A simple associative network.

ple associative processes assumed by the British empiricists could not be the basis for our detailed, highly structured knowledge of the world.

Modern memory theorists dealing with the understanding of prose have proposed rules for constructing deep-structure representations bearing family resemblance to those of the empiricist philosophers, but more sophisticated in several ways. Some notable theoretical attempts are those by Anderson and Bower (1973), Kintsch (1974), and Norman and Rumelhart (1975). These approaches are all similar in the way certain basic problems are solved. To illustrate, we shall examine one of them in some detail. This is the theory called HAM (for Human Associative Memory), proposed by Anderson and Bower (1973).

HAM has been partly realized as a computer program which takes in information in sentence form, constructs deep-structure representations of that information which it stores in its memory, and answers questions about the information it has learned. The main interest in the theory is centered on its deep-structure representation. Although it is similar to the much older associative theory in postulating that ideas are connected by associations, it is different in three important respects.

First, HAM makes use of *labeled associations*. To the British empiricist philosophers, all associations were of the same type. Later, some S–R theorists distinguished between "forward" and "backward" associations; but proponents of the computer analogy find it useful to postulate the existence of several different types of associations—each distinguished by a label that specifies exactly *how* the two ideas are related.

Consider Figure 12.10a. This HAM encoding can represent either sentence (7) or (8). It uses five kinds of associations: *subject, predicate, relation, object,* and *word.* Word links simply connect ideas with their corresponding words. The other four types of association give structure to the representation. A basic unit of information in HAM is the *proposition* (a kind of simple "abstract sentence"). Idea (A) stands for the entire proposition in Figure 12.10a. Each proposition must have both a *subject* and a *predicate.* The predicate, in turn, may be made up of two elements: a *relation* and an *object.* The labels on the links make it clear that idea (B) is the subject, and that it has a certain relation (D) to the object (E). Tracing out the word links allows us to relate the memory structure to actual words. Notice that Figures 12.10a and 12.10b clearly refer to different situations. Sentence (7) and (8) would be

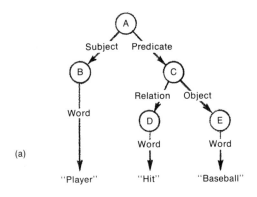

(a)

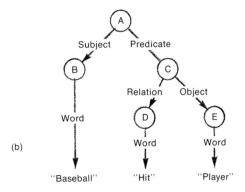

(b)

Figure 12.10 HAM deep structures for two different situations.

encoded as in panel (a); but sentences (9) and (10) would be encoded as in panel (b). Thus, through labeled associations, the HAM deep structure can encode in different ways sentences that are understood differently, and encode in the same way sentences whose meanings are the same.

A second important way that HAM differs from early associationism is in its *hierarchical structure*. This feature allows propositions to be embedded, one within another, to any degree of complexity. For example, the situation described by:

> (11)   *The baseball hit the player,*
> *and this angered the fans*

asserts that a complex event (the hitting of the player by the baseball) caused the fans to become angry. Since in HAM a single idea stands for an entire proposition, that proposition can play a simple role in a higher-level proposition, as shown in Figure 12.11.

Here, idea (A), which stands for the hitting of the player by the baseball (everything within the dashed outline) is the subject of the higher-level proposition represented by idea (F). In principle, of course, this can go on indefinitely. So, by making idea (F) the subject of a still higher-level proposition, one could represent the fact that the incident in (11) was reported in the Morning Bugle, and so on. Some hierarchical method of embedding such as this is obviously needed to deal adequately with the complexity of our real-world knowledge.

A third way in which HAM and other modern theories of prose memory differ from early associationism is in making what is called the *type-token distinction*. Consider the sentence:

> (12)   *One player hit the baseball,*
> *and the baseball hit another player.*

It is important that the memory representation of (12) clearly show that there are two different players involved, and two instances of hitting. Yet we do not want to lose the information that both players belong to the same category. This is where the type-token distinction is

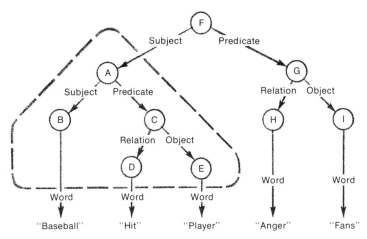

Figure 12.11 Two levels of propositions in a HAM associative network.

useful. A "type" is a general concept, and a "token" is a particular instance of that concept. Instead of associating a particular idea directly with its corresponding word (as was done for illustrative purposes in Figures 12.10 and 12.11), HAM includes an intermediate step. Each token is linked directly to the type to which it belongs, and the type idea is directly associated with the word. Associations between tokens and their types are labeled *is a* (for "is a member of the set") in Figure 12.12. The diagram indicates that ideas (B) and (I) are different tokens of the general type (J), referred to as "player"; and that ideas (D) and (H) are tokens of type (K), a relation called "hitting." Only one token of "baseball" is used (idea E), indicating that the *same* ball is involved in both propositions. Notice that the type-token distinction allows us to say things either about specific instances or about all members of a category. To include in Figure 12.12 information that baseballs are hard, for example, we would make idea (L) the subject of an additional proposition. To show that the player who hit the ball is named Willie Brezewski, we would add a word link connecting the name directly with idea (B).

Once HAM has some facts encoded in its memory, it can answer questions about what it has learned. It does this by constructing a propositional encoding of the question, matching it up with informa-

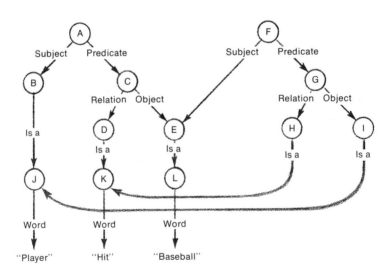

Figure 12.12 Use of the type-token distinction in HAM.

tion in memory, and reading out the information being sought. As an illustration, suppose HAM has learned:

(13)   *Wendy ate the sandwich,*

and now is asked:

(14)   *Who ate the sandwich?*

A tree structure of the question is constructed in the short-term store, as shown in Figure 12.13. HAM attempts to match this tree structure with one in the long-term store, by beginning with the information that has been supplied—namely, the words EAT and SANDWICH. It immediately finds that idea (f) matches (F), and idea (g) matches (G). It then proceeds to move up the tree, finding chains of ideas in long-term memory connected by the same labeled associations as those in the encoding of the question. Having matched ideas (a) and (A), HAM is ready to answer the question. An appropriate *subject* link is found,

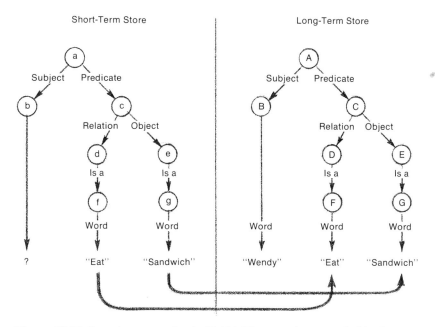

Figure 12.13 Question answering in HAM. The question, encoded in the STS, is matched up with information in the LTS.

leading to idea (B), and the corresponding word can be output in answer to the question. If a perfect match cannot be made (for instance, if the question in our example were "Who *made* the sandwich?"), HAM replies that it does not know.

How can a theory such as HAM be tested? The first step is to show that it performs as intended—in the case of HAM, to show that it will encode information input in sentence form and answer questions about it. This HAM does, for a limited set of kinds of English sentences. The second step is to derive predictions that can be tested using human subjects. Anderson and Bower (1973) have devised various experimental tests of predictions, most of them related to the structures of the propositional trees in which HAM encodes information. One such prediction is that ideas close together in the tree structure (for example, verbs and objects) are more likely to be forgotten together than are ideas that are further apart (for example, subject and object, or subject and verb). Another prediction is that the amount of time it takes subjects to say that two words are from the same sentence should depend on how many associations separate them in memory. The HAM theory has been only moderately successful in surviving such experimental tests, and as a result some of its basic assumptions have undergone change. This is as it should be; one cannot expect the first steps toward a comprehensive theory in any area to meet with immediate success.

Inference

But research on the understanding and retention of prose has revealed a problem more fundamental than the ones to which the experimental tests of HAM have been addressed. This problem affects not only HAM, but similar deep-structure theories, as well. In our discussion, we shall call this the *problem of inference*. Stated briefly, the problem of inference is this: When we read a passage of connected discourse, our understanding of that passage consists of much more information than is actually given. What we remember is produced by an interaction between the information in the passage and our pre-existing knowledge. It is sometimes said that we "read between the lines." What recent research suggests is that "reading between the lines" is not something that we do only occasionally—it is fundamental to the understanding process itself.

That prose understanding involves inference has been shown by numerous experiments. Only two will be mentioned here for illustration. Johnson, Bransford, and Solomon (1973) had the subjects of their experimental group read passages such as the following:

(15) *John was trying to fix the bird house. He was pounding the nail when his father came out to watch him and to help him do the work.*

The control subjects read the following passage, nearly identical in its surface structure to (15):

(16) *John was trying to fix the bird house. He was looking for the nail when his father came out to watch him and to help him do the work.*

Finally, subjects in both groups were given a recognition-memory test, including the following sentence:

(17) *John was using the hammer to fix the bird house when his father came out to watch him and to help him do the work.*

The experimental subjects were nearly three times as likely to incorrectly accept sentence (17) as "old" as were the control subjects. Why were they so fooled by this lure? The apparent reason is that "pounding the nail" clearly suggests a hammer, while "looking for the nail" does not. In neither original sentence, however, is a hammer directly mentioned. It is an inference, based on the subject's knowledge of the world—but it is part of his understanding of sentence (15), and thus part of its deep-structure representation.

In another experiment, Bransford and Johnson (1972) had subjects read the passage given in Figure 12.14. (Stop and read it before going further.) There were three conditions: In one, the passage was presented as is, with no topic provided; in another, the subjects were told after reading the passage that it was about washing clothes; in the third, they were given this information before reading the passage. All subjects then attempted to recall the passage. Those in the third group recalled more than twice as much as those in the other two. Knowing the topic while reading the passage helped comprehension and recall considerably; learning it only after reading the passage was of no help at all. Again, we see here the importance of inferences based on pre-existing knowledge. A sentence such as "Eventually they will be used once more and the whole cycle will have to be repeated" takes on a

The procedure is actually quite simple. First you arrange things into different groups. Of course, one pile may be sufficient depending on how much there is to do. If you have to go somewhere else due to lack of facilities that is the next step, otherwise you are pretty well set. It is important not to overdo things. That is, it is better to do too few things at once than too many. In the short run this may not seem important but complications can easily arise. A mistake can be expensive as well. At first the whole procedure will seem complicated. Soon, however, it will become just another facet of life. It is difficult to foresee any end to the necessity for this task in the immediate future, but then one can never tell. After the procedure is completed one arranges the materials into different groups again. Then they can be put into their appropriate places. Eventually they will be used once more and the whole cycle will then have to be repeated. However, that is part of life.

Figure 12.14 Passage used in an experiment by Bransford and Johnson (1972).

new meaning when one realizes it has to do with clothes, that "using" clothes means wearing them, that clothes can get dirty when being worn, and so on. Without this contribution from previous knowledge, the passage is vague and difficult to understand. (A current anecdote, possibly apocryphal, is that a psychologist explaining his work on comprehension to a Washington bureaucrat gave him the passage in Figure 12.14 to read. Asked whether he understood it, the bureaucrat said he did—it was a description of his job.)

The role of inference in comprehension is well illustrated by the following (from D. W. Chafe, cited in Minsky, 1975):

> (18) *There was once a Wolf who saw a Lamb drinking at a river and wanted an excuse to eat it. For that purpose, even though he himself was upstream, he accused the Lamb of stirring up the water and keeping him from drinking.*

What is involved in understanding this passage? In the first place, we know some common stereotypes about wolves (that they are cunning, greedy, and so on) and about their relationship with lambs that lend some plausibility to what is said. (If the words "wolf" and "lamb" were interchanged, the passage would sound quite bizarre.) Also, we must know something about rivers—that they contain flowing water, for example, and usually have a bottom of mud. We must know that animals drink water, that when water is stirred up sediment such as mud can change its appearance and possibly its flavor, making it less palatable. We must also know that water flows downstream, and carries material with it (hence, the wolf is lying—he has no valid reason for complaint). In addition, there are the facts that eating the lamb necessitates killing it, and that killing might be viewed, in a primitive sense of justice, as punishment for some offense. Finally, some of our knowledge is violated by the passage, since wolves cannot talk and presumably do not feel the need to justify their actions. In a folk tale, however, animals may speak and take on all sorts of human characteristics; and when this interpretation is given the passage, these peculiarities become acceptable.

If the understanding process is this complex, how are we to account for it theoretically? It is clear that the HAM theory is inadequate. It is much too "literal"—that is, the deep-structure encodings HAM constructs are too closely tied to the actual linguistic input. For humans, the linguistic input is not the entire message—indeed, it seems to be treated only as a set of clues regarding what message the sender (the speaker or writer) intends to convey. The message sender implicitly *assumes* that the receiver knows certain things, and tries to restrict his actual linguistic output to information the receiver will need to construct the intended message out of what he already knows. (Too much information will bore the receiver, too little will confuse him.) Thus, a theory of human comprehension will have to include mechanisms for *constructing* underlying meanings, by combining the linguistic input with prior relevant knowledge.

Conceptual Dependency Theory

Schank (1975, 1976) has proposed an ingenious approach to the problem of inference, which he calls *conceptual dependency theory*. He assumes that the deep structure into which linguistic input is transformed consists of a sequence of "conceptualizations." Each conceptualization has an *actor* and an *action,* and may include other information such as an *object* of the action, a *recipient* of the object, *direction* of the action, and so on. The action is of central importance in Schank's system. He proposes that there are only eleven basic actions, called *primitive acts.* Out of these, all conceptualizations are built.

These eleven acts are common to all normal adult humans, regardless of their culture. According to Schank, the universal nature of this set of basic units enables us to translate any thought from one language into another. Schank's eleven primitive acts are listed and described briefly in Figure 12.15.

Much of Schank's work has attempted to show how events expressed in ordinary language can be mapped onto the eleven primitive acts. These efforts have relied primarily on Schank's own intuitive judgments; and indeed, it is through careful analysis of his own intuitions about meanings that Schank arrived at the particular set of primitive actions given in the figure. The basic goal of this type of analysis is to show that the similarities and differences among conceptualizations can be understood in terms of the configurations of the underlying acts.

Consider, for example, the following two sentences:

(19) *John gave his car to Bill.*

(20) *John sold his car to Bill.*

Act	Description
PTRANS	Transfer of physical location of an object (for example, go, fly).
PROPEL	Application of physical force to an object (for example, push, pull, kick). May result in PTRANS.
ATRANS	Transfer of an abstract relationship such as ownership (for example, give, take, buy).
MTRANS	Transfer of information between animals or within mental structures of one animal (for example, remember, forget, see, tell, read).
MBUILD	Construction, within the mind, of new information from old information (for example, decide, imagine, consider, answer).
ATTEND	Direction or focusing of a sense organ towards a particular stimulus (for example, look, listen). Usually results in MTRANS.
SPEAK	Production of a sound. May result in MTRANS.
MOVE	Movement by an animal of a part of its own body.
GRASP	Physical grasping of an object.
INGEST	Intake of an object into an animal's body (for example, eat, breathe, smoke).
EXPEL	Ejection of something from the body (for example, spit, cough, sweat). Opposite of INGEST.

Figure 12.15 Schank's eleven primitive acts. [Adapted from Schank, 1976.]

According to Schank, our understanding of (19) consists of one ATRANS action, having *actor* John, *object* ownership of car, *recipient* Bill, and *direction* from John to Bill. Our understanding of (20) consists of two ATRANS actions, that which underlies (19) plus another, with *actor* Bill, object *ownership* of money, *recipient* John, and *direction* from Bill to John.

The power of Schank's conceptual system to make inferences comes from the fact that information can be fit together only in certain ways. The restrictions are such that "guesses" about the nature of missing information have a good chance of being correct. Every act, for example, must have an *actor* and *object;* some acts require a *recipient, direction,* and *instrument,* as well. Furthermore, there are rules determining how acts are causally related. The usual result of ATTEND is MTRANS for example, and MTRANS can lead to MBUILD. MOVE must be preceded by MBUILD (usually involving the intention of the movement). MOVE may result in PROPEL, if certain conditions have been satisfied. For example, MOVEment of the arm can result in the PROPELing of a rock only if the rock was previously GRASPed in the hand.

Rieger (1975) has demonstrated the inferential power of Schank's theory in a computer program which uses these rules to guess at information that is missing in the linguistic input itself. Beginning with the input, the program generates chains of inferences that expand both backward and forward in time. The inferences are assumed to be made automatically, as a kind of "reflex" of the mind triggered by linguistic input. The kinds of inferences made by Rieger's program seem much like those humans might make while reading.

For example, given as input the sentence "John told Mary that Bill wants a book," the program generates: "John believes that Bill wants a book," "Mary now knows that Bill wants a book," "Bill wants a book," "Bill might want to know the concepts contained in the book," "Mary might give Bill a book," "John may want Mary to give Bill a book," "John and Mary may have been together recently," and so on.

Many theorists see serious problems with this approach. For one thing, it seems inefficient to have so much information generated—most of it unnecessary and some of it invalid, as inferences frequently are—whenever a simple sentence is understood. For another, there seem to be no reasonable rules about where or when the process should stop. Clearly, it must. It would be unreasonable for the above example to be expanded to encompass the possibility that Mary will phone Bill to suggest he join the Book-of-the-Month Club, that Bill will go to the post office to buy a stamp so he can join the Club, and so forth.

One might abandon the assumption of *automatic inference,* and adopt instead an *inference-on-demand* approach, in which inferences are drawn only when they are required for understanding. A basic shortcoming of an inference-on-demand mechanism, however, is that there is no way to determine when an optimal level of understanding has been reached. The inference mechanism may be satisfied with a superficial analysis of the situation, and so stop short of making interesting discoveries about interrelations among current and past events, people's actions and their possible motives, and so on. If humans were strictly inference-on-demand devices, they would not enjoy reading a good mystery story, for the hidden intricacies of the plot would all escape their notice.

Frame Theory

Whether or not one accepts the basic assumptions of Schank's conceptual dependency theory, it is clear that much of the world knowledge we use in drawing inferences is of a higher level than represented by the simple conceptualizations we have discussed so far. Consider this beginning of a children's story:

(24) *Jane was invited to Jack's birthday party. She wondered if he would like a kite. She went to her room and shook her piggy bank. It made no sound.*

To understand this passage we must know what a typical children's birthday party is like.

Investigators working on the problem of computer understanding of prose have proposed that such knowledge be represented in a highly organized data structure, variously called a *frame* (Minsky, 1975), a *script* (Schank, 1976), or a *schema* (Rumelhart and Ortony, 1976). Schank says:

> A script is a giant causal chain of conceptualizations that have been known to occur in that order many times before. Scripts can be called up from memory by various words in the correct context, by visual inputs, or by expectancies generated through inferences. What a script does is to set up expectations about events that are likely to occur in a given situation. These events

can be predicted because they have occurred in precisely this fashion before. Scripts are associated, then, with static everyday events such as restaurants, birthday parties, classrooms, bus riding, theater going, and so on (Schank, 1976, pp. 180–181).

And Minsky describes the frame as follows:

> A *frame* is a data-structure for representing a stereotyped situation, like being in a certain kind of living room, or going to a child's birthday party. Attached to each frame are several kinds of information. Some of this information is about how to use the frame. Some is about what one can expect to happen next. Some is about what to do if these expectations are not confirmed. . . . The "top levels" of a frame are fixed, and represent things that are always true about the supposed situation. The lower levels have many . . ."slots" that must be filled by specific instances or data (Minsky, 1975, p. 212).

The frame, then, underlies much of what we have called generic memory: our stereotypes about people, the pattern of our daily or weekly or yearly routine, our knowledge of certain forms of literature (sonnets, folk tales), music (fugues, symphonies, rock tunes), architecture (typical churches, service stations), and games (chess, hopscotch, basketball). All can presumably be represented by structured frames.

The frame for a child's birthday party includes some "slots" that must be filled in, such as an adult hostess (or host), the child who is having the birthday, and the guests (number unspecified), as well as a cake with candles, and the ritual in which the candles are blown out and the birthday song is sung. Other slots are optional, but still highly likely, such as a gift from each guest (for which price and type are only loosely specified but which must be gift wrapped, and should be something the guest of honor would like), food (hot dogs, ice cream), games, and decorations.

How, then, is passage (24) understood? The first sentence is assumed to retrieve the "birthday party" frame from memory; Jack is filled in as the guest of honor, and Jane as one of the invited guests. The slot that "kite" best fits into is the one for gifts, and this judgment is confirmed by the fact that Jane wonders whether Jack would like one. The purpose of the kite, and its likely future role, can be guessed at only by reference to the general knowledge summarized by the birthday party frame.

Frame theory appears, to many, to be the best current answer to the question of how inferences are made when we understand linguistic input. It promises to provide computers with a powerful representation of world knowledge, and to help psychologists understand how knowledge is organized in human memory and how it is used in perception and comprehension. With the frame concept, memory theory may at last make real contact with the educational process—for the kind of structural, meaningful information taught in school is the kind that is best represented in frames. Despite this promise, however, frame theory is still vague and in need of development. The power of this representation system has not yet been adequately demonstrated. As frame theory is developed, unforeseen difficulties may be encountered. Furthermore, little attention has yet been given to the important problem of how frames are learned in the first place. We have seen how frames might be used in learning new information, but have not considered how the frames themselves are learned. This is a topic of current theoretical interest, and one or more solutions will likely be proposed in the next few years.

13

Current Trends and Future Projections

In his best-selling book *Future Shock*, Alvin Toffler criticizes educators for giving youth the skills and knowledge needed to cope with the past, rather than with the future. Educators are reluctant—and understandably so—to deal in speculations about the future, when they have much more certain knowledge of the past. There is, however, another reason to reflect on the past: it is only by relating the past to the present that one can determine the directions of trends that are likely to continue. This is why this book has concerned itself not only with the present state of the field of learning and memory but with the past developments, as well.

We have seen that the experimental psychology of learning and memory emerged from two parent disciplines—philosophy and biology; that the new field inherited from philosophy the approach we have called cognitivism and from biology the approach we have called behaviorism—the first stressing mental events and the second stressing the biological mechanisms underlying behavior. The most extreme form of cognitivism is introspectionism, which is interested only in subjectively observable mental events; the most extreme form of behaviorism is descriptive behaviorism, which is interested only in objectively observable behavior. Most cognitive psychologists require objective observations, but attempt to explain those observations in mentalistic terms. Behaviorists, by contrast, prefer mechanistic explanations of behavior. In recent years we have seen the fusion of mentalistic and mechanistic accounts of behavior in the computer analogy—a theoretical development that has given impressive new vigor to the cognitivist approach.

COGNITIVISM VERSUS BEHAVIORISM

In its beginning, in the late nineteenth and early twentieth centuries, psychology had a strongly cognitivist orientation. Indeed, it was in this period that the technique of introspection was most popular. Gradually, disaffection with the cognitive approach grew, and behaviorism became popular, reaching a peak in the 1940s and 1950s. Since 1960, the pendulum has swung in the other direction at an accelerating rate. The psychology of learning and memory today is dominated by cognitivism nearly as strongly as it was by behaviorism thirty years ago.

Cognitivist Inroads into Animal Learning

Evidence for the dominance of cognitivism can be seen in certain current trends in the field of animal learning. Not too long ago, students of human learning and memory got their theoretical inspiration from animal learning theories such as that of Clark Hull. The conditioning analogy suggested that the learning and forgetting of serial and paired–associates lists be accounted for in terms of S–R bonds. Today, the situation is reversed. Cognitive accounts of animal learning are becoming increasingly popular. As was pointed out in Chapter 6, several recent animal conditioning theories bear more than a superficial resemblance to Tolman's expectancy theory; but in addition, animal memory is becoming the focus of much experimental and theoretical work, and the inspiration for this work clearly derives from the study of human memory. Published articles have titles such as, "Short-term Visual Memory in the Pigeon," and "Proactive Interference of Bar-pressing in the Mouse." More and more, animal learning researchers are coming to distinguish between short-term and long-term memory stores, and between visual, auditory, and other memory modalities. Writers discuss retroactive and proactive interference in animal memory, and stress the importance of retrieval cues (for example, Spear, 1971). Papers on classical conditioning are even blossoming with box-and-arrow diagrams of the hypothetical flow of information in the nervous system (for example, Grant, 1972).

But animal learning theorists have not begun discussing memory simple because it is now fashionable to do so; there are experimental data that strongly suggest that animal learning is at least partly a matter of "episodic memories," of individual events, and not just of "habit strength." An excellent illustration of this point is given by the work of Capaldi (1967, 1971) on the partial-reinforcement effect. The partial-reinforcement effect, as we saw in Chapter 4, is the finding that resistance to extinction is greater following intermittent than following continuous reinforcement. Capaldi accounts for the effect with a *sequential hypothesis*, which assumes, in effect, that the animal can remember something of the trial-to-trial sequence of events to which it has been exposed.

Suppose a rat runs down a straight-alley runway and finds no food. According to Capaldi's sequential hypothesis, when the animal is placed in the start box on the next trial, the start box cues retrieve from memory the traces of events that occurred on the last trial, including the fact that there was no reward. If the rat traverses the runway on this trial and finds food, then it learns that nonreward (N) is sometimes followed by reward (R). This is something an animal given continuous reinforcement does not learn; since only R trials are given during training, it never experiences an NR transition. Capaldi's prediction of the partial-reinforcement effect follows directly from these assumptions. During extinction, only N trials are given. The partially reinforced animal has learned to run in the presence of memories of N; the continuously reinforced animal has not. Hence, the running of the partially reinforced animal extinguishes more slowly. The hypothesis is more complex than this, however; an animal can remember several N trials in a row. Thus, a rat given the sequence NNNNR learns not only that N is followed by R, but also that NN, NNN, and NNNN are followed by R. (The number of N's followed by an R is called "N-length.") It is assumed, moreover, that there is generalization among memory traces, determined by the variable, N-length. Thus, NN is more similar to NNN than it is to NNNN, and so on. A prediction of the hypothesis, then, is that the longer the N-length used in training, the greater will be the resistance to extinction. This prediction and several others made by the sequential hypothesis have been confirmed experimentally (see Capaldi, 1967, 1971). While the hypothesis does not explain all the phenomena surrounding partial reinforcement, it makes more correct, detailed predictions about effects of particular patterns of reinforcement than its competitors. Capaldi and his colleagues have concluded that animals remember not only whether they were rewarded or not on the previous trial, but also how large the reward was, what response was made, and what the time interval was between trials. These are all particular aspects of experience, of the kind that supposedly characterize episodic memory, as discussed in Chapter 12.

Cognitivism in Behavior Modification

With the area of human memory dominated by cognitivism, and even students of animal conditioning invoking cognitive explanations of behavior, it would be surprising if advocates of behavior modification and behavior therapy could resist the cognitive trend. Chapter 7 pointed out some of the problems of accounting for complex human behavior in terms of operant conditioning, as some have tried to do. Most leaders of the behavior modification movement recognize these problems. They have, increasingly, adopted a point of view in which cognitive processes play a prominent role.

Foremost among those who have attempted to develop a systematic understanding of behavior modification techniques has been Bandura (1969, 1971, 1977). The approach Bandura favors is called *social learning theory*. He contrasts it with the strict behavioristic approach as follows:

> A more valid criticism of the extreme behavioristic position is that, in a vigorous effort to eschew spurious inner causes, it neglected determinants of man's behavior arising from his cognitive functioning. Man is a thinking organism possessing capabilities that provide him with some power of self-direction. To the extent that traditional behavioral theories could be faulted, it was for providing an incomplete rather than an inaccurate account of human behavior. . . .
>
> Social learning theory . . . places special emphasis on the important roles played by vicarious, symbolic, and self-regulatory processes, which receive relatively little attention even in most contemporary theories of learning (Bandura, 1971, p. 2).

The work for which Bandura is best known concerns *observational learning*—that is, "vicarious" learning from the experience of others. In a typical experiment conducted by Bandura, a young child is allowed to observe the behavior of another person (the model) and is later tested to see whether he imitates the model. Bandura and his colleagues find that the tendency to imitate aggressive, hostile behavior is quite strong. (This research has been used to support the argument that violence should be banned from children's movies and television.) Degree of imitation has been found to be determined by a number of factors, including characteristics of the model, the particular behavior the model engages in, and the reward or punishment he receives for his actions.

In the operant conditioning interpretation of observational learning, the modeled stimulus is assumed to become, somehow, a discriminative stimulus (S^D) for the imitative behavior. Bandura (1971) rejects this approach as superficial, proposing instead a combination of four subprocesses:

1. *Attention.* The observer must attend closely to the particular behaviors to be imitated. Prestige of the model is an important determinant of attention. Some methods of presentation (for example, television) capture attention especially well.

2. *Retention.* The observer must remember the behavior. The information can be encoded either in the form of images or in verbal form. Rehearsal often plays a role in retention of imitative behavior.

3. *Motor skills.* The observer must be able to reproduce the remembered behavior at the appropriate time. Often, the attempts are crude at first, but become more refined through practice with feedback.

4. *Motivation.* If there are sanctions against the observed behavior, or if the incentive to produce it is too weak, it may not occur. The role of reinforcement is thus essentially the same as in Tolman's theory.

Social learning theory, as developed by Bandura and others, is compatible with most of the work that has been done on behavior modification; at the same time, it recognizes the role of cognitive processes in complex social behavior. It provides a framework within which both "behavior modifiers" and "information-processing psychologists" can fit. Furthermore, it directs attention toward important questions of how cognitive processes and behavior interact. In American psychology, divided as it has been between behaviorist and cognitivist approaches, these questions have been largely ignored.

The Future Role of Behaviorism

All this should not be understood to mean that cognitivism will take over completely, and behaviorism disappear. As we have seen, theoretical trends have a way of reversing themselves. In addition, however, a continuing role can be seen for the behavioristic approach. Behaviorism is more compatible than cognitivism with biology, and the ties between biology and the psychology of learning are strong. Evidence of these ties is seen in the profound effects that ethology is having on animal learning theory, as discussed in Chapter 7. If different species possess specialized learning mechanisms, each adapted to a particular ecological niche, then there is a temptation to try to understand what the genetic differences are, how they affect the chemistry or structure of the brain, and how this particular characteristic of the brain is linked to the behavior. At this level, mentalistic explanations clearly will not do. There is also the question of the nature of learning in simple organisms. Should mentalistic theories be applied to protozoa, to worms, or to lower vertebrates such as fish? For such creatures, surely, behaviorist theories are more appropriate than cognitivist ones.

The Biological Basis of Learning

The behavioristic approach of seeking mechanistic explanations is also kept alive by the engrossing search for the biological nature of learning. This book has had little to say about this subject. A number of researchers, however—in the fields of neurophysiology, biochemistry, and physiological psychology—are seeking to determine what physical change occurs in the brain with learning. This is perhaps the greatest mystery still facing biological science.

The problem, however, has proven to be enormously difficult (see the collection of articles edited by Rosenzweig and Bennett, 1976). The brain is a mass of some twelve billion neurons, each connected to an estimated average of ten thousand others—not in an entirely random fashion, but in a complex patterned network that no one yet understands. Even more numerous than neurons are glial cells, which are intertwined around the neurons. Electrical potentials are passed from neuron to neuron across tiny gaps called synapses; chemicals that are released to carry the impulse across the synapse are called neurotransmitters. It is generally believed, although it has not been proven, that the changes that underlie learning take place at these synapses. Electrical activity has also been recorded from glial cells, however, and both neurons and glia are affected by and produce a large number of chemical substances, many of which remain to be identified.

How might one go about identifying the biological basis of learning and memory? One way is to look for differences between a brain that has learned and one that has not. Early experience is known to affect the behavior of rats. Animals raised in an environment "enriched" with objects to manipulate and other rats to socialize with are better at learning mazes than are rats raised in isolation. This *may* be due to a difference in "intelligence" resulting from a difference in the amount of previous learning. (It may also be due to differences in excitability, hormone levels, motivation, or the ability to attend to distant visual cues—but it is often assumed that the difference is one of previous learning.) A comparison of the brains of rats raised in enriched and isolated environments shows that enriched animals have a thicker cortex, more glial cells, neurons with more branches and synapses, and more neuronal RNA. There are also differences in the activities of various enzymes. Such differences are suggestive, but nothing more.

Formal training procedures, interestingly enough, produce some similar effects. Typically, an experimental animal will be put through a learning task, such as passive avoidance or learning to use its nonpreferred paw to reach for food. A control animal is treated as similarly as possible, without being required to learn. Brain materials from these animals are then analyzed and compared. A number of differences have been reported: trained animals' brains have more RNA, or different kinds of RNA, more of various proteins, and different amounts of certain enzymes and transmitter substances. Again, differences may not reflect learning. Is it reasonable to assert that the control animal learned nothing? How do we know the observed differences are not due to different levels of stress? Indeed, how do we know they aren't artifacts of the experimental procedure? Sometimes, investigators discard from the experimental group those animals that do not learn—a procedure that could be responsible for some physiological differences between experimental and control animals that have been reported.

It is frequently suggested, because of such evidence, that the change underlying learning somehow involves RNA— perhaps in the role it plays in protein synthesis. Drugs that facilitate RNA synthesis, injected after a learning experience, often facilitate retention, while drugs that inhibit the synthesis of RNA or of proteins produce apparent amnesia. (Many such drugs also make animals very sick. Some of the effects of these drugs on behavior may be due to effects of the sickness on activity levels or motivation, or to side effects such as learned taste aversions of the kind discussed in Chapter 7.) Some drugs produce amnesia only for relatively weak habits; and amnesia due to protein synthesis inhibitors can sometimes be reversed, suggesting that it is retrieval rather than memory formation that has been affected. The drugs used in all these studies could affect, either directly or indirectly, any number of different chemical reactions in which proteins, hormones, and neurotransmitters may all be involved. Without knowing more about the biochemistry of the brain than we now know, therefore, about all we can conclude is that some change must be going on in the brain. RNA and proteins may be involved somehow, but the evidence for even so weak a statement is still indirect.

Even if one could identify specific substances as of central importance, and establish that they affected learning, rather than stress, motivation, or retrieval, there would remain the problem of determining exactly how they produce their effects. Where does the physical change take place? Is it at specific synapses, or distributed haphazardly through the brain? If it is at a specific synapse, is it within the surrounding glial cells or in the neurons themselves? If it is in a neuron, which one: the sender (pre-synaptic) or receiver (post-synaptic) of the impulse? Is learning a matter of "turning on" the synapses to be used, or turning a myriad of unwanted connections off? If it is the former, how is it done? Do adjacent surfaces grow closer together, do they grow fatter, or is the working synapse supplemented by other redundant ones? Or is the synaptic change not one of growth but one of setting up the cellular machinery for producing the transmitter substance? These are a few of the basic questions that are still open. We know very little of the biological basis of memory at this time.

It is not even obvious that a single answer to this question exists. Kety (1976) has this to say:

> So profound and powerful an adaptation as learning or memory is not apt to rest upon a single modality. Rather, I suspect that advantage is taken of every opportunity provided by evolution. There were forms of memory before organisms developed nervous systems, and after that remarkable leap forward it is likely

that every new pathway and neural complexity, every new neurotransmitter, hormone, or metabolic process that played upon the nervous system and subserved a learning process was preserved and incorporated (Kety, 1976, pp. 321–322).

The possibility Kety raises here, at the level of brain processes, is reminiscent of Razran's (1971) analysis, at the level of behavior. In simple organisms only one biological learning mechanism may exist; in more complex organisms several may coexist—underlying different kinds of learning, underlying the same habit at different ages, or simultaneously serving the same function. Such a hypothesis is as consistent with the evidence as any other.

But all these questions could be misleading. The ultimate answer could turn out to be quite different from what most investigators in this area expect. It is generally believed that a change in the efficiency of active synapses underlies learning. RNA and proteins are assumed to be involved somehow in this change. But what if information were encoded into the molecular structure itself? The hypothesis is generally discounted as implausible, because it is difficult to see how such a mechanism would work. But in a famous series of experiments—as celebrated in science fiction as in psychology—McConnell (1962) reported that when classically conditioned planaria are ground up and fed to another planarian, the "cannibal" worm (or recipient) by this means acquires the habit the original worms (or donors) learned. These studies are highly controversial, for several reasons. Perhaps most important is the doubt that planaria can be classically conditioned. What was transferred in the McConnell studies may have been sensitization, or general excitability, rather than the encoding of a specific habit.

Nevertheless, the possibility that memories might be transferred from a donor animal to a recipient has been pursued by other investigators. The most spectacular success using this approach has been reported by Ungar and several colleagues (for example, Ungar, 1973). These researchers have investigated the transfer of several habits, including dark avoidance in rats. Ungar claims to have isolated, analyzed, and synthesized in the laboratory a specific protein—a peptide consisting of fifteen amino acids—which produces dark avoidance when injected into the brains of recipient animals. The substance (dubbed *scotophobin,* after the Greek words for "fear of the dark") has also been reported to produce dark avoidance in mice and, remarkably enough, in goldfish. The exact meaning of these results is difficult to determine. If scotophobin really does encode dark avoidance, then the isolation and identification of other memory molecules may not be far in the future. But there have been some failures to replicate, and Ungar's reasoning and his procedures have been criticized (for example, Goldstein, 1973). In addition, most investigators feel certain that learning is based on changes at particular synaptic sites, and it is difficult to see how a substance like scotophobin, simply injected into the brain, would find its way to the appropriate locations. Despite the potential importance of Ungar's claim, therefore, it is widely disbelieved.

The controversy surrounding the evidence for memory-encoding molecules may be resolved within the next several years. But it would be foolish to predict a final solution to the problem of the biological basis of learning in the near future. Progress in biochemistry and related fields suggests that the problem will eventually be solved, but whether it will take fifteen or fifty years, or longer, is difficult to guess. Pavlov (1927) thought he had nearly solved the problem—and while we are probably closer to a solution than he was, there is no way to be sure.

We have been arguing that, although cognitivism has made extensive inroads into behaviorism's territory, there are areas where the behavioristic approach is so obviously appropriate that it is safe from cognitivist attack. These include investigations of learning in lower organisms, attempts to relate animal behavior to genetics, and attempts to explain animal learning in terms of the underlying machinery of the brain. In these areas, where the psychology of learning blends in with biology, the mentalistic flavor of cognitive psychology is out of place.

TRENDS IN THE PSYCHOLOGY OF MEMORY

How is the study of human memory likely to change in the next several years? Some trends were discussed in Chapter 12 which are likely to grow in importance. First, if the evidence continues to suggest that certain modalities of memory (for example, visual, olfactory, motor) obey laws different from those for verbal materials, special theories are likely to be developed to deal with them. A unified theory of human memory based on a few simple principles may be as elusive as a unified theory of animal learning has been. Second, there is likely to be increasing emphasis on how episodic and generic memory differ from each other and how they interrelate. Theories will either have to deal with this intuitively compelling dichotomy with two somewhat different mechanisms or show how the same processes can be used to explain them both. Third, interest in meaningful learning in general, and in processes of comprehension in particular, will undoubtedly continue to grow.

The computer analogy, we have seen, is a dominant force in modern cognitive psychology. How researchers conceive of this analogy, therefore, will surely determine, to some extent, the directions their research takes.

The Development of Memory

A distinction that is becoming increasingly important in memory theory is the distinction between the structural characteristics of the memory system and the *control processes*, which direct the processing of information within the system. Human adults have developed nearly optional strategies for encoding, rehearsal, and retrieval, which they can decide to use when appropriate to the demands of the task. More often than not, memory researchers have treated memory strategies as annoyances, to be eliminated by exerting strict control over the subject's processing activities. However, with research on mnemonic devices, strategies have emerged as a focus of interest in themselves.

Control processes have become an especially important topic in the study of the development of memory in children. Here, the interest is not so much in whether the child can be trained to use powerful mnemonic techniques as it is in how the child spontaneously discovers techniques and integrates them into his cognitive repertoire. Strategies discovered by the child apparently play a central role in the development of the ability to remember.

Studying the mental abilities of children is especially difficult, and this is the main reason so little has been said about memory development in this book. A child may do poorly on an experimental task because of a lack of motivation, an inability to concentrate, a failure to understand the instructions, or even a failure of the experimenter to understand the child's responses. But careful research that takes such problems into account has made some interesting observations about memory development in children. Memory performance improves with age, of course, but the degree of improvement varies considerably, depending on the nature of the task. Brown (1975) has identified two factors that limit a young child's memory performance. One is the degree of involvement of generic, or semantic, memory required by a task. The larger the vocabulary required, or the more general the knowledge, the greater is the effect of age. The other factor is the degree of "strategic involvement" required. The more performance in the task can be improved by mnemonic strategies, the greater is the improvement with age.

This analysis suggests that tasks in which mnemonic strategies have little, if any, effect should show little, if any, developmental improvement. One such task is recognition memory for unrelated pictures. Several investigations have failed to find a developmental trend in this task. For example, Nelson (1971) tested first-, fourth-, and seventh-grade children on memory for realistic pictures, abstract paintings, and puzzle pieces, using a two-alternative forced-choice recognition test, administered either immediately or 14 days after presentation. He found no reliable differences in performance among the three age levels (68.1 percent, 68.3 percent, and 69.7 percent correct, respectively). He found large age differences, however, in performance on a pattern-reconstruction task, which presumably involved strategies of encoding and retrieval. A second memory task that presumably should be affected little by strategies is the recency-discrimination task, described in Chapter 8. Brown (1973) presented pictures to first, second, and fourth graders, and college students, testing them on pairs on which they were required to pick either the "oldest" or the "newest" of the two pictures. Overall percentages correct for the four age groups were remarkably constant: 70.8 percent, 71.6 percent, 69.5 percent, and 72.5 percent, respectively. A third task that seems relatively strategy free is frequency judgments. Hasher and Chromiak (1977) found no change in accuracy of frequency judgments over an age range from second grade to college. Thus, there is considerable support for the hypothesis that certain tasks show little improvement with age.

Another implication of Brown's analysis is that, in tasks that are sensitive to strategy, one should be able to observe the development of strategies with age. This is indeed the case. Flavell, Friedrichs, and Hoyt (1970) tested nursery school, kindergarten and second- and fourth-grade children on a serial-recall task, in which objects were displayed in a horizontal row of windows, each of which could be illuminated by the subject by pressing a button directly below it. Subjects were allowed to study the objects until they felt they were ready to recall their names in order. A hidden observer recorded the subjects' behavior in detail. The nursery school and kindergarten children approached the task with no real strategy; they studied by simply illuminating the pictures and naming the objects aloud. Older children—particularly the fourth graders—began by naming the objects, but then tested themselves to see whether they could anticipate the objects in the windows, and rehearsed the names, often pointing at each of the windows in turn. The younger children, when asked to estimate their memory spans, were very unrealistic. Over half predicted errorless recall of 10 or more (versus a true average span of 3.5). Of the fourth graders, in contrast, only 21 percent predicted spans greater than 10 (versus an actual span of 5.5).

Observations such as these have led Flavell and Wellman (1976) to argue that there is little change in the "hardware" of memory with age—that the most profound changes take place in control processes, based upon the child's awareness of his own memory and its limitations, and of the ways that he can use it effectively. Such knowledge they call *"metamemory."* The argue that the very young child may lack control processes not only because he has had little opportunity to practice them, but—more profoundly—because it never occurs to him to try deliberately to retrieve information or to prepare for future retrieval at all. With experience, the child gradually learns that some things are easier to remember than others, that retrieval cues can be effective aids to remembering, that large amounts of material and long retention intervals make remembering difficult, that rehearsal and self-testing improve retention, and so on. It is not until he has some awareness of his mnemonic abilities and limitations that he will begin to develop the control processes that characterize memorization in the adult.

If these ideas are correct, then an understanding of control processes will be essential to an understanding of cognitive development. It may also be that control processes—which are often viewed as tricks employed by wily subjects to bewilder the memory researcher—can best be analyzed and understood by concentrating on the abilities of children, instead of those of the intelligent and sophisticated adult. In this way, we may isolate and identify basic, elementary control processes, and then show how they are combined in the complex strategies that adults employ.

The Future of the Computer Analogy

Not all the theoretical predispositions brought about by the computer analogy have fared as well as the concept of control processes. Psychologists have tended to ignore the fact that computers and human brains originated in completely different ways. Many have taken for granted, as it has been said, "that men and computers are merely two different species of a more abstract genus called 'information-processing systems.' " The computer analogy, however, must be used with great caution. While it may be true that the human brain is a computer *of some kind,* there is no reason to believe that it is much like the electronic digital computers with which present-day theorists are familiar. Indeed, there are reasons to believe that it is quite different.

The assumption of discrete, multiple memory stores, as suggested by the computer analogy, has been questioned on several grounds, as we saw in Chapter 11. The assumption of strict all-or-none learning likewise has been questioned, and the behavioral evidence seems to weigh against it. It has been argued that since neurons fire in an all-or-none manner, the assumption has neurophysiological support—but a neuron's *readiness* to fire is not all-or-none (the more impulses received from other neurons, the more likely the neuron is to fire), and the *rate* of firing appears to be continuously variable. Recent evidence suggests that much of the information processing in the brain may involve graded changes in electrical potential, rather than all-or-none neural impulses (Schmitt, Dev, and Smith, 1976). Thus, even this supposed neurophysiological support for all-or-none storage is extremely weak.

The assumption that all information is represented in memory in propositional form has been hotly debated. While no one today seriously makes the opposite claim—that all internal representations are analogue (for example, images)—it is often claimed that propositional and analogue representations coexist in memory. According to the dual-coding theory (for example, Paivio, 1971, 1975), verbal information and visual images are stored in separate representational systems—the verbal system specialized for dealing with abstract concepts and sequential information, and the imagery system specialized for representing concrete objects and spatial information. The two systems are assumed to be independent but interconnected, probably located in different cerebral hemispheres (an assumption for which there is considerable evidence).

A fundamental problem with the notion that images are stored in memory is that the retrieval of information from an image would seem to require a "little man in the head" to scan, analyze, and interpret the image. This point has been emphasized especially by advocates of the computer analogy (for example, Pylyshyn, 1973). Workers in the fields of computer simulation and artificial intelligence have struggled with baffling problems of visual perception (that is, scene analysis), and seem quite perturbed at the notion that, after carrying out the sophisticated analyses that perception seemingly involves, the brain would go ahead and encode into memory the raw picture instead of the information already extracted from the picture. It may be that the images we experience are more abstract and less picture-like than they seem. Still, there remain many experimental findings—such as data on serial learning and on the linear-ordering effect—that are interpreted more easily in terms of analogue than propositional representations. It is known that certain sensory qualities have analogue representations in the cortex (the visual field and the auditory pitch dimension are given spatial representation on the cortex, for example, and stimulus intensities are represented in several modalities by neural firing rate). It is not unreasonable to suppose that analogue forms of representation are used in "deeper" processing, as well. It seems likely, therefore, that theories based on computer analogy eventually will have to come to grips with the problems of analogue representation.

The assumption that the brain is strictly a serial processing device is almost certainly incorrect. Although some mental acts—particularly those requiring conscious attention—may be done sequentially, the evidence suggests that much of the information processing done by the brain is parallel. Collins and Quillian (1972), for example, reject the hypothesis that the search for information in long-term memory involves examination of one associative link at a time, and propose instead that "activation" spreads out in all directions along established pathways, demanding conscious attention for evaluation only when potentially interesting information has been found. Evidence for such automatic activation is found, for example, in the Stroop effect, discussed in Chapter 10.

Collins and Quillian also comment on a striking and profound difference between computers and animals: the difference in their ability to generalize and to learn discriminations. Humans easily recognize a visual stimulus such as the letter "R" whether it is light on a dark ground or dark on a light ground, at the middle, top, bottom, left, or right of the visual field, regardless of its size, and despite various degrees of distortion. Likewise, we recognize an auditory stimulus such as the tune "Turkey in the Straw" whether it is played on a flute, cello, or tuba, at a slow or fast speed, and under the various rhythmic distortions characteristic of different musical styles. It is extremely difficult to get a computer to make these generalizations which people find so natural.

This difference in the ability to generalize may reflect the quite different purposes for which computers were developed and brains evolved. A living organism exists in an ever-changing environment, in which two equivalent experiences are seldom if ever exactly the same. Food and danger must be recognized in new situations if the animal is to survive, and learning is of value only if it contributes to survival. Computers have been developed as strictly logical devices. It is their rigor and precision for which they are praised (and sometimes lauded as superior to humans). Any device that extrapolates wildly in order to bring past experience to bear on the present situation is bound to make many errors, and errors are what computers were designed to avoid.

Yet the ability and willingness to make such extrapolations are very likely an important aspect of human intelligence. Just as we can see the "same" letter under different distortions, we also can see the "same" principle underlying very different types of experience. Reasoning by analogy has long been recognized as essential to productive, creative thought. (It underlies much foolish thinking, as well.) Analogy and metaphor are now being recognized as of crucial importance in language comprehension. The sentence:

(1) *The waves cast by a pebble of thought spread until they reach even the nitwits on the shores.*

and the newspaper headline:

(2) *Dodgers pulverize Giants*

are not to be taken literally. They can be understood correctly only if certain remote similarities are noticed between two very different situations. A computer with intellectual abilities matching those of human will have to be able to see such similarities, as well. The great advantage of the computer, then—its rigor and precision—is also a disadvantage. "Fuzzy thinking" is perhaps more worthwhile than we have been led to believe. Indeed, recent developments in mathematics—"fuzzy set theory" and (built upon it) "fuzzy logic"—are being explored as ways of making too-logical and too-literal computers more like the human mind.

There is a further problem concerning the computer analogy that deserves mention here. The problem is how to characterize the mechanism that governs or controls the information-processing system. This is a problem that no theorist seems adequately to have faced. In the TOTE-unit theory of Miller, Galanter, and Pribram (1960), for example, it was assumed that what is learned is a plan or behavioral program, in which feedback loops called TOTE units are organized, sequentially and hierarchically, in a way that is likely to accomplish an overall goal. Very little is said, however, about how the program is put together. Presumably, there must be some kind of program-writing program, of considerable power, that accomplishes this; but no account is given of how such a program might work. Similarly, in the two-process memory theory of Atkinson and Shiffrin (1968, 1971) control processes such as rehearsal, the use of imagery, and memory search are discussed. But nothing is said about the mechanism that decides when and how these control processes are to be used. Shakey, the SRI robot (see Chapter 6), plans its own sequences of actions—but these plans are designed always to reach goals stated by its human masters. A complete theory of human cognition must explain how the highest-level goals are formulated, for they are what determine the overall direction behavior will take.

Information-processing theorists typically either ignore this problem altogether, or attribute the overall planning to an *"executive routine."* The purpose here is apparently to equate high-level human planning to the function of the executive routine of a computer—a program that decides how to allocate memory storage, which user to serve next, and so on. The analogy is a very weak one, however. The term "executive routine" is used as though it were an explanation, but it is not. Until someone demonstrates that a computer program can carry out creative planning on the highest level, without human direction, it is probably best to think of "executive routine" as nothing more than a substitute for terms such as "volition," the "will," or the "soul," used by earlier writers in essentially the same way.

Limitations of the Computer Analogy

At present, the computer analogy may be as useful for what it tells us that humans are not as for what it tells us we are. But computers are certain to change. In the not-too-distant future we may have parallel-process, analogue, learning computers, that formulate and carry out their own plans. But even then there are likely to be severe limits to what the computer analogy can tell us about the human mind. Weizenbaum (1976), himself a worker in the field of artificial intelligence, has discussed several reasons for believing that this is so. Two of his arguments are worth presenting here—one has to do with complexity, and the other with implicit knowledge.

The complexity argument is essentially this: Much of human cognition is extremely complex. A computer program capable of simulating it in any detail, therefore, must itself be complex. But the more complex the program is, the less adequate it will be as a scientific theory. Theories must be parsimonious—not simply for aesthetic reasons, but for practical reasons as well. A theory that is too complex cannot be understood. If the theorist does not understand the theory, he cannot figure out why its predictions fail, and therefore does not know how to modify it to make it work. Perhaps worse, he cannot explain it to his fellow scientists. Thus, the more adequate the simulation program becomes in one sense, the less satisfactory it becomes in the other sense. It is possible for the behavior of a complex program to be just as mysterious as the human behavior the program was intended to help explain.

The implicit-knowledge argument says that there are some things we know simply because we are human beings—things we cannot adequately describe, and therefore could never communicate to a computer. Human beings are all of the same species. Our nervous systems have the same structure, and we experience similar environments. Nearly all of us know the appearance of the nighttime sky, how it feels to be wet and cold, to be sleepy, to be happy, to be physically exhausted, to feel pain, to feel panic or pleasurable excitement, to fear death. We can communicate about such things with each other, but only because of our common experience. Even a computer with vast world knowledge could never understand such things in the sense that another human can. Thus, it is argued that computer simulation will be of little use where human emotion is involved. The computer could not possess the skills of a good psychotherapist, or understand the meaning of a lyric poem.

The proponent of the computer analogy might answer by saying, "If you can explain in detail how a system works, I can write a program to simulate it." This is undoubtedly true. The computer is a general symbol-manipulating device of great power. To argue that computer simulation of the human mind is inherently limited is to argue that there are inherent limits to the scientific understanding of the mind. No one should be surprised at such a conclusion, since there are known to be limits to knowledge in other fields (mathematics and physics). For now, however, speculation about the limits of psychological knowledge is of no real practical consequence, since we have only begun to explore those aspects of the human mind that are potentially within our reach.

BASIC ATTITUDES

We have seen how early cognitivism, which included introspective observation, gave way during the behaviorist revolution to a constellation of attitudes including: (a) a stress on mechanistic explanations of behavior, (b) a rejection of introspectionism, and (c) an emphasis on environment, instead of heredity, as the primary determinant of behavior. During the last several years, cognitivism has again gained the upper hand. What has been the fate of these attitudes of behaviorism?

The first, we have argued, is present in subdued form in the computer analogy. In this form, mechanistic explanation is not viewed as the antithesis of mentalistic explanation; they are seen as complementary. But what about introspectionism? Will the trend toward mentalistic explanations be accompanied by a return of subjective observation? And what about the almost total emphasis on learning, as opposed to "instinct" and "innate ideas"? Let us first consider subjective observation.

Subjective Versus Objective Observation

The crumbling of early introspectionism, as was pointed out in Chapter 2, resulted from a lack of agreement among observers regarding just what the data were. In the experimental psychology of learning and memory, the fate of early introspectionism has not been forgotten. To be sure, cognitive psychologists sometimes ask subjects for introspective reports on how they did an experimental task, and they often perform the task themselves to gain insights into how it is done. But they do this primarily to get ideas about what kind of mental events may lie behind the objective, behavioral data. Thus, subjective observation is viewed as an aid to theory building, but seldom is it seen as a direct source of data.

Present-day linguists—particularly Chomsky and his followers—make use of subjective observations for deciding the grammatical acceptability of sentences. The grammar of a language is that set of rules that will generate all acceptable sentences of the language and no unacceptable ones. To determine the rules of the language, then, one needs many crucial sentences, some known to be grammatical and others known to be ungrammatical. In deciding whether a sentence is grammatical, the linguist uses his own "linguistic intuition," assuming the intuitive judgments of other native speakers of the language will necessarily be the same. If this were so, there would be no problem, as there would be a substantial body of data agreed upon by all observers.

But as grammatical theory has developed, crucial distinctions have become more and more subtle, and agreement—even among trained linguists—has not always been assured. Perhaps more importantly, the judgments of linguists, because of their training, may not be the same as those of the linguistic community in general. Indeed, Spencer (1973) had college students judge the grammatical acceptability of 150 sentences given in linguistics papers as "clear cases" of acceptable or unacceptable utterances. While the subjects agreed with each other fairly well, they disagreed with the authors of the papers on fully 59 of the examples (39 percent). Thus, it may be an error for linguists, as it apparently was for the introspectionists, to rely entirely on their own subjective observations to generate data.

Despite these cautions, there are some who would like to expand the very limited role now played by subjective observation in experimental psychology. Tart (1972), in what must be one of the most unusual papers the journal *Science* has ever published, advocates that "altered states of consciousness" such as dreams and hypnosis, experiences of "ecstasy" and "space-and-time transcendence," and alcohol, marijuana and LSD intoxication, be investigated by establishing what he terms "state-specific sciences." Each state of consciousness, in his proposal, would have its own science, in which specially trained observers would conduct introspective observations and construct theories only while they themselves were in the state under investigation. No such "state-specific science" currently exists, and it is doubtful that one ever will. Even if the many other difficulties could be overcome (for example, knowing when two individuals are in the same state of consciousness), there would remain the problem of interobserver agreement regarding the data. If the introspectionists—all highly trained observers in controlled situations and in their normal, rational state—sometimes failed to agree, one can imagine the anarchy and confusion Tart's proposal would entail. It is doubtful that any attempt to bring back introspection as the primary method of observation will succeed.

Heredity Versus Environment

We saw in Chapter 2 that the philosophical roots of the experimental psychology of learning lay in British empiricism, which stressed experience as the source of all knowledge. This emphasis on the environment became particularly strong in the writings of John B. Watson, who essentially denied that heredity had any important role in determining behavior. While the empiricist doctrine has always been dominant in the field of learning, the position of the European rationalists, emphasizing innate determinants of conscious experience and behavior, has also had its effects. This general point of view has found its way from European philosophy into American psychology through a number of circuitous routes: Research on instincts by the ethologists—particularly Konrad Lorenz—was influenced by Kant's doctrine of innate ideas. Likewise, Sigmund Freud's analysis of instincts in humans, Jean Piaget's theory of stages of cognitive development, and the emphasis in Gestalt psychology on innate principles of organization in perception and memory all show the influence of rationalist philosophy. And the linguist Noam Chomsky, who sees the immediate problem of linguistics and psychology as the discovery of the innate mental structure—unique to humans—that makes language acquisition possible, emphatically aligns himself with rationalist, and against empiricist, philosophy.

   The field of behavior genetics has also contributed to this trend. In animals such as the rat, activity level, susceptibility to seizures, preference for alcohol, and ability to learn mazes are to some extent inherited. In humans, several abnormalities of the nervous system (for example, Down's syndrome and color blindness) are known to be genetically determined, and there is some evidence that I.Q., as well, is partly a product of heredity.

Unfortunately, thinking in this area seems to become bound up in some people's minds with political beliefs. Most often, it is assumed that proponents of genetic determinants of behavior will have right-wing political views—apparently because arguments for the inheritance of mental abilities can be distorted to justify racial, ethnic, and sex discrimination. However, Chomsky, the modern champion of rationalist philosophy, relates his linguistic views to leftist-anarchist politics, and blames empiricist thinking (especially that of behaviorism) for many of the ills of American society, including its involvement in the Vietnamese War. If positions concerning the genetic determinants of behavior were inextricably tied to political beliefs, it is hard to see how Chomsky (1968) could cite with approval the ethological contributions of Konrad Lorenz, who once wrote papers seeking to justify the prohibition by the Nazis of intermarriage between Germans and Jews. Positions on the psychological issue, on the one hand, and the political issue, on the other, come in all combinations. Relationships between them, it seems safest to conclude, are probably imaginary.

Despite the apparently misguided attempts to politicize this issue, the various rationalist influences have had their effects. It has become more and more acceptable for psychologists to consider the extent to which abilities may be innately determined. Even theorists working on the comprehension of prose have found it necessary to postulate a number of "primitive" concepts and operations which exist before any knowledge has been acquired through experience. Examples of such primitive concepts are the labels on associations used in the HAM theory of Anderson and Bower (1973), and the primitive acts postulated by Schank (1976). These correspond roughly to the innate categories that Kant assumed determine the nature of our experience. The increasing acceptance of such a notion could lead, in the future, to a major experimental and theoretical effort to determine which are the "true" innate categories of the human mind.

Bibliography

Aarons, L. Sleep-assisted instruction. *Psychological Bulletin,* 1976, *83,* 1–40.

Amsel, A. The role of frustrative nonreward in noncontinuous reward situations. *Psychological Review,* 1962, *69,* 306–328.

Anderson, J. R. and Bower, G. H. *Human Associative Memory.* Washington, D.C.: V. H. Winston & Sons, 1973.

Anderson, R. C., and Myrow, D. L. Retroactive inhibition of meaningful discourse. *Journal of Educational Psychology Monographs,* 1971, *62,* No. 1.

Andrews, L. M., and Karlins, M. *Psychology: What's in It for Us?* New York: Random House, 1975.

Anisfeld, M., and Knapp, M. Association, synonymity, and directionality in false recognition. *Journal of Experimental Psychology,* 1968, *77,* 171–179.

Asch, S. E. Reformulation of the problem of association. *American Psychologist,* 1969, *24,* 92–102.

Atkinson, R. C., and Shiffrin, R. M. Human memory: A proposed system and its control processes. In K. W. Spence and J. T. Spence (Eds), *The Psychology of Learning and Motivation.* Vol. 2. New York: Academic Press, 1968.

Atkinson, R. C., and Shiffrin, R. M. The control of short-term memory. *Scientific American,* 1971, *225,* 82–90.

Ausubel, D. P. *The Psychology of Meaningful Verbal Learning.* New York: Grune & Stratton, 1963.

Ausubel, D. P., Stager, M., and Gaite, A. J. H. Retroactive facilitation in meaningful verbal learning. *Journal of Educational Psychology,* 1968, *59,* 250–255.

Ayer, A. J. *The Problem of Knowledge.* London: Macmillan, 1956.

Ayllon, T., and Azrin, N. H. *The Token Economy: A Motivational System for Therapy and Rehabilitation.* New York: Appleton-Century-Crofts, 1968.

Baddeley, A. D. Short-term memory for word sequences as a function of acoustic, semantic, and formal similarity. *Quarterly Journal of Experimental Psychology,* 1966, *18,* 362–365.

Baddeley, A. D., and Hitch, G. Working memory. In G. H. Bower (Ed.), *The Psychology of Learning and Motivation.* Vol. 8. New York: Academic Press, 1974.

Baddeley, A. D., and Warrington, E. K. Amnesia and the distinction between long- and short-term memory. *Journal of Verbal Learning and Verbal Behavior,* 1970, *9,* 176–189.

Bandura, A. *Principles of Behavior Modification.* New York: Holt, Rinehart & Winston, 1969.

Bandura, A. *Social Learning Theory.* New York: General Learning Press, 1971.

Bandura, A. Self-efficacy: Toward a unifying theory of behavioral change. *Psychological Review,* 1977, 84, 191–215.

Barber, T. X. Hypnotic age regression: A critical review. *Psychosomatic Medicine,* 1962, *24,* 286–299.

Barbizet, J. *Human Memory and Its Pathology.* San Francisco: W. H. Freeman & Co., 1970.

Barnes, J. M., and Underwood, B. J. "Fate" of first-list associations in transfer theory. *Journal of Experimental Psychology,* 1959, *58,* 97–105.

Bartlett, F. C. *Remembering.* Cambridge: Cambridge University Press, 1932.

Bateson, P. P. G. Internal influences on early learning in birds. In R. A. Hinde and J. Stevenson-Hinde (Eds.), *Constraints on Learning: Limitations and Predispositions.* London: Academic Press, 1973.

Beatty, J. Similar effects of feedback signals and instructional information on EEG activity. *Physiology and Behavior,* 1972, *9,* 151–154.

Beck, E. C., and Doty, R. W. Conditioned flexion reflexes acquired during combined catalepsy and de-efferentation. *Journal of Comparative and Physiological Psychology,* 1957, *50,* 211–216.

Begg, I., and Wickelgren, W. A. Retention functions for syntactic and lexical vs. semantic information in sentence recognition memory. *Memory & Cognition*, 1974, *2*, 353–359.

Beh, H. C. and Barratt, P. E. H. Discrimination and conditioning during sleep as indicated by the electroencephalogram. *Science*, 1965, *147*, 1470–1471.

Bergson, H. *Matter and Memory*. Translated by N. M. Paul and W. S. Palmer. New York: Macmillan, 1911.

Bigham, J. Memory: Studies from Harvard (II). *Psychological Review*, 1894, *1*, 453–461.

Bitterman, M. E. The comparative analysis of learning. *Science*, 1975, *188*, 699–709.

Bjork, R. A., and Whitten, W. B. Recency-sensitive retrieval processes in long-term free recall. *Cognitive Psychology*, 1974, *6*, 173–189.

Blake, M. J. F. Time of day effects on performance in a range of tasks. *Psychonomic Science*, 1967, *9*, 349–350.

Blough, D. S. A method for obtaining psychophysical thresholds from the pigeon. *Journal of the Experimental Analysis of Behavior*, 1958, *1*, 31–43.

Bolles, R. C. Species-specific defense reactions and avoidance learning. *Psychological Review*, 1970, *77*, 32–48.

Boneau, C. A. Paradigm regained? Cognitive behaviorism restated. *American Psychologist*, 1974, *29*, 297–309.

Bousfield, W. A. The occurrence of clustering in the recall of randomly arranged associates. *Journal of General Psychology*, 1953, *49*, 229–240.

Bower, G. H. Partial and correlated reward in escape learning. Journal of Experimental Psychology, 1960, *59*, 126–130.

Bower, G. H. Imagery as a relational organizer in associative learning. *Journal of Verbal Learning and Verbal Behavior*, 1970, *9*, 529–533.

Bransford, J. D., and Johnson, M. K. Contextual prerequisites for understanding: Some investigations of comprehension and recall. *Journal of Verbal Learning and Verbal Behavior*, 1972, *11*, 717–726.

Bregman, E. An attempt to modify the emotional attitude of infants by the conditioned response technique. *Journal of Genetic Psychology*, 1934, *45*, 169–198.

Breland, K., and Breland, M. A field of applied animal psychology. *American Psychologist*, 1951, *6*, 202–204.

Breland, K., and Breland, M. The misbehavior of organisms. *American Psychologist*, 1961, *16*, 681–683.

Brimer, C. J. Disinhibition of an operant response. *Learning and Motivation*, 1970, *1*, 346–371.

Broadbent, D. E. *Perception and Communication*. London: Pergamon Press, 1958.

Broadbent, D. E. The magical number seven after fifteen years. In A. Kennedy and A. Wikes, *Studies in Long-Term Memory*. London: John Wiley & Sons, 1975.

Brogden, W. J. Sensory pre-conditioning. *Journal of Experimental Psychology*, 1939, *25*, 323–332.

Brown, A. L. Judgments of recency for long sequences of pictures: The absence of a developmental trend. *Journal of Experimental Child Psychology*, 1973, *15*, 473–480.

Brown, A. L. The development of memory: Knowing, knowing about knowing, and knowing how to know. In H. W. Reese (Ed.), *Advances in Child Development and Behavior*. Vol. 10. New York: Academic Press, 1975.

Brown, J. Some tests of the decay theory of immediate memory. *Quarterly Journal of Experimental Psychology*, 1958, *10*, 12–21.

Brown, P. L., and Jenkins, H. M. Auto-shaping of the pigeon's keypeck. *Journal of the Experimental Analysis of Behavior*, 1968, *11*, 1–8.

Brown, R., and McNeill, D. The "tip of the tongue" phenomenon. *Journal of Verbal Learning and Verbal Behavior*, 1966, *5*, 325–337.

Bugelski, B. R. Images as mediators in one-trial paired-associate learning. II: Self-timing in successive lists. *Journal of Experimental Psychology*, 1968, *77*, 328–334.

Burtt, H. E. An experimental study of early childhood memory: Final report. *Journal of Genetic Psychology*, 1941, *58*, 435–439.

Buschke, H. Relative retention in immediate memory determined by the missing scan method. *Nature*, 1963, *200*, 1129–1130.

Calkins, M. W. Association. *Psychological Review*, 1894, *1*, 476–483.

Calkins, M. W. Association: An essay analytic and experimental. *Psychological Review Monograph Supplements*, 1896, No. 2.

Capaldi, E. J. A sequential hypothesis of instrumental learning. In K. W. Spence and J. T. Spence (Eds.), *The Psychology of Learning and Motivation*. Vol. 1. New York: Academic Press, 1967.

Capaldi, E. J. Memory and learning: A sequential viewpoint. In W. K. Honig and P. H. R. James (Eds), *Animal Memory*. New York: Academic Press, 1971.

Cermak, L. S., Butters, N., and Goodglass, H. The extent of memory loss in Korsakoff patients. *Neuropsychologia*, 1971, *9*, 307–315.

Chase, W. G., and Simon, H. A. Perception in chess. *Cognitive Psychology*, 1973, *4*, 55–81.

Chomsky, N. *Syntactic Structures*. The Hague: Mouton, 1957.

Chomsky, N. *Language and Mind*. New York: Harcourt Brace Jovanovich, 1968.

Chorover, S. L., and Schiller, P. H. Short-term retrograde amnesia in rats. *Journal of Comparative and Physiological Psychology*, 1965, *59*, 73–78.

Collins, A. M., and Loftus, E. F. A spreading-activation theory of semantic processing. *Psychological Review*, 1975, *82*, 407–428.

Collins, A. M., and Quillian, M. R. Retrieval time from semantic memory. *Journal of Verbal Learning and Verbal Behavior*, 1969, *8*, 240–247.

Collins, A. M., and Quillian, M. R. How to make a language user. In E. Tulving and W. Donaldson (Eds.), *Organization of Memory*. New York: Academic Press, 1972.

Conrad, R. Acoustic confusions in immediate memory. *British Journal of Psychology*, 1964, *55*, 75–84.

Conrad, R. Short-term memory processes in the deaf. *British Journal of Psychology*, 1970, *61*, 179–195.

Cook, J. O. "Superstition" in the Skinnerian. *American Psychologist*, 1963, *18*, 516–518.

Craik, F. I. M., and Kirsner, K. The effect of speaker's voice on word recognition. *Quarterly Journal of Experimental Psychology*, 1974, *26*, 274–284.

Craik, F. I. M., and Lockhart, R. S. Levels of processing: A framework for memory research. *Journal of Verbal Learning and Verbal Behavior*, 1972, *11*, 671–684.

Craik, K. J. W. *The Nature of Explanation*. Cambridge: Cambridge University Press, 1943.

Crespi, L. P. Quantitative variation of incentive and performance in the white rat. *American Journal of Psychology*, 1942, *55*, 467–517.

Cronholm, B. Post-ECT amnesias. In G. A. Talland and M. C. Waugh (Eds.), *The Pathology of Memory*. New York: Academic Press, 1969.

Davis, M., and Wagner, A. R. Habituation of startle response under incremental sequence of stimulus intensities. *Journal of Comparative and Physiological Psychology*, 1969, *67*, 486–492.

Deese, J., and Kaufman, R. A. Serial effects in recall of unorganized and sequentially organized verbal material. *Journal of Experimental Psychology*, 1957, *54*, 180–187.

de Groot, A. D. *Thought and Choice in Chess*. The Hague: Mouton, 1965.

Deutsch, J. A. *The Structural Basis of Behavior*. Chicago: University of Chicago Press, 1960.

Deutsch, J. A. and Deutsch, D. *Physiological Psychology.* Homewood, Ill.: Dorsey Press, 1973.

DiCara, L. V. Learning in the autonomic nervous system. *Scientific American,* 1970, *222,* 30–39.

Dickinson, A., Hall, G., and Mackintosh, N. J. Surprise and the attenuation of blocking. *Journal of Experimental Psychology: Animal Behavior Processes,* 1976, *2,* 313–322.

Dimond, S. J., and Beaumont, J. G. (Eds.) *Hemisphere Function in the Human Brain.* London: Paul Elik (Scientific Books), 1974.

Dmitriev, A. S., and Kochigina, A. M. The importance of time as a stimulus of conditioned reflex activity. *Psychological Bulletin,* 1959, *56,* 106–132.

Dollard, J., and Miller, N. E. *Personality and Psychotherapy.* New York: McGraw-Hill, 1950.

Drachman, D. A., and Arbit, J. Memory and the hippocampal complex, II. *Archives of Neurology,* 1966, *15,* 52–61.

Dulany, D. E. Awareness, rules and propositional control: A confrontation with S–R behavior theory. In T. R. Dixon and D. L. Horton (Eds.), *Verbal Behavior and General Behavior Theory.* Englewood Cliffs, N.J.: Prentice-Hall, 1968.

Ebbinghaus, H. *Grundzüge der Psychologie.* Vol. I 3rd Ed. Leipzig: Verlag von Veit and Company, 1911.

Ebbinghaus, H. *Über das Gedächtnis.* Leipzig: Duncker & Humbolt, 1885. Translated by H. Ruyer and C. E. Bussenius. New York: Columbia Teachers College, 1913.

Ebenholtz, S. M. Position mediated transfer between serial learning and a spatial discrimination task. *Journal of Experimental Psychology,* 1963, *65,* 603–608.

Emlen, S. T. The stellar-orientation system of a migratory bird. *Scientific American,* 1975, *233,* 102–111.

Emmons, W. H., and Simon, C. W. The non-recall of material presented during sleep. *American Journal of Psychology,* 1956, *69,* 76–81.

Engen, T., and Ross, B. M. Long-term memory of odors with and without verbal descriptions. *Journal of Experimental Psychology,* 1973, *100,* 221–227.

Entwisle, D. R., and Huggins, W. H. Interference in meaningful learning. *Journal of Educational Psychology,* 1964, *55,* 75–78.

Eysenck, H. J. The effects of psychotherapy: An evaluation. *Journal of Consulting Psychology,* 1952, *16,* 319–324.

Feigenbaum, E. A., and Simon, H. A. A theory of the serial position effect. *British Journal of Psychology,* 1962, *53,* 307–320.

Ferster, C. B., and Skinner, B. F. *Schedules of Reinforcement.* New York: Appleton-Century-Crofts, 1957.

Fingerman, P., and Levine, M. Nonlearning: The completion of the blindness. *Journal of Experimental Psychology,* 1974, *102,* 720–721.

Flavell, J. H., Friedrichs, A. G., and Hoyt, J. D. Developmental changes in memorization processes. *Cognitive Psychology,* 1970, *1,* 324–340.

Flavell, J. H., and Wellman, H. M. Metamemory. In R. V. Kail, Jr. and J. W. Hagen (Eds.), *Perspectives on the Development of Memory and Cognition.* Hillsdale, N. J.: Lawrence Erlbaum Associates, 1976.

Fodor, J. A., Bever, T. G., and Garrett, M. F. *The Psychology of Language.* New York: McGraw-Hill, 1974.

Fouts, R. S. Language: Origins, definitions and chimpanzees. *Journal of Human Evolution,* 1974, *3,* 475–482.

Fowler, R. L., and Kimmel, H. D. Operant conditioning of the GSR. *Journal of Experimental Psychology,* 1962, *63,* 563–567.

Franks, J. J., and Bransford, J. D. Abstraction of visual patterns. *Journal of Experimental Psychology,* 1971, *90,* 65–74.

Freedman, J. L., and Landauer, T. K. Retrieval of long term memory: "Tip-of-the-tongue" phenomenon. *Psychonomic Science,* 1966, *4,* 309–310.

Galton, F. Psychometric experiments. *Brain,* 1879–1880, *2,* 149–162.

Garcia, J., Ervin, F. R., and Koelling, R. A. Learning with prolonged delay of reinforcement. *Psychonomic Science,* 1966, *5,* 121–122.

Garcia, J., and Koelling, A. Relation of cue to consequence in avoidance learning. *Psychonomic Science,* 1966, *4,* 123–124.

Gardner, B. T., and Gardner, R. A. Evidence for sentence constituents in the early utterances of child and chimpanzee. *Journal of Experimental Psychology: General,* 1975b, *104,* 244–267.

Gardner, R. A., and Gardner, B. T. Teaching sign language to a chimpanzee. *Science,* 1969, *165,* 664–672.

Gardner, R. A., and Gardner, B. T. Early signs of language in child and chimpanzee. *Science,* 1975a, *187,* 752–753.

Gibson, E. J. A systematic application of the concepts of generalization and differentiation to verbal learning. *Psychological Review,* 1940, *47,* 196–229.

Glassman, W. E. Subvocal activity and acoustic confusions in short-term memory. *Journal of Experimental Psychology,* 1972, *96,* 164–169.

Godden, D. R., and Baddeley, A. D. Context-dependent memory in two natural environments: On land and underwater. *British Journal of Psychology,* 1975, *66,* 325–331.

Goldstein, A. Comments on the "Isolation, identification and synthesis of a specific-behavior-inducing brain peptide." *Nature,* 1973, *242,* 60–62.

Grant, D. A. A preliminary model for processing information conveyed by verbal conditioned stimuli in classical conditioning. In A. H. Black and W. F. Prokasy (Eds.), *Classical Conditioning III: Current Research and Theory.* New York: Appleton-Century-Crofts, 1972.

Grice, G. R. The relation of secondary reinforcement to delayed reward in visual discrimination learning. *Journal of Experimental Psychology,* 1948, *38,* 1–16.

Grice, G., and Reynolds, B. Effects of varying amounts of rest on conventional and bilateral transfer "reminiscence." *Journal of Experimental Psychology,* 1952, *44,* 247–252.

Grings, W. W., Schell, A. M., and Carey, C. A. Verbal control of an autonomic response in a cue reversal situation. *Journal of Experimental Psychology,* 1973, *99,* 215–221.

Groves, P. M., and Thompson, R. F. Habituation: A dual-process theory. *Psychological Review,* 1970, *77,* 419–450.

Gustavson, C. R., Garcia, J., Hankins, W. G., and Rusiniak, K. W. Coyote predation control by aversive conditioning. *Science,* 1974, *184,* 581–583.

Guthrie, E. R. *The Psychology of Learning.* Rev. Ed. New York: Harper & Row, 1952.

Hall, J. F. *Verbal Learning and Retention.* Philadelphia: Lippincott, 1971.

Hanson, H. M. Effects of discrimination training on stimulus generalization. *Journal of Experimental Psychology,* 1959, *58,* 321–334.

Hart, J. T. Memory and the feeling-of-knowing experience. *Journal of Educational Psychology,* 1965, *56,* 208–216.

Hasher, L., and Chromiak, W. The processing of frequency information: An automatic mechanism? *Journal of Verbal Learning and Verbal Behavior,* 1977, *16,* 173–184.

Heath, R. G. Electrical self-stimulation of the brain in man. *American Journal of Psychiatry,* 1963, *120,* 571–577.

Hebb, D. O. *Organization of Behavior.* New York: John Wiley & Sons, 1949.

Hefferline, R. F., Keenan, B., and Harford, R. A. Escape and avoidance conditioning in human subjects without their observation of response. *Science,* 1959, *130,* 1338–1339.

Herb, F. H. Latent learning-nonreward followed by food in blinds.

Journal of Comparative and Physiological Psychology, 1940, *29,* 247–255.

Hilgard, E. R., and Bower, G. H. *Theories of Learning.* 3rd Ed. New York: Appleton-Century-Crofts, 1966.

Hinrichs, J. V., and Buschke, H. Judgment of recency under steady-state conditions. *Journal of Experimental Psychology,* 1968, *78,* 574–579.

Hintzman, D. L. Explorations with a discrimination net model for paired-associate learning. *Journal of Mathematical Psychology,* 1968, *5,* 123–162.

Hintzman, D. L. Apparent frequency as a function of frequency and the spacing of repetitions. *Journal of Experimental Psychology,* 1969a, *80,* 139–145.

Hintzman, D. L. Backward recall as a function of stimulus similarity. *Journal of Verbal Learning and Verbal Behavior,* 1969b, *8,* 384–387.

Hintzman, D. L. Theoretical implications of the spacing effect. In R. L. Solso (Ed.), *Theories in Cognitive Psychology: The Loyola Symposium.* Potomac, Md,: Lawrence Erlbaum Associates, 1974.

Hintzman, D. L., and Block, R. A. Repetition and memory: Evidence for a multiple-trace hypothesis. *Journal of Experimental Psychology,* 1971, *88,* 297–306.

Hintzman, D. L., Block, R. A., and Inskeep, N. R. Memory for mode of input. *Journal of Verbal Learning and Verbal Behavior,* 1972, *11,* 741–749.

Hintzman, D. L., and Summers, J. J. Long-term visual traces of visually presented words. *Bulletin of the Psychonomic Society,* 1973, *1,* 325–327.

Hirsch, R. The hippocampus and contextual retrieval of information from memory: A theory. *Behavioral Biology,* 1974, *12,* 421–444.

Hoffman, H. S., and Ratner, A. M. A reinforcement model of imprinting: Implications for socialization in monkeys and men. *Psychological Review,* 1973, *80,* 527–544.

Hogan, J. A. How young chicks learn to recognize food. In R. A. Hinde and J. Stevenson-Hinde (Eds.), *Constraints on Learning: Limitations and Predispositions.* London: Academic Press, 1973.

Hogan, J. A. Responses in Pavlovian conditioning studies. *Science,* 1974, *186,* 156–157.

Houston, J. P. Proactive interference and undetected retention interval rehearsal. *Journal of Experimental Psychology,* 1969, *83,* 511–514.

Hull, C. L. *Principles of Behavior: An Introduction to Behavior Theory.* New York: Appleton-Century-Crofts, 1943.

Hull, C. L. *A Behavior System.* New Haven: Yale University Press, 1952.

Hull, C. L., Hovland, C. I., Ross, R. T., Hall, M., Perkins, D. T., and Fitch, F. B. *Mathematico-Deductive Theory of Rote Learning.* New Haven, Conn.: Yale University Press, 1940.

Hyde, T. S., and Jenkins, J. J. Differential effects of incidental tasks on the organization of recall of a list of highly associated words. *Journal of Experimental Psychology,* 1969, *82,* 472–481.

James, W. *The Principles of Psychology.* New York: Holt, Rinehart & Winston, 1890.

Jenkins, H. M., and Moore, B. R. The form of the auto-shaped response with food or water reinforcers. *Journal of the Experimental Analysis of Behavior.* 1973, *20,* 163–181.

Jenkins, J. G., and Dallenbach, K. M. Obliviscence during sleep and waking. *American Journal of Psychology,* 1924, *35,* 605–612.

Jensen, A. R. Spelling errors and the serial-position effect. *Journal of Educational Psychology,* 1962, *53,* 105–109.

Jerison, H. *Evolution of the Brain and Intelligence.* New York: Academic Press, 1973.

Johnson, M. K., Bransford, J. D., and Solomon, S. K. Memory for tacit implications of sentences. *Journal of Experimental Psychology,* 1973, *98,* 203–205.

Jones, M. C. The elimination of children's fears. *Journal of Experimental Psychology,* 1924, *7,* 382–390.

Kamiya, J. Conditioned discrimination of the EEG alpha rhythm in humans. Paper read at the meeting of the Western Psychological Association, 1962.

Kaufman, A., Baron, A., and Kopp, R. E. Some effects of instructions on human operant behavior. *Psychonomic Monograph Supplements,* 1966, *1,* 243–250.

Kellogg, W. N. Communication and language in a home-raised chimpanzee. *Science,* 1968, *162,* 423–427.

Kent, G. H., and Rosanoff, A. J. A study of association in insanity. *American Journal of Insanity,* 1910, *67,* 37–96, 317–390.

Keppel, G., and Underwood, B. J. Proactive inhibition in short-term retention of single items. *Journal of Verbal Learning and Verbal Behavior,* 1962, *1,* 153–161.

Kety, S. S. Biological concomitants of affective states and their possible role in memory processes. In M. R. Rosenzweig, and E. L. Bennett, (Eds.), *Neural Mechanisms of Learning and Memory.* Cambridge, Mass.: M.I.T. Press, 1976.

Kimble, G. A. *Hilgard and Marquis' Conditioning and Learning.* New York: Appleton-Century-Crofts, 1961.

Kimmel, H. D. Reflex "habituability" as a basis for differentiating between classical and instrumental conditioning. *Conditional Reflex,* 1973, *8,* 10–27.

King, M. C., and Wilson, A. C. Evolution at two levels in humans and chimpanzees. *Science,* 1975, *188,* 107–116.

Kintsch, W. *The Representation of Meaning in Memory.* Hillsdale, N. J.: Lawrence Erlbaum Associates, 1974.

Kirkpatrick, E. A. An experimental study of memory. *Psychological Review,* 1894, *1,* 602–609.

Koestler, A. *The Ghost in the Machine.* New York: Macmillan, 1967.

Koffka, K. *The Growth of the Mind.* Translated by R. M. Ogden. London: Kegan, Paul, Trench, Trubner, 1924.

Koffka, K. *Principles of Gestalt Psychology.* New York: Harcourt Brace Jovanovich, 1935.

Köhler, W. *The Mentality of Apes.* Translated by E. Winter. New York: Harcourt Brace Jovanovich, 1925.

Köhler, W. *Gestalt Psychology.* New York: Liveright, 1929.

Kolers, P. A. Pattern-analyzing memory. *Science,* 1976, *191,* 1280–1281.

Krechevsky, I. "Hypotheses" in rats. *Psychological Review,* 1932, *39,* 516–532.

Kuhn, T. S. *The Structure of Scientific Revolutions.* Chicago: University of Chicago Press, 1962.

Lane, H. *The Wild Boy of Aveyron.* Cambridge, Mass.: Harvard University Press, 1976.

Lapides, J., Sweet, R. B., and Lewis, L. W. Role of striated muscle in urination. *Journal of Urology,* 1957, *77,* 247–250.

Lashley, K. S. The effect of strychnine and caffeine upon rate of learning. *Psychobiology,* 1917, *1,* 141–170.

Lashley, K. S., and Ball, J. Spinal conduction and kinesthetic sensitivity in the maze habit. *Journal of Comparative Psychology,* 1929, *9,* 71–105.

Lawrence, D. M., and Banks, W. P. Accuracy of recognition memory for common sounds. *Bulletin of the Psychonomic Society,* 1973, *1,* 298–300.

Lehrman, D. S. A critique of Konrad Lorenz's theory of instinctive behavior. *Quarterly Review of Biology,* 1953, *28,* 337–363.

Leuba, C., Birch, L., and Appleton, J. Human problem solving during complete paralysis of the voluntary musculature. *Psychological Reports,* 1968, *22,* 849–855.

Light, L. L., and Carter-Sobell, L. Effects of changed semantic context on recognition memory. *Journal of Verbal Learning and Verbal Behavior,* 1970, *9,* 1–11.

Locke, D. *Memory.* Garden City, N.Y.: Doubleday, 1971.

Locke, E. A. Is "behavior therapy" behavioristic? (An analysis of Wolpe's psychotherapeutic methods.) *Psychological Bulletin,* 1971, *76,* 318–327.

Loess, H., and Waugh, N. C. Short-term memory and intertrial interval. *Journal of Verbal Learning and Verbal Behavior,* 1967, *6,* 455–460.

Loftus, E. F. Leading questions and the eyewitness report. *Cognitive Psychology,* 1975, *7,* 560–572.

Lorenz, K. Z. *King Solomon's Ring.* New York: T. Y. Crowell, 1952.

MacFarlane, D. A. The role of kinesthesis in maze learning. *University of California Publications in Psychology,* 1930, *4,* 277–305.

Maier, S. F., and Seligman, M. E. P. Learned helplessness: Theory and evidence. *Journal of Experimental Psychology: General,* 1975, *105,* 3–46.

Marler, P. A comparative approach to vocal learning: Song development in white-crowned sparrows. *Journal of Comparative and Physiological Psychology Monograph,* 1970, *71,* No. 2, part 2.

Marslen-Wilson, W. D., and Teuber, H. L. Memory for remote events in anterograde amnesia: Recognition of public figures from newsphotographs. *Neuropsychologia,* 1975, *13,* 353–364.

McConnell, J. V. Memory transfer through cannibalism in planarians. *Journal of Neuropsychiatry,* 1962, *3* (Supplement 1), 542–548.

Mc Crary, J. W., Jr., and Hunter, W. S. Serial position curves in verbal learning. *Science,* 1953, *117,* 131–134.

McGeoch, J. A. Forgetting and the law of disuse. *Psychological Review,* 1932, *39,* 352–370.

McGeoch, J. A., and Irion, A. L. *The Psychology of Human Learning.* New York: David McKay, 1952.

McLaughlin, J. P. The von Restorff effect in serial learning: Serial position of the isolate and length of list. *Journal of Experimental Psychology,* 1966, *72,* 603–609.

McNamara, H. J., Long, J. B., and Wike, E. L. Learning without responses under two conditions of external cues. *Journal of Comparative and Physiological Psychology,* 1956, *49,* 477–480.

Meehl, P. E. On the circularity of the law of effect. *Psychological Bulletin,* 1950, *47,* 52–75.

Melton, A. W., and Irwin, J. McQ. The influence of degree of interpolated learning on retroactive inhibition and the overt transfer of specific responses. *American Journal of Psychology*, 1940, *53*, 173–203.

Menzel, E. W. Chimpanzee spatial memory organization. *Science*, 1973, *182*, 943–945.

Merton, P. A. How we control the contraction of our muscles. *Scientific American*, 1972, *226*, 30–37.

Miller, G. A. The magical number seven, plus or minus two: Some limits on our capacity for processing information. *Psychological Review*, 1956, *63*, 81–97.

Miller, G. A., Galanter, E., and Pribram, K. A. *Plans and the Structure of Behavior*. New York: Holt, Rinehart & Winston, 1960.

Miller, N. E. Studies of fear as an acquired drive: I. Fear as motivation and fear-reduction as reinforcement in the learning of new responses. *Journal of Experimental Psychology*, 1948, *38*, 89–101.

Miller, N. E. Learning of visceral and glandular responses. *Science*, 1969, *163*, 434–445.

Miller, N. E., and Dworkin, B. Visceral learning: Recent difficulties with curarized rats and significant problems for human research. In P. A. Obrust, A. Black, J. Brener, and L. V. DiCara (Eds.), *Cardiovascular Psychophysiology*. Chicago: Aldine, 1974.

Miller, S., and Konorski, J. On a particular type of conditioned reflex. *Proceedings of the Biological Society* (Polish Section, Paris), 1928, *99*, 1155–1157.

Milner, B., Corkin, S., and Teuber, H. L. Further analysis of hyppocampal amnesic syndrome: 14 year follow-up study of H. M. *Neuropsychologia*, 1968, *6*, 215–234.

Minsky, M. A framework for representing knowledge. In P. H. Winston (Ed.), *The Psychology of Computer Vision*. New York: McGraw-Hill, 1975.

Moltz, H. Latent extinction and the fractional anticipatory response mechanism. *Psychological Review*, 1957, *64*, 229–241.

Moltz, H. Imprinting: Empirical basis and theoretical significance. *Psychological Bulletin*, 1960, *57*, 291–314.

Moltz, H. Imprinting: An epigenetic approach. *Psychological Review*, 1963, *70*, 123–138.

Moore, B. R. The role of directed Pavlovian reactions in simple instrumental learning in the pigeon. In R. A. Hinde and J. Stevenson-Hinde (Eds.), *Constraints on Learning: Limitations and Predispositions*. London: Academic Press, 1973.

Mulholland, T. B., and Peper, E. Occipital alpha and accommodative vergence, pursuit tracking, and fast eye movements. *Psychophysiology*, 1971, *8*, 556–575.

Murdock, B. B., Jr. The distinctiveness of stimuli. *Psychological Review*, 1960, *67*, 16–31.

Murdock, B. B. Jr. The retention of individual items. *Journal of Experimental Psychology*, 1961, *62*, 618–625.

Nagge, J. W. An experimental test of the theory of associative interference. *Journal of Experimental Psychology*, 1935, *18*, 663–682.

Nelson, K. E. Memory development in children: Evidence from nonverbal tasks. *Psychonomic Science*, 1971, *25*, 346–348.

Nickerson, R. S. A note on long-term recognition memory for pictorial material. *Psychonomic Science*, 1968, *11*, 58.

Norman, D. A. *Memory and Attention*. 2nd ed. New York: John Wiley & Sons, 1976.

Norman, D. A., and Rumelhart, D. E. *Explorations in Cognition*. San Francisco: W. H. Freeman & Co., 1975.

Oberly, H. S. A comparison of the spans of "attention" and memory. *American Journal of Psychology*, 1928, *40*, 295–302.

O'Keefe, J. and Nadel, L. Maps in the brain. *New Scientist*, 1974, *62*, 749–751.

Olds, J., and Milner, P. Positive reinforcement produced by electrical stimulation of septal area and other regions of rat brain. *Journal of Comparative and Physiological Psychology*, 1954, *47*, 419–427.

Overmeier, J. B., and Seligman, M. E. P. Effects of inescapable shock upon subsequent escape and avoidance learning. *Journal of Comparative and Physiological Psychology*, 1967, *63*, 23–33.

Paivio, A. Mental imagery in associative learning and memory. *Psychological Review*, 1969, *76*, 241–263.

Paivio, A. *Imagery and Verbal Processes*. New York: Holt, Rinehart & Winston, 1971.

Paivio, A. Imagery and long-term memory. In R. A. Kennedy and A. Wilkes (Eds.), *Studies in Long Term Memory*. New York: John Wiley & Sons, 1975.

Paivio, A., Yuille, J. C., and Rogers, T. B. Noun imagery and meaningfulness in free and serial recall. *Journal of Experimental Psychology*, 1969, *79*, 509–514.

Parkinson, S. R. Short-term memory while shadowing: Multiple-item recall of visually and of aurally presented letters. *Journal of Experimental Psychology*, 1972, *92*, 256–265.

Paskewitz, D. A., and Orne, M. T. Visual effects on alpha feedback training. *Science,* 1973, *181,* 361–363.

Pavlov, I. P. *The Work of the Digestive Glands.* Translated by W. H. Thompson. London: Charles Griffin, 1902.

Pavlov, I. P. *Conditioned Reflexes.* Translated by G. V. Anrep. London: Oxford University Press, 1927.

Peckham, G. W., and Peckham, E. G. Some observations on the mental powers of spiders. *Journal of Morphology,* 1887, *1,* 383–419.

Penfield, W. The permanent record of the stream of consciousness. *Acta Psychologica,* 1955, *11,* 47–69.

Penfield, W. *The Mystery of the Mind.* Princeton, N.J.: Princeton University Press, 1975.

Peterson, L. R., and Peterson, M. J. Short-term retention of individual verbal items. *Journal of Experimental Psychology,* 1959, *58,* 193–198.

Piaget, J., and Inhelder, B. *Memory and Intelligence.* Translated by A. J. Pomerans. New York: Basic Books, 1973.

Plotkin, W. B. On the self-regulation of the occipital alpha rhythm: Control strategies, states of consciousness, and the role of physiological feedback. *Journal of Experimental Psychology: General,* 1976, *105,* 66–99.

Posner, M. I., and Keele, S. W. Retention of abstract ideas. *Journal of Experimental Psychology,* 1970, *83,* 304–308.

Posner, M. I., and Konick, A. F. On the role of interference in short-term retention. *Journal of Experimental Psychology,* 1966, *72,* 221–231.

Posner, M. I., and Mitchell, R. F. Chronometric analysis of classification. *Psychological Review,* 1967, *74,* 392–401.

Postman, L. The present status of interference theory. In C. N. Cofer (Ed.), *Verbal Learning and Verbal Behavior.* New York: McGraw-Hill, 1961.

Postman, L., and Phillips, L. W. Short-term temporal changes in free recall. *Quarterly Journal of Experimental Psychology,* 1965, *17,* 132–138.

Potts, G. R. Storing and retrieving information about ordered relationships. *Journal of Experimental Psychology,* 1974, *103,* 431–439.

Premack, A. J., and Premack, D. Teaching language to an ape. *Scientific American,* 1972, *227,* 92–99.

Premack, D. Reinforcement theory. In M. R. Jones (Ed.), *Nebraska Symposium on Motivation: 1965.* Lincoln: University of Nebraska Press, 1965.

Premack, D. A functional analysis of language. *Journal of the Experimental Analysis of Behavior,* 1970, *14,* 107–125.

Premack, D. Language in chimpanzee? *Science,* 1971, *172,* 808–822.

Pylyshyn, Z. W. What the mind's eye tells the mind's brain: A critique of mental imagery. *Psychological Bulletin,* 1973, *80,* 1–24.

Quartermain, D., McEwen, B. S., and Azmitia, E. C., Jr. Recovery of memory following amnesia in the rat and mouse. *Journal of Comparative and Physiological Psychology,* 1972, *79,* 360–370.

Rachlin, H. *Behavior and Learning.* San Francisco: W. H. Freeman & Co., 1976.

Raphael, B. *The Thinking Computer.* San Francisco: W. H. Freeman & Co., 1976.

Razran, G. *Mind in Evolution.* Boston: Houghton Mifflin, 1971.

Reiff, R., and Scheerer, M. *Memory and Hypnotic Age Regression.* New York: International Universities Press, 1959.

Reitman, J. S. Without surreptitious rehearsal, information in short-term memory decays. *Journal of Verbal Learning and Verbal Behavior,* 1974, *13,* 365–377.

Rescorla, R. A. Probability of shock in the presence and absence of CS in fear conditioning. *Journal of Comparative and Physiological Psychology,* 1968, *66,* 1–5.

Restorff, H. von, Analyse von Vorgangen in Spurenfeld. I. Über die Wrikung von Bereichsbildung im Spurenfeld. *Psychologische Forschung,* 1933, *18,* 299–342.

Revusky, S. H., and Bedarf, E. W. Association of illness with prior ingestion of novel foods. *Science,* 1967, *155,* 219–220.

Ribback, A., and Underwood, B. J. An empirical explanation of the skewness of the bowed serial position curve. *Journal of Experimental Psychology,* 1950, *40,* 329–335.

Rieger, C. J. III. Conceptual memory and inference. In R. C. Schank (Ed.), *Conceptual Information Processing.* Amsterdam: North-Holland, 1975.

Riley, D. A. Memory for form. In L. Postman (Ed.), *Psychology in the Making,* New York: Alfred A. Knopf, 1963.

Rimm, D. C., and Masters, J. C. *Behavior Therapy.* New York: Academic Press, 1974.

Roll, D. L., and Smith, J. C. Conditioned taste aversion in anesthetized rats. In M. E. P. Seligman and J. L. Hager (Eds.), *Biological Boundaries of Learning.* New York: Appleton-Century-Crofts, 1972.

Rosenzweig, M. R., and Bennett, E. L. (Eds.) *Neural Mechanisms of Learning and Memory.* Cambridge, Mass.: M.I.T. Press, 1976.

Rozin, P., and Kalat, J. Specific hungers and poison avoidance as adaptive specializations of learning. *Psychological Review*, 1971, *78*, 459–486.

Rubenstein, R., and Newman, R. The living out of "future" experiences under hypnosis. *Science*, 1954, *119*, 472–473.

Rumbaugh, D. M., Gill, T. V., von Glasersfeld, E., Warner, H., and Pisani, P. Conversations with a chimpanzee in a computer-controlled environment. *Biological Psychiatry*, 1975, *10*, 627–641.

Rumelhart, D. E., and Ortony, A. The representation of knowledge in memory. In R. C. Anderson, R. J. Spiro, and W. E. Montague (Eds.), *Schooling and the Acquisition of Knowledge*. Hillsdale, N.J.: Lawrence Erlbaum Associates, 1976.

Russell, W. R., and Nathan, P. W. Traumatic amnesia. *Brain*, 1946, *69*, 280–300.

Sachs, J. S. Recognition memory for syntactic and semantic aspects of connected discourse. *Perception and Psychophysics*, 1967, *2*, 437–442.

Saltzman, I. J. Maze learning in the absence of primary reinforcement: A study of secondary reinforcement. *Journal of Comparative and Physiological Psychology*, 1949, *42*, 161–173.

Sameroff, A. J. Can conditional responses be established in the newborn infant: 1971? *Developmental Psychology*, 1971, *5*, 1–12.

Schactel, E. On memory and childhood amnesia. *Psychiatry*, 1947, *10*, 1–26.

Schank, R. C. (Ed.) *Conceptual Information Processing*. Amsterdam: North-Holland, 1975.

Schank, R. C. The role of memory in language processing. In C. R. Cofer (Ed.), *The Structure of Human Memory*. San Francisco: W. H. Freeman & Co., 1976.

Schmitt, F. O., Dev, P., and Smith, B. H. Electrotonic processing of information by brain cells. *Science*, 1976, *193*, 114–120.

Seidel, R. J. A review of sensory preconditioning. *Psychological Bulletin*, 1959, *56*, 58–73.

Seligman, M. E. P. On the generality of the laws of learning. *Psychological Review*, 1970, *77*, 406–418.

Seligman, M. E. P. *Helplessness*. San Francisco: W. H. Freeman & Co., 1975.

Seligman, M. E. P., and Hager, J. L. *Biological Boundaries of Learning*. New York: Appleton-Century-Crofts, 1972.

Seligman, M. E. P., and Johnston, J. C. A cognitive theory of avoidance learning. In F. J. McGuigan and D. B. Lumsden (Eds.), *Contemporary Approaches to Conditioning and Learning*. Washington, D.C.: V. H. Winston & Sons, 1973.

Seward, J. P., and Levy, N. Sign learning as a factor in extinction. *Journal of Experimental Psychology*, 1949, *39*, 660–668.

Shaffer, W. O., and Shiffrin, R. M. Rehearsal and storage of visual information. *Journal of Experimental Psychology*, 1972, *92*, 292–296.

Shapiro, M. M., and Herendeen, D. L. Food-reinforced inhibition of conditioned salivation in dogs. *Journal of Comparative and Physiological Psychology*, 1975, *88*, 628–632.

Shepard, R. N. Recognition memory for words, sentences and pictures. *Journal of Verbal Learning and Verbal Behavior*, 1967, *6*, 156–163.

Shulman, H. G. Semantic confusion errors in short-term memory. *Journal of Verbal Learning and Verbal Behavior*, 1972, *11*, 221–227.

Simon, H. A. How big is a chunk? *Science*, 1974, *183*, 482–488.

Simon, H. A., and Feigenbaum, E. A. An information processing theory of some effects of similarity, familiaritization, and meaningfulness in verbal learning. *Journal of Verbal Learning and Verbal Behavior*, 1964, *3*, 385–396.

Skinner, B. F. Two types of conditioned reflex: A reply to Konorski and Miller. *Journal of General Psychology*, 1937, *16*, 272–279.

Skinner, B. F. *The Behavior of Organisms*. New York: Appleton-Century-Crofts, 1938.

Skinner, B. F. "Superstition" in the pigeon. *Journal of Experimental Psychology*, 1948, *38*, 168–172.

Skinner, B. F. Are theories of learning necessary? *Psychological Review*, 1950, *57*, 193–216.

Skinner, B. F. How to teach animals. *Scientific American*, 1951, *185*, 26–29.

Skinner, B. F. *Science and Human Behavior*. New York: Macmillan, 1953.

Skinner, B. F. The science of learning and the art of teaching. *Harvard Educational Review*, 1954, *24*, 86–97.

Skinner, B. F. A case history in scientific method. *American Psychologist*, 1956, *11*, 221–233.

Skinner, B. F. Pigeons in a pelican. *American Psychologist*, 1960, *15*, 28–37.

Skinner, B. F. What is psychotic behavior? Theory and treatment of the psychoses. *Cumulative Record:* Rev. Ed. New York: Appleton-Century-Crofts, 1961.

Skinner, B. F. *The Technology of Teaching*. New York: Appleton-Century-Crofts, 1968.

Skinner, B. F. *Contingencies of Reinforcement: A Theoretical Analysis*. New York: Appleton-Century-Crofts, 1969.

Skinner, B. F. *Beyond Freedom and Dignity*. New York: Alfred A. Knopf, 1971.

Skinner, B. F. *About Behaviorism*. New York: Alfred A. Knopf, 1974.

Smith, T. L. On muscular memory. *American Journal of Psychology*, 1896, *7*, 453–490.

Smith, W. G. The relation of attention to memory. *Mind*, 1895, *4*, 47–73.

Spalding, D. A. Instinct, with original observations on young animals. *Macmillan's Magazine*, 1873, *27*, 282–293. (Reprinted in *British Journal of Animal Behavior*, 1954, *2*, 2–11.)

Spear, N. E. Forgetting as retrieval failure. In W. K. Honig and P. H. R. James (Eds.), *Animal Memory*. New York: Academic Press, 1971.

Spelke, E., Hirst, W., and Neisser, U. Skills of divided attention. *Cognition*, 1976, *4*, 215–230.

Spence, K. W. *Behavior Theory and Conditioning*. New Haven, Conn.: Yale University Press, 1956.

Spencer, N. J. Differences between linguists and nonlinguists in intuitions of grammaticality-acceptability. *Journal of Psycholinguistic Research*, 1973, *2*, 83–98.

Squire, L. R., Slater, P. C., and Chase, P. M. Retrograde amnesia: Temporal gradient in very long-term memory following electroconvulsive therapy. *Science*, 1975, *187*, 77–79.

Staddon, J. E. R., and Simmelhag, V. L. The "superstition" experiment: A reexamination of its implications for the principles of adaptive behavior. *Psychological Review*, 1971, *78*, 3–43.

Standing, L. Learning 10,000 pictures. *Quarterly Journal of Experimental Psychology*, 1973, *25*, 207–222.

Sternberg, S. High-speed scanning in human memory. *Science*, 1966, *153*, 652–654.

Sternberg, S. Memory scanning: New findings and current controversies. *Quarterly Journal of Experimental Psychology*, 1975, *27*, 1–32.

Stroop, J. R. Studies of interference in serial verbal reactions. *Journal of Experimental Psychology*, 1935, *18*, 643–662.

Sulzbacher, S. I., and Houser, J. E. A tactic to eliminate disruptive behaviors in the classroom: Group contingent consequences. *American Journal of Mental Deficiency*, 1968, *73*, 88–90.

Tart, C. T. States of consciousness and state-specific sciences. *Science*, 1972, *176*, 1203–1210.

Terrace, H. S. Stimulus control. In W. H. Honig (Ed.), *Operant Behavior: Areas of Research and Application*. New York: Appleton-Century-Crofts, 1966.

Testa, T. J. Effects of similarity of location and temporal intensity pattern of conditioned and unconditioned stimuli on the acquisition of conditioned suppression in rats. *Journal of Experimental Psychology: Animal Behavior Processes*, 1975, *1*, 114–121.

Thistlethwaite, D. A critical review of latent learning and related experiments. *Psychological Bulletin*, 1951, *48*, 97–129.

Thompson, R. F., and Spencer, W. A. Habituation: A model phenomenon for the study of neuronal substrates of behavior. *Psychological Review*, 1966, *73*, 16–43.

Thorndike, E. L. Animal intelligence: An experimental study of the associative processes in animals. *Psychological Monographs*, 1898, *2*, No. 8.

Thorndike, E. L. *Educational Psychology: The Psychology of Learning*. Vol. 2. New York: Teachers College, 1913.

Thorndike, E. L. *The Psychology of Learning*. New York: Teachers College, 1914.

Thorndike, E. L. *The Fundamentals of Learning*. New York: Teachers College, 1932.

Thorndike, E. L. Expectation. *Psychological Review*, 1946, *53*, 277–281.

Tinklepaugh, O. L. An experimental study of representative factors in monkeys. *Journal of Comparative Psychology*, 1928, *8*, 197–236.

Toffler, A. *Future Shock*. New York: Random House, 1970.

Tolman, E. C. *Purposive Behavior in Animals and Men*. New York: Appleton-Century-Crofts, 1932.

Tolman, E. C. The determiners of behavior at a choice point. *Psychological Review*, 1938, *45*, 1–41.

Tolman, E. C. Cognitive maps in rats and men. *Psychological Review*, 1948, *55*, 189–208.

Tolman, E. C. Principles of purposive behavior. In S. Koch (Ed.), *Psychology: A Study of a Science*. Vol. 2. New York: McGraw-Hill, 1959.

Tolman, E. C., and Honzik, C. H. "Insight" in rats. *University of California Publications in Psychology*, 1930a, *4*, 215–232.

Tolman, E. C., and Honzik, C. H. Introduction and removal of reward, and maze performance in rats. *University of California Publications in Psychology*, 1930b, *4*, 257–275.

Trapold, M. A., Carlson, J. G., and Myers, W. A. The effect of noncontingent fixed- and variable-interval reinforcement upon subsequent acquisition of the fixed-interval scallop. *Psychonomic Science*, 1965, *2*, 261–262.

True, R. M. Experimental control in hypnotic age regression states. *Science*, 1949, *110*, 583–584.

Tulving, E. Subjective organization in free recall of "unrelated" words. *Psychological Review*, 1962, *69*, 344–354.

Tulving, E. Episodic and semantic memory. In E. Tulving and W. Donaldson (Eds.), *Organization of Memory*. New York: Academic Press, 1972.

Tulving, E. Cue-dependent forgetting. *American Scientist*, 1974, *62*, 74–82.

Tulving, E., and Watkins, M. J. Continuity between recall and recognition. *American Journal of Psychology*, 1973, *86*, 739–748.

Twitmyer, E. B. A study of the knee jerk. *Journal of Experimental Psychology*, 1974, *103*, 1047–1066.

Underwood, B. J. "Spontaneous" recovery of verbal associations. *Journal of Experimental Psychology*, 1948, *38*, 429–439.

Underwood, B. J. Interference and forgetting. *Psychological Review*, 1957, *64*, 49–60.

Underwood, B. J. An evaluation of the Gibson theory of verbal learning. In C. N. Cofer (Ed.), *Verbal Learning and Verbal Behavior*. New York: McGraw-Hill, 1961.

Underwood, B. J. False recognition produced by implicit verbal responses. *Journal of Experimental Psychology*, 1965, *70*, 122–129.

Underwood, B. J., and Freund, J. S. The effect of temporal separation of two tasks on proactive inhibition. *Journal of Experimental Psychology*, 1968, *78*, 50–54.

Underwood, B. J., and Postman, L. Extraexperimental sources of interference in forgetting. *Psychological Review*, 1960, *67*, 73–95.

Underwood, B. J., and Schulz, R. W. *Meaningfulness and Verbal Learning*. Philadelphia: Lippincott, 1960.

Ungar, G. Molecular mechanisms in central nervous system coding. In G. B. Ansell and P. B. Bradley (Eds.), *Macromolecules and Behavior*. Baltimore: University Park Press, 1973.

Walsh, D. H. Interactive effects of alpha feedback and instructional set on subjective state. *Psychophysiology*, 1974, *11*, 428–435.

Walter, W. G. *The Living Brain*. New York: Norton, 1953.

Washburn, M. F. Social psychology of man and the lower animals. In *Studies in Psychology: Titchener Commemorative Volume*. Worcester, Mass.: Louis N. Wilson, 1917.

Wasserman, E. A. Pavolvian conditioning with heat reinforcement produces stimulus-directed pecking in chicks. *Science*, 1973, *181*, 875–877.

Watson, J. B. Psychology as the behaviorist views it. *Psychological Review*, 1913, *20*, 158–177.

Watson, J. B. *Psychology from the Standpoint of a Behaviorist.* Philadelphia: Lippincott, 1919.

Watson, J. B. *Behaviorism.* New York: Norton, 1925.

Watson, J. B. What the nursery has to say about instincts. In C. Murchison (Ed.), *Psychologies of 1925.* Worcester, Mass.: Clark University Press, 1926.

Watson, J. B. *Behaviorism.* Rev. Ed. New York: Norton, 1930.

Watson, J. B., and McDougall, W. *The Battle of Behaviorism.* New York: Norton, 1929.

Watson, J. B., and Rayner, R. Conditioned emotional reactions. *Journal of Experimental Psychology,* 1920, *3,* 1–14.

Waugh, N. C., and Norman, D. A. Primary memory. *Psychological Review,* 1965, *72,* 89–104.

Weizenbaum, J. *Computer Power and Human Reason.* San Francisco: W. H. Freeman & Co., 1976.

Wickelgren, W. A. Multitrace strength theory. In D. A. Norman (Ed.), *Models of Human Memory.* New York: Academic Press, 1970.

Wickelgren, W. A. Single-trace fragility theory of memory dynamics. *Memory & Cognition,* 1974, *2,* 775–780.

Wickelgren, W. A. Alcoholic intoxication and memory storage dynamics. *Memory & Cognition,* 1975, *3,* 385–389.

Wickens, D. D. Encoding categories of words: An empirical approach to meaning. *Psychological Review,* 1970, *77,* 1–15.

Wickens, D. D., and Clark, S. E. Osgood dimensions as an encoding class in short-term memory. *Journal of Experimental Psychology,* 1968, *78,* 580–584.

Wilcoxin, H. C., Dragoin, W. B., and Kral, P. A. Illness-induced aversions in rat and quail: Relative salience of visual and gustatory cues. *Science,* 1971, *171,* 826–828.

Wilkins, W. Desensitization: Social and cognitive factors underlying the effectiveness of Wolpe's procedure. *Psychological Bulletin,* 1971, *76,* 311–317.

Williams, D. R., and Williams, H. Auto-maintenance in the pigeon: Sustained pecking despite contingent non-reinforcement. *Journal of the Experimental Analysis of Behavior,* 1969, *12,* 511–520.

Winkelman, J. H., and Schmidt, J. Associative confusions in mental arithmetic. *Journal of Experimental Psychology,* 1974, *102,* 734–736.

Wollen, K. A., Weber, A., and Lowry, D. H. Bizarreness versus interaction of mental images as determinants of learning. *Cognitive Psychology,* 1972, *3,* 518–523.

Wolfe, J. B. Effectiveness of token-rewards for chimpanzees. *Comparative Psychology Monographs,* 1936, *13,* No. 60.

Wolpe, J. *Psychotherapy by Reciprocal Inhibition.* Stanford, Calif.: Stanford University Press, 1958.

Wolpe, J., and Lazarus, A. *Behavior Therapy Techniques.* New York: Permagon Press, 1968.

Wulf, F. Über die Veränderung von Vorstellungen. *Psychologische Forschung,* 1922, *1,* 333–373.

Wundt, W. *Lectures on Human and Animal Psychology.* Translated by J. E. Creighton and E. B. Titchener. New York: Macmillan, 1896.

Yntema, D. B., and Trask, F. Recall as a search process. *Journal of Verbal Learning and Verbal Behavior,* 1963, *2,* 65–74.

Young, R. K. Tests of three hypotheses about the effective stimulus in serial learning. *Journal of Experimental Psychology,* 1962, *63,* 307–313.

Young, R. K. Serial learning. In T. R. Dixon and D. L. Horton (Eds.), *Verbal Behavior and General Behavior Theory.* Englewood Cliffs, N.J.: Prentice-Hall, 1968.

Zeaman, D. Response latency as a function of the amount of reinforcement. *Journal of Experimental Psychology,* 1949, *39,* 446–483.

Author Index

Subject Index